This 5th edition of *Hadrian's Wall Path* Daniel McCrohan. His work built upon the first four editions of this book.

DANIEL MCCROHAN is a widely published travel writer with a passion for hiking and a penchant for ancient walls. For more than a decade he lived in Beijing, under the shadow of the Great Wall of China, another breathtaking bastion which he has hiked much of the way along, and written about for numerous publications, including Lonely Planet. Back in the UK, he jumped at the chance to size up Britain's very own great wall – and brought his family along for the ride. With their nephew and two friends from Beijing they all descended on Newcastle one sunny summer's day and hiked and camped their way along the entire route. Eight days later they concluded that Hadrian's Wall was in pretty good nick considering it was more than a thousand years older than its Ming-Dynasty counterpart in China – but were thankful it wasn't quite as long.

This is Daniel's third Trailblazer guide – and his 32nd guidebook in total. You can keep track of his travels at danielmccrohan.com or on Twitter (@danielmccrohan). To listen to a podcast about Daniel hiking Hadrian's Wall, go to www.traveltapethepodcast.com.

Born in Chatham, Kent, **HENRY STEDMAN** has been writing guidebooks for 20 years now and is the author or co-author of over half a dozen Trailblazer titles including *Kilimanjaro*, *Coast to Coast Path*, *Dales Way* and all three books in the *South-West Coast Path* series. On most walks he's accompanied by Daisy. Two parts trouble to one part Parson's Jack Russell, Daisy has now completed Hadrian's Wall Path, Coast to Coast, Dales Way, Offa's Dyke and the entire South-West Coast Path.

When not travelling or writing, Henry lives in Battle, maintaining his Kilimanjaro website and arranging climbs on the mountain through his company, Climb Mount Kilimanjaro.

Authors

Hadrian's Wall Path First edition: 2006; this fifth edition: 2017

Publisher Trailblazer Publications
The Old Manse, Tower Rd, Hindhead, Surrey, GU26 6SU, UK
info@trailblazer-guides.com, 📞 www.trailblazer-guides.com

British Library Cataloguing in Publication Data
A catalogue record for this book is available from the British Library

ISBN 978-1-905864-85-0

© Trailblazer 2006, 2008, 2011, 2014, 2017: Text and maps

Editing & Layout: Anna Jacomb-Hood **Proofreading**: Jane Thomas
Cartography & illustrations pp76-7: Nick Hill **Index**: Jane Thomas & Daniel McCrohan
Photographs (flora): C1 bottom right © Henry Stedman, all others © Bryn Thomas
All other photographs: © Daniel McCrohan (unless otherwise indicated)

All rights reserved. Other than brief extracts for the purposes of review no part of this book may be reproduced in any form without the written consent of the publisher and copyright owner.

The maps in this guide were prepared from out-of-Crown-copyright Ordnance Survey maps amended and updated by Trailblazer.

Acknowledgements

I was immensely fortunate to be able to bring with me on this trip so many of my nearest and dearest; it made for a unique experience that I will treasure forever. I was accompanied every step of the way by my darling wife, Taotao, our two fabulously energetic children, Dudu and Yoyo, and our strong-as-an-ox nephew Zhang Yi, whose tent-carrying capabilities and general good humour were invaluable throughout our 84-mile Roman ramble. I was also very lucky to be joined for much of the trip by my dear friends Qing Jing and Zhou Dao. I just hope that backpacking across rain-swept northern England hasn't put you off travelling for life! Thank you too to my wonderful mum for all her support over such a hectic summer, and to Sam and Heidi, and Catherine, Ron and Pat for being so accommodating when descended upon by the whole Hadrian's Wall crew!

Huge thanks, as always, goes to Bryn Thomas for commissioning me to write this book. Also at Trailblazer, I'd like to thank Anna Jacomb-Hood, Jane Thomas and Nick Hill for all their fantastic work on the editing and mapping, and to fellow author Henry Stedman for his magnificent work on previous editions. We're also grateful to David McGlade, National Trail Officer, and to all those readers who wrote in with comments and suggestions for this book, particularly Tom Anderson, Jared Bond, George Bowers, Giles Cooper, Anne Devecchi, Keith Dunbar, Sharon Dunn, Mike Durrans, Ken, Rich & Sophie Eames, Keith Frayn, Jim Horstman, Roger Kennington, Unni Oberhofer, Kornelie Oostlander-Vos, Henry Purbrick, John Nichols, Cathy Rooke, Michael Scarlatos, Robert Stonehouse, Ingrid Strobl, Rick & Mel Toyer, Murray Turner, Pam & Stephen Turner and David Twine.

A request

The author and publisher have tried to ensure that this guide is as accurate and up to date as possible. Nevertheless, things change. If you notice any changes or omissions, please write to Trailblazer (address above) or email us at 📧 info@trailblazer-guides.com. A free copy of the next edition will be sent to persons making a significant contribution.

Warning: long-distance walking can be dangerous

Please read the notes on when to go (pp13-15) and outdoor safety (pp68-70). Every effort has been made by the author and publisher to ensure that the information contained herein is as accurate and up to date as possible. However, they are unable to accept responsibility for any inconvenience, loss or injury sustained by anyone as a result of the advice and information given in this guide.

Updated information will be available on: 🌐 www.trailblazer-guides.com

Photos – Front cover: Following a fine stretch of Wall near Turret 45A.
This page: Hiking past Sewingshields Crags. **Overleaf**: Hikers near Walltown Quarry.

Printed in China; print production by D'Print (📞 +65-6581 3832), Singapore

Hadrian's Wall
PATH

59 large-scale maps & guides to 29 towns and villages
PLANNING – PLACES TO STAY – PLACES TO EAT
WALLSEND TO BOWNESS-ON-SOLWAY

HENRY STEDMAN
& DANIEL McCROHAN

TRAILBLAZER PUBLICATIONS

INTRODUCTION

About the Hadrian's Wall Path
How difficult is the Hadrian's Wall Path? 10 – How long do you need? 12 – Hadrian's Wall highlights 13 – When to go 13

PART 1: PLANNING YOUR WALK

Practical information for the walker
Route finding 17 – Accommodation 17 – Food and drink 21
Money 23 – Information for foreign visitors 24 – Other services 26
Walking companies 26

Budgeting 29

Itineraries
Village and town facilities table 30 – Suggested itineraries 33
Which direction? 35 – Taking dogs along the Hadrian's Wall Path 35

What to take
Keep your luggage light 36 – How to carry it 36 – Footwear 37
Clothes 38 – Toiletries 38 – First-aid kit 38 – General items 39
Camping gear 39 – Money and documents 39 – Hadrian's Wall Passport 40 – Maps 40 – Recommended reading 41 – Sources of further information 43

Getting to and from the Hadrian's Wall Path
National transport 44 – Getting to Britain 45 – Local transport 48

PART 2: HADRIAN'S WALL

History
The decision to build the Wall 49 – Hadrian builds his Wall 50
The Wall post-Hadrian 54 – The Romans in Britain 55
After the Romans 60

PART 3: MINIMUM IMPACT WALKING & OUTDOOR SAFETY

Minimum impact walking
Hadrian's Wall Code of Respect 64 – Economic impact 64
Environmental impact 65 – Access 67

Outdoor safety
Avoidance of hazards 68 – Weather forecasts 69 – Blisters 70
Hypothermia, hyperthermia and sunburn 70

PART 4: THE ENVIRONMENT & NATURE

Conservation
Government agencies and schemes 71

Flora and fauna
Mammals 73 – Reptiles and fish 75 – Birds 75 – Trees 77 – Flowers 79

PART 5: NEWCASTLE

City guide
Arrival 81 – Transport 82 – Services 83 – Where to stay 83
Where to eat and drink 89 – Entertainment 93 – What to see and do 94

PART 6: ROUTE GUIDE AND MAPS

Using this guide 99

Wallsend to Heddon-on-the-Wall 101
Segedunum 101 – Wylam 115 – Heddon-on-the-Wall 116

Heddon-on-the-Wall to Chollerford 118
East Wallhouses 122 – Corbridge–Hexham–Acomb alternative 126
(Corbridge 126, Corbridge Roman Town 130, Hexham 133,
Acomb 137) – Wall 142 – Chollerford 144 – Chesters 145

Chollerford to Steel Rigg (for Once Brewed) 146
Housesteads 156 – Once Brewed 160 – Vindolanda 162

Steel Rigg to Banks 163
Haltwhistle 167 – Greenhead 172 – Gilsland 174 – Birdoswald 178
Banks 180

Banks to Carlisle 182
Walton 184 – Brampton 186 – Crosby-on-Eden 189 – Carlisle 194

Carlisle to Bowness-on-Solway 201
Burgh-by-Sands 205 – Boustead Hill 210 – Drumburgh 210
Glasson 212 – Port Carlisle 212 – Bowness-on-Solway 214

APPENDICES

Glossary 217 – GPS Waypoints 218 – Taking a dog 221

MAP KEY 222 INDEX 223

OVERVIEW MAPS & PROFILES 230

ABOUT THIS BOOK

This guidebook contains all the information you need. The hard work has been done for you so you can plan your trip from home without the usual pile of books, maps and guides.

When you're all packed and ready to go, there's comprehensive public transport information to get you to and from the trail and 59 detailed maps (1:20,000) and town plans to help you find your way along it. The guide includes:

- All standards of accommodation with reviews of campsites, bunkhouses, hostels, B&Bs, guesthouses and hotels
- Walking companies if you want an organised tour and baggage-transfer services if you just want your luggage carried
- Itineraries for all levels of walkers
- Answers to all your questions: when to go, degree of difficulty, what to pack, and how much the whole walking holiday will cost
- Walking times and GPS waypoints
- Cafés, pubs, tearooms, takeaways, restaurants – and shops for buying supplies
- Rail, bus and taxi information for all villages and towns along the path
- Street plans of the main towns both on and off the Wall: Newcastle, Wylam, Corbridge, Hexham, Haltwhistle, Brampton and Carlisle
- Historical, cultural and geographical background information
- GPS waypoints

❏ MINIMUM IMPACT FOR MAXIMUM INSIGHT

Man has suffered in his separation from the soil and from other living creatures ... and as yet he must still, for security, look long at some portion of the earth as it was before he tampered with it.
Gavin Maxwell, *Ring of Bright Water*, 1960

Why is walking in wild and solitary places so satisfying? Partly it is the sheer physical pleasure: sometimes pitting one's strength against the elements and the lie of the land. The beauty and wonder of the natural world and the fresh air restore our sense of proportion and the stresses and strains of everyday life slip away. Whatever the character of the countryside, walking in it benefits us mentally and physically, inducing a sense of well-being, an enrichment of life and an enhanced awareness of what lies around us.

All this the countryside gives us and the least we can do is to safeguard it by supporting rural economies, local businesses, and low-impact methods of farming and land-management, and by using environmentally sensitive forms of transport – walking being pre-eminent.

In this book there is a detailed and illustrated chapter on the wildlife and conservation of the region and a chapter on minimum-impact walking, with ideas on how to tread lightly in this fragile environment; by following its principles we can help to preserve our natural heritage for future generations.

INTRODUCTION

Just when you think you are at the world's end, you see a smoke from East to West as far as the eye can turn, and then under it as far as the eye can stretch, houses and temples, shops and theatres, barracks and granaries, trickling along like dice behind – always behind – one long, low, rising and falling, and hiding and showing line of towers. And that is the Wall!
Rudyard Kipling, Puck of Pook's Hill

On 23 May 2003, Britain's 13th National Trail, Hadrian's Wall Path, was opened in the border country between England and Scotland. The trail (84 miles/135km from end to end) follows the course of northern Europe's largest-surviving Roman monument, a 2nd-century fortification built on the orders of Emperor Hadrian in AD122. The Wall marked the northern limits of Hadrian's empire – an empire that stretched for 3000 miles across Europe and the Mediterranean all the way to the Euphrates.

The trail follows the course of northern Europe's largest surviving Roman monument

To say that creating such a path was problematic would be something of an understatement. This was the first National Trail to follow the course of a UNESCO World Heritage Site. As such, every time a fencepost, signpost or waymark was driven into the ground, an

Hiking beside a stretch of 'Clayton Wall' (see pp61-2) near Housesteads.

8 Introduction

The walk begins at Segedunum, the most easterly fort on the Wall, and follows the River Tyne through Newcastle and past the city's seven bridges. This is the 'winking eye' Millennium Bridge, seen from the BALTIC gallery.

archaeologist had to be present to ensure that the integrity of the Wall was not in any way compromised. To give you an indication of just how careful they had to be, it took *ten years* before the Hadrian's Wall Path was finally opened to the public. By comparison, it took the 2nd and 6th legions of the Roman army only six years to build the actual Wall!

Since its opening many have walked the trail and all seem to agree that the difficulties involved in its creation were well worth it, allowing the walker to follow in the sandal-steps of those who built it with the trail itself rarely diverting from the course of the Romans' barrier by more than a few hundred metres. And, though there's only about ten miles of the Wall left and it hardly ever rises to more than half its original height, it – or at least the route it would have taken – makes for a fascinating hiking companion.

It's an incredible feat of engineering, best appreciated in the section from Housesteads to Cawfield Quarry

Punctuated by forts, milecastles and turrets spaced evenly along its length, the Wall snaked over moor and down dale through Northumberland and Cumbria, between the Roman fort of Segedunum (at the appropriately named Newcastle suburb of Wallsend) in the east and the mouth of the Solway River in the west. It's an incredible feat of engineering, best appreciated in the section from Housesteads to Cawfield Quarry where the landscape is so bleak and wild that human habitation and farming never really took a hold. It is here that the Wall stands most intact, following the bumps and hollows of the undulating countryside – as integral a part of the scenery now as the whinstone cliffs on which it is built. Here, too, are some of the best-preserved fortresses, from the vast archaeological trove at Vindolanda, set just off the Wall to the south, to the subtle charms at Birdoswald and the beautifully situated Housesteads itself.

Journey's end! A small shelter and a little garden mark the end of the walk on Banks Promenade at Bowness-on-Solway.

After the Romans withdrew the Wall fell into disrepair. What we see as a unique and awe-inspiring work of military architecture was to the local landowners a convenient source of ready-worked stones for their own building purposes. The Wall is part of the fabric of many of the major constructions built after the Romans left: the churches, priories and abbeys that lie just off the Wall, such as those at Hexham and Lanercost; the Norman castles at Carlisle and Newcastle; the Military Road which you follow for part of the

There are numerous cafés, tearooms and pubs to detain you along the way.

walk; the stronghouses at Thirlwall and Drumburgh – all beautiful, historically important buildings. And all of them incorporate stones from the Wall. Yet even where its destruction was total, the Wall's legacy continues to echo through the ages in the names of the villages that lie along the route: Wallsend, Wallend, Wallhouses, Walton, Wall village and Oldwall are just some of the place names that celebrate the Wall. The past, it seems, is inseparable from the present.

Quite apart from the architectural and historical interest, all around the Wall is scenery of breathtaking beauty, from the sophisticated cityscape of Newcastle to the wild, wind-blasted moors of Northumberland, the pastoral delights of Cumbria and

> **Quite apart from the architectural and historical interest, all around the Wall is scenery of breathtaking beauty**

the serenity of Bowness-on-Solway, an Area of Outstanding Natural Beauty and a haven for birdwatchers and those seeking peaceful solitude. After all, what other national trail passes through Paradise (a suburb of Newcastle), Eden (the river flowing through Carlisle) and the site of the Battle of Heavenfield (before Chollerford).

Yet perhaps the best feature of the Wall is that all its treasures are accessible to anyone with enough get-up-and-go to leave their armchair. The path itself is regarded as one of the easiest National Trails, a week-long romp on a grassy path through rolling countryside with the highest point, Green Slack, just 345m above sea level. The waymarking is clear and, with the Wall on one side and a road a little distance away on the other, it's very difficult to lose one's way. There are good facilities, from lively pubs to cosy B&Bs, friendly, well-equipped bunkhouses and idyllic little tearooms. And for those for whom completing the entire trail is over-ambitious, there are good transport connections, including a special Hadrian's Wall Country bus (the AD122). With a little planning, you can arrange a simple stroll along a short section of the trail, maybe take in a fort or museum on

> **For those for whom completing the entire trail is over-ambitious, there are good public transport connections (see pp46-8)**

the way, then catch a bus back to 'civilisation'. While for those who prefer not to follow any officially recognised National Trail, the path also connects to 43 other walks, details of which are readily available from one of the tourist information offices serving the trail.

So, while the Wall no longer defines the border between Scotland and England (90% of Northumberland, an English county, actually lies to the north of the Wall, and at no point does the Wall actually coincide with the modern Anglo-Scottish border), it nevertheless remains an inspiring place and a monument to the breathtaking ambition of both Hadrian, the youthful dynamic emperor, and of Roman civilisation itself. And there can be few greater ways to appreciate it than by walking along this trail.

How difficult is the Hadrian's Wall Path?

The Hadrian's Wall Path is, for experienced hikers, just a long walk. Indeed, many rate this as the easiest of the national trails in the UK. It only takes about a week to complete it, and for some no more than four days. And there's a guy

How difficult is the Hadrian's Wall Path? 11

called Elvis from Haltwhistle who completed it in one 30-hour stretch for charity.

The waymarking is clear and it's very difficult to lose one's way

Age seems to be no barrier to completing the walk either. While updating the third edition of this book Henry Stedman walked with his friend, Peter Fenner, who was just a month shy of his 78th birthday. And while updating this fifth edition, Daniel McCrohan was joined by his whole family, including his six-year-old daughter Yoyo. So there's no need for crampons, ropes, ice axes, oxygen bottles or any other climbing paraphernalia, because there's no climbing involved. All you need to complete the walk is some suitable clothing, a bit of money, a rucksack full of determination and a half-decent pair of calf muscles.

The route is well marked with the familiar National Trail 'acorn' signposts, arrows and other waymarks, so keeping to the trail shouldn't really be a problem. That said, it is a fairly wild walk in places. Regarding safety, there are few places on the regular trail where it would be possible to fall from a great height, unless you stray from the path near the crags; and with the Wall on one side and a road on the other, it's difficult to get lost, too. Nevertheless, you may find a compass or

There's a great variety of scenery on this walk: it's not just about the Wall. On some stretches, such as between Carlisle and Bowness-on-Solway (**below**, see pp214-6), almost all evidence of the Wall has disappeared.
(Photo © Henry Stedman)

12 How difficult is the Hadrian's Wall Path?

The trig point at Green Slack (see p164), at 345m, is the highest point on the path.
(Photo © Henry Stedman)

GPS unit (see p17) useful. Your greatest danger will likely come from those sections where the trail follows or crosses a main road. These points are few and far between, but care should be take on them nonetheless. Sadly you will pass one roadside memorial to a hiker who was hit and killed by a vehicle while walking by a stretch of the B6318 at East Wallhouses.

Your greatest inconvenience will no doubt come from the weather, which can also be hazardous at times. It is very important that you dress for inclement conditions and always carry a set of dry clothes with you. Not pushing yourself too hard is important too, as over-exertion leads to exhaustion and all its inherent dangers; see pp68-70.

But really, while it is no mean achievement to complete this walk, it is nevertheless a straightforward but fairly exhausting stroll by the standards of other hikes in northern Britain and should be enjoyed and appreciated as such.

How long do you need?

Most people take around six days to complete the walk, making it one of the shorter national trails. Of course, if you're fit there's no reason why you can't go

Most people take around six days to complete the walk

a little faster, if that's what you want to do, and finish the walk in five days (or even less), though you will end up having a different sort of hike to most of the other people on the trail. For where theirs is a fairly relaxing holiday, yours will be more of a sport. What's more, you won't have as much time to enjoy the forts and other attractions; one of the main reasons for visiting the Wall in the first place.

When deciding how long to allow for the walk, those intending to camp and carry their own luggage shouldn't underestimate just how much a heavy pack can slow them down; bank on taking more like seven or eight days if carrying all your luggage. On pp32-4 there are some suggested itineraries covering different walking speeds. If you have only a few days, perhaps don't try to walk it all; consider concentrating instead on one particular area, such as the

See pp32-4 for some suggested itineraries covering different walking speeds

popular central section, or the quieter Cumbrian section from Carlisle to Bowness.

❏ HADRIAN'S WALL HIGHLIGHTS

Trying to pick one particular section that is representative of the entire trail is impossible because each is very different. Undoubtedly if I had to recommend one highlight it would be from **Chollerford to Steel Rigg** (see pp146-63), with its excellently preserved Wall, its milecastles and Wall forts. The landscape is the most dramatic here, too, as you ride the crests and bumps of the various crags. David McGlade, the National Trail Officer for Hadrian's Wall, prefers the **Walltown section** of the Wall (see pp170-3), **Birdoswald and Segedunum forts** (the former for the views, the latter for its presentation), and the **Solway Estuary** (see pp209-16) because of its birdlife.

But just because these sections are our favourites does not mean that the others should be dismissed. The cityscape and suburbs of Newcastle, the absorbing roadside tramp from Heddon-on-the-Wall to Chollerford, the gentle rolling countryside of Cumbria, and 'The Land that Time Forgot' near Bowness are all worth experiencing.

Henry Stedman

When to go

SEASONS

Britain is a notoriously wet country and the north of England is an infamously damp part of it. '*Hadrain*' as one witty souvenir T-shirt puts it and it's fair to say that few hikers manage to complete the walk without suffering at least one downpour; two or three per trip are more likely, even in summer. That said, it's equally unlikely that you'll spend a week in the area and not see any sun at all, and even the most cynical of hikers will have to admit that, during the hiking season at least, there are more

The hiking season runs from April to September

sunny days than showery ones. The **hiking season** starts at Easter and builds to a crescendo in August, before steadily tailing off in September. By September's end, few indeed are the hikers who attempt the whole trail, although there are plenty of people on day walks, and by the end of October many places close down for the winter.

Unusually, the authorities in charge of maintaining the path request that walkers do **not attempt the trail in winter** (which they define as October to April), when the path is at its most fragile; they do not, however, rule out walking in Wall country altogether; see the box on pp64-5 for more details.

There are two further points to consider when planning your trip. Firstly, remember that most people set off on the trail at a weekend. This means that you'll find the trail quieter **during the week** and as a consequence you may find it easier to book accommodation. Secondly, towards the western end of the walk, the trail through the Solway Marshes can be prone to flooding. While this won't affect when you set off (at least, not if you are starting at the eastern end of it), you do need to be aware of the time of the high tides and plan your walk through the marshes so that you are not there during particularly high-level tides; the box on p201 gives advice on how to do this.

Spring

Find a dry week in springtime (around the end of March to mid June) and you're in for a treat. The wild flowers are coming into bloom, lambs are skipping in the meadows, the grass is green and lush, and the path is not yet badly eroded. Of course, finding a dry week in spring is not easy but occasionally there's a mini-heatwave. Another advantage with walking at this time is that there will be fewer hikers and finding accommodation is relatively easy, though do check that the hostels/B&Bs have opened. Easter is the exception; the first major holiday in the year when people flock to the Wall.

Summer

Summer, on the other hand, can be a bit *too* busy but even over the most hectic weekend in August it's rarely insufferable. Still, the chances of a prolonged period of sunshine are of course higher at this time of year than any other, the days are much longer, all the facilities and public transport are operating and the heather is in bloom, turning some of the hills around the crags a fragrant purple. If you're flexible and want to avoid seeing too many people on the trail, avoid the school holidays, which basically means ruling out the tail end of July, all of August and the first few days of September. Alternatively, if you crave the company of other hikers, summer will provide you with the opportunity of meeting plenty of them, though do remember that you **must book your accommodation in advance**, especially if staying in B&Bs.

Despite the higher than average chance of sunshine, take clothes for any eventuality – it will probably still rain at some point.

Autumn

September is a wonderful time to hike, when many of the tourists have returned home, the path is clear and blackberries provide sustenance for the weary walker along the trail. The weather is usually fairly good too, at least at the beginning of September. The B&Bs and hostels will probably be open until the end of the month. By then the weather will begin to get a little wilder and the nights will start to draw in. The hiking season is almost at an end.

❏ **FESTIVALS AND ANNUAL EVENTS**
As one of the emptiest parts of England, it is perhaps not surprising that there is a dearth of traditional annual festivals, at least when compared to other parts of the country. That's not to say that events don't happen, it's just that the many fairs, festivals and other happenings do not have the weight of tradition or history behind them. Though many of the activities do take place annually, it's not necessarily at the same time each year. Nevertheless, a look at the official Hadrian's Wall website does give a reasonable list of things going on, from lectures to Easter-egg hunts, guided tours to Roman re-enactments, bat walks to falconry displays, and it's very possible that your trip will coincide with at least one event.

For more details and a complete list of what's on throughout the year, see 🖥 hadrianswallcountry.co.uk/events.

Winter

The National Trail authorities ask that you do not walk the trail during the winter, to give the path a rest and prevent damage. It is also a little more dangerous to walk it at this time, with few people around, a cold climate and a slippery trail. But while the advice discourages walking the actual trail, there is nothing to stop you trying one of the circular winter trails near the Wall. For leaflets with suggestions for walks you can take in Wall country that don't actually encroach on the main trail and any unexcavated archaeological treasures see 🖥 www.nationaltrail.co.uk/hadrians-wall-path/leaflets.

RAINFALL

At some point on your walk it will rain; if it doesn't, it's fair to say that you haven't really lived the full Hadrian's Wall experience properly. The question, therefore, is not whether you will be rained on but how often. As long as you dress accordingly and take note of the safety advice given on pp68-70, this shouldn't be a problem.

DAYLIGHT HOURS

If walking in autumn or early spring, you must take account of how far you can walk in the available light. It won't be possible to cover as many miles as you would in summer. Remember, too, that you will get a further 30-45 minutes of usable light before sunrise and after sunset depending on the weather.

In June, because the path is in the far north of England, those coming from the south may be surprised that there's enough available light for walking until at least 10pm. Conversely, in winter the nights draw in quickly. Bear this in mind if walking outside the summer season.

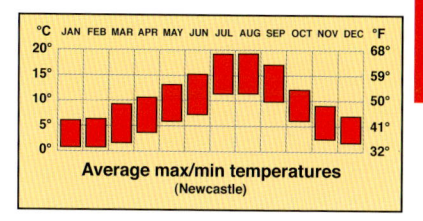

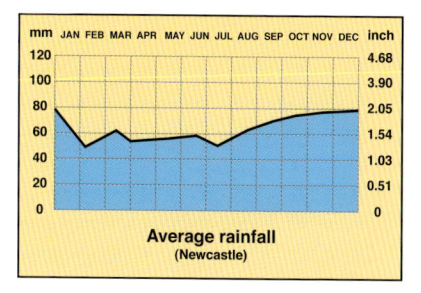

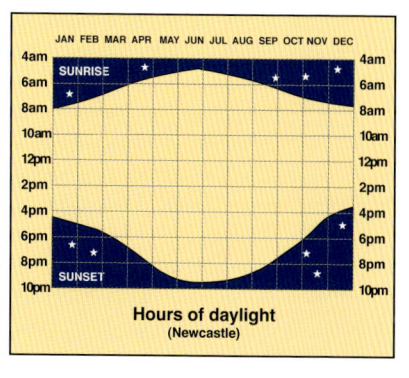

Average max/min temperatures
(Newcastle)

Average rainfall
(Newcastle)

Hours of daylight
(Newcastle)

❑ **DON'T WALK ON THE WALL**
There are plenty of ways in which hikers can help protect the Wall for future generations to enjoy (see pp64-5 **Caring for the Wall – the Hadrian's Wall Code of Respect** for more details), but the most important one to remember is never, ever walk along, or climb onto the Wall, even if it's just to get a better angle for a photo.

PLANNING YOUR WALK 1

Practical information for the walker

ROUTE FINDING

With the Wall to follow, it's difficult to get lost on this walk. The route is well marked with the familiar National Trail 'acorn' signposts, arrows and other waymarks, so keeping to the trail shouldn't really be a problem. Nevertheless, you may find a GPS unit (see box below) useful.

ACCOMMODATION

The trail guide (Part 6) lists a fairly comprehensive selection of places to stay along the length of the trail. You have three main options: camping, staying in hostels/bunkhouses/camping barns, or

---

❏ **Using GPS with this book**
I never carried a compass, preferring to rely on a good sense of direction ... I never bothered to understand how a compass works or what it is supposed to do ... To me a compass is a gadget, and I don't get on well with gadgets of any sort.   **Alfred Wainwright**

While Wainwright's acolytes may scoff, other walkers will accept GPS technology as an inexpensive, well-established if non-essential, navigational aid. To cut a long story short, within a minute of being turned on and with a clear view of the sky, **GPS receivers** will establish your position as well as elevation in a variety of formats, including the British OS grid system, anywhere on earth to an accuracy of within a few metres. These days most **smartphones** have a GPS receiver built in and mapping software available to run on it (see box p41).

The maps in the route guide include numbered waypoints; these correlate to the list on pp218-20, which gives the grid reference as well as a description. You can download the complete list of these waypoints for free as a GPS-readable file (that doesn't include the text descriptions) from the Trailblazer website: 🖳 www.trailblazer-guides.com.

Bear in mind that the vast majority of people who tackle the Hadrian's Wall Path do so perfectly successfully without a GPS unit. Instead of rushing out to invest in one, consider putting the money towards good-quality waterproofs or footwear instead.

(Opposite): Sycamore Gap (see p160), named after what is probably the most photographed tree in the Northumberland National Park.

using B&Bs/pubs/guesthouses/hotels. Few people stick to just one of these options the whole way, preferring, for example, to camp most of the time but spend every third night in a hostel, or perhaps use hostels where possible but splash out on a B&B every once in a while.

When booking accommodation, remember to ask if a pick-up and drop-off service is available (usually only B&Bs provide this service). Few of the B&Bs actually lie on the Wall, and at the end of a tiring day it's nice to know a lift is available to take you to your accommodation rather than having to traipse another two or three miles off the path to get to your bed for the night.

The facilities' table on pp30-1 provides a quick snapshot of what type of accommodation is available in each of the towns and villages along the way, while the tables on p33 provide some suggested itineraries. The following is a brief introduction to what to expect from each type of accommodation.

Camping

There are campsites all the way along the Hadrian's Wall Path except in Newcastle and Carlisle, and it is possible to complete the whole trail using nothing but campsites (perhaps with the exception of your first night in Newcastle itself). However, some sections between campsites can be quite long, especially if you're hiking with a heavy rucksack, tent and cooking equipment, so although there's no need to book campsites in advance, some advance planning is advisable, especially given that **wild camping is not allowed**. See the 'Carry on Camping' itinerary in the box on p34 for one potential way to plot your route.

A lot of people choose to camp some nights, rather than every night on the trail. You're almost bound to get at least one night where the rain falls relentlessly, soaking equipment and sapping morale, and it is then that many campers opt to spend the next night drying out in a hostel or B&B. There are, however, many advantages with camping the whole way. It's much more economical, for a start, with most campsites charging £5-10pp. And, although it's wise to phone ahead in the morning to check your planned campsite has space for that night, there's almost never any need to actually book a pitch at a campsite, unless perhaps you're hiking in a large group with a number of tents.

Campsites vary; some are just the back gardens of B&Bs or pubs; others are full-blown caravan sites with a few spaces put aside for tents. Showers are usually available, occasionally for a fee though more often than not included in the rate. Note that wild camping (ie not in a regular campsite) is not allowed.

Camping independently affords you a lot of freedom; if you find yourself ahead of schedule one day, you can simply push on to the next campsite. Likewise, if you're feeling particularly exhausted, you can stop earlier than planned if you pass a campsite halfway along that day's stage. However, carrying your accommodation around with you is not an easy option; the route is wearying enough without a huge, heavy rucksack on your back. So some hikers choose to employ one of the baggage-transfer companies mentioned on p26. Of course this does mean it will cost more and that you will lose a certain amount of freedom as you have to inform the company, at least a day before, of your next destination – and stick to it – so that you and your bag can be reunited every evening. What's more, make sure that the baggage transfer companies deliver to campsites – not all of them do. Hadrian's Wall Ltd (see p27) offers a camping-based walking holiday.

Bunkhouses/camping barns and hostels

The terms '**bunkhouse**' and '**camping barn**' can mean many different things, though usually they mean simple dormitory-style bunk-bed accommodation in a converted barn in a farmer's field or in the annex of a country house. Sleeping bags are usually necessary in these places, although some do provide bedding at extra cost. While not exactly the lap of luxury, a night in a bunkhouse is probably the nearest non-campers will get to sleeping outside, while at the same time providing campers with shelter from the elements should the weather look like taking a turn for the worse. Some of the better bunkhouses provide a shower and simple kitchen with running water and perhaps a kettle, and occasionally pots, pans, cutlery and crockery.

Hostels generally have a mix of dorms and private rooms; facilities are generally shared for dorms but some rooms are now en suite. They have self-catering facilities and rates may include a light toast-and-cereal breakfast. Independent hostels come with less restrictive rules regarding things like curfews and mixed dorms than YHA hostels do. However, since the first edition of this guide, the number of YHA hostels (☎ 01629-592700, 🖳 www.yha.org.uk) on the trail has dropped alarmingly. There is now only one, at Once Brewed (see p160), and even that was closed for reconstruction at the time of research.

The cost of staying in a hostel usually works out at around £20 per person per night; the rate at a YHA hostel is about £3pp less for YHA members. For solo travellers, this is a lot cheaper than staying in a B&B, but if you are walking as a couple or in a group, and usually share the cost of a room, the price of a cheap B&B may not be much more in total.

Bed and breakfast

Bed and Breakfasts (B&Bs) are a great British institution and many of those along the Hadrian's Wall Path are absolutely charming, with buildings often three or four hundred years old and some even made with Wall stones! There's nothing mysterious about a B&B; as the name suggests, they provide you with a bed in a private room and a cooked breakfast (see p21) – unless you specify otherwise beforehand – though they range in style enormously.

Rooms usually contain either a double bed (known as a double room), or two single beds (known as a twin room) though sometimes twin beds can be pushed together to make a double bed. Some rooms sleep three (Tr) or four people (Qd); these are often called family rooms. Generally this means there is a double bed (which two people may need to share) with one or two single beds, or bunk beds. Rooms are often en suite but in some cases the facilities are shared or private, though even with the latter the bathroom is never more than a few feet away. Most rooms have a TV and tea/coffee-making facilities.

An evening meal (usually around £12-20) is often provided at the more remote or bigger places, at least if you book in advance. If not, there's nearly always a pub or restaurant nearby or, if it's far, the B&B owner may give you a lift to and from the nearest place with food.

B&B rates B&Bs in this guide start at around £30 per person (pp) based on two people sharing a room, but most charge around £35-45pp. Solo trekkers should take note: single rooms are not so easy to find so if you are on your own you will often end up occupying a double/twin room, for which you'll usually have to pay a single occupancy (sgl occ) rate, often amounting to the full room rate, minus the cost of one breakfast (usually £10-15). Some places are more generous towards solo travellers, though, and will let you stay for closer to the per-person rate. Rates are sometimes discounted for stays of two or more nights.

Guesthouses, hotels, pubs and inns

The difference between a B&B and a guesthouse is minimal, though some of the better guesthouses are more like hotels, offering evening meals and a lounge for guests. Pubs and inns also offer bed and breakfast accommodation and prices are no more than in a regular B&B.

Hotels usually do cost more, however, and some can be a little irritated with a bunch of smelly hikers turning up and treading mud into their carpet. Most on the Hadrian's Wall Path, however, are used to seeing walkers and welcome them warmly. Prices in hotels start at around £35-40pp, though occasionally you can get some special deals with the larger hotel chains in Newcastle and Carlisle that can be as low as £25 for a room. Hotel and pub rates usually include breakfast, but not always.

❑ **Should you book your accommodation in advance?**

Apart from if camping it's essential that you have your night's accommodation booked by the time you set off in the morning. Nothing is more deflating than to arrive at your destination at the day's end only to find that you've then got to walk a further five miles or so, or even take a detour off the route, because everywhere in town is booked.

That said, there's a certain amount of hysteria regarding the booking of accommodation, with many websites, B&Bs and other organisations suggesting you book at least six months in advance. There really is no need for this, and it leaves you vulnerable to changing circumstances, which may lead to you being left with a trail of lost deposits. By not booking so far in advance, you give yourself the chance to shift your holiday plans to a later date should the unforeseen arise.

Unlike on some other national trails, the lack of accommodation is not as bad on the Hadrian's Wall Path, at least not outside the high season (ie the summer period coinciding with the long school holidays in the UK). Outside this period, and particularly in April/May or September, as long as you're flexible and willing to take what's offered, with maybe even a night or two in a hostel if that's all there is, you should get away with booking just a few nights in advance, or indeed just the night before. The exceptions to this rule are at weekends, when everywhere is busy, and where accommodation is very limited.

Campers, however, have much more flexibility and can usually just turn up and find a space, though phoning ahead in the morning gives you some reassurance. You should always phone ahead out of season, though, just to check your intended campsite is open.

Airbnb

The rise and rise of Airbnb (💻 www.airbnb.co.uk) has seen private homes and apartments opened up to overnight travellers on an informal basis. While accommodation is primarily based in cities, the concept is spreading to tourist hotspots in more rural areas, but do check thoroughly what you are getting and the precise location. While the first couple of options listed may be in the area you're after, others may be too far afield for walkers. At its best, this is a great way to meet local people in a relatively unstructured environment, but do be aware that these places are not registered B&Bs, so standards may vary, and prices may not necessarily be any lower than the norm.

FOOD AND DRINK

Breakfast and lunch

Stay in a B&B and you'll be filled to the gills with a cooked **English breakfast**. This usually consists of a bowl of cereal followed by a plateful of eggs, bacon, sausages, mushrooms, tomatoes and possibly baked beans or black pudding, with toast and butter, and all washed down with coffee, tea and/or juice. Enormously satisfying the first time you try it, by the fourth or fifth morning you may start to prefer a lighter continental breakfast. If you have had enough of these cooked breakfasts and/or plan an early start, ask if you can have a packed lunch instead of breakfast. Some B&Bs are happy to provide a **packed lunch** (indicated by the Ⓛ symbol in the text) at an additional cost (unless it's in lieu of breakfast), though of course there's nothing to stop you preparing your own (but do bring a penknife if you plan to do this), or going to a pub (see below) or café.

Remember to plan ahead; certain stretches of the walk are virtually devoid of eating places (the stretch from Chollerford to Housesteads for example – save for a couple of vans that sometimes set up in summer along the way – and from there to Walltown Quarry) so read ahead about the next day's walk in Part 6 to make sure you never go hungry.

Cream teas

Whatever you do for lunch, don't forget to leave some room for a cream tea or two, a morale, energy and cholesterol booster all rolled into one delicious package: a pot of tea accompanied by scones served with cream and jam, and sometimes a cake or two. The jury is out on whether you should put the jam on first or the cream but either way do not miss the chance of at least one cream tea.

Evening meals

Pubs are as much a feature of the walk as moorland and sheep, and in some cases the pub is as much a tourist attraction as any Roman fort or ruined priory. ***Robin Hood Inn*** (see p122) at East Wallhouses, is one example, as are ***The Keelman*** (see p110) at Newburn and ***The Hadrian Hotel*** (see p142) at Wall (both just off the trail), the historic ***Twice Brewed Inn*** (see p160) at Once Brewed, ***Samson Inn*** (see p177) at Gilsland, and ***Drover's Rest*** (see p205) in Monkhill, near Beaumont.

There are also several great pubs in the towns and cities near the path, such as ***Golden Lion*** and ***The Wheatsheaf Hotel*** (see p129) at Corbridge, the cosy ***Black Bull Inn*** (see p169) at Haltwhistle, and the fabulously unassuming ***Crown Posada*** (see p92) in Newcastle.

Most pubs have become highly attuned to the desires of hikers and offer lunch and evening meals (often with a couple of local dishes and usually some vegetarian options), some locally brewed beers, a garden to relax in on hot days and a roaring fire to huddle around on cold ones. The standard of the food varies widely, though is usually served in big portions, which is often just about all hikers care about at the end of a long day. In many of the villages the pub is the only place to eat out. Note that pubs may close in the afternoon, especially in the winter months, so check in advance if you are hoping to visit a particular one, and also if you are planning lunch there as food serving hours can change.

That other great British culinary institution, the **fish 'n' chip shop**, can be found in Newcastle, Carlisle, and towns off the Wall such as Haltwhistle, Brampton and Hexham; as can Chinese and Indian **takeaways**, which are usually the last places to stop serving food, staying open until at least 11pm.

Self-catering on the trail

Except for when the trail passes through the cities of Newcastle and Carlisle, there aren't actually that many shops where you can buy provisions along the path. Heddon-on-the-Wall has a small supermarket that's combined with its petrol station and Chollerford likewise (though even smaller). There's also a shop at Cottage & Glendale Holiday Park (see p212) near Port Carlisle, but by then you're almost done. The only other places where you can buy anything to eat are the gift shops at the forts of Chesters, Housesteads, Birdoswald and Carvoran, at some cafés, such as House of Meg in Gilsland (see p177), and at the informal **refreshment stalls** established at such places as Haytongate Farm, Bleatarn, Crosby-on-Eden, Grinsdale and Drumburgh (this last one known as Laal Bite). These refreshment stalls are, on occasion, absolute lifesavers: the biggest, such as Haytongate, Crosby-on-Eden and Drumburgh, provide a small hut in which hikers can cower from the elements and take advantage of the refrigerated cans, chocolate bars, crisps, even a hot drinks machine. The other ones, such as those at Bleatarn and Grinsdale, are little more than small boxes in which the provisions are kept. All of them, however, are unsupervised, and thus rely on an honesty-box system (where you put the correct money into a tin or moneybox to pay for what you've consumed). As some of these 'stalls' are actually run by the children of local families, please don't abuse their trust by walking off without paying. See Part 6 for more details.

❑ Local breweries
When it comes to drinking, there are any number of local breweries competing to slake the thirst of trekkers with real ales, stouts and bitters. Of particular interest to trekkers, maybe, is **Hadrian and Border Brewery** (🖥 www.hadrian-border-brewery.co.uk), based in Newcastle. A merger of two breweries, Hadrian and Border's beers include Coast to Coast (4.4%), Reiver's IPA (4.4%) and Rampart (4.8%).

Wylam Brewery (🖥 www.wylambrewery.co.uk) once based in Heddon-on-the-Wall has now moved to Newcastle and is located just north of the city centre in Exhibition Park (see map p84). Brews include some seriously strong craft beers, such as the Club of Slaughters (8.8%), as well as cask ale classics like the Angel Amber Ale (4.3%). Brewery tours (£10) are held on Saturdays.

Also in Northumberland, and only a short hike from the trail, **High House Farm Brewery** (see p122; 🖥 www.highhousefarmbrewery.co.uk) is based on a farm in the village of Matfen and boasts a well-stocked bar from where you can sample one (or more) of their beers, many of which are named after the farm's animals such as Ferocious Fred (4.8%), the farm bull, and the seriously strong Cyril the Magnificent (5.5%), named in honour of the cat.

Another that will be of interest to Wall Walkers is **Big Lamp Brewery** (🖥 biglampbrewers.co.uk), the North-East's oldest micro-brewery, based at The Keelman pub (see p110) just off the trail at Newburn. Brews include the delicious Summerhill Stout and the appropriately named Blackout (11%!).

Another brewer from this neck of the Wall, **Mordue** (🖥 www.morduebrewery.com), produces the divine Workie Ticket (4.5%), 2013 Champion Best Bitter of Britain and a cracking pint.

Heading into Cumbria, another brewery of interest is Cockermouth's **Jennings Brewery** (🖥 www.jenningsbrewery.co.uk), the most ubiquitous brewer in Cumbria.

Further boosting Cumbria's reputation for fine brewing, **Geltsdale Brewery** (🖥 www.geltsdalebrewery.com) is based in part of the Old Brampton Brewery (which was originally founded in 1785), from where they produce eight different brews including a lager, AD78, which is named after the year that Governor Agricola finally brought Britain under control.

Drinking water
There are plenty of ways of perishing on the Hadrian's Wall Path but given how damp the north of England is, thirst probably won't be one of them. Be careful, though, for on a hot day in some of the remoter parts after a steep climb or two you'll quickly dehydrate, which is at best highly unpleasant and at worst mightily dangerous. Always carry some water with you and in hot weather drink three or four litres a day. Don't be tempted by the water in the streams; if the cow or sheep faeces in the water don't make you ill, the chemicals from the pesticides and fertilisers used on the farms almost certainly will. Using iodine or another purifying treatment will help to combat the former, though there's little you can do about the latter. It's a lot safer to fill up from taps instead.

MONEY

Outside Newcastle and Carlisle, **banks** (and ATMs) are few and far between on the Hadrian's Wall Path – indeed, there is only one place, Heddon-on-the-Wall, which boasts an ATM, though there are plenty in the towns (Hexham, Corbridge, Haltwhistle and Brampton) that lie a mile or two off the trail; see the table on pp30-1 for details. However, you can get cash (by debit card) for free at any **post office** counter if you bank with most UK banks or building societies. For details see 🖳 www.postoffice.co.uk/branch-finder.

❑ **Information for foreign visitors**

● **Currency** The British pound (£) comes in notes of £50, £20, £10 and £5, and coins of £2 and £1. The pound is divided into 100 pence (usually referred to as 'p', pronounced 'pee') which come in 'silver' coins of 50p, 20p, 10p and 5p, and 'copper' coins of 2p and 1p. Cash is the most welcome form of payment though debit/credit cards are accepted in some places. Up-to-date currency **exchange rates** can be found on 🖳 www .xe.com/ucc, at some post offices, and at most banks and travel agents.

● **Business hours** Most **village shops** are open Monday to Friday 9am-5pm and Saturday 9am-12.30pm, though some open as early as 7.30/8am; many also open on Sundays but not usually for the whole day. Occasionally you'll come across a local shop that closes at lunchtime on one day during the week, usually a Wednesday or Thursday; this is a throwback to the days when all towns and villages had an 'early closing day'. **Supermarkets** are open Monday to Saturday 8am-8pm (sometimes longer) and on Sunday from about 9am to 5 or 6pm, though main branches of supermarkets generally open 10am-4pm or 11am-5pm.

Main **post offices** generally open Monday to Friday 9am-5pm and Saturday 9am-12.30pm; **banks** typically open at 9.30/10am Monday to Friday and close at 3.30/4pm, though in some places both post offices and banks may open only two or three days a week and/or in the morning, or limited hours, only. **ATMs** (**cash machines**) located outside a bank, shop, post office or petrol station are open all the time, but any that are inside will be accessible only when that place is open. However, ones that charge, such as Link machines, may not accept foreign-issued cards.

Pub hours are less predictable as each pub may have different opening hours. However, most pubs on the Path open daily 11am-11pm (some close at 10.30pm on Sunday) but **some close in the afternoon**. The last entry time to most **museums and galleries** is usually half an hour, or an hour, before the official closing time.

● **Public (bank) holidays** Most businesses are shut on 1 January, Good Friday (March/April), Easter Monday (March/April), the first and last Monday in May, the last Monday in August, 25 December and 26 December.

● **School holidays** School holiday periods in England are generally: a one-week break late October, two weeks around Christmas/New Year, a week in mid February, two weeks around Easter, a week in late May/early June (to coincide with the bank holiday on the last Monday in May), and six weeks from late July to early September. Private-school holidays fall at the same time, but tend to be slightly longer.

● **Travel/medical insurance** The **European Health Insurance Card** (EHIC) entitles EU nationals (on production of the EHIC card) to necessary medical treatment under the UK's National Health Service while on a temporary visit here. However, this is not a substitute for proper medical cover on your travel insurance for unforeseen bills and for getting you home should that be necessary. Also consider cover for

Another way of getting money in your hand is to use the **cashback** system: find a store that will accept a debit card and ask them to advance cash against the card. However, you will almost always need to buy something. Some pubs can also do this. Note that, with few local stores, pubs or B&Bs accepting credit or debit cards, and few places where you can get money out along the way, it is essential to carry plenty of **cash** with you, though do keep it safe and out of sight (preferably in a moneybelt). A chequebook could prove very useful as back-up, so that you don't have to keep on dipping into your cash reserves, especially as most B&Bs don't accept credit cards.

---

loss or theft of personal belongings, especially if you're camping or staying in hostels, as there will be times when you'll have to leave your luggage unattended.

● **Documents** If you are a member of a National Trust organisation in your country bring your membership card as you should be entitled to free entry to National Trust properties and sites in the UK. However, being a member of English Heritage (EH) is more useful for this walk as most of the forts/sites are managed by EH.

● **Weights and measures** Milk in Britain is still sometimes sold in pints (1 pint = 568ml), as is beer in pubs, though most other **liquids** including petrol (gasoline) and diesel are sold in litres. Road **distances** are given in miles (1 mile = 1.6km) rather than kilometres, and yards (1yd = 0.9m) rather than metres. The population remains divided between those who still use inches (1 inch = 2.5cm) and feet (1ft = 0.3m) and those who are happy with centimetres and millimetres; you'll often be told that 'it's only a hundred yards or so' to somewhere, rather than a hundred metres or so. Most **food** is sold in metric weights (g and kg) but the imperial weights of pounds (lb: 1lb = 453g) and ounces (oz: 1oz = 28g) are often displayed too. The **weather** – a frequent topic of conversation – is also an issue: while most forecasts predict temperatures in °C, some people continue to think in terms of °F (see temperature chart on p15 for conversions).

● **Time** During the winter the whole of Britain is on Greenwich Meantime (GMT). The clocks move one hour forward on the last Sunday in March, remaining on British Summer Time (BST) until the last Sunday in October.

● **Smoking** Smoking in enclosed public places is banned. The ban relates not only to pubs and restaurants, but also to B&Bs, hostels and hotels. These latter have the right to designate one or more bedrooms where the occupants can smoke, but the ban is in force in all enclosed areas open to the public – even in a private home such as a B&B. Should you be foolhardy enough to light up in a no-smoking area, which includes pretty well any indoor public place, you could be fined £50, but it's the owners of the premises who suffer most if they fail to stop you, with a potential fine of £2500.

● **Telephones** The international access code for Britain is ☎ 44, followed by the area code minus the first 0, and then the number you require. Within the UK, to call a number with the same code as the landline phone you are calling from, the code can be omitted: dial the number only. It is cheaper to ring at weekends (from midnight on Friday till midnight on Sunday), and after 7pm and before 7am on weekdays. If you're using a **mobile (cell) phone** that is registered overseas, consider buying a local SIM card to keep costs down. Mobile phone reception is generally good on and around Hadrian's Wall Path; also remember to bring a universal adaptor so you can charge your phone.

● **Emergency services** For police, ambulance, fire and mountain rescue dial ☎ 999, or the EU standard number ☎ 112.

OTHER SERVICES

An increasing number of places offer **internet access** and/or **wi-fi** including most accommodation options. Most villages away from the Wall have a **grocery store**, often with a **post office** in part of it, and nearby you'll usually find a **phone box**. There are **outdoor equipment shops** in Carlisle, Newcastle and Hexham; **pharmacies/chemists** in those towns as well as Corbridge and Brampton; and **tourist information centres** (see box p43).

WALKING COMPANIES

It is, of course, possible to turn up with your boots and backpack at Wallsend and just start walking, with little planned save for your accommodation (see box on p20). The following companies, however, are in the business of making your holiday as stress-free and enjoyable as possible.

Baggage transfer and accommodation booking

There are several **baggage-transfer companies** serving the Hadrian's Wall Path, from national organisations such as Sherpa Van Project to companies that consist of little more than one man and his van. With all these services you can book up to the last moment, usually up to around 8pm the previous evening, though it's cheaper if you book in advance. Do shop around as the costs (usually around £8 to take your bag to your next destination) and maximum weight (17-20kg) vary between companies. Most also stipulate a minimum number of bags that they will transfer from the same address (this is usually two).

Nearly all these companies offer **accommodation booking** as well. Alternatively you can contact the tourist information centres as most also offer accommodation booking in their area (see box p20).

- **BaggageTransfer Plus** (☎ 07545 086857, 🖥 www.baggagetransferplus.com)
- **Brigantes Walking Holidays** (☎ 01756-770402, 🖥 www.brigantesenglish walks.com)
- **Hadrian's Haul** (☎ 07967-564823, 🖥 www.hadrianshaul.com)
- **Sherpa Van Project** (baggage transfer ☎ 01748-826917, accommodation booking ☎ 01609-883731, 🖥 www.sherpavan.com)
- **Walkers' Baggage Transfer Co Ltd** (☎ 016977-42341, 🖥 www.walkersbags .co.uk)

Self-guided holidays

Self-guided basically means that the company will organise accommodation, baggage transfer, transport to and from the walk, and various maps and advice, but leave you on your own to actually walk the path. Most companies offer walks between March/April and the end of October. In addition to the 'standard' itineraries summarised on p33, just about all the companies can tailor your holiday to suit your requirements and offer the walk in both directions.

- **Absolute Escapes** (☎ 0131-240 1210, 🖥 www.absoluteescapes.com; Edinburgh) Trips of 5-8 days along the whole of the Wall in either direction.

- **BookMyTrail** (☎ 078523 29015, 🖳 bookmytrail.com/portfolio-item/hadrians-wall-path; Notts) Specialise in the national trails. Complete Wall walks in 6-10 days. No single supplement.
- **Brigantes Walking Holidays** (see opposite) Complete Wall walks lasting 4-10 days.
- **British & Irish Walks** (☎ 01242-254353, 🖳 www.britishandirishwalks.com; Glos) Offers an itinerary along the entire Wall in 7 days.
- **Celtic Trails** (☎ 01291-689774, 🖳 www.celtictrailswalkingholidays.co.uk; Chepstow) A 4-day 'Best of the Wall' walk and complete Wall walks of 6-11 days. They also offer two standards of accommodation.
- **Contours Walking Holidays** (☎ 01629-821900, 🖳 www.contours.co.uk; Derbyshire) Walks along the entire Wall (5-11 days) as well as a Best of/highlight tours (5-6 days/4-5 days) and a 'Short Break' (2-3 days).
- **Discovery Travel** (☎ 01983 301133, 🖳 www.discoverytravel.co.uk; Isle of Wight) Offer standard self-guided walks of 6-9 nights as well as a 5-night 'Highlights of Hadrian's Wall' package.
- **Explore Britain** (☎ 01740-650900, 🖳 www.explorebritain.com; Co Durham) Two walks of four and five days covering just the Wall's picturesque centre and also offers the whole path.
- **Footpath Holidays** (☎ 01985-840049, 🖳 www.footpath-holidays.com; Wilts) Run single-centre guesthouse-based self-guided (selected parts) walks for 5-7 days with Hexham as the base and also the whole path, inn-to-inn.
- **Freedom Walking Holidays** (☎ 07733 885390, 🖳 www.freedomwalkingholidays.co.uk; Goring-on-Thames) Trips of 6-7 days' walking.
- **Hadrian's Wall Ltd** (☎ 01434-603499, 🖳 www.walkthewall.uk; Northumberland) As the name suggests, this company specialises in Hadrian's Wall. They offer all kinds of treks with a range of accommodation levels and are the only company to offer **camping treks** (end May-mid Aug; 4-6 nights).
- **Hillwalk Tours** (☎ +353 91 763994, 🖳 www.hillwalktours.com; Republic of Ireland) Walks (4-11 days) graded by level – gentle, moderate and challenging – and includes the Hadrian's Wall Passport (see box p40).
- **Let's Go Walking** (☎ 01837-880075, 🖳 www.letsgowalking.com; Devon) Offers 7- to 10-day walks along the entire Wall.
- **Macs Adventure** (☎ 0141-530 8886, 🖳 www.macsadventure.com; Glasgow) A range of itineraries from a 'Best of the Wall' trip along the central section between Corbridge and Gilsland to the whole Wall in 6-11 days. They give clients the Hadrian's Wall Passport (see box p40).
- **Mickledore Travel** (☎ 01768-772335, 🖳 www.mickledore.co.uk; Keswick) A number of self-guided tours ranging from a 3-day short break on the most dramatic central section of the wall, between Humshaugh and Gilsland, to a walk of 6-10 days (in either direction) over the entire length of the path. Packed lunches are optional.
- **Load Off Your Back** (☎ 01707-386726, 🖳 www.loadoffyourback.co.uk; Herts) The 'self-guiding' arm of Ramblers Walking Holidays (see p28) offers trips of 5-9 days.

- **NorthWestWalks** (☎ 01257-424889, 🖳 www.northwestwalks.co.uk; Wigan) Itineraries from 5 nights/4 days' walking to 10 nights/9 days' walking.
- **Responsible Travel** (☎ 01273-823700, 🖳 www.responsibletravel.com; Brighton) A 'Best of the Wall' holiday (4 walking days), based at Haltwhistle.
- **Roman Wall Walks** (☎ 07949-564124, 🖳 www.romanwallwalks.com; Heddon-on-the-Wall) A local company based on the Wall offering walks of any length according to clients' needs.
- **Shepherds Walks Holidays** (☎ 01669-621044, 🖳 www.shepherdswalks.co.uk; Northumberland) Trips of 5-10 days along the whole of the Wall as well as 'highlights' tours. Give clients the Hadrians' Wall Passport (see box p40).
- **Sherpa Expeditions** (☎ 020-8577 2717, 🖳 www.sherpaexpeditions.com; London) Offers 8- and 10-day 'Inn-to-Inn' walking tours along the whole Wall.
- **The Carter Company** (☎ 01296-631671, 🖳 www.the-carter-company.com; Buckinghamshire) Offer a luxury trip of 8 nights/7 days' walking.
- **The Walking Holiday Company** (☎ 01600-713008, 🖳 www.thewalkingholidaycompany.co.uk; Monmouth) Trips of 4-10 days along the whole of the Wall in either direction.
- **Wandering Aengus Treks** (☎ 01697-478443, 🖳 www.watreks.com; Caldbeck, Cumbria) A 'Best of the Wall' holiday in 3-5 days' walking, and the complete Wall in 6-9 days' walking.

Group/guided walking tours

If you don't trust your map-reading skills or simply prefer the company of other walkers as well as an experienced guide, the following may be of interest. Packages nearly always include meals, accommodation, transport arrangements, minibus back-up and baggage transfer.

Have a good look at each of the companies' websites before booking as each has their own speciality. Note that there is nearly always a single supplement for solo travellers.

- **Great Guided Tours** (☎ 01228-670578, 🖳 www.greatguidedtours.co.uk) Carol Donnelly MBE has been guiding tours along the Wall for over 35 years; she runs a 2- to 3-hour 'ramble' and also a guided bus tour along the Wall.
- **Hadrian's Wall Ltd** (see p27) They offer a range of guided and part-guided walks; the guide will accompany walkers for one day.
- **HF Holidays** (☎ 0345 470 8558, 🖳 www.hfholidays.co.uk; Penrith) Offers a 'Best of the Wall' 6 nights, centre-based holiday located in Haltwhistle.
- **NorthWestWalks** (see above) Offers one itinerary each year of 7 nights/6 days' walking.
- **Ramblers Walking Holidays** (☎ 01707-331133, 🖳 www.ramblersholidays.co.uk; Herts) A 6-day walk (Apr-Aug approx once a month; Heddon-on-the-Wall to Bowness) based at a hotel near Hexham and one in Carlisle.
- **Shepherds Walks Holidays** (see above) Offer guided walks along the whole trail and also highlights.

Budgeting

England is not a cheap place to go travelling and while the north may be one of the cheaper parts, the towns and villages on the Hadrian's Wall Path are more than used to seeing tourists and charge accordingly. You may think before you set out that you are going to try to keep your budget to a minimum by camping every night where possible and cooking your own food but it's a rare trekker who sticks to this rule. Besides, the B&Bs and pubs on the route are amongst the path's major attractions and it would be a pity not to sample the hospitality in at least some of them.

If the only expenses of this walk were accommodation and food, budgeting for the trip would be a piece of cake. Unfortunately, in addition, there are all the little **extras** that push up the cost of your trip: getting to and from the path, beer, cream teas, stamps and postcards, internet use (though this is often free now), buses here and there, baggage transfer, phone calls, laundry, memory card(s) for your camera, souvenirs, entrance fees (to minimise these it is worth being a member of English Heritage/National Trust (see box p72) ... it's surprising how much these add up.

CAMPING

You can survive on less than £15pp per day if you use the cheapest campsites, don't visit any pubs, avoid all the museums and tourist attractions in the towns, and cook all your own food. Even then, unforeseen expenses will probably nudge your daily budget above this figure. Include the occasional pint, and perhaps a pub meal every now and then, and the figure will be nearer £20 a day.

BUNKHOUSES/CAMPING BARNS AND HOSTELS

The charge for staying in a bunkhouse/camping barn or hostel varies according to its quality and range of facilities, but they tend to cost £15-25 per person. Breakfast is usually extra, at least in the cheaper bunkhouses. Overall, it is likely to cost around £30-40 per day, factoring in the odd beer and going out for the occasional meal.

B&Bs, PUBS, GUESTHOUSES AND HOTELS

B&B rates start at £30pp per night but can easily be at least twice this, particularly if you are walking by yourself and are thus liable to pay single supplements. Add on the cost of lunch and dinner and you should reckon on about £60pp minimum per day. Staying in a guesthouse or hotel would probably push the minimum up to £70pp.

Note that B&B rates are often discounted for stays of two or more nights.

30 Itineraries

VILLAGE AND

Place name (Places in brackets are a short walk off Hadrian's Wall Path)	Distance from previous place § approx miles/km	Bank/ Cash Machine (ATM) £=charge	Post Office (✔) = limited service	Tourist Information Centre (TIC) National Park Centre (NPC)
Newcastle/Wallsend		✔	✔	TIC
Newburn	**11/18**			
(Wylam)	(1/1.6)	✔£	✔	
Heddon-on-the-Wall	**4/6**	✔£	✔	
East Wallhouses	**6/9.5**			
Corbridge–Hexham–Acomb alternative route				
(Corbridge)	(3/4.8 from Halton)	✔	✔	TIC
(Hexham)	(4.5/7.2)	✔	✔	TIC
(Acomb)	(1.5/2.4 + 2.25/3.5 back to Path)		✔	
Port Gate (A68)	**4/6.4**			
Wall	**4/6.4**			
Chollerford	**1/1.6**			
(Humshaugh)	(1/1.6)			
(Old Repeater Stn)	(0.5/0.8)			
(Grindon)	(2/3.2)			
Housesteads	**9/14.5**			
Steel Rigg	**4/6.4**			
(Once Brewed)	(0.25/0.4)			NPC/TIC
(Haltwhistle)	(2/3.2)	✔	✔	TIC
Carvoran	**5.5/8.8**			
(Greenhead)#	(0.3/0.5)			
Gilsland	**2.5/4**	✔	(✔)	
Birdoswald	**2/3.2**			
Banks	**2.5/4**			
(Lanercost Priory)	(0.75/1.25)			Visitor Centre
Walton	**2.5/4**			
Newtown	**2/3.2**			
(Brampton)	(2/3.2)	✔	✔	TIC
(Laversdale)	(0.6/1)			
Crosby-on-Eden	**5/8**			
Carlisle	**5/8**	✔	✔	TIC
Grinsdale	**3.5/5.6**			
Beaumont (& Monkhill)	1/1.6			
Burgh-by-Sands	**1.5/2.5**			
(Boustead Hill)	(0.3/0.5)			
Drumburgh	**2.5/4**			
Glasson	**1/1.6**			
Port Carlisle	**2.5/4**			
Bowness-on-Solway	**1/1.6**			

TOTAL DISTANCE   84 miles/135.5km

§ Distances in **bold** are between places directly on the trail; distances in brackets are the distances off the path but not necessarily from the previous place mentioned.

TOWN FACILITIES

Eating Place ✔=1 ✔✔=2 ✔✔✔=3+ (✔)= seasonal	Food Store	Campsite	Hostels YHA/ H (IndHostel)/ B (Barn or Bunkhouse)	B&B-style accommodation ✔=1 ✔✔=2 ✔✔✔=3+	Place name (Places in brackets are a short walk off Hadrian's Wall Path)
✔✔✔	✔		H	✔✔✔	**Newcastle/Wallsend**
✔✔				✔	**Newburn**
✔✔	✔	✔(*)		✔✔	(Wylam)
✔✔	✔		H	✔✔	**Heddon-on-the-Wall**
✔✔✔		✔			**East Wallhouses**
Corbridge–Hexham–Acomb alternative route					
✔✔✔	✔			✔✔✔	(Corbridge)
✔✔✔	✔			✔✔✔	(Hexham)
✔✔				✔✔	(Acomb)
(✔)					**Port Gate (A68)**
✔		✔		✔	**Wall**
✔✔	✔	✔		✔	**Chollerford**
✔	✔			✔	(Humshaugh)
		✔(u)		✔	(Old Repeater Stn)
				✔	(Grindon)
				✔	**Housesteads**
					Steel Rigg
✔		✔	YHA & B	✔✔	(Once Brewed)
✔✔✔	✔	✔		✔✔✔	(Haltwhistle)
✔					**Carvoran**
✔✔		✔	H & B	✔✔	# (Greenhead)
✔✔✔			B	✔✔✔	**Gilsland**
(✔)					**Birdoswald**
		✔		✔	**Banks**
✔				✔	(Lanercost Priory)
(✔)		✔	B	✔	**Walton**
	✔(r)			✔	**Newtown**
✔✔✔	✔			✔✔✔	(Brampton)
		✔			(Laversdale)
✔	✔(r)	✔		✔	**Crosby-on-Eden**
✔✔✔	✔		H	✔✔✔	**Carlisle**
	✔(r)				**Grinsdale**
				✔	(Monkhill &) **Beaumont**
✔	✔				**Burgh-by-Sands**
✔					
		✔	B	✔✔	(Boustead Hill)
	✔(r)				**Drumburgh**
✔	✔				**Glasson**
✔		✔	B		**Port Carlisle**
(✔✔)		✔	B	✔✔✔	**Bowness-on-Solway**

(*) (in Ovingham); ✔(u) = no official campsite though can camp nearby; ask the locals
✔(r) = unmanned refreshments stall with honesty box or vending machine
(Greenhead) this includes Holmhead which is on the Wall

Itineraries

Part 6 of this book has been written from east to west, though there is of course nothing to stop you from tackling it in the opposite direction, and there are advantages in doing so – see p35. To help you plan your walk the colour maps at the back of the book have **profile charts**; there is also a **distance chart** and a **planning map**. The **table of village/town facilities** (pp30-1) gives a rundown on the essential information you will need regarding accommodation possibilities and services.

You could follow one of the suggested itineraries (see opposite) which are based on preferred type of accommodation and walking speeds or, if tackling the entire walk seems a bit ambitious, you can tackle it a day or two at a time, using public transport to get to the start and end of the walk. The public transport map and service details are on pp44-8. Once you have an idea of your

❏ **Visiting the forts – a walker's view**
To many or even most people on the Hadrian's Wall path, the various forts and museums are little more than milestones on the trail: places to tick off as they pass by rather than places to actually stop at and visit. However, some of our readers – many not even particularly interested in Roman history (or at least not before the trail) – write in to tell us how much they enjoyed the various museums on the way. The following from Jane Johnson was one such letter:

'To get an idea of the Roman remains we decided it would be good to have visited the sites before commencing the walk, establishing their location as well as those of the Roman roads. We camped for a week, basing ourselves at Haltwhistle; this enabled us to visit Chesters, Vindolanda (5hrs), Corbridge etc as well as the smaller off route places such as the bridge abutment across from Chesters. From Haltwhistle it was an easy train ride to Newcastle to visit the sites along the West Road and the Great North Museum: Hancock with its new displays.

We didn't do the actual walk until the following year but even with the gap in time we really appreciated having been to the main sites as we had some knowledge of things. Before setting off we spent two nights in Newcastle to see the rest of the sites around there. Arriving at the station in the early afternoon we hopped on the metro to South Shields to reach Arbeia, well worth visiting, before settling in to the city.

The next day we went to Segedunum and then did the short walk back to the city (not the most inspiring start to a walk!) leaving a 10-mile stretch to Heddon on the second day. This means you can visit Segedunum and walk the first five miles without baggage. What an easy start to the walk. Both Arbeia and Segedunum are great, especially having the reconstructions as they give an idea of the size of buildings. We wanted to stay in B&Bs for the actual walk and used a baggage transfer company to take our bags. Of course all this could be done in about two weeks' holiday if you have both the time and finance.' **Jane Johnson**

While Jane's itinerary may be a bit extreme for some tastes, her email is at least further testimony that it is worth visiting some of the forts on the way.

Suggested itineraries

STAYING IN B&B-STYLE ACCOMMODATION

Relaxed		Medium		Fast	
Place / Night	Approx Distance miles/km	Place	Approx Distance miles/km	Place	Approx Distance miles/km
0 Newcastle		Newcastle		Newcastle	
1 Newburn	11/18	Heddon	15/24	Chollerford	30/48
2 East Wallhouses	7.5/12	Chollerford	15/24	Gilsland	21/34
3 Chollerford	11.5/18.5	Once Brewed	12/19.5	Carlisle	19/30.5
4 Once Brewed	12/19.5	Walton	16/26	Bowness	14/22.5
5 Gilsland	9/14.5	Carlisle	12/19.5		
6 Newtown	9/14.5	Bowness	14/22.5		
7 Carlisle	10/16				
8 Bowness	14/22.5				

STAYING IN BUNKHOUSES/CAMPING BARNS/HOSTELS

Relaxed		Medium		Fast	
Place / Night	Approx Distance miles/km	Place	Approx Distance miles/km	Place	Approx Distance miles/km
0 Newcastle		Newcastle		Newcastle	
1 Heddon	15/24	Heddon	15/24	Heddon	15/24
2 Black Carts	16/25.5	Old Repeater Stn	19/30.5	Once Brewed	27/43.5
3 Old Repeater Stn	3/5	Greenhead	15/24	Walton	16/25.5
4 Once Brewed	8/13	Crosby*	14/22.5	Carlisle	12/19.5
5 Greenhead	7/11	Boustead Hill	14/22.5	Bowness	14/22.5
6 Walton	9/14.5	Bowness	7/11		
7 Carlisle	12/19.5				
8 Bowness	14/22.5				

* Only option is camping or B&B

CAMPING

Relaxed		Medium		Fast	
Place / Night	Approx Distance miles/km	Place	Approx Distance miles/km	Place	Approx Distance miles/km
0 Ovingham *		Ovingham *		Ovingham *	
1 Ovingham *	15/24	Ovingham *	15/24	East Wallhouses	21/34
2 East Wallhouses	11/18	Chollerford	21/33	Once Brewed	22/35
3 Chollerford	11/18	Once Brewed	14/23	Crosby-on-Eden	18/29
4 Once Brewed	14/23	Walton	16/26	Bowness	22/35
5 Greenhead	7/11	Beaumont	16/28		
6 Walton	9/14	Bowness	11/18		
7 Crosby-on-Eden	6/10				
8 Beaumont	11/18				
9 Bowness	11/18				

* See box p34. With no campsite in Newcastle you'd need to spend two nights in Ovingham and commute to and from the Path.

34 Itineraries

approach turn to Part 6 for detailed information on accommodation, places to eat and other services in each village and town on the route. Also in Part 6 you will find summaries of the route to accompany the detailed trail maps.

SUGGESTED ITINERARIES

The itineraries in the boxes on p33 are based on different accommodation types: camping, hostels and B&Bs, with each one divided into three alternatives depending on walking speed. They are only suggestions so feel free to adapt them. See also box p32 for a reader's itinerary and if planning to camp see also the box below. It is also possible to plan a walk with fixed bases, such as Hexham, Haltwhistle and around Carlisle; this would mean using public transport, but you wouldn't need to carry your luggage every day. Whatever you do **don't forget** to add your travelling time before and after the walk.

❏ **Carry on camping**

If you want to camp every night, it is possible, but it takes a little bit of forward planning due to the scarcity of campsites on some stretches of the trail, and the fact that **wild camping is not allowed**. The following is one possible option, with fairly evenly spaced campsites never more than 15 miles apart. Remember, it's a lot harder walking long distances when you're carrying all your camping gear, plus food and water, so unless you're super fit and very much accustomed to long-distance 'through hiking', don't expect to be able to walk much more than 15 miles in one day.

This itinerary is, of course, only one option. There are plenty of other campsites besides these, allowing you to stay at numerous other points on the trail.

- **Days 0 & 1: Ovingham – 15 miles** (High Hermitage Caravan Park, p115) Since there are no campsites in, or even close to Newcastle, one option is for you to spend your first two nights here (two miles from the trail, just beyond Wylam) and to use the train, or local buses (see pp46-8) to get you to the start of the trail in the morning before hiking back to your tent. The campsite is about 15 miles (24km) from Wallsend, and 4 miles (6km) from Heddon-on-the-Wall.
- **Day 2: East Wallhouses – 11 miles** (Robin Hood Inn or Wellhouse Farm Camping, both p122) Wellhouse is better equipped, but about a mile south of the trail.
- **Day 3: Chollerford – 11 miles** (Riverside Campsite, p144) Note, you'll need to stay here for two nights if you also want to walk the Corbridge loop. Also note, you could push on an extra three miles to reach the excellent Green Carts Farm Campsite (p147), and help reduce the length of the next day's walk.
- **Day 4: Once Brewed – 14 miles** (Winshields Farm Campsite, p162).
- **Day 5: Greenhead – 7 miles** (Holmhead B&B, p172) This stretch is hillier than most so don't overdo the mileage. It's also a Wall-filled stage to be savoured, so best not to rush through it. Note, this campsite is very small so can fill up.
- **Day 6: Walton – 9 miles** (Sandysike, p184) You could push on to Crosby-on-Eden if you're feeling energetic.
- **Day 7: Crosby-on-Eden – 6 miles** (Crosby Camping, p189) This is the last campsite before Carlisle.
- **Day 8: Beaumont – 11 miles** (Roman Wall Lodges, p205).
- **Day 9: Bowness-on-Solway – 11 miles** (Wallsend Guest House, p216) You may have time to catch public transport back home from Bowness after your final day's walk, thereby negating the need to use this final campsite.

WHICH DIRECTION?

It's more common for Wall walkers attempting the entire trail to start from Newcastle and head west. The main reason seems to be because the official trail guide and the majority of those guidebooks that have followed in its wake were written from east to west. The justification put forward by the author of the official guide is that it seems 'more natural' to walk out of a big city into the open country, and there is some truth in that. Around 60% of Wall walkers seem to agree. Furthermore, the scenery improves the further west you go – up to a point – and the turrets and milecastles are also numbered from east to west (see box p116) as that is the direction that the Romans built the Wall. What's more, as it's more popular to walk from east to west, those trekkers who prefer a bit of company will find more people heading in their direction.

But, that said, there are arguments that could be made for walking the other way, from Bowness-on-Solway to Wallsend; for one thing, the prevailing winds in the UK tend to blow in from the west, and thus will be at your back if walking from west to east, which is preferable to struggling against a force nine (though, to be fair, the winds aren't too severe in summer). Secondly, just as the official guide says that it's better to walk out of a city into the countryside, it could also be argued that a big city makes a suitably grand place to finish a hike – and Newcastle certainly has any number of places in which to celebrate the completion of a successful walk. Thirdly, some argue that you get a better view of the crags (on your way into Thirlwall) and can understand a little more how the Wall was laid out by travelling in this direction (and yes, of course, you can just look back and see the same view if travelling westwards – but it's a rare hiker who actually does). It's also a lot easier getting away from Newcastle at the end of the trail than it is from Bowness – and struggling to find a bus or lift that will take you away from the Solway and back to 'civilisation' is not something you want to be doing after you've walked 84 miles. Finally, isn't there something poetic about finishing a walk along the Wall at a place called Wallsend?

As the majority of trekkers continue to walk from east to west, that is the way this book has been written. That said, those who prefer to swim against the tide of popular opinion and walk west to east should find it easy to use this book too.

TAKING DOGS ALONG THE HADRIAN'S WALL PATH

The Hadrian's Wall Path is actually not that dog-friendly. Much of the land through which the path passes is grazed by livestock and dogs must be kept on a lead; the number of B&Bs, bunkhouses, guesthouses and even campsites that accept dogs is surprisingly low; and even the odd pub refuses to allow dogs inside, leaving you to sup your shandy in a storm while other walkers crowd around the open fire inside. Furthermore, there are few litterbins on the trail where you can throw away poo bags after you've cleaned up after your dog.

It's fair to say that dog owners must be a resilient breed to put up with the privations they suffer for the sake of their pet. Still, despite all the moans it *is* possible to walk from one end to the other with your dog and many are the rewards that await those prepared to make the extra effort required to bring their best friend with them. Don't underestimate the extra work involved in bringing your pooch to the path. Just about every decision you make will be influenced by the fact you've got a dog: how you plan to travel to the start of the trail, where you're going to stay, how far you're going to walk each day, where you're going to rest and where you're going to eat in the evening etc etc. The decision-making begins well before you've set foot on the trail. For starters, you have to ask – and be honest with – yourself: can your dog really cope with walking ten-plus miles a day, day after day, for a week or more? And just as importantly, will he or she actually enjoy it? If you think the answer is yes to both, you need to start preparing accordingly.

For detailed information about taking a dog along the path see pp221-2.

What to take

Deciding how much to take can be difficult. Experienced walkers know that you should take only the bare essentials but at the same time you must ensure you have all the equipment necessary to make the trip safe and comfortable.

KEEP YOUR LUGGAGE LIGHT

Experienced backpackers know that there is some sort of complicated formula governing the success of a trek, in which the enjoyment of the walk is inversely proportional to the amount carried. Carrying a heavy rucksack slows you down, tires you out and gives you aches and pains in parts of the body that you never knew existed. It is imperative, therefore, that you take a good deal of time packing and that you are ruthless when you do; if it's not essential, don't take it.

HOW TO CARRY IT

If you are using one of the baggage-transfer services (see p26), you must contact them beforehand to find out what their regulations are regarding the weight and size of the luggage you wish them to carry. Even if you are using one of these services, you will still need to carry a small **daypack**, filled with those items that you will need during the day: water bottle or pouch, this book, map, sun-screen, sun hat, wet-weather gear, some food, camera, money and so on.

If you have decided to forego the services of the baggage carriers you will have to consider your **rucksack** even more carefully. Ultimately its size will depend on where you are planning to stay and how you are planning to eat. If you are camping and cooking for yourself you will probably need a 70- to 95-litre rucksack, which should be large enough to carry a small tent, sleeping bag, cooking equipment, crockery, cutlery and food. Those not carrying their home with them should find a 40- to 60-litre rucksack sufficient.

When choosing a rucksack, make sure it has a stiffened back and can be adjusted to fit your own back comfortably. Don't just try the rucksack out in the shop: take it home, fill it with things and then try it out around the house and take it out for a short walk. Only then can you be certain that it fits. Make sure the hip belt and chest strap (if there is one) are fastened tightly as this helps distribute the weight more comfortably with most of it being carried on the hips. Carry a small daypack inside the rucksack, as this will be useful to carry things in when leaving the main pack at the hostel or B&B.

Don't forget to bring a **waterproof rucksack cover**. Most rucksacks these days have them 'built in' to the sack, but you can also buy them separately for less than a tenner. Lining your bag with a strong **bin liner** is another sensible, cut-price idea. Finally, it's also a good idea to keep everything wrapped in plastic bags inside the rucksack; that way, even if it does pour with rain, everything should remain dry.

FOOTWEAR

Boots

Most hikers choose to wear a decent pair of strong, durable trekking boots, but is perfectly possible to hike the trail in running shoes or cross-trainers, which are usually much more comfortable. The downside is that they are much less waterproof, if waterproof at all, so you will find you spend many an evening trying to dry them out in preparation for your next day's walk. Many hikers prefer boots with a good ankle support; the ground can occasionally be rough and stony and twisted ankles are commonplace. Whatever footwear you choose, it is essential that your shoes or boots are thoroughly 'broken in' so they're comfortable and not likely to cause blisters. Never, under any circumstances, attempt to start a hike like this one is new boots!

In addition, some people bring an extra pair of shoes or trainers (or even just sandals or flip-flops) to wear off the trail. This is not essential but if you've got room in your luggage, why not? If you're camping, a pair of flip-flops certainly comes in handy for walking around the campsite.

Socks

If you haven't got a pair of the modern hi-tech walking socks the old system of wearing a thin liner sock under a thicker wool sock is just as good. Bring a few pairs of each; you certainly don't want to start any day of hiking in socks that are anything other than clean and bone dry.

I have sent you ... pairs of socks from Sattua, two pairs of sandals and two pairs of underpants ...
Tablet 346 of the **Vindolanda Postcards** (see pp162-3)

CLOTHES

In a country notorious for its unpredictable climate it is imperative that you pack enough clothes to cover every extreme of weather, from burning hot to bloomin' freezing. Modern hi-tech outdoor clothes come with a range of fancy names and brands but they all still follow the basic two- or three-layer principle, with an inner base layer to transport sweat away from your skin, a mid-layer for warmth and an outer layer to protect you from the wind and rain.

A thin lightweight **thermal top** of a synthetic material is ideal as the base layer as it draws moisture (ie sweat) away from your body. Cool in hot weather and warm when worn under other clothes in the cold, pack at least one thermal top. Over the top in cold weather a mid-weight **polyester fleece** should suffice. Fleeces are light, more water-resistant than the alternatives (such as a woolly jumper), remain warm even when wet and pack down small in rucksacks; they are thus ideal trekking gear. Over the top of all this a **waterproof jacket** is essential. 'Breathable' jackets cost a small fortune (though prices are falling all the time) but they do prevent the build-up of condensation.

Leg wear

Some hikers find trekking trousers an unnecessary investment and any light, quick-drying trouser should suffice. Jeans are heavy and dry slowly thus are not recommended. A pair of **waterproof trousers** *is* more than useful, however, while on really hot sunny days you'll be glad you brought your shorts. Thermal **long johns** take up little room and could be vital if the weather starts to close in. **Gaiters** are not essential but, again, those who bring them are always glad they did, for they provide extra protection when walking through muddy ground and when the vegetation around the trail is dripping wet after bad weather.

Other clothes

Three or four changes of **underwear** is fine. Any more is excessive, any less unhygienic. Because backpacks can cause bra straps to dig painfully into the skin, women may find a **sports bra** more comfortable.

You may like to consider a woolly **hat** and **gloves** – you'd be surprised how cold it can get up on the moors, even in summer – and a **sun hat**.

TOILETRIES

Once again, take the minimum. **Soap**, **towel** (quick-dry micro-fibre camping towels are particularly useful as they pack up very small) a **toothbrush** and **toothpaste** are pretty much essential (although those staying in B&Bs will find that most provide soap and towels anyway). Some **toilet paper** could also prove vital on the trail, particularly if using public toilets (which occasionally run out).

Other items: **razor**; **deodorant**; **tampons/sanitary towels** and a high factor **sun-screen** should cover just about everything.

FIRST-AID KIT

A small first-aid kit could prove useful for those emergencies that occur along the trail. This kit should include **aspirin** or **paracetamol**; **plasters** for minor cuts; **moleskin**, **Second Skin** or some other treatment for blisters; a **bandage** or elasticated joint support for supporting a sprained ankle or a weak knee; **antiseptic wipes**; **antiseptic cream**; **safety pins**; **tweezers** and **scissors**.

You may sometimes encounter biting midges in the early morning or late evening between June and August so it's worth taking **insect repellent**.

GENERAL ITEMS
Essential
Everybody should have some **emergency food, a water bottle or pouch, torch and spare batteries, penknife, whistle** (see p69 for details of the international distress signal), and an **alarm** on a watch or phone.

If you know how to use it properly you may find a **compass** handy. Most people find a **mobile phone** invaluable too, particularly if it's a **smartphone** with GPS capabilities and a camera. Phone reception is usually good on the trail and it's extremely handy to be able to phone ahead in the mornings to confirm your accommodation for that night, or to be able to arrange a lift from the Wall to your B&B at the end of the day. Just don't forget your **phone charger**!

Useful items and luxuries
Those with weak knees may find a **walking pole** or **sticks** useful. Other things worth considering include a **map** (though of course this book has that covered), a **book** for days off, or on train and bus journeys, a **camera** (although most people's smartphones have this covered), a pair of **sunglasses**, **binoculars**, a **vacuum flask** for hot drinks and an **iPod/iPad** or **MP3 player**.

CAMPING GEAR

Both campers and those intending to stay in the various bunkhouses/camping barns en route will find a **sleeping bag** essential. A two- to three-season bag should suffice for summer. Campers will also need a decent bivvy bag or tent, a sleeping mat, fuel and stove, cutlery, pans, a cup and a scrubber for washing up. If you're more concerned about the weight of your bag than the cost of your trip, you could get away without bringing cooking equipment, as most campsites are either close to pubs or cafés that do food, or can provide food themselves. This does prove expensive, though, and takes half the fun out of a camping trip.

MONEY AND DOCUMENTS

(Also see Money, pp23-5) ATMs (cash machines) are infrequent along the Hadrian's Wall Path and, apart from pubs, few places along the trail accept **debit** or **credit cards** as payment either – though some B&Bs now do, and many shops, restaurants and cafés in the larger towns. As a result, you should always carry a fair amount of **cash** with you, just to be on the safe side. A **chequebook** from a British bank is useful in those places where credit cards are not accepted. Crime on the trail is thankfully rare but you may want to carry your money in a **moneybelt**, just to be safe.

Don't forget your **Hadrian's Wall Path Passport** (see box p40).

❑ Hadrian's Wall Path Passport

A simple piece of folded card, the Hadrian's Wall Path Passport not only provides walkers with a bit of fun, and proof that they walked the entire trail, but is also an important measure in protecting the Wall. It is available from May to October only, so encourages walkers to view the trail as a summertime-only activity, and the money raised from it goes towards support for the maintenance of the Path.

You can buy a Passport (£5) in person from Segedunum, Walltown Quarry Country Park, Carlisle TIC, or in Bowness at either the King's Arms or Wallsend Guesthouse/Tearoom. They are also available online: 🖳 www.shoptwmuseums.co.uk (£5.50 inc UK post and packing), or 🖳 www.trailgiftshop.co.uk (£5.99 inc UK P&P).

Open up the passport and you'll find seven blank spaces; the idea is to collect seven stamps from various places along the trail. Get the full set and you qualify for the right to purchase a commemorative badge and/or certificate; these are available from most of the above places or by post. The **'stamping stations'** are located at:

- **Segedunum, Wallsend** There is a stamp inside the main entrance to the museum, available during opening hours only, and also one by the rear entrance which is available outside these hours.
- **Robin Hood Inn** (East Wallhouses) In a box outside the front door.
- **Chesters Roman Fort** Inside the entrance to the museum during opening hours; outside these hours a stamping box is provided attached to the wall on the road at the entrance to the car park – though it's not easy to spot.
- **Housesteads** Outside the museum entrance.
- **Birdoswald Roman Fort** Inside the main entrance during opening hours; outside these hours a stamping box is provided by the main entrance.
- **Sands Sports Centre, Carlisle** Inside the café; available only during the centre's opening hours.
- **The Banks Promenade**, in Bowness, any time, or at **Wallsend Guesthouse/Tearoom, King's Arms, or Lindow Hall** during their relevant opening hours.

If you are a member of **English Heritage** or the **National Trust**, bring your **membership cards** (See box p72); membership of English Heritage in particular will save you money at the sights along the path, allowing free entrance to the Roman forts and other attractions.

MAPS

The hand-drawn maps in this book cover the trail at a scale of 1:20,000. This large scale, combined with the notes and tips written on the maps, should be more than enough to stop you losing your way. Nevertheless, some people like to have a separate map of the region; such maps can prove invaluable should you need to abandon the path and find the quickest route off the trail in an emergency. They also help in identifying local features and landmarks and devising possible side trips.

Perhaps the best map for the whole walk is *Hadrian's Wall Adventure Atlas*, published by A–Z (🖳 www.az.co.uk); this booklet includes the OS maps (1:25,000) spread over 38 pages with the path clearly marked; also included are distances and an index.

Also worth considering is *Hadrian's Wall Path* (XT40) strip map (1:40,000) published by Harvey Map Services (💻 www.harvey maps.co.uk); the bonus for this map is that it is waterproof.

Ordnance Survey (💻 www.ordnancesurvey.co.uk) also produce a waterproof strip map (OL43) that covers the central section of the trail (centred on Haltwhistle and Hexham) at a scale of 1:25,000 as part of their Explorer Outdoor Leisure series. In addition, you'll need Explorer Active maps 314, 315 and 316 to cover the rest of the trail. They also offer online maps which you can download and tailor to your requirements by plotting routes, adding notes and photos and so on. A one-month subscription for this service costs £3.99 (£19.99 for one year), but you can also get it as a free 7-day trial.

While it may be extravagant to buy all these maps, members of Ramblers' (see box p43) can make use of their library which allows them to borrow up to ten maps for up to six weeks free of charge. It is also possible you will be able to borrow them from your local public library.

Historic England publish *An Archaeological Map of Hadrian's Wall* (£9.99). Beautiful, fascinating and insightful, the map includes sites both along and near the Wall. It's probably only for those with a specialist interest in the Wall's history and archaeology, but is arguably the most absorbing map on the Wall and its surroundings.

RECOMMENDED READING

There is a wealth of books on the Wall, as you'd expect, so the following is a mere overview of the better, or at least newer, works. Some of these books can be found in the tourist information centres and at the reception desks of the

---

❑ **Digital mapping**

There are several software packages available on the market today that provide Ordnance Survey maps for a PC or smartphone. The two best known are Memory Map and Anquet, but more suppliers join the list every year. Maps are supplied not in traditional paper format, but electronically, on DVD or USB media, or by direct download over the Internet. The maps are then loaded into an application, also available by download, from where you can view them, print them and create routes on them. Additionally, the route can be viewed directly on a smartphone or uploaded to a GPS device. If your smartphone has a GPS chip, you will be able to see your position overlaid onto the digital map on your phone.

Many websites now have free routes you can download for the more popular digital mapping products. Anything from day walks to complete Long Distance Paths. It is important to ensure any digital mapping software on your smartphone uses pre-downloaded maps, stored on your device, and doesn't need to download them on-the-fly, as this may be expensive and will be impossible without a signal.

Smartphones and GPS devices should complement, not replace, the traditional method of navigation (a map and compass) as any electronic device is susceptible to failure and, if nothing else, battery failure. Remember that battery life will be significantly reduced, compared to normal usage, when you are using the built-in GPS and running the screen for long periods. **Stuart Greig**

42 What to take

Roman forts en route. As well as stocking many of the titles listed below, these places also have a number of books about the towns and villages en route, usually printed by local publishers. Furthermore, each of the visitor centres of the major English Heritage historical attractions, such as Housesteads, Chesters and Corbridge, publishes their own guidebook to the site.

The journalist and author Hunter Davies, who was born at the western end of the trail, has written the historical travelogue *A Walk Along the Wall* (Frances Lincoln; originally published in 1974), the result of spending a year trekking along and studying the wall. *Hadrian's Wall*, by David Breeze and Brian Dobson, is part of the Penguin History Series and deals with the history of the Wall as well as the day-to-day activities of those who lived in its shadow, both soldiers and locals, during the Roman occupation.

On a similar subject, *Hadrian's Wall in the Days of the Romans*, by Ronald Embleton and Frank Graham (WJ Williams & Son Books Ltd), does exactly what it says on the cover; *Hadrian's Wall AD122-410* by Nic Fields (Osprey Publishing) covers much the same ground. Newer, *The Wall: Rome's Greatest Frontier* (Birlinn Ltd) by Alistair Moffatt, also deals with the building of the

---

❏ Wall-related websites
- **www.hadrians.com** A website dedicated to the man who ordered the construction of the Wall, including studies of his family, as well as the food, clothes, homes and work of those who lived during his reign.
- **www.bbc.co.uk/history/ancient/romans** The BBC's website on the Romans, includes some useful timelines and interesting articles by various boffins. However, this is no longer updated.
- **www.britannia.com/history/h30.html** Described as the American gateway to the British Isles, this website is great for an overview of British history, with the address above dealing specifically with Roman Britain.

Trail-specific websites
- **www.nationaltrail.co.uk/hadrians-wall-path** The official site of the Hadrian's Wall Path and the essential first stop for those looking to walk the Wall. Check out the slideshow (trail gallery), trail video, trail officer's blog, maps, sections on accommodation and publications. Best of all, register with them and they'll send you newsletters.
- **www.hadrianswallcountry.co.uk** The most complete website on the Wall itself, this is the website of Hadrian's Wall Country – and thus, unlike the website above, is not specifically for walkers – with lists of tour agencies, accommodation, travel information, events, history and the latest news – though it does have a page on walking.
- **www.walltogether.org.uk** The website for Hadrian's Wall Association; this aims to promote and support the management and maintenance of the Hadrian's Wall Frontiers including the National Trail; they also publish an *Essential Services* guide.
- **www.perlineamvalli.wordpress.com** An information-packed blog about walking Hadrian's Wall from an archaeologist's point of view; the archaeologist in question being Mike Bishop. It also has a reading list.
- **www.heartofhadrianswall.com** Gives information about places to stay and eat as well as services in the central area of the Wall.
- **www.golakes.co.uk** Official website for the Lake District, Cumbria, though does contain pages on Carlisle and the Hadrian's Wall Path.

❑ SOURCES OF FURTHER INFORMATION

Tourist information centres (TICs)
Tourist information centres are based in towns throughout Britain and provide all manner of locally specific information. Most also provide an accommodation-booking service (in many cases a 10% deposit is payable which is deducted from the final bill and sometimes a booking charge as well). The centres listed here are on or close to the Hadrian's Wall Path: **Corbridge** (see p128); **Hexham** (see p135); **Haltwhistle** (p167); **Brampton** (see p186) and **Carlisle** (see p196).

Due to open in the latter half of 2017, the **Once Brewed** TIC will be part of a new, the state-of-the-art National Landscape Discovery Centre (see p160).

Organisations for walkers
- **Backpackers' Club** (🖥 www.backpackersclub.co.uk) A club aimed at people who are involved or interested in lightweight camping through walking, cycling, skiing and canoeing. They produce a quarterly magazine, provide members with a comprehensive advisory and information service on all aspects of backpacking, organise weekend trips and also publish a farm-pitch directory. Membership is £15 a year.
- **The Long Distance Walkers' Association** (🖥 www.ldwa.org.uk) An association of people with the common interest of long-distance walking. Membership includes a journal, *Strider*, three times per year giving details of challenge events and local group walks as well as articles on the subject. Individual membership is £13 a year (£19.50 for non-UK residents) whilst family membership for two adults and all children under 18 is £19.50 a year.
- **Ramblers** (formerly Ramblers' Association; 🖥 www.ramblers.org.uk) Looks after the interests of walkers throughout Britain. They publish a large amount of useful information including their quarterly *Walk* magazine (£3.60 to non-members), also available in pdf and audio format. Annual membership costs £34.50.

Wall and is perhaps the best read of the three and has a good section on the Vindolanda postcards. One of the leading Wall experts, Anthony R Birley, has produced a biography of the enigmatic man behind the Wall: *Hadrian, The Restless Emperor* (Routledge), though it must be said that the text is a little dry.

The Great Wall of Britain – A Walk Along Hadrian's Wall (Hayloft), by the illustrator Anton Hodge, is a travelogue-cum-geographical-historical-tour of the Roman Wall. You may find it locally, or you can visit the author's website: 🖥 antonhodge.co.uk/the-great-wall-of-britain. In a similar 'travelogue' vein is Bob Bibby's *On the Wall with Hadrian* (Eye Books).

English Heritage produce their own historical guide to the Wall, titled simply *Hadrian's Wall*, written by Stephen Johnson and published by BT Batsford.

Also worth looking at is *Hadrian's Wall: Everyday Life on a Roman Frontier* by Patricia Southern (Amberley Publishing).

Flora and fauna field guides
Collins Bird Guide, with its beautiful illustrations of British and European birds, continues to be the favourite field guide of both ornithologists and laymen alike. Its *Trees of Britain & Europe* is also OK if you've room in your rucksack and don't know your ash from your alder. Collins also produces guides to the above and *Mushrooms*, *Butterflies*, *Insects*, *Wild Flowers* and *Birds* as part of

44 What to take

their *Gem* series – a collection of cracking guides that are only slightly larger than a pack of playing cards and thus ideal for hiking with.

A rather odd book – but charming in its way – is John Miles's *Hadrian's Wildlife* (Whittles Publishing) which looks at the animals, birds and landscape that would have existed in the region when the Wall was being built.

There are also some field guide **apps** for smart phones and tablets, including those that can aid in identifying birds by their song as well as by their appearance.

DVDs

There's a very pleasant video, *Edge of Empire*, that's produced by Striding Edge and the Ordnance Survey, in which Eric Robson takes us on a journey through the Wall's two-millennia-long history. The *Lost Treasures of the Ancient World* series (Cromwell Productions) has a 48-minute documentary on the Wall; the DVD has features including a 'Test your Knowledge' section.

There is also a DVD dedicated to the trail itself, *Hadrian's Wall Path National Trail*, narrated by Anthony Burton. Best of all, however, is *Hadrian's Wall from the Air*, a 45-minute DVD of the Wall filmed from above. They have also produced a DVD, *Illuminating Hadrian's Wall* that celebrates the night of 13 March 2010 when the entire length of the Wall was lit by over a thousand volunteer torch-bearers and supporters.

Getting to and from the Hadrian's Wall Path

Carlisle and Newcastle are the main transport hubs for the trail and conveniently they all but bookend the path, with Carlisle near the western end and the Newcastle suburb of Wallsend at the eastern end. Both are well connected by public transport to the rest of the country and indeed Europe; see box opposite. However, it should be noted that some of the other places on the trail are less well connected, both east and west of Carlisle.

NATIONAL TRANSPORT

By train

Both Newcastle and Carlisle lie on the main England–Scotland rail links. All timetable and fare information can be obtained from **National Rail Enquiries** (☎ 03457-484950 – operates 24hrs; ⌨ www.nationalrail.co.uk), or the relevant train companies. Tickets can be bought through the train companies or from websites such as ⌨ www.thetrainline.com.

Newcastle is a stop on the **Virgin Trains East Coast** (⌨ www.virgintrains eastcoast.com) line which operates between London King's Cross and Inverness. There are 1-2 services an hour between London and Newcastle and the journey takes around three hours. There is approximately one service an hour from Edinburgh/Glasgow to Newcastle. In addition, the **TransPennine Express** (⌨ www.tpexpress.co.uk) operates from Liverpool/Manchester (inc

❏ GETTING TO BRITAIN

● **By air** Newcastle International Airport (🖥 www.newcastleairport.com) is the closest to the Hadrian's Wall Path, especially if walking east to west. From Manchester Airport (🖥 www.manchesterairport.co.uk) to Carlisle, on the western end of the walk, it's just over two hours by train. Manchester Airport is also connected to Newcastle by train (see below). Other airports that are fairly close include Leeds Bradford (🖥 www.leedsbradfordairport.co.uk) and Durham Tees Valley Airport (🖥 www.durhamteesvalleyairport.com).

● **From Europe by train** Eurostar (🖥 www.eurostar.com) operates the high-speed passenger service via the Channel Tunnel between Paris/Brussels and London. Conveniently, the terminal in London is St Pancras International, which is next to King's Cross, the station for departures to Newcastle. Euston, the station for trains to Carlisle, is only a 5-minute walk away in the other direction on Euston Rd.

For more information about rail services from Europe, contact your national rail provider or Railteam (🖥 www.railteam.eu).

● **From Europe by coach** Eurolines (🖥 www.eurolines.com) have a huge network of long-distance coach services connecting over 500 cities throughout Europe to London. Check carefully: often, once expenses such as food for the journey are taken into consideration, it doesn't work out much cheaper than flying, particularly when compared to the prices of some of the budget airlines.

● **From Europe by ferry (with or without a car)** There are numerous ferries plying routes between ports around the UK and those in Ireland and continental Europe. However, the most convenient for Hadrian's Wall Path is DFDS Seaways (🖥 www.dfdsseaways.co.uk) with a daily service connecting Amsterdam and Newcastle.

A useful website for further information is 🖥 www.directferries.com.

● **From Europe by car** Eurotunnel (🖥 www.eurotunnel.com) operates 'le shuttle' (the shuttle) train service for vehicles via the Channel Tunnel between Calais and Folkestone taking just 35 minutes.

Manchester Airport) to Newcastle (1-2/hr, journey time 2-3hrs) via York, Northallerton, Darlington & Middlesbrough.

Carlisle is connected to London Euston, Manchester and Glasgow via the West Coast main line, with services operated by **Virgin Trains** (🖥 www.virgintrains.co.uk; 1-2/hr); the fastest Euston to Carlisle service takes about 3¼ hours.

Northern Rail (🖥 www.northernrailway.co.uk) operates most lines in the north of England but perhaps most usefully of all, Hadrian's Wall Country Rail Line which connects Newcastle and Carlisle (see p48).

By coach

The principal coach (long-distance bus) operator in Britain is **National Express** (🖥 www.nationalexpress.com). Coach travel is generally cheaper (though with the excellent advance-booking train fares and special deals offered by the train companies, that is not always the case now) but the journey time is longer than if travelling by train (both London to Newcastle and London to Carlisle take at least six hours). National Express's services to **Newcastle** include: NX332/530 (from Birmingham, both 1/day); NX531 (from Plymouth, 1/day); NX580 (from Liverpool via Manchester, 5/day); NX534/329 (from Hull, both 1/day), NX425 (from Leeds, 1/day); NX425/435/591 from London, all 1-2/day). *(cont'd on p48)*

☐ PUBLIC TRANSPORT – BUS SERVICES

Notes: For details of Stagecoach's No 22 service in **Newcastle** see p82.
- **85/685** services may be on an Arriva or a Stagecoach bus and tickets are valid on both. The 85 operates to Haydon Bridge and the 685 from there but some 685 buses go from Newcastle to Carlisle. Even though the service number may change passengers do not need to change bus.
- Drivers of **Tynedale Links (TL)** services will stop where it is safe to do so. • Not all **AD122** services stop at all the places on the route.

85/685 ANE, SC	Newcastle to Carlisle via Lemington, Heddon-on-the-Wall, Corbridge, Hexham, Haydon Bridge, Bardon Mill, Haltwhistle, Greenhead & Brampton, Mon-Sat 1/hr, Sun 1/hr (85) to Hexham & 5/day (685) to Carlisle
X85 ANE	Newcastle to Hexham via Corbridge, Mon-Fri 2/day
10 GNE	Newcastle to Hexham via Blaydon & Corbridge, Mon-Sat 2/hr, Sun 1/hr
74 GNE	Newcastle to Hexham via Matfen, Halton & Errington Arms, Mon-Fri 4/day, Sat 5/day plus 1/day Newcastle to Matfen
X84 GNE (Tynedale Xpress)	Newcastle to Hexham via Denton Burn, Lemington, Throckley, Heddon-on-the-Wall, Wylam & Corbridge, Mon-Sat 1/hr
X85 GNE (Tynedale Xpress)	Newcastle to Hexham via Denton Burn, Heddon-on-the-Wall, Horsley, Wylam & Corbridge, Mon-Sat 1/hr
X85 ANE	Newcastle to Hexham via Corbridge, Mon-Fri 2/day
686 GNE (TL)	Prudhoe to Ovington via Wylam & Ovingham, Mon-Sat 2-3/day (not shown on map)
680 GNE (TL)	Hexham to Bellingham via Acomb, Wall, Humshaugh & Wark, Mon-Sat 7-8/day
682 GNE (TL)	Hexham to Acomb, Mon-Sat 4-6/day
687 GNE (TL)	Hexham to Corbridge, Mon-Sat 2/day
AD122 GNE	Hexham to Haltwhistle (circular route) via Chesters Fort, Housesteads, Once Brewed, Vindolanda, Milecastle Inn, Walltown (Roman Army Museum) & Greenhead, mid Apr to late Sep daily 4/day.
185 GNE	Haltwhistle to Gilsland via Walltown (Roman Army Museum) & Greenhead, Mon-Sat 3/day (+ to Birdoswald Apr-Sep)
BR1	Laversdale to Carlisle via Newtown, Irthington & Crosby-on-Eden, Tue & Fri 1/day
BR2	Laversdale to Carlisle via Newtown, Irthington, Brampton, Lanercost & Walton, Thur 1/day
BR3	Laversdale to Carlisle via Newtown, Irthington, Brampton, Lanercost, Banks, Birdoswald, Walltown (Roman Army Museum), Greenhead, Gilsland & Lanercost, Wed 1/day
93/93A SC	Carlisle to Bowness-on-Solway via Beaumont, Burgh-by-Sands, Dykesfield, Drumburgh, Glasson & Port Carlisle, Mon-Sat 3/day plus Carlisle to Bowness-on-Solway, Mon-Sat 2/day

Operator contact details: ANE = Arriva North East (☐ www.arrivabus.co.uk/north-east); **GNE** = Go North East (☐ www.gonortheast.co.uk); **SC** = Stagecoach (☐ www.stagecoachbus.com); **BR** = Border Rambler (☐ www.borderramblerbus.co.uk; volunteer-run service)

Local transport 47

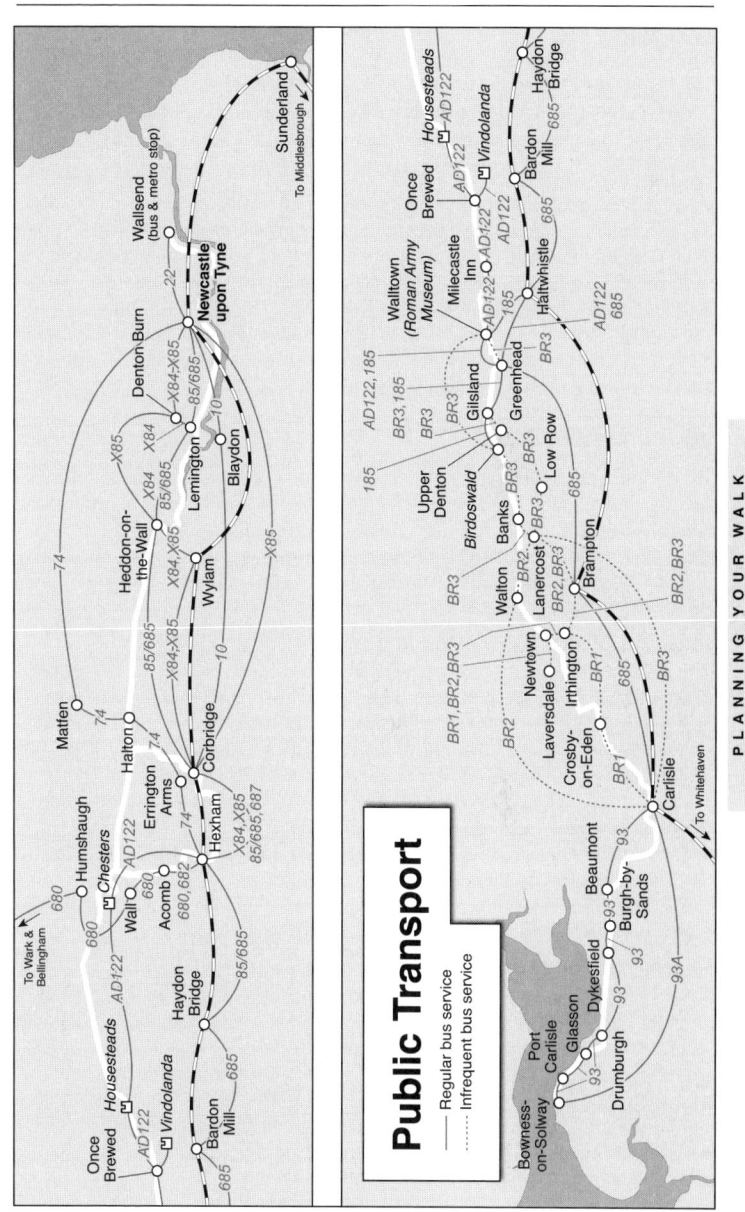

PLANNING YOUR WALK

(cont'd from p46) National Express's service to **Carlisle** is on the NX538 (Birmingham to Aberdeen, 1/day) and also from London the NX544 (to Glasgow, 1/day), and the NX590/592 (to Aberdeen, 2/day but one goes overnight).

Megabus (🖥 uk.megabus.com), a low-cost coach company, operates services between London and Newcastle (and beyond) but none to Carlisle.

By car

There are reasonable road connections to Hadrian's Wall. Access from the western side is along the M6 from the south (junctions 42, 43 and 44) and A74 (M) from Glasgow to Carlisle. Access from the eastern side is along the A1(M) to Newcastle; take the city-centre exit and follow signs for Wallsend; or take the A19 and follow the signs for Wallsend from there. The A68 links Edinburgh and Darlington and bisects the trail around Corbridge. Finally, the A69 between Newcastle and Carlisle runs parallel to the Wall, usually around 2-5 miles (3-8km) south of it, and is the main access route.

LOCAL TRANSPORT

With both a special Hadrian's Wall Country Bus service serving the middle section of the Wall, and good connecting bus services at either end as well as the Hadrian's Wall Country rail line (Newcastle to Carlisle – the oldest coast-to-coast service in the country), public transport along the trail is surprisingly good. At Hexham and Haltwhistle the services dovetail neatly, with the buses calling in at the railway stations.

Hadrian's Wall Country Bus AD122

This bus service, given the appropriate route number AD122, is operated (Easter to end Sep except bank holidays) by Go North East. The AD122 operates a round-trip route between Hexham and Haltwhistle. You can download a timetable, and get up-to-date information about the route, from the Hadrian's Wall Country website (🖥 hadrianswallcountry.co.uk/travel/bus).

A one-day **AD122 Rover ticket** (£12/9/6/25 for adults/student/children/family ie two adults and up to three children under 16) permits unlimited travel on the AD122. Three-day tickets (£24/18/12/50) are also available. You can also buy an **AD122 Rover Ticket +** which includes travel on Go North East's services X84, X85 and 10 services between Newcastle and Hexham, and Tynedale Links services (see 🖥 www.gonortheast.co.uk).

Hadrian's Wall Country Rail Line

Services on this line are operated by **Northern** (see p45). A **Day Ranger ticket** allowing unlimited day travel on rail services between Sunderland and Whitehaven (which encompasses Newcastle to Carlisle) is available on trains, or from staffed stations, for £21/10.50/13.85 adult/child/railcard.
- Newcastle to Carlisle via Hexham & Haltwhistle, daily 1-2/hr, some services stop at Wylam, Corbridge, Haydon Bridge, Bardon Mill & Brampton.
- Middlesbrough to Hexham via Newcastle & Corbridge, Mon-Sat 1/hr.
- Whitehaven to Carlisle, Mon-Sat 11/day, Sun 4/day.

HADRIAN'S WALL 2

History

THE DECISION TO BUILD THE WALL

Though by far the most famous, Hadrian's Wall was in fact just one of four Roman frontiers built between the subjugated south of what is now called Britain and those tribes living in the northern part of the island,

> ❏ **A Haiku on Hadrian's Wall**
> don't like the neighbours?
> build a wall eighty miles long
> that should sort it out
> © **Henry Purbrick 2015**

known collectively as the Caledones. Since their invasion in AD43, the Romans had at one time or another conquered just about all the tribes living on the island of Britannia. But the area we now call Scotland, once defeated, proved more difficult to keep under control. Even a potentially decisive victory in AD84 somewhere north of the Tay at a place they called Mons Graupius failed to quell the ongoing insurrection by the Caledones.

Emperors came and went before the pragmatic Domitian (who reigned AD81-96) decided that maintaining a grip over all of the island would ultimately require too many troops; troops that could be more usefully employed in other parts of the empire. It was thus decided to draw a line across the island and establish a border to separate the controllable south from those 'lawless' lands to the north. Initially that boundary was drawn to watch over the glens – the main gateways into and out of the Highlands – a border known as the **Gask Frontier**. However, as more and more troops were withdrawn from Britannia to fight in other parts of the Empire, the border by necessity receded south to the area now known, appropriately enough, as the Borders.

Soon after his accession, Emperor Trajan (AD97-117) decided to move the border still further south, choosing as his frontier the **Stanegate** (though this was not what the Romans called it), the east–west road that ran between the Roman settlements of Carlisle and Corbridge. Built during the governorship of Agricola in AD80, the Stanegate was an important trade route that needed protecting. Trajan's troops set about building a line of turf and timber forts to guard the Stanegate, including Vindolanda (see p162) and Corbridge Roman Town (p130).

HADRIAN BUILDS HIS WALL

Having completely transformed the soldiers, in royal fashion, he made for Britain, where he set right many things and – the first to do so – drew a wall along a length of eighty miles to separate barbarians and Romans. **Aelius Spartianus**, *The Augustan History*

During Trajan's reign, his fortified border was used less as a defensive barrier than as a launchpad for incursions into Scotland; an *attacking* border, if you like. His successor and adopted son, Hadrian (AD117-138), however, saw it as more of a traditional border; as both a defensive barrier and a physical marker for the northern limit of his territories. Following a tour of his dominions in AD122, Hadrian ordered the refortification of Trajan's border with the building of a wall to the north of it along the line of the Whin Sill ridge, a geological fault running across the centre of Britain. This wall was to extend beyond the limits of the Stanegate, to stretch across the entire island. And thus the Wall that we know today began to take shape.

The building of the Wall was something of an organic process, evolving as the geology and political climate dictated. This is best illustrated by the curious size of the foundations, which for much of the first half of the walk (from Newcastle west to the River Irthing, which was the first section to be built) are far too broad for the wall that was eventually built upon them, suggesting, of course, that the Romans initially had plans to construct a much bigger barrier. The materials used in the Wall's construction changed too, depending on where it was built. In the east of the country, a core of rubble and puddled clay was used, whereas a limestone mortar core was prevalent in the middle of the country and in the western half of the country an all-turf wall was built (though this, too, was later converted to stone sometime in the second half of the second century AD as the infrastructure improved and the supply of building materials to the line of the Wall became more efficient).

To carry out all this construction, three legions were employed: the Second Augusta from Caerleon in South Wales, the Twentieth Valeria Victrix from Chester and the Sixth Victrix from York. It was their task to clear the ground of

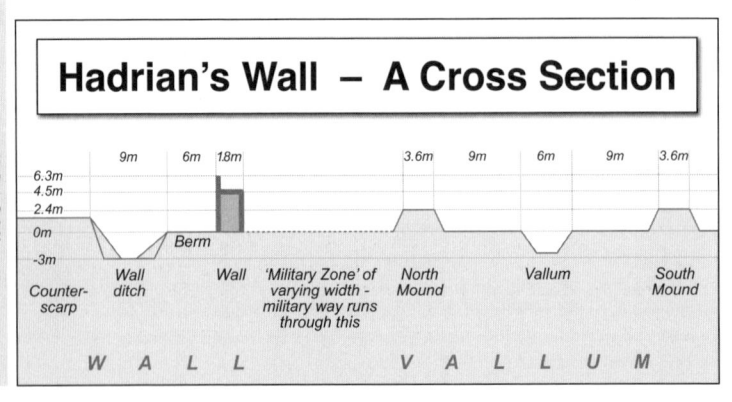

Hadrian's Wall – A Cross Section

trees and scrub where necessary and quarry, transport and organise the estimated 25 million facing stones that were used in the Wall, each approximately 10" long, 6" high and 20" deep (25cm by 15cm by 50cm respectively). These were then set into the core of the Wall. As a measure of the legions' efficiency, an experiment was conducted recently in which a section of the Wall was rebuilt

> ❑ **Hadrian's Wall ... or is it?**
> It should be stated here that there are some who believe that the refortification of Trajan's turf-and-timber wall by Hadrian actually took place *before* the latter visited Britain. The history of the Wall is full of minor controversies like this because, as you'll see when you read this book and other accounts, much of the history of Hadrian's Wall is still open to conjecture. Indeed, up until the 19th century or so, it was actually known as the **Wall of Severus** after the emperor who ruled at the beginning of the 3rd century AD. It was just prior to Severus's reign, in AD197, that the Wall was overrun for the first time, leading to an extensive overhaul and rebuilding of the Wall between AD205 and 208 – which explains why, until archaeological discoveries proved conclusively otherwise, the Wall was originally attributed to Severus. Indeed, it was only in 1839 and the publication of *History of Northumberland* by **John Hodgson**, a local vicar, that people began to accept that the Wall might be Hadrian's baby after all. In the book, produced in six volumes over more than twenty years, the reverend wrote a lengthy footnote in the final volume presenting all the evidence he'd amassed that the Wall was Hadrian's – and nobody has convincingly argued against his theory ever since. Unfortunately, Hodgson's health was failing him after working for so many years on a loss-making book, and he died while this final volume was being printed.
>
> While on the one hand people may find it astonishing that nobody knew who was responsible for such a massive feat of civil engineering, on the other hand it's perhaps not that surprising: there are no contemporary accounts of the construction of the Wall that have yet been discovered, with the earliest mentions having been written in the late 4th century, over 150 years later (such as that by Spartianus, as quoted opposite). What's more, these later authors weren't beyond rewriting history if it suited them. It is believed, for example, that Severus's son, Caracalla, could have been one of the sources for the rumour that his father was the originator of the Wall and not Hadrian. He and Severus had spent three years in northern Britain, and particularly Caledonia, trying to conquer the whole island without success. In 211, the emperor himself was killed at York and Caracalla had to retreat back to Rome with his tail between his legs. However, in later texts this was portrayed as a victory, such as this example from the late 4th century:
>
> '... *after driving out the enemy, he* [Severus] *fortified Britain, as far as it was useful, with a wall led across the island to each end of the Ocean.*'
> **Aurelius Victor**, *Liber de Caesaribus*
>
> One can only assume, therefore, that this and all the other histories written at this time that claim the Wall for Severus were using the same deceitful source, namely Caracalla or one of his followers, who wanted to present the campaign as a success.
>
> All of which goes to prove just how difficult it is to compile an accurate chronology of the Roman Empire in Britain. So, with the following account of the Wall's construction and history, it's worth bearing in mind that not all of it should be taken as gospel but merely as a version of events currently accepted by the majority of Wall experts. Furthermore, don't be surprised if some of the 'facts' written here are contradicted by accounts in other books.

52 Hadrian builds his Wall

using some original facing stones. It concluded that a gang of 80 men needed 32 wagons and 64 oxen to keep them supplied with enough lime, water and stone to build the Wall. Yet despite all the effort required, the original construction took as little as six years to complete.

It's a level of efficiency that becomes even more impressive when one considers the sheer enormity of the Wall (or *Vallum Aelium* as the Romans may have called it, Aelium being Hadrian's family name). An estimated one ton of stone had to be dragged up for every single yard of it. Stretching from the Solway Firth to the North Sea, the Wall was 80 Roman miles long (73 modern miles) and stood at around 20ft (6m) high and just under 10ft (3m) thick. And just to ensure the security of the Wall, a 20ft (6m) **ditch** (Hadrian's ha-ha, perhaps?) was dug on the northern 'Scottish' side along its length (though not, it must be said, around many of the crags, where the crags themselves were considered an adequate defence). A typical Roman defence, this ditch would probably have had a 'false floor' under which sharp spikes would have been concealed. Spikes were also placed in the **Berm**, the flat area between the ditch and the Wall.

Such manifold defences are impressive. Yet even so, Hadrian's Wall could act as an effective barrier only if it was sufficiently manned. So while the bulk of the men continued to be stationed in the old forts built by Trajan along the Stanegate road, **milecastles** (see box p116) with a capacity for 32 men were built along the entire length of the Wall at intervals of, as their name suggests, one Roman mile (the equivalent of a thousand paces); thus there were a total of 80 milecastles in all. And evenly spaced between each one were two **turrets** or observation posts, 161 all told along the Wall's entire length and always made of stone, regardless of the material of the Wall draped between them. Each was capable of holding 10 men. Estimates suggest that it would have taken just 2½ minutes to run from one fort to the next, so messages could have been relayed along the Wall speedily.

Improving the Wall

Just a couple of years after the wall was finished the defences were strengthened, possibly in response to pressure from either the Caledones to the north of the Wall or the Brigantes – whose territory the Wall crossed. Specifically, a series of **16 forts**, each housing 500 to 1000 men, was constructed at irregular intervals along the Wall. These, in many cases, replaced the forts along the Stanegate, which were either converted into supply bases or abandoned altogether. The Wall was extended at its eastern end too, beyond Pons Aelius to Segedunum (see pp101-4).

In addition, 50 to 100 yards (46-91m) south of the Wall two 10ft (3m) high walls of earth were constructed, with a 10ft (3m) deep, 120ft (36m) wide ditch between them. This earthwork is known as the **Vallum** which, confusingly, means 'wall' in Latin; the name was given by the Venerable Bede, an 8th-century monk and early English historian who was the first to write about the Wall's dimensions. (Incidentally, Bede wrote his *Ecclesiastical History of the English People* at his monastery in Jarrow, a building that was constructed, at

Hadrian's Wall in Roman times 53

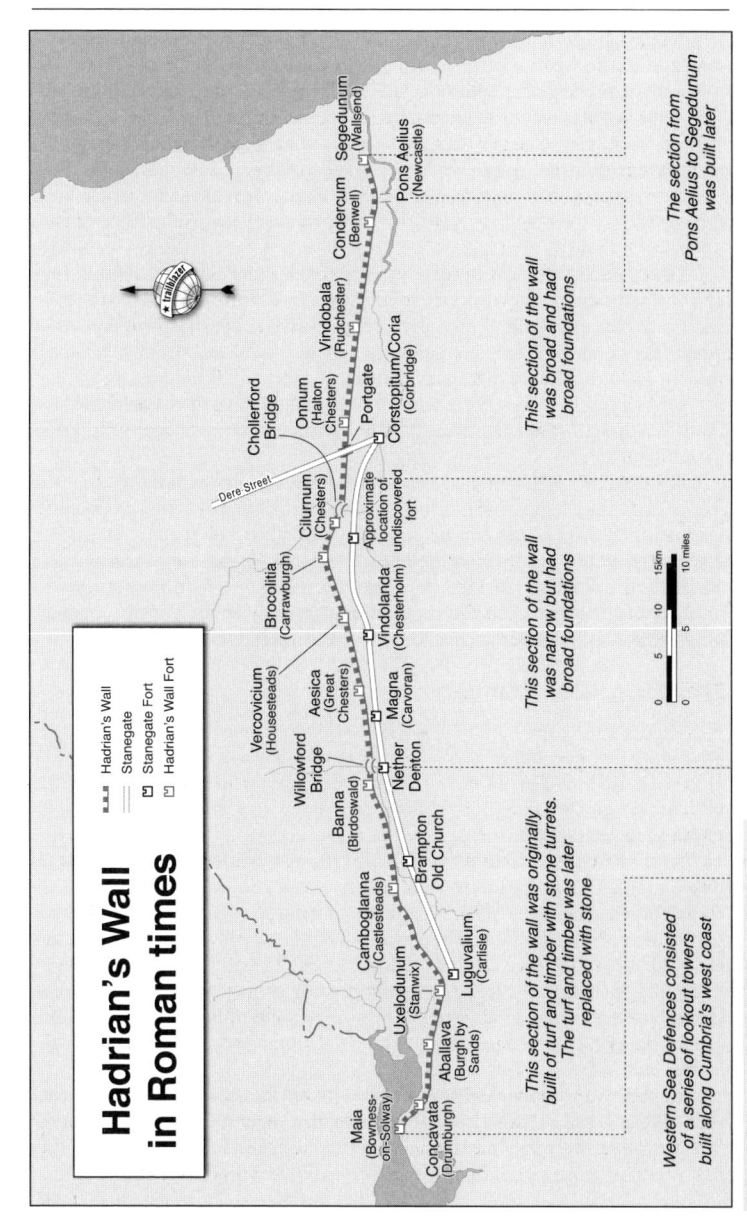

least in part, from stones taken from the Wall.) Nobody is completely sure what the Vallum is for; as it is on the south side of the Wall it is unlikely to have been a defensive barrier; nor, with both the Stanegate and, later, the Military Way (see p58) nearby, would it have made much sense to construct a road here. Recent theories have suggested that the Vallum marked the border between the civilian territory and a sort of 'military no-go zone' surrounding the Wall. Another suggestion is that it was used to stop conscripted British soldiers, forced against their will to serve the Romans along the Wall, from running away.

The character of the Wall had now changed. From a lengthy but fairly flimsy construction whose primary purpose was a lookout from which to keep an eye on the locals, the Wall now became a defensive, heavily fortified barrier; while the number of soldiers stationed on the Wall went from a relatively measly 3000 to a much more intimidating 15,000 – a 500% increase in manpower. As a result, it is estimated that around 10% of the entire imperial Roman army was based in Britain, even though the island accounted for only 4% of their total territory.

It should be noted here that although Roman soldiers built the Wall, it was Rome's auxiliary legions who actually manned it. These soldiers were recruited from various parts of the empire – on the Wall alone you'll come across evidence of auxiliary legions from Belgium, Germany, Spain, Iraq, Syria and elsewhere. These auxiliary soldiers were not officially Roman citizens, at least not until they had served a certain length of time (usually about 25 years, the minimum term of service for an auxiliary) in the army and had retired.

THE WALL POST-HADRIAN

Whatever the original intentions of Hadrian, the defensive obligations of the Wall soon became rather secondary to more mundane yet lucrative duties. Following Hadrian's death in AD138 his successor, Antoninus Pius, decided to push the Empire's frontier further north once more, to a line stretching from the Clyde to the Firth of Forth.

Not to be outdone, Antoninus fortified his new border with a 'Wall' of his own (AD142-4), the **Antonine Wall**, made of turf. So, just 10 years after the completion of Hadrian's Wall, its primary purpose as a border-cum-defensive-barrier was all but finished. The character of Hadrian's original fortifications changed too. Some forts, such as Housesteads, no longer on the front line, were left to languish and developed more into trading posts than military positions. Others, however, such as Corbridge, two miles south of the Wall, prospered as supply bases for the Roman troops stationed further north along Antoninus's border.

Markets were established near all the forts and the local tribe, the Brigantes, soon set up small villages, called *vici* (singular: *vicus*), in the shadow of the Wall to take advantage of the trading opportunities afforded them by the world's first professional army, staffed by regularly paid, full-time soldiers.

(cont'd on p58)

❏ THE ROMANS IN BRITAIN

It took the Romans a while to reach Britain. Expanding in every direction from their base on the west coast of what we now call Italy, conquering the cold, windswept island in the top left-hand corner of the known world was never really a priority for them. And even when the Romans did eventually decide to invade, it wasn't the beauty of the land or the treasures it contained that lured them here. Instead, it could be said that the invasion was instigated by the whim of one man who was looking for a way to impress his friends and fellow citizens and strengthen his political position at home.

That man was Julius Caesar, and the year was 55BC. At that time Julius Caesar was one of a triumvirate, along with Pompey and Crassus, vying for supreme power in Rome; and the best way to improve your standing at home at that time was to win a battle abroad. So casting his eye around for a suitably easy yet seemingly impressive land to conquer, Julius hit upon Britannia.

Iron-Age Britain was a dynamic society of hillforts and nascent towns characterised by a grid of streets each flanked with houses, places of worship, forges and workshops, and each populated by traders, craftsmen, warriors and druid priests. Metalwork was the Britons' signature craft, whether for vanity and decoration, such as the beautiful brooches that now sit in museums across the land, or for more belligerent purposes, such as horned helmets, swords and spears. The Romans described the country as 'uncivilised', but to them that simply meant that the inhabitants didn't live in cities.

To Caesar, Britain was the perfect victim for his invasion. He knew it wasn't the land of popular imagination, a land peopled by a barbaric yet united race that would fight tooth and nail to defend their homeland. Instead, he surmised that it was inhabited by a disparate set of tribes who were too busy with their own internecine squabbles to care too much about foreigners arriving on their shores, and whose squabbling would make them easy to divide, conquer and rule. Unfortunately, things didn't quite pan out the way Caesar had imagined. Firstly, the weather – that most fickle of British facets – intervened. Storms across the channel smashed much of Caesar's army before it had even caught sight of land; those troops that did make it across found the locals would not stand and fight, as the Romans had hoped, but preferred instead to engage in guerrilla warfare, which hardly seemed fair at all. Thus their first invasion in 55BC was abandoned almost as soon as it had begun. A second campaign the following year was only slightly more successful: though they managed to get across the Channel in greater numbers this time, the might of the Roman Empire reached only as far as the Thames at Brentford – which, as anybody who's been to Brentford recently will agree, is a poor return for all that effort. Confronted with the might of the Catuvellauni tribe, the Romans were forced to retreat with their imperial tail between their legs, the only trophies they had to show for their invasion being a couple of tributes and taxes paid by a few piddling little tribes in southern England.

Claudius and the conquest

So it was left to one of Julius Caesar's successors, the divine Emperor Claudius, finally to invade and occupy in AD43, using a massive force of some 40,000 men. The disparate tribes of Britain in the 1st century AD were no match for the professionalism and discipline of the Roman legions. The Romans knew this; so, too, did many of the British tribes, or at least the smarter ones who, rather than engaging the Imperial legions in battle – a route that could lead only to certain defeat and possible annihilation – opted instead to live in peace and relative freedom, albeit under the rule of Rome, and enjoy the advantages that acquiescence brings.   *(cont'd overleaf)*

❏ THE ROMANS IN BRITAIN

(cont'd from p55) Thus, for the first decade or two, things went pretty much to plan for the empire. True, the west and north of the island still lay beyond their control. But the tribes in that portion of Britain which they *had* conquered seemed to find living under the Romans to be no bad thing, and played the part of meek and obedient subjects rather well. And they probably would have done for much longer too, had Nero not ascended to the Imperial throne in AD54. Corrupt and oppressive, Nero's brutal administration caused the Britons to rise up against their rulers. The leader of this revolt was Boudicca (aka Boadicea), queen of the Iceni tribe, who rampaged through the province in AD60 destroying key Roman settlements one by one as she went, including Camulodunum (Colchester), Londinium (London), where thousands of Romans were massacred) and Verulamium (St Albans). Though the uprising was soon quashed the entire affair had exhausted both sides. Boudicca, witnessing the slaughter of her own troops at the final battle, took her own life and now lies buried, so it is said, under Platform 10 of London's King's Cross Station.

What's more, further upheaval back in Rome forced the empire to rethink its ambitions and a halt to its expansionist policy in Britain was called – even though the west and north still remained unconquered and alive with the enemies of Rome and its empire.

The accession of Vespasian in AD68 saw a return to stability and a consequent reinvigoration of Rome's ambitions to subjugate the British Isles; just a decade later Rome was again launching successful campaigns into the lands we now know as Wales, Cumbria and Scotland, under the rule of the new governor, Gnaeus Julius Agricola. Of the three regions, it was Caledonia (now called Scotland that proved the most stubborn and even after a decisive victory against the Caledones at Mons Graupius (believed by some historians to be Bennachie in Aberdeenshire) the survivors were able to flee and regroup in the relative safety of the Highlands.

Recognising the difficulty of flushing the Caledones out from their remote base, Emperor Domitian opted instead for a policy of containment, building a line of fortifications known as the **Gask Frontier**, which ran south-west to north-east across Perthshire in Scotland. The idea of the frontier was to watch over the Scottish glens – the main exit and entry points into the Highlands – thereby effectively placing the Caledones under house arrest. Yet even this newer, more realistic strategy was soon deemed to be too ambitious and, as other parts of the empire came under attack from various tribes, the decision was made to withdraw one of the four legions stationed in Scotland and to pull back from the Gask Frontier.

Trajan and expansion

With the death of Domitian (possibly at the hands of his wife) in AD96, and the brief reign of Nerva, who ruled for less than two years, Marcus Ulpius Traianus, or Trajan, a career soldier, was anointed emperor in AD98. As his military background would suggest, Trajan's style was aggressive and focused largely on the continuing expansion of Rome's borders. Indeed, the empire was never larger than it was under his reign, as Armenia, Romania and Mesopotamia were brought under his rule.

Once again, however, in order to achieve these victories Trajan was forced to reduce his army's presence in Scotland, and in order to do this the empire's northern frontier was once again redrawn further south. This time a road known as the Stanegate (Saxon for 'Stone Road') was chosen as the frontier. Built in AD80 to link the towns of Corbridge and Carlisle, the road cut across the two main military routes heading north, one on either side of the Pennines.

To suggest that Trajan ignored Britain, however, is wrong. Indeed, his unquenchable ambition simply would not allow him to be content with only half the island. So, while it is true that under his reign the northernmost boundary of his empire receded south into what we now know as England, Trajan did not view this Stanegate Frontier as a defensive border but more of an offensive one, as a base from which to launch further raids into Scotland. Indeed the Stanegate road became an essential military line of communication, enabling the Romans to move troops quickly across the Pennines from one major north–south road to the other. To guard the road, forts and watchtowers were placed at intervals along the Stanegate – the forerunner, of course, to Hadrian's Wall and its forts.

As for the land to the south of the Stanegate, Trajan was content to continue with what was known as the Flavian policy (the Flavians being the imperial dynasty that preceded Trajan and included Emperor Vespasian): allowing Roman culture and society to influence the development of the province, so that in time Britain would come to identify more closely with its masters and therefore, hopefully, be less inclined to rebel.

Hadrian and his Wall

With the death of Trajan in AD117, another Spanish military man and a relative of Trajan, Publius Aelius Hadrianus, was chosen as heir. Though no less competent, militarily speaking, than Trajan, where the latter was consumed by an ambition to push back the frontiers of his empire, Hadrian was content to adopt a more defensive approach and protect all the gains made in his predecessor's reign. This change in policy heralded a period of almost 100 years of continuous peace; it also, of course, led to the building of one of the greatest military constructions of them all: a wall of stone along the empire's northernmost border, a frontier that up until now had been defended merely by hastily built turf and timber forts and watchtowers.

The end of Roman Britain

The Romans survived in Britain for almost another 400 years after Hadrian, until the start of the 5th century. Indeed, it's fair to say that they did more than just survive: they positively prospered. And so, too, did their subjects, who found that the Roman way of doing things, particularly when it came to matters of architecture, road-building, cooking, drinking, trading, educating and organising society in general, was often the best way (see box pp58-9). Far from an extended swansong, the last 200 years of Roman rule left behind some of the empire's most impressive pieces of work in Britain, such as the mosaics at Bignor Villa in Sussex. In fact, some historians have even gone as far as to declare that, by the time the Romans departed, Britain was one of the most 'Romanised' of its territories, and its people the most prosperous and peaceful.

So what drove the Romans out from this most compliant of provinces? The truth is that nothing did, or at least nothing within Britain itself. Instead, as the Empire crumbled and its borders were attacked from all sides, the Romans found themselves unable to hold on to all their territories; just as Britain was one of the last places to succumb to Roman rule, so it became one of the first to be dispensed with when the going got tough.

As they withdrew, other invaders filled the vacuum. In particular, the Anglo-Saxons from across the North Sea, Picts from northern Scotland and invaders from Ireland all penetrated Roman Britain's borders. Attempts to restore some sort of Roman law and order went on for the next two centuries or so. But by then, the Golden Age of Roman Britain was well and truly over.

(cont'd from p54) The new, non-military character of these forts continued even after the Antonine Wall was abandoned, about AD160, just 20 years after its inception, having been repeatedly overrun. For the next 200 years after this, Hadrian's Wall remained the definitive limit of the Roman Empire. In addition, a second road, the **Roman Military Way**, was built around AD160 between the Stanegate and the Wall, often along the northern earthwork of the Vallum (which by now had been largely decommissioned). Such a road would be vital for the rapid transport of troops along the Wall and eventually replaced the Stanegate as the primary artery adorning the neck of Britain.

It would be wrong, therefore, to think of the Wall purely as a means of defence, a place to shelter from the spears of the Barbarians to the north. Because, whatever Hadrian's original intention for his Wall, it had evolved to become more of a checkpoint, a place to watch the comings and goings of the locals as they crossed the border, and to collect tolls and customs duties from the traders.

❏ Life in Roman Britain

Though the number of Roman troops who occupied Britannia was relatively small compared to the total population, their influence was all-pervasive. Roman cities sprouted on England's green and pleasant land, filled with quintessentially Roman buildings – basilicas, villas, baths and forums – that employed the latest Roman construction methods, exuded an architectural style that was intrinsically Roman, and were all crowded with local people who dressed in the Roman style, spent Roman money, measured distances in Roman miles (the word itself derived from the Latin for 1000 paces, the Roman mile being slightly shorter than the modern one) and ate Roman food.

Over the heather the wet wind blows,
I've lice in my tunic and a cold in my nose.

The rain comes pattering out of the sky,
I'm a Wall soldier, I don't know why.

The mist creeps over the hard grey stone,
My girl's in Tungria; I sleep alone.

Aulus goes hanging around her place,
I don't like his manners, I don't like his face.

Piso's a Christian, he worships a fish;
There'd be no kissing if he had his wish.

She gave me a ring but I diced it away;
I want my girl and I want my pay.

When I'm a veteran with only one eye
I shall do nothing but look at the sky.
                    WH Auden, *Roman Wall Blues*

Nor did Roman influence end there, for towards the end of their empire the descendants of many who had prospered under Roman rule even began to worship Roman gods and speak Latin as a first language!

And you can't blame them; without deriding the traditional British culture that had thrived before the invasion, life under the Romans certainly seemed a more comfortable affair. Rough, muddy tracks became sleek metalled roads. Buildings, previously made of timber, thatch and mud now became imposing, stone-made constructions with such novel features as windows and columns, with indoor plumbing and warmth provided by underfloor heating rather than the dangerous and unhealthy open hearth. The Romans brought with them a complete change in the organisation of

Severus's restoration

That is not to say that the Wall had entirely forsaken its military duties; indeed, following a successful breach by invaders sometime around the end of the 2nd century AD, it was decided to restore, renovate and refortify Hadrian's Wall. This took place at the beginning of the 3rd century under the reign of Emperor Severus.

Amongst the improvements was a rebuilding of the Wall using a super-hard white mortar which allowed it to be much narrower than before. The Wall had never looked so good, nor so impregnable; it's been estimated that 3,700,000 tons (30,138,000kg) of stone was used in its construction. Indeed, so comprehensive was the renovation that the original construction of the Wall was for over 1500 years wrongly ascribed to – and even named after! – Severus; prior to conclusive proof that the Wall was built during the reign of Hadrian, it had always been assumed that Hadrian had ordered the construction of the Vallum only and that it was Severus who had built the actual Wall (see box on p51).

British society, from the family-based 'clan' system so popular among the 'primitive' tribes to a highly stratified civil and military structure.

Other innovations that were introduced include canals, water mills, factories and even such basics as new cereals and vegetables. And when they went they took much of their technology with them, including glass-making (the secret of which wasn't rediscovered until the 13th century), lighthouses (reintroduced in the 19th century), lavatories and central heating (commonplace again only in the 20th century).

Indeed, so pervasive was their influence that their currency became the legal tender of Britain just as it was across the rest of the empire, and Latin became the *lingua franca* of traders in this remote northern outpost. Furthermore, as the merchants and traders of Britain learned Latin, so they learned the advantages of literacy and the written record. Nor was that the only benefit reaped by the traders of the occupied provinces. The fact that there were now thousands of foreign troops on their land was in itself a business opportunity and soon local villages were springing up near Roman strongholds to take advantage.

Of course, while Britain enjoyed great prosperity, it was still forced to play the part of the conquered; because while there was some integration and mixing of the two sides – an integration that grew the longer the Romans remained in Britain – there was still very much an 'us and them' mentality on both sides. For the Romans, inevitably, there was a sense of snobbery when it came to discussing the Brits, whom the former frequently came to sneer at as the Britunculli – a translation of which would be something like 'wretched little Brits'. The Brits, too, while happy to adopt much that was good about the Roman way of life, still identified themselves first and foremost with their tribes. The Brigantes occupied the region that today we think of as northern England (Lancashire, Yorkshire, Cumbria and parts of Derbyshire) while the Hadrian's Wall region was shared with the Carvetii. But the 'independence' of these tribes depended to a large extent on their obedience to Rome: the more supine the tribe, the greater the control they had over their affairs, with the more compliant even allowed to establish their own governing body, able to wield at least partial power over the affairs of their territory.

AFTER THE ROMANS

Unfortunately, after the Romans had gone their greatest monument on these shores suffered. Though it had been overrun only three or four times (nobody is sure exactly how many) since its original construction, when the Empire crumbled and the troops were withdrawn in AD409 the Wall was subjected to all manner of depredations and indignities. For one thing, local landowners started to remove the stone for their own purposes. Hexham Abbey (see p133) was just one beneficiary of this pilfering, with the crypt constructed entirely of Wall stone. And where the locals left the Wall untouched, the elements took their toll as wind and rain gradually wore down the remaining structure. Today, only around 10 miles of the Wall are still visible.

And so it stood for centuries, forlorn and neglected if not exactly ignored. Soon it even lost its duty as a boundary between countries as the border gradually drifted north and the country beyond – now called 'Scotland' after the Scots tribe from Ireland who migrated centuries after the Romans had left – shrank.

Interest in the Wall was first revived, at least in print, in 1600 with the publication of *Britannia* by William Camden, then headmaster of Westminster School in London, who attempted to explain the form, function and construction of the Wall. His work was built on a century later by the Rev John Horsley and the publication of *Britannia Romana*, in which, of course, the Wall featured heavily.

The General wades in

Horsley's work revived great interest in the Wall amongst the reading public but it was not enough to prevent further damage being visited upon it during the Jacobite Uprising. In 1745, Bonnie Prince Charlie smashed his way from Scotland down through Carlisle and on to Derby before turning back. The ease with which he was able to advance so far had much to do with the fact that his adversaries, General Wade and his men, were hunkered down in Newcastle waiting to ambush him there, having assumed that Charlie would choose the eastern road for his advance.

As a result of Charlie's success, Wade's troops constructed the Military Road (the modern B6318) across the Pennines to enable the swift movement of troops from one side of the country to the other. (This Military Road should not be confused with the Romans' Military *Way* – see p58 – though this lies nearby and performed much the same job almost 1700 years earlier.) To build this road, the Royal forces of George II removed sections of the Wall to pave their new highway. In fact, not only did they plunder the Wall for building material, they even built their road on top of it! (It should be noted that, though Wade is most associated with this road, it was actually built three years *after* his death.)

The Wall's modern pioneers

Once peace had returned to Britain, Camden's and Horsley's works encouraged others to look at the Wall anew. Among them was the shopkeeper William Hutton who in 1802 walked from his home in Birmingham to the Wall, walked

'Wall of Severus, near Housetead [sic], Northumberland' (19th century engraving)

along it and back, and then walked all the way home again – a total journey of about 600 miles (966km). Taking 35 days to complete, it was an impressive feat by any standards, particularly when one considers that he was 78 years old at the time and wore the same pair of socks for the entire walk!

The product of his adventure was a book, *The History of the Roman Wall which crosses the Island of Britain from the German Ocean to the Irish Sea, Describing its Antient* [sic] *State and its Appearance in the Year 1801* – a title almost as long as the Wall itself – in which his love of Severus's Wall (as it was still called) and his interest in its history shines through. John Hodgson and John Collingwood Bruce (whose *Wallet Book of the Roman Wall*, printed in 1863 and later renamed *Handbook to the Roman Wall*, was still being published over a hundred years later) also contributed to our knowledge with texts on the history and archaeology of the Wall and it was Hodgson who first definitively proved that the Wall was built during Hadrian's reign and not Severus's.

Then there was John Clayton, a Newcastle town clerk in the late 19th century, who bought four of the Wall forts and to whom we owe a great debt of gratitude; without his excavation and restoration work much of the Wall still extant would have been lost. That's not to say Clayton's work is unanimously admired today. In particular, his attempts to rebuild much of the Wall, taking great liberties and using largely non-Roman methods and materials, make more than one modern archaeologist weep; Clayton preferred to rebuild without mortar, so in effect the sections of Wall he rebuilt resemble a 'modern' drystone wall, still common around northern England, rather than the original Roman Wall. Clayton's efforts may have ensured that there is more of the Wall visible today but it can also be argued that what we are looking at is not really the Roman Wall at all but a 19th-century reconstruction, with almost none of the Wall's original inner core remaining. Nevertheless, to the layman, Clayton's work is vital, the miles he 'reconstructed' helping us to imagine what the Wall must have looked like when first built.

The work of Clayton was continued in the 20th century by individuals such as FG Simpson (of Stead & Simpson shoeshop fame), Eric Birley and Sir Ian Richmond, and later by bodies such as the National Trust, English Heritage and the Tyne and Wear Museums Service, organisations which concentrated less on the Wall and more on its accompanying forts and other buildings.

A proper survey of the Wall, recording every surviving remain and ruin, was conducted in 1985 to ensure there was a complete record of what exactly the authorities had in their care. And then, in 1987, UNESCO announced that the Wall was to become a World Heritage Site, thereby placing it alongside such wonders as the magnificent ruined city of Petra in Jordan, the awe-inspiring Pyramids of Giza in Egypt, Cambodia's mesmerising temples at Angkor Wat, Peru's fabled lost city of Machu Picchu, the architectural dream that is India's Taj Mahal and that other Great Wall, in northern China. The establishment in 2003 of a national trail running along the entire length of the Wall has once more brought it into the spotlight, and its instant success should ensure that millions more will enjoy the Wall's grandeur for years to come.

MINIMUM IMPACT & OUTDOOR SAFETY

Minimum impact walking

In April 2005 Britain was given a rude awakening by UNESCO, when it threatened to have Hadrian's Wall placed on their 'in danger' list of World Heritage sites. The warning was something of a national embarrassment, for at the time there were only 29 out of the then total 600 World Heritage sites on this list and only one in the so-called 'developed world' (Cologne Cathedral in Germany).

Thankfully, the threat seems to have abated somewhat since 2005; the Wall (which is now entered as part of the 'Frontiers of the Roman Empire' which also covers the Antonine Wall) has stayed off the 'in danger' list, which now numbers 55 sites (including the nearby Maritime Mercantile City in Liverpool) out of a total of 1052.

UNESCO's concern about the Wall arose largely because of the huge and sudden influx of walkers hiking alongside the Wall. The thousands of people who have walked along the National Trail since it opened (on 23 May 2003) have left their mark on the area, eroding the land and endangering the archaeological sites that are as yet unexcavated (and the majority of the Wall and its fortifications remain unexcavated; indeed, according to one expert only about 5% of the Wall and it accompanying buildings have been examined). The soil in this part of the world is particularly thin and the climate rather damp. Combine this with thousands of pairs of boots and you have the recipe for some serious erosion. Vegetation is trampled, exposing not just the soil but also, over time, archaeological deposits.

Nor is the Wall itself exempt from the depredations of walkers: in 2004, a team of 800 Dutch bankers walked *on* the Wall between Steel Rigg and Housesteads as part of a team-building exercise, sparking fury amongst conservationists and historians alike. To be fair to the bankers, they have returned since and abided by the Hadrian's Wall Code of Respect much more closely – see the box on pp64-5 – splitting their group up into more manageable sizes and keeping off the Wall itself.

The controversy is only exacerbated by the fact that there was so much opposition to the creation of the path in the first place, particularly amongst historians worried about protecting the Wall. Their fears were allayed only when they received assurances that the Wall and its earthworks would be protected; unfortunately, the resources just haven't been available to protect it properly.

Though some may blame the authorities for the current crisis, accusing them of inadequate preparation and provision, this doesn't mean we as walkers can't do our bit as well. The Hadrian's Wall Code of Respect, known as **Every Footprint Counts**, helps visitors minimise their impact on the trail. But the preservation of the Wall, while of overriding importance, should not be the only concern of walkers. The whole area is affected, economically, socially and culturally, by the arrival of walkers. By following a few simple guidelines while walking the trail, you can minimise your impact on it and have a positive effect on the local communities and the environment hereabouts.

ECONOMIC IMPACT

Rural businesses and communities in Britain have been hit hard in recent years by a seemingly endless series of crises. Most people are aware of the Countryside Code (see p67); not dropping litter and closing the gate behind you are still as pertinent as ever. But in light of the economic pressures that local countryside businesses are under, there is something else you can do: buy local.

❏ Caring for the Wall – the Hadrian's Wall Code of Respect

Overriding all other concerns about caring for the natural environment is the need to protect the Wall itself, and all the forts, milecastles, turrets, earthworks and ditches that go to make up the Roman defences – whether excavated or still buried beneath the soil.

With these considerations uppermost, the following code – known as **Every Footstep Counts** – has been formulated and endorsed by government agencies, English Heritage, the National Trust, local authorities, farmers, conservation and user groups concerned with the Wall.

● **Don't climb or walk on the Wall** Please don't walk on the Wall or climb it for a better view or to take a photograph of yourself, no matter how tempting.

● If walking only part of the trail, consider following a circular route or setting off from a place other than the usual starting points. This will limit the general wear and tear.

● **Don't walk the Wall in winter** The ground (and the unexcavated archaeological sites still buried within it) is more fragile and liable to damage then. Again, consider a nearby circular walk or visit one of the off-Wall Roman sites instead, such as Corbridge or Vindolanda. This is why the passport scheme runs only from May to October.

● **Visit the Roman forts along the way**, which will help to relieve the pressure suffered by the Wall itself.

● **Stay and eat locally** and use local services when visiting the Wall; that way the local economy will benefit from your visit.

● **Keep to waymarked and signposted paths** and trails only.

● **Keep dogs under close control** and on a lead when walking through fields with sheep; on National Trust land this is compulsory. Only let go of the lead if you're threatened by a farm animal.

● **Never light fires**, and **always take litter away** with you.

Support local businesses

Look and ask for local produce to buy and eat; not only does this cut down on the amount of pollution and congestion that the transportation of food creates (the so-called 'food miles'), but also ensures that you are supporting local farmers and producers; the very people who have moulded the countryside you have come to see and who are in the best position to protect it. If you can find local food which is also organic so much the better.

It's a fact of life that money spent at local level – perhaps in a market, or at the greengrocer, or in an independent pub – has a far greater impact for good on that community than the equivalent spent in a branch of a national chain store or restaurant. While no-one would advocate that walkers should boycott the larger supermarkets, which after all do provide local employment, it's worth remembering that businesses in rural communities rely heavily on visitors for their very existence. If we want to keep these shops and post offices, we need to use them.

ENVIRONMENTAL IMPACT

A walking holiday in itself is an environmentally friendly approach to tourism. The following are some ideas on how you can go a few steps further in helping to minimise your impact on the environment while walking the Hadrian's Wall Path. See also box below.

- Use **public rather than private transport** whenever you can.
- Leave all **farm gates** as you find them.

In addition to the above rules, there are some other important guidelines that need to be followed to minimise the damage hikers do to the archaeological deposits.
- Camping is allowed only on official sites. **Don't 'wild camp'** near the Wall.
- If the path resembles a worn line in the grass, walk alongside it to avoid exacerbating the erosion. In other words, **keep on the grass!** This is one of the most important rules – and also one of the most unusual, for on most trails you are usually told to stick to the path to prevent widening of the trail and the spreading of erosion. However, Hadrian's Wall is, of course, not your usual path and the authorities' main concern is not to preserve the state of the path but to protect the as-yet unexcavated archaeological treasures that lie beneath. This is why the path is a green sward, as it was felt that this was one of the best surfaces to protect the unexcavated treasures. But if that protective layer is eroded away, those treasures are put in danger. The erosion mats that have been placed on some of the muddier parts do a reasonable job but they can't be 100% successful. So avoid walking on a worn or eroded part of the trail and **walk side by side, not in single file**.
- Similarly, **don't walk on any nearby ridge or hillock**. Just as the trail cuts a delicate path through the Wall's numerous unexcavated mounds so you should avoid treading on any raised ground.
- If you find anything that might conceivably be of historical or archaeological interest on the trail, report your find(s) to a Wall guardian, trail officer or possibly a nearby museum. Do not, whatever you do, keep the find for yourself as a keepsake.
- Do not chip off a bit of stone or other matter from the Wall as a souvenir.

Use public transport whenever possible
Public transport along the Wall is not bad (though it can be infrequent), with most places served by at least one bus or train a day. It is preferable to using private cars as it benefits everyone: visitors, locals and the environment.

Never leave litter
Leaving litter shows a total disrespect for the natural world and others coming after you. As well as being unsightly, litter kills wildlife, pollutes the environment and can be dangerous to farm animals. Please carry a degradable plastic bag so you can dispose of your rubbish in a bin in the next village. It would be very helpful if you could pick up litter left by other people too.

● **Is it OK if it's biodegradable?** Not really. Apple cores, banana skins, orange peel and the like are unsightly, encourage flies, ants and wasps and ruin a picnic spot for others.

● **The lasting impact of litter** A piece of orange peel left on the ground takes six months to decompose; silver foil 18 months; a plastic bag 10 years; clothes 15 years; and an aluminium can 85 years.

Respect all wildlife
Care for all wildlife you come across along the path; it has as much right to be there as you. As tempting as it may be to pick wild flowers, leave them in place so the next people who pass can enjoy them too. Don't break branches off or damage trees in any way.

If you come across wildlife, keep your distance and don't watch for too long. Your presence can cause considerable stress, particularly if the adults are with young, or in winter when the weather is harsh and food is scarce. Young animals are rarely abandoned. If you come across young birds, keep away so that their mother can return.

Outdoor toiletry
Public toilets are marked on the trail maps in this guide and you will also find facilities in pubs, cafés and campsites along the trail. As a result, there shouldn't be any need to 'go' outdoors. This is very important. Normally, when caught short outdoors and with no public facilities nearby, considerate hikers would dig a small hole in the ground in which to bury their excrement. However, as previously mentioned many of Hadrian's Wall's treasures are as yet unexcavated.

For this reason, **it is forbidden to dig anywhere near the Wall**! And this point cannot be emphasised enough.

● **Toilet paper, tampons and sanitary towels** These take a long time to decompose, whether buried or not, and even if they are buried are easily dug up by animals and may then blow into water sources or onto the path.

The best method for dealing with any of these is to **pack it out**. Put the used item inside a paper bag which you then place inside a plastic bag (or two if you're worried about ruptures). Then simply empty the contents of the paper bag at the next toilet you come across and throw the bag away.

Wild camping
Wild camping is not allowed along the Wall and, with the number of campsites serving the trail, there's no need to either.

ACCESS

Britain is a crowded cluster of islands with few places where you can wander as you please. Most of the land is a patchwork of fields and agriculture and the environment through which the Hadrian's Wall Path marches is no different. However, there are countless public rights of way, in addition to the main trail, that criss-cross the land. This is fine, but what happens if you feel a little more adventurous and want to explore the moorland, woodland and hills that can also be found near the walk?

Right to roam
The Countryside & Rights of Way Act 2000 (CRoW), or 'Right (or Freedom) to Roam' as dubbed by walkers, came into effect in full on 31 October 2005 after a long campaign to allow greater public access to areas of countryside in England and Wales deemed to be uncultivated open country. This essentially means moorland, heathland, downland and upland areas. Some land is covered by restrictions (ie high-impact activities such as driving a vehicle, cycling and horse-riding are not permitted) and some land is excluded, such as gardens, parks and cultivated land. For further details visit 💻 www.gov.uk/right-of-way-open-access-land. With more freedom in the countryside comes a need for more responsibility from the walker. Remember that wild open country is still the workplace of farmers and home to all sorts of wildlife. Have respect for both and avoid disturbing domestic and wild animals.

Countryside code
The countryside is a fragile place which every visitor should respect. The Countryside Code, originally described in the 1950s as the Country Code, was revised and relaunched in 2004, in part because of the changes brought about by the CRoW Act (see above); it was updated again in 2012, 2014 & 2016. The Code seems like common sense but sadly some people still appear to have no understanding of how to treat the countryside they walk in. An adapted version of the 2016 Code (💻 www.gov.uk/government/publications), launched under the logo 'Respect. Protect. Enjoy.', is given here.

❑ **THE COUNTRYSIDE CODE**

Respect other people
● Consider the local community and other people enjoying the outdoors
● Leave gates and property as you find them and follow paths unless wider access is available; bear in mind the Hadrian's Wall Code of Respect (see box pp64-5)

Protect the natural environment
● Leave no trace of your visit and take your litter home
● Keep dogs under effective control (see also pp35-6 and pp221-2)

Enjoy the outdoors
● Plan ahead and be prepared
● Follow advice and local signs

Other points to consider on the Path

- **Keep to paths across farmland** Stick to the official path across arable or pasture land, though do bear in mind the Hadrian's Wall Code of Respect (see box pp64-5).
- **Use gates and stiles to cross fences, hedges and walls** The path is well supplied with stiles where it crosses field boundaries. On some of the side trips you may find the paths less accommodating. If you have to climb over a gate because you can't open it always do so at the hinged end.
- **Walk side by side and on healthy grass** In other words don't walk in single file and don't walk on worn areas.
- **Help keep all water clean** Leaving litter and going to the toilet near a water source can pollute people's water supplies.
- **Take special care on country roads** Drivers often go dangerously fast on narrow winding lanes. To be safe, walk facing the oncoming traffic and carry a torch or wear highly visible clothing when it's getting dark.
- **Protect wildlife, plants and trees** Care for and respect all wildlife you come across. Don't pick plants, break tree branches or scare wild animals. If you come across young birds that appear to have been abandoned leave them alone.
- **Make no unnecessary noise** Enjoy the peace and solitude of the outdoors by staying in small groups and acting unobtrusively.

Outdoor safety

AVOIDANCE OF HAZARDS

Though the Hadrian's Wall Path passes through some pretty wild countryside, the good waymarkings, proximity of the B6318 (the so-called Military Road) and the A69 highways to the south and the lack of any major highlands, fells or mountains mean that it is unlikely you're going to get lost or come to grief on the trail. Indeed, perhaps the biggest threat to your life is provided by the roads which cut across the path, particularly on the section between Heddon-on-the-Wall and Chollerford, and there's already been one memorial erected by the Robin Hood pub to a walker who was hit and killed by a vehicle on this road.

That said, there are some hazards that beset trekkers on even the easiest trails. But with good planning and preparation these can be avoided. This information is just as important for those out on a day walk as for those walking the entire Hadrian's Wall Path.

In addition to the points listed opposite, always make sure you have suitable **clothes** (see p38) to keep you warm and dry whatever the conditions and a spare change of inner clothes. Carrying plenty of **food and water** is vital too. A **compass**, **whistle**, **torch**, **map** and **first-aid kit** should be carried; see pp38-9.

Safety on the Hadrian's Wall Path

Sadly every year people are injured walking along the trail, though usually it's nothing more than a badly twisted ankle. The most dangerous section is from Sewingshields to Walltown, where the unpredictable weather can leave hikers in difficulty – though with a road never far away, there's nothing too serious to worry about. Abiding by the following rules, however, should minimise the risks:

- Avoid walking on your own if possible.
- Make sure that somebody knows your plans for every day you are on the trail. This could be a friend or relative whom you have promised to call every night or the B&B or hostel you plan to stay in at the end of each day's walk. That way, if you fail to turn up or call, they can raise the alarm.
- If the weather closes in suddenly and fog or mist descends while you are on the trail, particularly on the moors or fells, and you become uncertain of the correct trail, do not be tempted to continue. Just wait where you are and you'll find that mist often clears, at least for long enough to allow you to get your bearings. If you are still uncertain and the weather does not look like improving, return the way you came to the nearest point of civilisation and try again another time when conditions have improved.
- Always fill your water bottle or pouch at every available opportunity and ensure you have plenty of food such as high-energy snacks.
- Always carry a torch, compass, map, whistle and first-aid kit (see pp38-9). The **international distress signal** is six blasts on the whistle or six flashes with a torch.
- Always take wet-weather gear with you and a spare change of inner clothes.
- Use footwear with good grip, and consider wearing sturdy hiking boots with ankle support.
- Be extra vigilant with children.
- For information on walking safely with dogs, see pp35-6 and pp221-2.

Dealing with an accident

- Use basic first aid to treat the injury to the best of your ability.
- Work out exactly where you are. If possible leave someone with the casualty while others go to get help. If there are only two people, you have a dilemma. If you decide to get help, leave all spare clothing and food with the casualty.
- In an emergency dial ☎ 999 or ☎ 112.

WEATHER FORECASTS

The trail suffers from extremes of weather so it's vital that you always try to find out what the weather is going to be like before you set off for the day. Many B&Bs and tourist information centres will have pinned up somewhere a summary of the weather forecast. You can get an online forecast through 💻 www.bbc.co.uk/weather or 💻 www.metoffice.gov.uk. Pay close attention to it and alter your plans for the day accordingly. That said, even if the forecast is for a fine sunny day, always assume the worst and pack some wet-weather gear.

BLISTERS

It is important to break in new footwear before embarking on a long trek. Make sure your boots or shoes are comfortable and try to avoid getting them wet on the inside. Air your feet at lunchtime, keep them clean and change your socks regularly. If you feel any hot spots, stop immediately and apply a few strips of zinc oxide tape and leave on until it is pain free or the tape starts to come off.

If you have left it too late and a blister has developed you should surround it with 'moleskin' or any other blister kit to protect it from abrasion. Popping it can lead to infection. If the skin is broken keep the area clean with antiseptic and cover with a non-adhesive dressing material held in place with tape.

HYPOTHERMIA, HYPERTHERMIA & SUNBURN

Also known as exposure, **hypothermia** occurs when the body can't generate enough heat to maintain its normal temperature, usually as a result of being wet, cold, unprotected from the wind, tired and hungry. It is usually more of a problem in upland areas such as the moors. Hypothermia is easily avoided by wearing suitable clothing, carrying and eating enough food and drink, being aware of the weather conditions and checking the morale of your companions.

Early signs to watch for are feeling cold and tired with involuntary shivering. Find some shelter as soon as possible and warm the victim up with a hot drink and some chocolate or other high-energy food. If possible give them another warm layer of clothing and allow them to rest until feeling better.

If allowed to worsen, strange behaviour, slurring of speech and poor coordination will become apparent and the victim can quickly progress into unconsciousness, followed by coma and death. Quickly get the victim out of any wind and rain, improvising a shelter if necessary. Rapid restoration of bodily warmth is essential and best achieved by bare-skin contact: someone should get into the same sleeping bag as the patient, both having stripped to their underwear, putting any spare clothing under or over them to build up heat. Send urgently for help.

Hyperthermia occurs when the body generates too much heat, eg heat exhaustion and heatstroke. Not ailments that you would normally associate with the north of England, these are serious problems nonetheless. Symptoms of **heat exhaustion** include thirst, fatigue, giddiness, a rapid pulse, raised body temperature, low urine output and, if not treated, delirium and finally a coma. The best cure is to drink plenty of water. **Heatstroke** is more serious. A high body temperature and an absence of sweating are early indications, followed by symptoms similar to hypothermia such as a lack of coordination, convulsions and coma. Death will follow if treatment is not given instantly. Sponge the victim down, wrap them in wet towels, fan them and get help immediately.

Sunburn can happen, even up here and even on overcast days. The way to avoid it is to stay wrapped up but that's not really an option. What you must do, therefore, is to wear a hat and smother yourself in sunscreen (with a minimum factor of 15); apply it regularly throughout the day.

Don't forget your lips, nose, the back of your neck and even under your chin to protect you against rays reflected from the ground.

THE ENVIRONMENT & NATURE

4

Conservation

GOVERNMENT AGENCIES AND SCHEMES

Natural England
Natural England (🖥 www.gov.uk/government/organisations/natural-england) is the single body responsible for identifying, establishing and managing: National Parks, Areas of Outstanding Natural Beauty, National Nature Reserves and Sites of Special Scientific Interest.

The highest level of landscape protection is the designation of land as a **national park** (🖥 www.nationalparksengland.org.uk), which recognises the national importance of an area in terms of landscape, biodiversity and as a recreational resource. At the time of writing there were 10 national parks in England. The Hadrian's Wall Path passes through one: the 1049 sq km Northumberland National Park (🖥 www.northumberlandnationalpark.org.uk), England's most remote national park, and an area that contains some of the best-preserved parts of the Wall. But there is an extra dimension to that designation in Northumberland National Park – the sky. In 2013, the park was awarded the title of **Northumberland Dark Sky Park** (see box p146).

The second level of protection is **Area of Outstanding Natural Beauty** (AONB; 🖥 www.landscapesforlife.org.uk), of which there are 33 wholly in England (plus the Wye Valley which straddles the English-Welsh border) covering some 15% of England and Wales. The only AONB on the trail is the exquisite Solway Coast (🖥 www.solwaycoastaonb.org.uk), west of Carlisle, though the trail also brushes the northern edge of England's second largest AONB, North Pennines (🖥 www.northpennines.org.uk), which begins just to the south of the road running between Brampton and Hexham. Their primary objective is conservation of the natural beauty of a landscape.

Other levels of protection include: **National Nature Reserves** (NNRs), of which there are 224 in England, including Greenlee Lough NNR, the largest freshwater lake in Northumberland, situated north of Housesteads in Northumberland National Park; Muckle Moss NNR, a 'mire' or peat bog close by between Stanegate and

Vindolanda; Drumburgh Moss NNR, south of the trail and the hamlet of the same name; and South Solway Mosses NNR, just south of Bowness at the western end of the walk, which is a composite of three large lowland raised bogs – peat bogs – and also form the **South Solway Mosses Special Area of Conservation** (SAC).

Overlapping many of the NNRs are **Sites of Special Scientific Interest** (SSSIs). These range in size from little pockets protecting wild flower meadows, important nesting sites or special geological features, to vast swathes of upland, moorland and wetland.

On the trail there are several (the following descriptions all assume you are heading west along the trail): Close House, Riverside, the riverbank area by the Tyne before you head onto the golf course; Brunton Bank Quarry, to the north of the path just past Planetrees; Roman Wall Loughs, Roman Wall Escarpments and Muckle Moss which together form one large SSSI stretching from just east of Sewing Shields to Cawfields Quarry; Allolee to Walltown (beginning about half a mile west of Chesters fort and stretching for about 1¼ miles along the Wall from the crags at Walltown); the Tipalt Burn that crosses the path at the

---

❏ Campaigning and conservation bodies/organisations

● **English Heritage** (🖥 www.english-heritage.org.uk) English Heritage looks after, champions and advises the government on historic buildings and places. However, in April 2015 it was divided into a new charitable trust that retains the name English Heritage and a non-departmental public body, Historic England (see below).

English Heritage is responsible for nearly all the Roman forts along the Wall that are open to the public – though in one notable instance shares this duty with the National Trust.

● **Historic England** (🖥 historicengland.org.uk) Created in April 2015 as a result of dividing the work done by English Heritage (see above). Historic England is the government department responsible for looking after and promoting England's historic environment and is in charge of the listing system, giving grants and dealing with planning matters.

● **National Trust** (NT; 🖥 www.nationaltrust.org.uk) A charity that aims to protect, through ownership, threatened coastline, countryside, historic houses, castles and gardens, and archaeological remains for everybody to enjoy. In particular the NT cares for about 775 miles of British coastline, over 250,000 hectares of countryside and 300 historic buildings, monuments, parks, gardens and reserves, including: George Stephenson's birthplace in Wylam, Northumberland; Housesteads and six miles of the Wall itself!

● **Royal Society for the Protection of Birds** (RSPB; 🖥 www.rspb.org.uk) The largest voluntary conservation body in Europe focusing on providing a healthy environment for birds and wildlife and with over 200 reserves in the UK and more than a million members.

● The umbrella organisation for the 47 wildlife trusts in the UK is **The Wildlife Trusts** (🖥 www.wildlifetrusts.org). Two relevant to the Hadrian's Wall path are **Cumbria Wildlife Trust** (🖥 www.cumbriawildlifetrust.org.uk) and **Northumberland Wildlife Trust** (🖥 www.nwt.org.uk).

lovely Thirlwall Castle; the River Eden and its tributaries (first encountered at the River Irthing, west of Gilsland); White Moss, Crosbymoor (on the way into Crosby-on-Eden); and the Upper Solway Flats and Marshes, Drumburgh Moss, Glasson Moss and Bowness Common at the far western end of walk.

Flora and fauna

Northumberland and Cumbria are England's two 'wildest' counties so, as you would probably expect, much of the nation's native flora and fauna is more abundant here than elsewhere. Furthermore, given the variety of habitats that you pass through on the trail, from woodland and grassland to heathland, moor and bog, the variety of flora and fauna present is also commensurately greater.

The following is not in any way a comprehensive guide, but merely a brief run-down of the more commonly seen flora and fauna on the trail, together with some of the rarer and more spectacular species.

MAMMALS

One of the great attractions of walking any long-distance trail in Britain is the opportunity it affords of seeing a native animal in its natural environment, and the Hadrian's Wall Path is no different. That said, spotting the wildlife is another matter. Many of Britain's native species are nocturnal and those which aren't are often very shy and seldom encountered. Then of course there are those – the otter, for example, or the water vole – that are few in number anyway and sightings are always very rare.

Nevertheless, with a bit of luck and patience, on the quieter parts of the trail you may well be rewarded with a sighting or two of something fluffy. One creature that you will definitely see along the walk is the **rabbit** (*Oryctolagus cuniculus*). It was actually the Romans who brought the first rabbits to Britain. Timid by nature, most of the time you'll have to make do with nothing more than a brief and distant glimpse of their white tails as they race for the nearest warren at the sound of your footfall. Because they are so numerous, however, the laws of probability dictate that you will at some stage during your walk get close enough to observe them without being spotted; trying to take a decent photo of one of them, however, is a different matter.

Rabbits and Romans have a shared history as the Romans brought rabbits with them to use as the main ingredient in gourmet dishes. And now, 2000 years later, the descendants of those first rabbits are said to be one of the main threats to the Wall, their burrows destroying its foundations from below ground just as the boots of hikers damage them from above. The situation is said to be so serious, some scientists are calling for a reintroduction of myxomatosis, the disease that wiped out 99% of the rabbit population in the 1950s. If you're lucky you

74 Flora and fauna

may also come across **hares** (*Lepus europaeus*), often mistaken for rabbits but they are much larger, with longer bodies, ears and back legs.

Northumberland and Cumbria play host to a number of creatures that are found in few other places in England. In particular, there's the **red squirrel** (*Sciurus vulgaris*), which has been seen by hikers in the trees near Birdoswald Fort. Elsewhere in the country this small, tufty-eared native has been usurped by its larger cousin from North America, the **grey squirrel** (*Sciurus carolinensis*), but in the north of England and Scotland the red squirrel maintains a precarious foothold. Fears for their survival on these shores have prompted the establishment of Red Alert, a charity aimed at protecting the species. For more information see 🖳 rsst.org.uk.

Two other creatures that are subject to long-term protection programmes are the otter and the water vole. Previously persecuted because it was (wrongly) believed to have an enormously detrimental effect on fish stocks – indeed, it was hunted with dogs up until 1977 – the **otter** (*Lutra lutra*) is enjoying something of a renaissance thanks to some concerted conservation efforts. At home both in saltwater and freshwater, they are a good indicator of a healthy unpolluted environment and are said to be well established on the banks of the North Tyne in Northumberland National Park.

As for the **water vole** (scientifically known as *Arvicola terrestris*, but better known as 'Ratty' from Kenneth Grahame's classic children's story *Wind in the Willows)*, this is another creature, like the red squirrel, that's fallen foul of an alien invader, in this case the **mink** (*Mustela vison*) from North America which has successfully adapted to the British countryside after escaping from local fur farms. Unfortunately, the mink not only hunts water voles but is small enough to slip inside their burrows. Thus, with the voles afforded no protection, the mink is able to wipe out an entire riverbank's population in a matter of months. This is another reason why protecting the otter is important: they kill mink.

Other creatures you might see include the ubiquitous **fox** (*Vulpes vulpes*), now just as at home in the city as it is in the country. While generally considered nocturnal, it's not unusual to encounter a fox during the day too, often lounging in the sun near its den.

Another creature of the night that you may *occasionally* see in the late afternoon is the **badger** (*Meles meles*). Relatively common throughout the British Isles, these sociable mammals with their distinctive black-and-white striped muzzles live in large underground burrows called setts, appearing around sunset to root for worms and slugs.

One creature that is strictly nocturnal, however, is the **bat**, of which there are 17 species in Britain, all protected by law. Your best chance of spotting one is at dusk while there's still enough light in the sky to make out their flitting forms as they fly along hedgerows, over rivers and streams and around street lamps in their quest for moths and insects. The commonest species in Britain is the **pipistrelle** (*Pipistrellus pipistrellus*).

In addition to the above, keep a look out for other fairly common but little-seen species such as the carnivorous **stoat** (*Mustela erminea*), its diminutive cousin the **weasel** (*Mustela nivalis*), the **hedgehog** (*Erinaceus europaeus*) – these days, alas, most commonly seen as roadkill – and any number of species of **voles**, **mice** and **shrews**.

Finally, a surprisingly large number of hikers encounter deer on their walk. Mostly this will be the **roe deer** (*Capreolus capreolus*), a small native woodland species, though it can also be seen grazing in fields. As with most creatures, your best chance of seeing one is very early in the morning, particularly in Northumberland National Park: there are said to be 6000 in Kielder Forest alone! Britain's largest native land mammal, the **red deer** (*Cervus elaphus*), is rarely seen on the walk though it does exist in small pockets in Cumbria.

REPTILES AND FISH

The **adder** (*Vipera berus*) is the only common snake in the north of England, and the only poisonous one of the three species in Britain. They pose very little risk to walkers – indeed, you should consider yourself extremely fortunate to see one, providing you're a safe distance away. They bite only when provoked, preferring to hide instead. The venom is designed to kill small mammals such as mice, voles and shrews, so deaths in humans are very rare but a bite can be extremely unpleasant and occasionally dangerous to children or the elderly. You are most likely to encounter them in spring when they come out of hibernation and during the summer when pregnant females warm themselves in the sun. They are easily identified by the striking zigzag pattern on their back. Should you be lucky enough to encounter one, enjoy it but leave it undisturbed.

Salmon (*Salmo salar*) thrive in the clean waters of Northumberland National Park.

BIRDS

The woods, moorland and hedgerows along the Hadrian's Wall Path provide homes for a wealth of different species.

While Northumberland is famed for its birdlife, in order to appreciate its richness it's often necessary to leave the trail, either by heading to one of the offshore islands or visiting the forest at Kielder. The former is one of the best birdwatching venues in Britain and the latter's not bad either, though in Kielder it's fair to say that often you can't see the birds for the trees. Nevertheless, the area is particularly rich in raptors, including **sparrowhawks** (*Accipiter nisus*), **goshawks** (*Accipiter gentilis*), **merlins** (*Falco*

SKYLARK
L: 185MM/7.25"

columbarius), **peregrines** (*Falco peregrinus*) and **kestrels** (*Falco tinnunculus*).

At the northern end of Kielder Water, Bakethin Reservoir has been declared a nature reserve and attracts **ospreys** as well as more common residents including wildfowl and gulls. The conifer forests at Kielder play host to the **crossbill** (*Loxia curvirostra*), while the deciduous, lower areas of the North Tyne Valley are popular with the **pied flycatcher** (*Ficedula hypoleuca*) and **redstart** (*Phoenicurus phoenicurus*).

Occasionally, some of these species may be glimpsed on the trail but in the main it's the usual 'garden' species that dominate: the **great tit** (*Parus major*), **coal tit** (*Parus ater*), **blue tit** (*Parus caeruleus*), **blackbird** (*Turdus merula*), **mistle thrush** (*Turdus philomelos*) and **robin** (*Erithacus rubecula*).

You may also see, but are more likely to hear, the continuous and rapid song of the **skylark** (*Alauda arvensis*). They tend to move from moorland to lower agricultural land in the winter. Just bigger than a house sparrow, they have brown upper parts and chin with dark flakes and a white belly.

As for Cumbria, the AONB (Area of Outstanding Natural Beauty) along the Solway Firth at the western end of the trail is renowned as a haven for birdlife. The most famous, or at least the most voluble, inhabitant is the **barnacle goose** (*Branta leucopsis*). The goose is actually only a winter visitor, as it flees its nesting sites on the cliffs of Svalbard, Norway, to enjoy Cumbria's milder climate. Up to 30,000 of the birds arrive in November, heading back to Norway in mid-April.

LAPWING/PEEWIT
L: 320MM/12.5"

Other species you might encounter on this shoreline include **ducks**, **swans**, **ringed plovers** (*Charadrius hiaticula*), **oystercatchers** (*Haematopus ostralegus*) and **lapwings** (*Vanellus vanellus*). The latter is black and white with iridescent green upper parts and is approximately the size of a pigeon or tern. Its most distinctive characteristic, however, is the male's tumbling, diving, swooping flight pattern when disturbed, believed to be either a display to attract a female or an attempt to distract predators from its nest, which is built on the ground. Common in Solway, you can also find them on the moors in Northumberland.

CURLEW
L: 600MM/24"

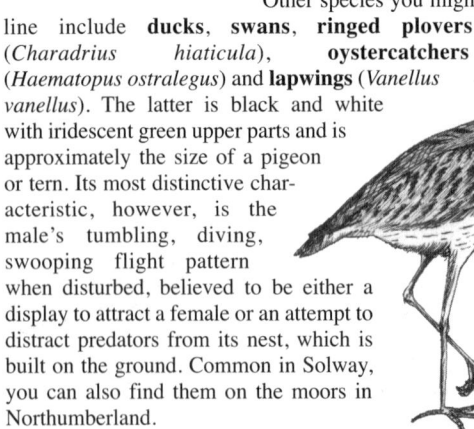

One of the most common birds seen on the path is the **pheasant** (*Phasianus colchicus*). The male is distinctive thanks to his beautiful long, barred tail feathers, brown body and glossy green-black head with red flashes, while the female is a dull brown. Another way to distinguish them is by the distinctive strangulated hacking sound they make together with the loud beating of wings as they fly off. Another moorland favourite is the rare **black grouse** (*Tetrao tetrix*). Feeding on cotton grass and tree shoots, in spring they gather together in 'leks' – display grounds – where the males conduct a spectacular courtship display. Its much commoner relative, the **red grouse** (*Lagopus lagopus scoticus*), is one of the few birds that stays on the moors year-round.

Less common but still seen by many hikers is the **curlew** (*Numenius arquata*). The largest of the British wading birds, it's the emblem of Northumberland National Park and lives on the moors there throughout spring and summer, returning to the coast in autumn. With feathers uniformly streaked grey and brown, the easiest way to identify this bird is by its thin elongated, downward curving beak.

BLACK GROUSE
L: 580MM/23"

Other birds that make their nest on open moorland and in fields include the **redshank** (*Tringa totanus*), **golden plover** (*Pluvialis apricaria*), **snipe** (*Gallinago gallinago*), **dunlin** (*Calidris alpina*) and **ring ouzel** (*Turdus torquatus*).

TREES

In the main, the Wall passes through bleak moorland bereft of any plantlife that can rise higher than the carpet of heather, though there are patches of woods and forest along the way, particularly in Northumberland National Park and towards the western end of the trail in Cumbria. Indeed, woodland in Cumbria is estimated to cover a surprisingly large 65,000 hectares, or 9.5% of the land in the county, though a storm at

❏ **Oak leaves showing galls**
Oak trees support more kinds of insects than any other tree in Britain and some affect the oak in unusual ways. The eggs of gall-flies cause growths known as galls on the leaves. Each of these contains a single insect. Other kinds of gall-flies lay eggs in stalks or flowers, leading to flower galls, growths the size of currants.

the beginning of 2005 which blew down 500,000 trees probably reduced these figures. Even more surprising, Cumbria's woodland cover has actually *increased* over the past two decades. Conifer woodland makes up the majority, though there's also a fair bit of broadleaf woodland. Popular species include willow, oak, beech and maple.

Hazel (with flowers)

Birch (with flowers)

Oak woodland is a diverse habitat and not exclusively made up of oak. Other trees that flourish here include **downy birch** (*Betula pubescens*), its relative the **silver birch** (*Betula pendula*), **holly** (*Ilex aquifolium*) and **hazel** (*Corylus avellana*) which has traditionally been used for coppicing (the periodic cutting of small trees for harvesting).

Further east there are some examples of limestone woodland. **Ash** (*Fraxinus excelsior*) and oak dominate, along with **wych elm** (*Ulmus glabra*), **sycamore** (*Acer pseudoplatanus*) and some **yew** (*Taxus baccata*). The **hawthorn** (*Crataegus monogyna*) also grows along the path, usually in isolated pockets on pasture. These species are known as pioneer species and they play a vital role in the ecosystem by improving the soil. It is these pioneers – the hawthorn and its companion the **rowan** (*Sorbus aucuparia*) – that you will see growing alone on inaccessible crags and ravines. Without interference from man, these pioneers would eventually be succeeded by longer-lived species such as the oak.

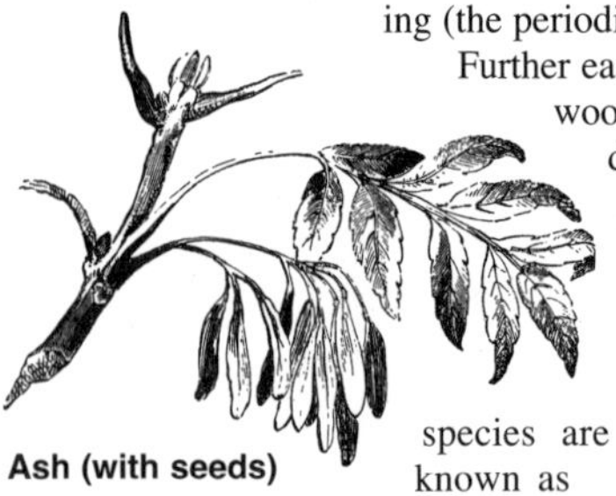

Ash (with seeds)

Alder (with flowers)

In wet, marshy areas and along rivers and streams you are more likely to find **alder** (*Alnus glutinosa*). Finally, in Northumberland National Park there are a few examples of the **juniper** tree (*Juniperus communis*), one of only three native British species of conifer, the blue berries of which are used to flavour gin.

FLOWERS

Spring is the time to come and see the spectacular displays of colour on the Hadrian's Wall Path, when most of the flowers are in bloom. Alternatively, arrive in August and you'll see the heathers carpeting patches of the moors in a blaze of purple flowers.

Juniper (with berries)

Woodland, hedgerows and riverbanks

From March to May **bluebells** (*Hyacinthoides non-scripta*) proliferate in some of the woods along the trail, providing a wonderful spectacle. The white **wood anemone** (*Anemone nemorosa*) – wide open flowers when sunny, closed and drooping when the weather's dull – and the yellow **primrose** (*Primula vulgaris*) also flower early in spring. **Red campion** (*Silene dioica*), which flowers from late April, can be found in hedgebanks along with **rosebay willowherb** (*Epilobium angustifolium*) which also has the name fireweed due to its habit of colonising burnt areas.

In scrubland and on woodland edges you will find **bramble** (*Rubus fruticosus*), a common vigorous shrub responsible for many a ripped jacket thanks to the sharp thorns and prickles. **Blackberry** fruits ripen from late summer to autumn. Fairly common in scrubland and on woodland edges is the **dog rose** (*Rosa canina*) which has a large pink flower, the fruits of which are used to make rose-hip syrup.

In streams or rivers look out for the white-flowered **water crow-foot** (*Ranunculus penicillatus pseudofluitans*) which, because it needs unpolluted, flowing water, is a good indicator of the cleanliness of the stream.

Other flowering plants to look for in wooded areas and in hedgerows include the tall **foxglove** (*Digitalis purpurea*) with its trumpet-like flowers, **forget-me-not** (*Myosotis arvensis*) with tiny, delicate blue flowers, and **cow parsley** (*Anthriscus sylvestris*), a tall member of the carrot family with a large globe of white flowers which often covers roadside verges and hedgebanks.

Perhaps the most ubiquitous plant on the trail, however, is none of the above – nor is it even a British native. **Himalayan balsam** (*Impatiens glandulifera*) is a tall plant that can reach to well over head height and produces pink flowers with pods that 'explode' when squeezed, scattering their seeds. Introduced in 1839, it particularly enjoys riverbanks where it thrives, often suffocating out any other plant.

Heathland and scrubland

There are three species of heather. The most dominant is **ling** (*Calluna vulgaris*) with tiny flowers on delicate upright stems. The other two species are **bell heather** (*Erica cinera*) with deep purple bell-shaped flowers and **cross-leaved heath** (*Erica tetralix*) with similarly shaped flowers of a lighter pink, almost white colour. Cross-leaved heath prefers wet and boggy ground. As a result, it usually grows away from bell heather which prefers well-drained soils.

Heather is an incredibly versatile plant which is put to many uses. It provides fodder for livestock, fuel for fires, an orange dye and material for bedding, thatching, basketwork and brooms. It is still sometimes used in place of hops to flavour beer and the flower heads can be brewed to make good tea; it is also used in the production of some varieties of honey. It is incredibly hardy and thrives on the denuded hills, preventing other species from flourishing. Indeed, at times highland cattle are brought to certain areas of the moors to graze on the heather, allowing other species a chance to grow.

Not a flower but worthy of mention is the less attractive species **bracken** (*Pteridium aquilinum*), a vigorous non-native fern that has invaded many heathland areas to the detriment of native species.

Grassland

There is much overlap between the hedge/woodland-edge habitat and that of pastures and meadows. You will come across **common birdsfoot-trefoil** (*Lotus corniculatus*), **Germander speedwell** (*Veronica chamaedrys*), **tufted** and **bush vetch** (*Vicia cracca* and *V. sepium*) and **meadow vetchling** (*Lathyrus pratensis*) in both. Often the only species you will see in heavily grazed pastures are the most resilient.

Of the thistles, in late summer you should come across the **melancholy thistle** (*Cirsium helenoides*) drooping sadly on roadside verges and hay meadows. Unusually, it has no prickles on its stem.

The **yellow rattle** is aptly named, for the dry seedpods rattle in the wind, a good indication for farmers that it is time to harvest the hay.

Other widespread grassland species include **harebell** (*Campanula rotundifolia*), delicate yellow **tormentil** (*Potentilla erecta*), which often spreads onto the lower slopes of mountains along with **devil's-bit scabious** (*Succisa pratensis*). Also keep an eye out for orchids such as the **fragrant orchid** (*Gymnadenia conopsea*) and **early purple orchid** (*Orchis mascula*).

Common flora C1

Herb-Robert
Geranium robertianum

Meadow Cranesbill
Geranium pratense

Heartsease (Wild Pansy)
Viola tricolor

Lousewort
Pedicularis sylvatica

Red Campion
Silene dioica

Common Dog Violet
Viola riviniana

Germander Speedwell
Veronica chamaedrys

Heather (Ling)
Calluna vulgaris

Harebell
Campanula rotundifolia

Early Purple Orchid
Orchis mascula

Bell Heather
Erica cinerea

Himalayan Balsam
Impatiens glandulifera

C2 Common flora

Gorse
Ulex europaeus

Meadow Buttercup
Ranunculis acris

Marsh Marigold (Kingcup)
Caltha palustris

Bird's-foot trefoil
Lotus corniculatus

Water Avens
Geum rivale

Tormentil
Potentilla erecta

Primrose
Primula vulgaris

Ox-eye Daisy
Leucanthemum vulgare

Cotton Grass
Eriophorum angustifolium

Common Ragwort
Senecio jacobaea

Hemp-nettle
Galeopsis speciosa

Cowslip
Primula veris

Common flora C3

Yellow Rattle
Rhinanthus minor

Dog Rose
Rosa canina

Forget-me-not
Myosotis arvensis

Scarlet Pimpernel
Anagallis arvensis

Self-heal
Prunella vulgaris

Thrift (Sea Pink)
Armeria maritima

Ramsons (Wild Garlic)
Allium ursinum

Common Hawthorn
Crataegus monogyna

Sea Campion
Silene maritima

Bluebell
Hyacinthoides non-scripta

Yarrow
Achillea millefolium

Hogweed
Heracleum sphondylium

C4 Common flora

Common Vetch
Vicia sativa

Honeysuckle
Lonicera periclymemum

Rowan (tree)
Sorbus aucuparia

Foxglove
Digitalis purpurea

Common Knapweed
Centaurea nigra

Rosebay Willowherb
Epilobium angustifolium

Colour photos (following pages)

● **C5 Top**: Hiking above Crag Lough (see p159). **Middle**: Nosy neighbour at Winshields Farm Campsite. **Bottom left**: One of the locals near Grindon Turret 34A. **Right**: A decent stretch of Roman Wall at Willowford Farm, just outside Gilsland. (Photo © Henry Stedman).

● **C6-7 Top**: Looking east towards Housesteads Fort (behind the trees) from Cuddy's Crags. Note the 'Clayton Wall' here, named after John Clayton (see p61) who 'restored' it in the 1800s, adding the turf top. **Left**: Although the Hadrian's Wall Path is probably the least challenging of all the national trails, 84 miles is still a long way to walk and there are numerous stiles and steps to negotiate. **Right**: An impressive high section of unrestored Wall near Turret 45A.

● **C8 Top**: Picturesque riverside setting of the well-preserved Roman baths (see p145), Chesters Fort. **Middle**: Trying the latrines for size at the baths at Chesters. **Bottom left**: St Michael's Church (see p214), in Bowness on Solway, stands on the site of the Roman fort which marked the western end of the Wall. **Bottom right**: The brooding remains of Thirlwall Castle (see p172), constructed in the 14th century largely from Roman Wall stones. (Photo © Henry Stedman).

● **C9 Top**: The unique arched gateway of Milecastle 37 (see p158), one of the best preserved on the Wall. **Bottom**: The granary at Housesteads Fort (see p156; photo © Henry Stedman).

● **C10** A fine view on a summer's day: looking back towards Housesteads Fort and beyond. (Photo © Henry Stedman).

C5

C6

C7

C8

C9

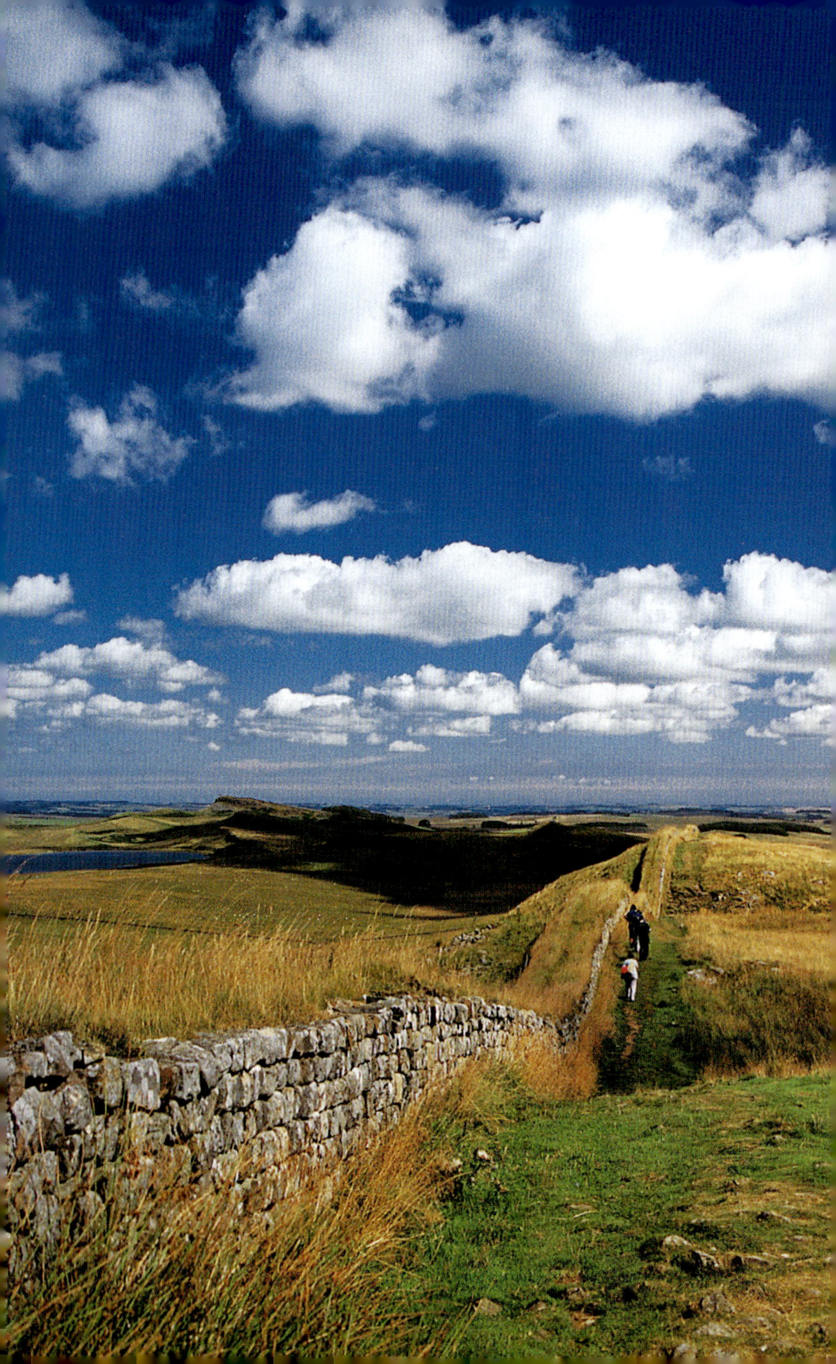

C10

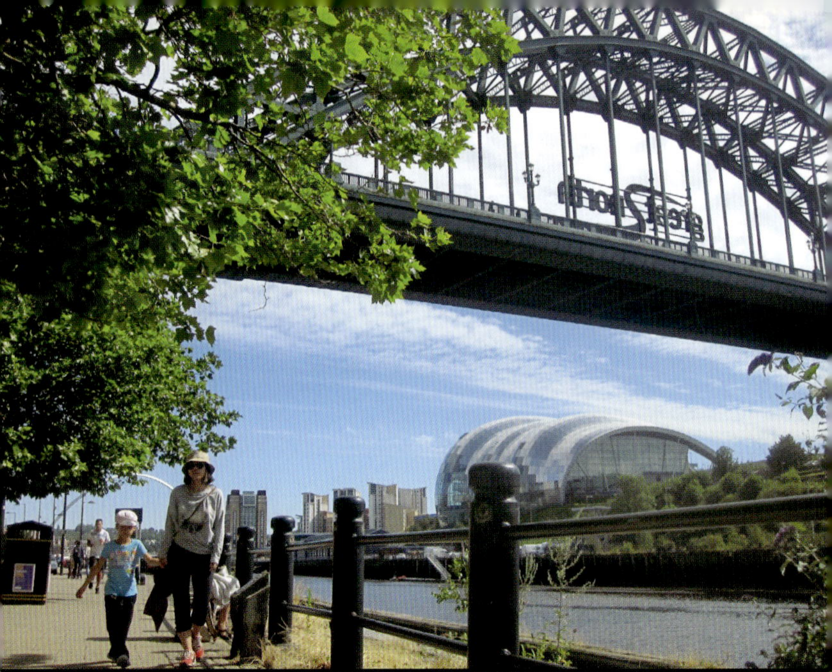

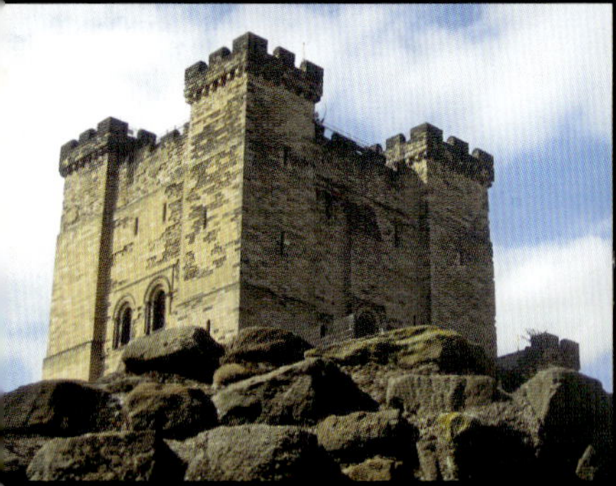

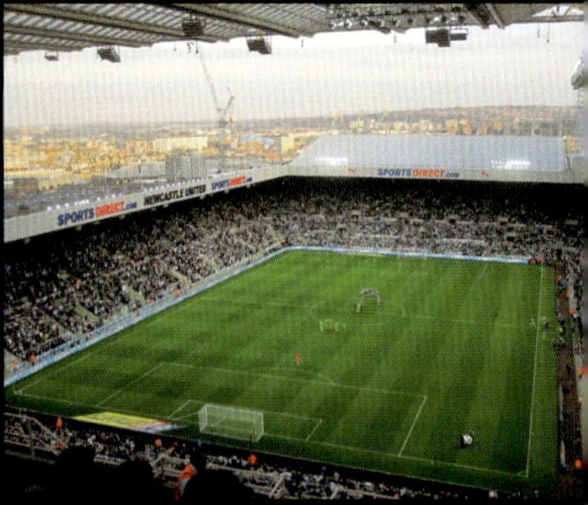

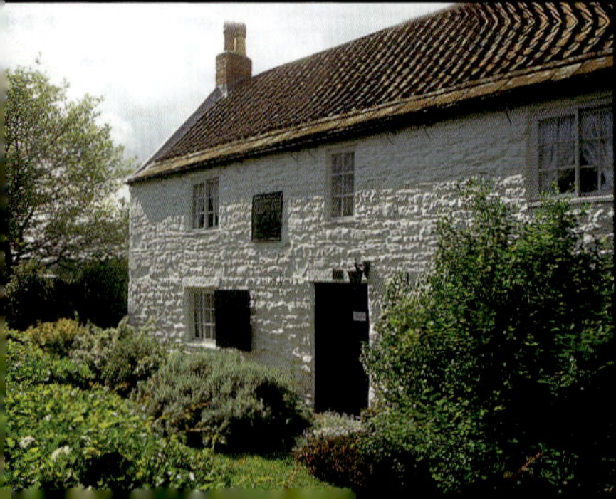

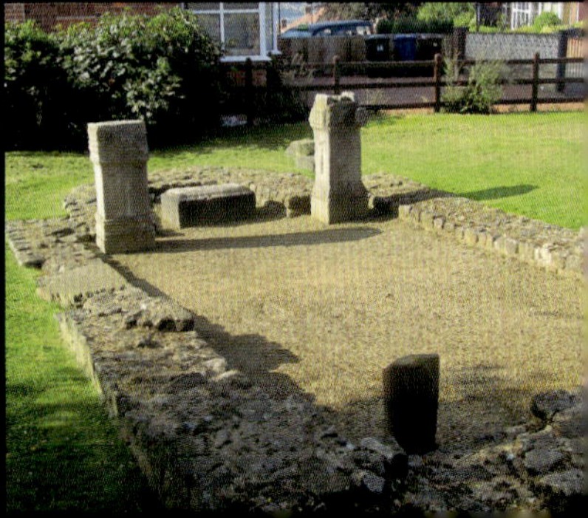

NEWCASTLE

5

City guide

A fittingly grand location to begin an epic walk, or the perfect venue for a post-trek knees-up, Newcastle is a large, buzzing city with plenty of history, a thriving food-and-drink scene and a pleasantly attractive riverside waterfront.

Arriving by train, the first thing you'll see as you cross the Tyne is an eclectic mix of river bridges, followed by an untidy jumble of roofs; an interesting but somewhat messy skyline that belies the uniform elegance of much of the city centre with its stylish Classical 19th-century façades interspersed here and there with the latest in cutting-edge municipal designs. Yet Newcastle is like that; a city that is forever defying those who dismiss it as merely a home for brown ale, football and fun-runs. As the starting point for a major trek it's ideal: functional, convenient, with great amenities and plenty to keep you occupied round-the-clock. The Great North Museum: Hancock, see p94, is also the perfect introduction to the Wall and its history (and like just about every other museum and gallery in the city, it's free), while if you are coming to the end of your Hadrian's Wall odyssey and Newcastle is your last stop, there couldn't be a better place to celebrate than the revamped Quayside, home to numerous cafés, bistros and bars.

ARRIVAL

Most visitors alight at Newcastle's **Central Station** and it's hard to imagine a more appropriate place to arrive in this city. Built in 1850, the station stands in the heart of a metropolis that will forever be associated with George Stephenson (see box p114), the 'Father of the Railways' who was born in nearby Wylam, and which thrived on the back of the railways in the glory days of the late 19th century. The terminus, lying just to the north of the River Tyne, has cafés, ATMs and its own metro station. The **National Express coach station** stands a five-minute walk to the west on St James Boulevard.

(**Opposite**) **Top**: Beneath the iconic Tyne Bridge in Newcastle's Quayside. **Middle left**: Castle Keep (see p94), Newcastle. **Middle right**: St James' Park, home to Newcastle United Football Club. **Bottom left**: George Stephenson, the father of the railways, grew up in this cottage near Wylam (see p114, © Henry Stedman). **Bottom right**: The remains of Benwell Roman Temple (see pp96-7) in the suburbs of Newcastle.

The **ferry terminus** (Port of Tyne International Passenger Terminal/DFDS Ferry Terminal) is 7 miles (11km) east of the city centre; the nearest metro station is Percy Main, a 20-minute walk away (or 5 minutes on Go North East's bus 19). From Percy Main it's 15-20 minutes by metro to Central Station. It's much easier, however, to take DFDS Seaways Bus (🖥 www.dfdsseaways.co.uk/ferry extras; click on Extras ashore, then Bus transfers), which waits for disembarking passengers outside the ferry terminal before conveying them to Bewick St in front of Central Station. Going the other way, the bus departs from Bewick St 2¼ and 1¼ hours before the ferries to Amsterdam are scheduled to depart.

The **airport** (see box p45) lies 25 minutes away from the city centre by metro; the best way into the city. However, if you prefer bus, Stagecoach's X78, (Mon-Sat 2/hr, Sun 1/hr) stops on the road outside the airport and goes to Eldon Square Bus Station.

TRANSPORT

Within the city

Newcastle, or at least its centre, is a fairly compact place and the chances are you'll be walking most of the time. The main local **bus** station (Eldon Square) can be accessed through Intu Eldon Square Shopping Centre, which fronts Eldon Square itself. A second, Haymarket, is 100 metres to the north.

There is also a pretty efficient **metro** (underground) service connecting most parts of the city, which runs daily from approximately 5am to midnight. A metro map can be found in most brochures and, of course, in the stations themselves.

Shields Ferry costs £1.50 one-way (Day Saver £2.80) and runs daily (Mon-Sat from about 6.45am to 8pm but later on Thur-Sat, Sun from about 10am to 5.45pm; 2/hr; approx 7 mins).

Fares (£1.70-3.30 single) depend on the distance travelled. Alternatively, you may wish to buy a **Metro DaySaver** (£2.90-5, depending on the number of zones covered), which enables unlimited travel on the metro and the Shields Ferry. Or there's the **Network One Day Rover** (£7), which allows unlimited one-day access on all metro, ferry and bus lines.

General information about all public transport in and around Newcastle can be found on **Nexus** (🖥 www.nexus.org.uk), the organisation responsible for all public transport in Tyne and Wear.

Getting to the start of the walk and further afield

You are likely to use the metro or the bus to get to the start of the walk. For the metro take a train on the Tyne loop via Monument to Wallsend station. Alternatively, one of the most useful bus services is Stagecoach's No 22 (2-6/hr) which goes to Wallsend Forum (High Street West, near the Metro) from Grainger St (near Central Station).

There are also lots of bus services from Newcastle to places on or near the Path. Most go as far as Hexham (Arriva's No 85 & X85; Go North East's Nos 10 and 74), but Arriva's/Stagecoach's No 685 goes all the way to Carlisle. See pp44-8 for further information.

SERVICES

Tourist information

Somewhat surprisingly for a city of this size, there is no longer a tourist information centre, but you can get comprehensive tourist information online at 🖳 www.newcastlegateshead.com. You'll also find leaflets at information points and kiosks dotted around the city, including at some bus stations and the railway station.

Other services

You'll have no trouble finding a **bank/ATM** in the city centre: they're everywhere. There are also plenty of **post office** branches including one in WH Smith on Northumberland St and a second, slightly further north on the same street, with handy extended opening hours (Mon-Fri 6am-8.30pm, Sat 6.30am-7.30pm, Sun 6.30am-5.30pm).

You can use the **internet** and **wi-fi** for free at Newcastle's impressive **City Library** (☎ 0191-277 4100, 🖳 www.newcastle.gov.uk, click on Libraries and leisure; Mon-Thur 10am-7pm, Fri to 5pm, Sat to 4pm, Sun 11am-4pm; see map p85). Most cafés, bars, hotels and hostels have free wi-fi too.

For self-catering or sandwich supplies, either head to one of the numerous **supermarkets** dotted around town – there's a Sainsbury's Local on Northumberland St, a Tesco Express just off it, and a Waitrose inside Intu Eldon Square Shopping Centre as well as one in Jesmond on Osborne Rd (Mon-Sat 8am-10pm, Sun 11am-5pm). Alternatively, visit the fabulous **Grainger Market** (🖳 www.graingermarket.org.uk; Mon-Sat 7am-5pm), a traditional covered market with cafés, delicatessens, fishmongers, bakers, fruit-and-veg stalls, and even a Chinese dumplings bar.

There are several **outdoor/camping/trekking shops** in town, including two on Northumberland St – Field & Trek (which is inside Sports Direct), and a large branch of Cotswold Outdoor – and a military-gear camping shop called Kommand Outdoors on Bigg Mkt. For **chemists** there's Boots, with branches all over the city, including one on Northumberland St near Haymarket metro station. Walkers in need of a pre- or post-hike rub-down can get an authentic Chinese **massage** at the **Traditional Chinese Treatment Centre** (☎ 0191-230 5388; Mon-Sat 10am-5.30pm; 30-min full-body massage £30) in Chinatown. Alternatively, **Tea Sutra Teahouse** (see Where to eat and drink) has a wellness therapy room where one-hour massages cost from £30.

WHERE TO STAY

Most places do not accept one-night bookings on a Saturday night. Note that rates can change depending on the day of the week or the time of the year.

City Centre [see map pp84-5]

Hostels Remember that if you book well in advance you may be able to get a room in a hotel chain such as Travelodge for about the same price as you would pay to stay in a hostel dormitory. *(cont'd on p86)*

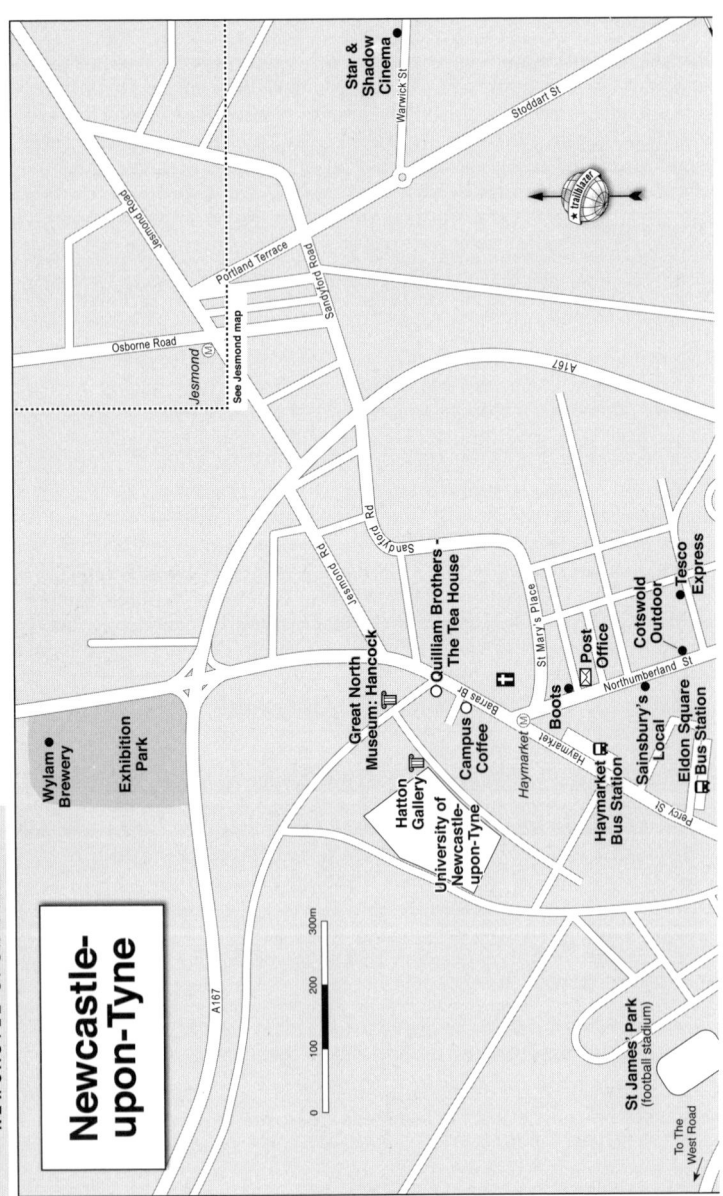

84 Newcastle-upon-Tyne city guide

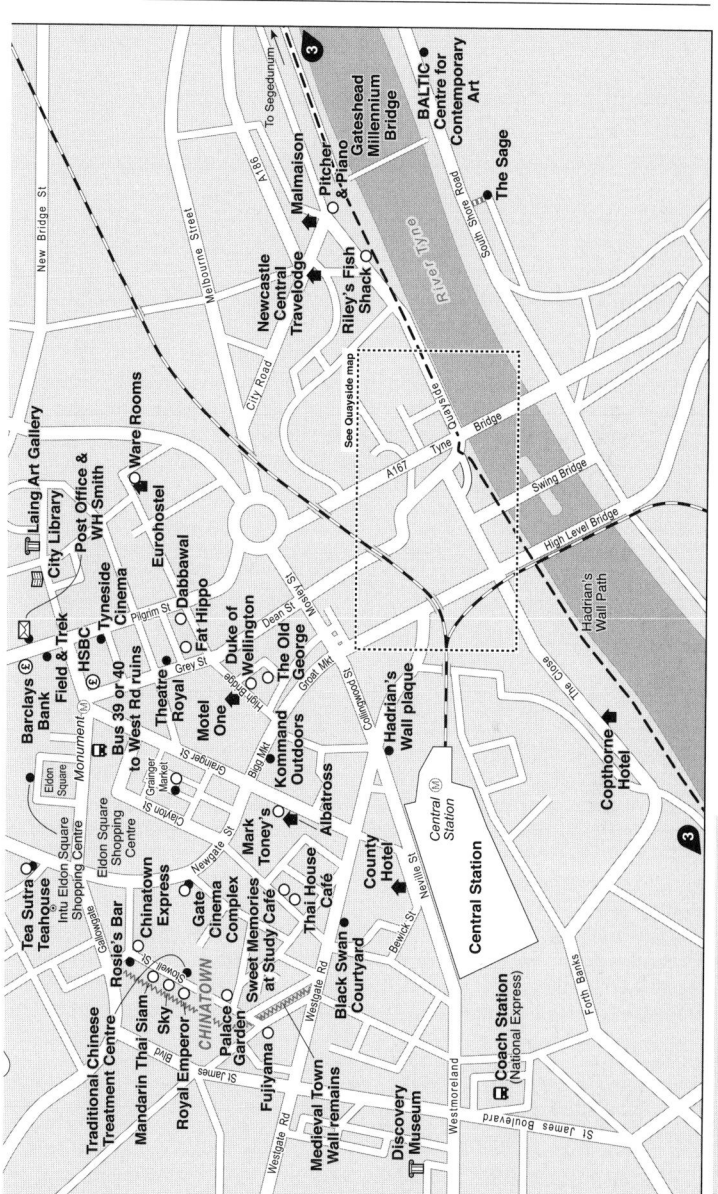

Newcastle-upon-Tyne map 85

(cont'd from p83) There is little to choose between the two hostels here but the more central of the two is the 176-bed ***Albatross*** (☎ 0191-233 1330, 🖥 albatrossnewcastle.co.uk; 2- to 12-bed dorms; WI-FI), on Grainger St, with free toast, tea and coffee, kitchen, and a satellite TV and pool table in the comfy lounge. It's housed inside the 150-year-old building of a former bank so has some character, although the rooms themselves are spartan to say the least. The cost of a bed (£16.50-27.90pp) depends on when you stay and the size of the dorm.

The other option, also pretty central, is ***Eurohostel*** (☎ 0845 4900 371, 🖥 www.eurohostels.co.uk/newcastle; shared dorms for 4-10 people; private rooms for 1-14 people, all en suite; WI-FI) at 17 Carliol Square. Dorm beds (female or mixed dorms) go from £16 but cost £25 at the weekend (contact them for rates for private rooms). There are laundry facilities but no kitchen. However, there is an amazingly good-value bar-restaurant called The Ware Rooms (see Where to eat) attached to the hostel.

Hotels Although the rooms can be rather soulless, you can sometimes get good deals at ***Newcastle Central Travelodge*** (☎ 0871-984 6164, 🖥 www.travelodge.co.uk; 203D or Tr, all en suite, 🛁; WI-FI £3 for 24hrs; 🐕), especially if you book far in advance. It has a good location too, close to the river and, therefore, the Hadrian's Wall Path. Room rates (for up to three people sharing) vary and depend in part how far you book in advance: 'Flexible' rates are around £68-72; 'Saver' rates, which are non refundable and must be paid for in advance, cost about £42-50. Breakfast costs £8.25pp.

Also fairly funky but much more slick and altogether more comfortable, is ***Motel One*** (☎ 0191-211 1090, 🖥 www.motel-one.com/en/hotels/newcastle; 222D, all en suite; WI-FI; 🐕 small), a centrally located boutique-type hotel in a quiet lane off Bigg Mkt. Rates start at £37pp (sgl occ from £59), but like all the other hotels can vary depending on the time of year. The continental breakfast buffet costs £9.50pp extra; the cocktails in the lounge bar get rave reviews.

County Hotel (☎ 0191-232 2471, 🖥 www.countyhotel.co.uk; 4S/77D/27D or T/6Tr, all en suite, 🛁; WI-FI; 🐕), on Neville St opposite the Central Station entrance, is in a 19th-century building. As with many of Newcastle's hotels of this calibre, their tariff depends on demand and can be as low as £35pp (sgl/sgl occ £55), but rates tend to start at around £50pp (sgl occ room rate). Breakfast costs £10pp.

Copthorne Hotel (☎ 0191-222 0333, 🖥 www.millenniumhotels.com; 156D or T, all en suite, 🛁; WI-FI) sits in a great location on The Close, right on the Tyne (and Hadrian's Wall Path) and just a couple of minutes west of the fun at the Quayside. Ugly as sin on one side, the side facing the water is better and the

---

❑ **Where to stay: the details**
In the descriptions of accommodation in this book: 🛁 means at least one room has a bath; 🐕 signifies that dogs are welcome in at least one room but also subject to prior arrangement, an additional charge may also be payable; WI-FI means wi-fi is available in the property, though not always (reliably) in every room. See also p100.

Where to stay 87

interior is decent, with rooms (every one of which overlooks the water) equipped with everything you'd expect from a hotel of this standard. There's also a gym and more than one restaurant. Rates start at £50pp (sgl occ rates on request) but the actual cost depends on availability and when you book.

Perhaps at the top of the pile, however, is *Malmaison* (☎ 0191-245 5000, 🖳 www.malmaison.com/locations/newcastle; 122D or T, all en suite, ⬛; WI-FI; 🐾), a sophisticated place housed in the old Co-operative building on the Quayside overlooking the Millennium Bridge. Facilities are top-notch and service is excellent. Weekday/weekend rack rates start at £42.50/60pp (sgl occ rates on request).

Quayside [see map below]

Hotels *Premier Inn Newcastle Quayside* (☎ 0871-527 8804, 🖳 www.premier inn.com; 133D/19T, all en suite; ⬛; WI-FI), by the foot of the Tyne Bridge on Lombard St, is central and offers early booking deals from £35 for a double, although rack rates are more like £60-85 for a room.

Rivalling this is a new, funkier hotel chain called *Tune Hotel* (☎ 0191-229 9210, 🖳 www.tunehotels.com/newcastle; 104D or T, all en suite; WI-FI), which has a branch in the heart of the Quayside action, close to the best pub in town (Crown Posada; see Where to eat and drink). The rooms are small, but it's still good value when you consider you can sometimes pay as little as £25 for two people sharing. Room rates are more like £35-89 (no single occupancy discount) most of the time, though what you pay depends in part on what add ons, such as TV, wi-fi and air-con you have. Also note that 13 of the cheapest rooms are interior rooms and come without windows. Breakfast is not available here.

Vermont Hotel (☎ 0191-233 1010, 🖳 www.vermont-hotel.com; 73D/27T, all en suite; ⬛; WI-FI), up by Castle Keep (see pp94-5), is a classy-looking place in a central yet quiet location beside the castle. The rooms are very smart and well equipped; the hotel offers 24-hour room service, has a restaurant, a couple of bars and a fitness centre. As with other places here the rates change every day, but expect to pay at least £60pp (sgl occ room rate), plus £10pp for breakfast.

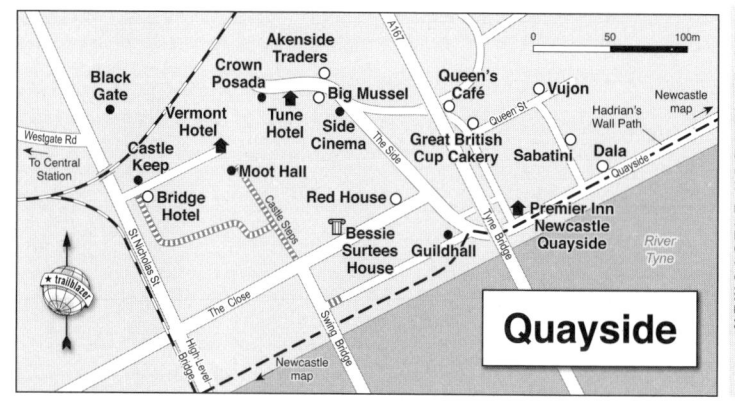

Jesmond [see map below]

B&Bs and hotels If it's a B&B you're after, the chances are you're going to end up in Jesmond, a smart residential area to the north of the city centre.

On Osborne Ave, on the corner of Manor House Rd, *Avenue Guest House* (☎ 0191-281 1396, ✉ avenue.newcastle@yahoo.co.uk; 4S/3T/3D/1Qd, all en suite; WI-FI) is a long-established place with well-appointed rooms and views over the cricket pitch. B&B costs £35pp (£45 for a single, sgl occ from £50), but three/four sharing is £30pp.

Jesmond Park Guest House (☎ 0191-281 2821, ✉ www.jesmond-park.co.uk; 6S/3T/4D/2Tr/3Qd, most en suite, rest share facilities; WI-FI; 🐾), 74-76 Queens Rd, is a small guest house that does B&B for as little as £24.75-32.50pp (sgl £36-46, sgl occ from £50, three/four sharing £75-99/90-130).

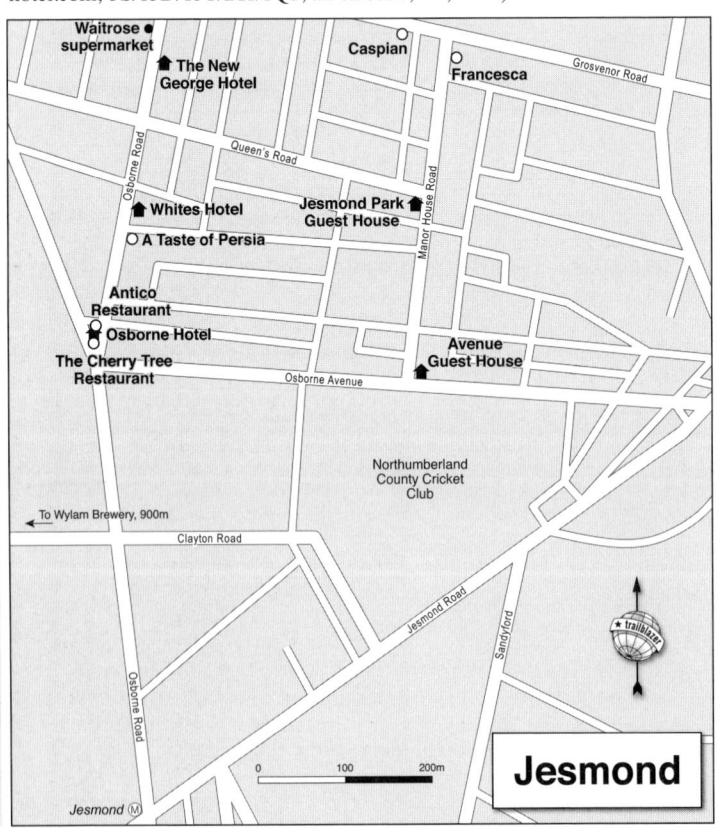

Another cheap option is *Whites Hotel* (☎ 0191-281 5126, ✉ www.whiteshotel.com; 3S/15D/15T/2Tr/1Qd, all en suite; ☕; WI-FI) but it's a favourite for stag and hen groups, so it's perhaps wise to bring your ear plugs. Room rates vary so it is best to look at their website; expect to pay £21.50-36.50pp (sgl £30-49, sgl occ room rate, £22-30pp for three/four sharing). Rates do not include breakfast but this is available if prebooked (from £4.95pp). However, food is available from their bar (daily 11am-11pm), and they have road-side terraced seating.

Nearby *Osborne Hotel* (☎ 0191-281 3385, 🖥 www.theosbornehotel.co.uk; 14S/3T/4D/1Tr/1Qd, all en suite; ☛; WI-FI) at 13-15 Osborne Rd, is a much smarter choice; a large well-run hotel where rates are £32.50-42.50pp (sgl from £45, sgl occ £50-55, £105-115/125-130 for three/four sharing). They also run Antico restaurant (see p93) next door.

Further up Osborne Rd is *The New George Hotel* (☎ 0191-281 4442, 🖥 www.newgeorgehotel.com; 3T/2D/2Tr/6Qd/three rooms sleep up to five people, all en suite; ☛; WI-FI), a small hotel, with a modern, almost boutique-like finish to its rooms. B&B starts at £25pp (sgl occ £35-40, £75/90/112.50 for three/four/five sharing). Note, the sign out front still says The George Hotel.

WHERE TO EAT AND DRINK

Food and drink choices are excellent here, as you'd expect from a city of this size. There are plenty of cafés and pubs, as well as some decent restaurants, and even a small Chinatown. You can also eat at the excellent **Grainger Market** (see p83). There are also some great food deals to be had, making Newcastle the cheapest place to eat on the whole path. At *The Ware Rooms* (daily 8am-10pm), attached to Eurohostel (see p86), for example, you can get breakfast items, such as a bacon bap and a coffee, for £1 each (or 5 items for £4.50) and evening meals for two people for £10 (including a drink each; from £6.25 for one person).

City Centre [see map pp84-5]
Cafés & teahouses Up near the university, *Quilliam Brothers – The Tea House* (☎ 0191-261 4861, 🖥 www.quilliambrothers.com; Mon-Fri 10am-midnight, Sat 9am-midnight, Sun 10am-4pm) is a fantastic place that hosts film evenings, art exhibitions and live music evenings – as well as purveying some of the finest tea known to man and some decent food too. *Stotties* (buns) with various fillings are served with roast potatoes and salad and start at around £6. The wooden décor is all rather splendid too.

Another tea specialist is *Tea Sutra Teahouse* (🖥 www.teasutra.co.uk/theteahouse; Mon-Fri 11am-8pm, Sat 11am-7pm, Sun noon-5pm, kitchen Mon-Sat 11.30am-3pm & 3.30-6pm, Sun noon-4pm), which promises 'no coffee, no tea bags, no wi-fi', instead preferring to focus on quality loose-leaf teas (£3-4pp per pot) and good old-fashioned conversation (free). They also serve health-conscious salads, soups and sandwich wraps, plus homemade dairy-free cakes, and have a '**wellness therapy room**' in the same building (see p83).

Another health-conscious choice is *Sweet Memories at Study Café* (☎ 0191-221 2323, 🖥 www.sweetmemoriesatstudycafe.com; Mon-Sat 9am-6pm, Sun 9am-5pm), at 89 Clayton St. It's a friendly little place where all dishes are homemade using local and organic ingredients where possible, and where the vegan/vegetarian selection is excellent. They do tea, coffee, homemade scones (from £1.75), cakes from £2.50, plus wholesome lunches and full English breakfasts (from £8.75, veggie/vegan £7.45).

Next door, *Thai House Cafe* (☎ 0191-261 5717; daily noon-11pm) is a small café-restaurant serving authentic Thai cuisine including super-tasty house-speciality noodle soups (£7-10).

For a more straightforward coffee and sandwich, try *Campus Coffee* (Mon-Sat 7.30am-5pm in term time, to 4pm otherwise), just by the university on Barras Bridge, or *Mark Toney* (☎ 0191-232 7794, 🖥 www.marktoney.co.uk; Mon-Sat 7.30am-8pm, Sun 9.30am-8pm), next to Albatross Hostel on Grainger St. Mark Toney does all-day breakfasts including tea or coffee for £5.95, and is particularly well known for its range of ice-creams. You can also get great-value lunches and evening meals here (£6.95 including a drink).

For a surreal beach-like experience down by the river, head to *Riley's Fish Shack* (☎ 0191-257 1371, 🖥 rileysfishshack.com; Fed-Dec Wed-Mon 9.30-11.30am, noon-4pm & 6-10pm, Jan Wed-Mon 9.30am-5pm), a café-cum-bar that's situated beside a small manmade beach, close to Gateshead Millennium Bridge. The beach is free to sit on (it's sprinkled with free-to-use deck chairs), but the Fish Shack enables you to enjoy the 'Geordie seaside' with a coffee/beer/cocktail in hand. As the name suggests, they also also do a selection of barbecued fish dishes (£10-15; from noon onwards) plus some fish wraps (£5-10) and a few fish-based breakfast choices (until 11.30am).

Pubs & restaurants Although the pick of Newcastle's pubs is probably Crown Posada (see Quayside Pubs), the city centre also has some excellent drinking establishments.

Claiming the title of oldest pub in Newcastle is *The Old George* (☎ 0191-260 3035, 🖥 www.oldgeorgeinnnewcastle.co.uk; food served daily 11am-10pm, winter to 9pm), established in 1582 and hidden intriguingly down a narrow back-alley off High Bridge, which in turn is off Bigg Market. They do a selection of real ales. You can get some decent meal deals here too (two mains for £9.49 on weekdays, for example). Nearby, on High Bridge itself, is *Duke of Wellington* (🖥 www.dukeofwelly.co.uk), a traditional-style pub which also serves food and cask ales. Another real-ale specialist with bags of character, but no food, is *Rosie's Bar* just on the edge of Chinatown. For something more mainstream, *Pitcher & Piano* (🖥 www.pitcherandpiano.com), part of the nationwide chain, is a smart gastro-pub with a great location overlooking the river by the Millennium Bridge.

In a quiet lane off Grey St, you'll find *Dabbawal* (☎ 0191-232 5133, 🖥 www.dabbawal.com; Mon-Fri noon-2.30pm & 5-10.30pm, Sat noon-11pm, Sun 5-10.30pm), an award-winning Indian restaurant which specialises in Indian street food such as *bhaji* (spicy deep-fried fritters), *samosa* (triangular-shaped fried savouries) and the tapas-like *chaat*. They also do *roomali roti* (flatbread wraps) and *dosa* (south-Indian savoury crêpes), as well as more familiar Indian-restaurant curries.

> ❏ **Chinatown**
> Less of a 'town' than a single street (Stowell St, to be precise), Chinatown (see map p85), which runs alongside the best-preserved stretch of Newcastle's **medieval Town Wall**, is nevertheless chock full of restaurants; some sit-down, some takeaway, and a couple with enticing all-you-can-eat deals that are perfect for that end-of-trek blowout.
>
> Starting by the elaborate decorative Chinese archway at the northern end of Stowell St, the first place you come to is *China Town Express* (Sun-Wed noon-11.30pm, Thur-Sat noon-2am), a no-nonsense Chinese takeaway joint (there are one or two tables too) that offers 'happy hour' meals (daily noon-2pm & 4-6pm) for £6, and is often crammed with Chinese university students – always a good sign.
>
> Further south, *Mandarin Thai Siam* (☎ 0191-261 7960, 🖥 www.mandarin-new castle.com; daily noon-2.30pm & 5.30-11.30pm) offers authentic Thai cuisine alongside its Cantonese menu. Next door, *Sky* (☎ 0191-230 3288, 🖥 skychinese.co.uk; daily 11.30am-11pm) is a new Cantonese restaurant that's well regarded amongst the local Chinese population and includes some decent dim-sum on its menu.
>
> For arguably the best dim-sum in Newcastle, though, walk further south to the long-established *Palace Garden* (☎ 0191-221 2888, 🖥 www.palacegarden.co.uk; daily noon-11pm). They also do Peking duck here as well as some spicy Sichuanese dishes. Diagonally opposite is *Royal Emperor* (☎ 0191-232 0868; Sun-Fri noon-2pm & 5-10.30pm, Sat noon-11pm), good for a slap-up Chinese banquet if you're in a large group. They have numerous set-menu options, including a £7.50 lunchtime one.

Nearby, is the gourmet burger specialist *Fat Hippo* (☎ 0191-447 1161, 🖥 www.fathippo.co.uk; Mon-Thur noon-10pm, Fri-Sat 11am-10.30pm, Sun 11am-10pm) with a huge variety of burgers (including beef, chicken and veggie), all served with chips, costing £8-11. Lunch-time weekday burger and chips go for just £6.

Just beyond Chinatown (see box above), opposite the south end of the street on Bath Lane, *Fujiyama* (☎ 0191-233 0189, 🖥 www.fujiyama.restaurant; Mon-Fri noon-2pm & 6-11pm, Sat noon-11pm, Sun noon-3pm & 6-11pm) is a Japanese teppanyaki restaurant with sushi from £4 and set menus for £23.90 to £38.50.

Quayside [see map p87]

Cafés Underneath the shadow of iconic Tyne Bridge is a trio of cafés well worth checking out. *Queen's* (Mon-Sat 6.30am-3pm, Sun 7am-3pm) is housed on the ground floor of a delightful, wedge-shaped heritage building that's squeezed tightly underneath the northern approach of the bridge, on a quiet street corner at No 1 Queen St. It's a traditional no-frills café that's been serving its astonishingly good-value breakfasts (from £2.95) to hungry punters for years. Walkers who like to make an early start will appreciate that they open at 6.30am most days. Nearby, at 15 Queen St, is *Great British Cup Cakery* (☎ 0191-230 2151, 🖥 thegreatbritishcupcakery.co.uk; Mon-Fri 9.30am-5pm, Sat to 6pm, Sun 10am-5pm), a favourite with young mums. The homemade cakes are rightly popular, but the real specialities are the simply enormous, cream-tastic milkshakes, served in overflowing pint jugs.

For something more refined (and a whole lot healthier), wander down to the river to find *Dala* (Mon-Fri 8.30am-4pm, Sun 9.30am-4pm, closed Sat), a friendly Swedish café that does excellent coffee, sandwiches and freshly baked cinnamon buns.

Pubs Those who love traditional British pubs and quality cask ale should do their best to pay a visit to the wonderfully unassuming *Crown Posada* (🖥 sjf .co.uk/our-pubs/crown-posada; Mon-Wed noon-11pm, Thur 11am-11pm, Fri 11am-midnight, Sat noon-midnight, Sun noon-10.30pm), a narrow slip of a pub that's been in business for 230 years. With wood-panelled walls, stained-glass windows dating from the 1880s and music that's played exclusively on a 1930s record player, this place oozes character. As with all the best pubs, there's no food served here, and although they do stock lagers and a variety of other beers, around seven out of every ten pints they pour come from one of their six cask-ale taps. Ale drinkers rejoice!

Up by Castle Keep, the 100-year-old *Bridge Hotel* (☎ 0191-232 6400, 🖥 sjf.co.uk/our-pubs/bridge-hotel; food served Tue-Sun noon-4pm) also has a decent selection of cask ales, and serves good-value pub grub too. They also have stained-glass windows, although not quite as old or impressive as the ones found in the Posada. *Red House* (☎ 0191-261 1037, 🖥 www.theredhousencl.co .uk; food served daily noon-9pm) is a very popular pub close to Tyne Bridge. Again, there are plenty of real ales on tap, but they also have an unusual food menu, which includes nothing but pie, mash and peas (£8.25), albeit with numerous types of each. The pies are homemade, and rightly lauded. They have some road-side seating out the front too.

For something more mainstream, *Akenside Traders* (☎ 0191-260 3175, 🖥 www.akensidetradersnewcastle.co.uk; food served daily noon-late) does standard pub grub as well as drinks and has live sport on TV.

Restaurants Quayside is one of the nicest places to come for an evening meal, and there's plenty on offer.

Sabatini (☎ 0191-261 4415, 🖥 www.sabatinis.co.uk; Mon-Thur noon-9.30pm, Fri & Sat to 10pm) is a smart Italian restaurant, serving pizza and pasta for as little as £6.50 during 'happy hours' (noon-6.30pm, to 5pm on Sat). The rest of the time mains go for £10-20.

For Indian food, try *Vujon* (☎ 0191-221 0601, 🖥 vujon.com; Mon-Sat 11.30am-2pm, daily 5.30-11.30pm), on Queen St. It's also quite a classy place, with an unusual menu; try the chilli hot sea bass Goan style, where the fish is marinated in garlic, lemon rind and fresh herbs and served on garlic and pak choi.

Just to the west of Vujon is the wonderfully down-to-earth *Big Mussel* (☎ 0191-232 1057, 🖥 www.bigmussel.co.uk; Mon-Fri noon-2pm & 5.30-10.15pm, Sat noon-10.15pm, Sun noon-3pm & 5.30-10pm), a welcoming seafood bistro specialising in mussel dishes (though vegetarian and poultry options are on the menu too). It has a variety of special offers with a medium/large bowl of mussels just £6.50/9.50 before 7pm. Lunch mains cost around £7.

Jesmond [see map p88]

Restaurants There are some great little restaurants in this smart suburb, many of which are on or around Osborne Rd.

The area's most popular restaurant has to be ***Francesca*** (☎ 0191-281 6586; Mon-Sat noon-2.30pm & 5-9.30pm), a long-established pizzeria that's been serving local residents for over 25 years. They don't take bookings and you often have to queue, such is the popularity of this great little place, though it's worth the wait; the food is cheap and plentiful, with most pasta and pizza dishes costing around £5; for the indecisive there's a half-pizza-half-pasta option for £6.95.

Slightly more upmarket, ***Antico*** (☎ 0191-281 2990, 🖳 www.anticorestaurant.com; Mon-Tue 5-10pm, Wed-Sat noon-2pm & 5-10pm, Sun noon-3pm & 5-9pm), attached to Osborne Hotel (see Where to stay), is another good Italian restaurant with a reasonable wine list and smart décor. Pizzas cost £9.50, but they also offer a 2-/3-course meal for £15.95/20.95 (daily noon-2pm & 5-6.30pm).

Just the other side of the Osborne, ***The Cherry Tree*** (☎ 0191-239 9924, 🖳 www.thecherrytreejesmond.co.uk; Mon-Sat noon-2.30pm & 5-10pm, Sun noon-8pm) serves the best of British food using delicious local and seasonal produce; it's not particularly cheap (2-/3-course set menus cost £18.50/24 respectively), but the menu changes frequently and the food is often exquisite.

Further north on Osborne Rd is the hugely popular ***A Taste of Persia*** (☎ 0191-281 8181, 🖳 www.atasteofpersia.com; Mon-Fri 5-10pm, Sat & Sun 1-11pm), a cosy, welcoming restaurant serving wonderfully flavoursome contemporary Persian cuisine.

Round the corner, on Grosvenor Rd, is ***Caspian*** (☎ 0191-908 2744, 🖳 www.thecaspianrestaurant.co.uk; Mon-Fri noon-10pm, Sat noon-10.30pm, Sun noon-9.30pm), a cheap and cheerful Turkish restaurant on a quiet residential stretch, close to Francesca. Mezze costs £3-4 per dish, mains cost between £7 and £11, and their weekday lunchtime set-menu is just £6.95 for three courses.

ENTERTAINMENT

Opened in 1837, the Grade I listed **Theatre Royal** (☎ 08448-112121, 🖳 www.theatreroyal.co.uk; see map p85) is Newcastle's premier theatre. Productions include ballet, contemporary dance, drama, musicals and opera, and the Royal Shakespeare Company visits annually. Further north, across the river, **The Sage** (🖳 www.sagegateshead.com; see map p85) is a giant slug-shaped glass auditorium and concert venue close to the BALTIC art gallery (see p96).

For the latest Hollywood blockbusters, head to **Gate Cinema** (☎ 0871 471 4714, 🖳 thegatenewcastle.co.uk/empire; see map p85) in the town centre. For something more thought-provoking, seek out one of the city's independent cinemas: **Side Cinema** (☎ 0191-232 2208, 🖳 www.amber-online.com/side-cinema; see map p87), by the Quayside; the 1930s' Art Deco **Tyneside Cinema** (☎ 0191-227 5500, 🖳 www.tynesidecinema.co.uk; see map p84), near Monument; or the volunteer-run **Star & Shadow** (☎ 07938 257663, 🖳 www.starandshadow.org.uk; see map p84) on Warwick St, just south of Jesmond.

Football fans wanting to take in a game at Newcastle United's iconic 52,000-seater stadium, **St James' Park** (see map p84), should check the club website (🖥 www.nufc.co.uk) for fixture details. Walk-in tickets are sometimes available from the matchday box office.

WHAT TO SEE AND DO

There's so much to see and do in Newcastle; the following is a brief overview of the city's major highlights, with a bias towards those with a Roman or Wall connection. Alternatively, you can take one of the City Sightseeing **hop-on hop-off bus tours** (☎ 0191-228 8900, 🖥 www.city-sightseeing.com; Apr/May-late Oct daily 10.30am-3pm, 2/hr; weekends only rest of year; adult/child £8/4) which visit all the major sites in a one-hour loop, starting and finishing on Bewick St, near Central Station.

Great North Museum: Hancock [see map p84]

The first place any self-respecting Wall-walker should head is the rather clumsily titled Great North Museum: Hancock (☎ 0191-208 6765, 🖥 greatnorth museum.org.uk; Mon-Fri 10am-5pm, Sat to 4pm, Sun 11am-4pm; admission is free but a donation is appreciated) which houses the collections that were once scattered across various museums in the city, including the Museum of Antiquities and the Shefton Museum.

Occupying centre stage both on the ground floor and in Wall walkers' imaginations is the interactive model of Hadrian's Wall. Characters from Roman Britain discuss various topics – construction, religion, defence of the Wall etc – at the simple press of a button, while surrounding the model are various treasures dug up from the soil near the Wall and its accompanying forts. A highlight is an ivory folding knife in the shape of a gladiator found at South Shields. There's also a reconstruction of a Mithraeum (see box pp152-3) which really gives you a flavour of what a secretive, strange and sinister religion Mithraism was.

Perhaps the most impressive items are the various pieces of jewellery. They include the gold Aemilia finger ring from Corbridge, dating back to between the 2nd and 4th centuries AD, which is believed to be one of the oldest Christian artefacts ever found on British soil. There's also a beautiful 3rd-century cameo of a bear on sardonyx, found in 1877, and a whole jewellery 'set' including brooch, necklace, bracelet and rings – all of which you would believe could have been made yesterday, such is their condition. The case on arms and weaponry is also enlightening, including as it does a highly decorated cheek piece from an auxiliary's cavalry helmet, again found in South Shields, and even a tiny segment of scale armour. Other highlights include the model of the skeleton of *Tyrannosaurus rex* at the rear of the museum on the ground floor and the giant Japanese spider crab near the entrance.

Castle Keep (New Castle) [see map p87]

Perhaps better and more precisely known as the **Castle Keep** (🖥 www.new-castlecastle.co.uk; daily 10am-5pm), these are the most visible remains of the New Castle, the edifice that gave the city its name. Built during the reign of

Henry II (1168-78), this New Castle was established on the foundations of Castle Garth, built in 1080 by William the Conqueror's eldest son Robert Curthose. (Note that tickets can only be bought at the Black Gate).

Though impressive, the Keep itself, and the **Black Gate** (daily 10am-5pm; adult £6.50, concessions £5.50, child aged 5-15 £3.90 inc Castle Keep), that was part of the same fortifications, are perhaps of limited interest to the average, Roman-obsessed Wall walker. However, one case in the Keep's museum section does have a few Roman artefacts, including fragments of a figure of Mercury. There are also details of the extent of the original Roman fort which was built to guard the bridge nearby. This bridge was **Pons Aelius** (*Pons* being Latin for 'bridge', Aelius being Hadrian's family name), which stretched across the Tyne in approximately the same location as the small Swing Bridge that you see today. It was from this bridge that the Roman fort took its name; a bridge that would have been about 700ft long (210m) and 18ft (5.4m) wide and the most impressive of the three main bridges the Romans built to cross the Tyne (the others were at Corbridge and Chollerford). In the 19th century, two altars were found in the water near the site of the bridge, though there's nothing left there today. Having noted the extent of the Roman fort, pop upstairs to the roof to get a better idea of its size and layout, and for good rooftop views of the city, its river and bridges.

The South Bank [see map p85]

The regeneration of Newcastle's city centre is a thing of wonder. From a rundown and slightly sleazy area, the waterfront is now the most photographed part of the metropolis; its dilapidated, crumbling constructions spruced up and

❏ **The Tyne bridges** [see Map 3, p107]
Where once there was just one bridge across the Tyne in the area we now know as Newcastle – the Roman Pons Aelius that remained until 1248 – today there are seven bridges within reasonable distance of each other in the city centre.

The most eye-catching is also the one furthest east, **Gateshead Millennium Bridge**, which, despite the name, was formally opened in May 2002 by the Queen. One of the smallest (126m long and just 50m above water) this footbridge, also known as the 'Winking Eye', is one of the most revolutionary and even has its own cleaning mechanism: when the bridge is raised the rubbish collects in special receptacles which are then emptied.

Heading west, the next bridge is the iconic **Tyne Bridge**, opened in 1928 by George V and looking for all the world like its contemporary, Sydney Harbour Bridge. After that you come to the comparatively small **Swing Bridge**, built on the site of the Roman Pons Aelius in 1876. As its name might suggest, it rotates through 90° to allow ships to pass through. After this there's the oldest and arguably most impressive of Newcastle's seven crossings, **High Level Bridge**, built by Robert Stephenson, the son of George (see box p114), and opened by Queen Victoria in 1849. **Queen Elizabeth II Bridge**, which carries the Metro, comes next, followed by **King Edward VII Bridge**, built in nearby Middlesbrough and another railway bridge. Finally, **Redheugh Bridge** (pronounced 'Red-yuff') was built on the site of two previous bridges and was opened in 1983 by the late Diana, Princess of Wales.

given a new lease of life or replaced by some breathtaking works of modern architecture. From being the shame of the city, the waterfront is now a place to be celebrated.

Perhaps the most impressive manifestation of this regeneration is **BALTIC Centre for Contemporary Art** (☎ 0191-478 1810, 🖳 www.balticmill.com; galleries Wed-Mon 10am-6pm, Tue from 10.30am), once a disused grain warehouse, now a world-class centre for contemporary art. It's a delight and, like most of the museums and galleries, is free, though some of the exhibitions charge and you probably won't find it easy resisting the temptation to eat in one of the cafés, including the rooftop restaurant, or to buy something from the BALTIC's gift shop. Nearby is the strikingly surreal **Sage** building (see p93), an international music venue designed by architect Norman Foster that's been variously described as a glass wave, a blister and a giant slug.

Arbeia
(*☎ 0191-277 1410, 🖳 arbeiaromanfort.org.uk; Apr-Oct Mon-Fri 10am-5pm, Sat 11am-4pm, Sun 2-5pm; Nov-Mar closed; admission free*)
Though not strictly a Wall fort, being on the other side of the Tyne and four miles further east of the end of the Wall at Segedunum, Arbeia was, nevertheless, an

---

❏ **The West Road – the real Wall route**
Most people know that Hadrian's Wall did not follow the river, as the trail does, but originally ran through the heart of Newcastle. However, you'd struggle to find much in the way of evidence to back this up. There's a **plaque** near Central Station (head east past the George Stephenson statue and you'll find it on your right, under the Westgate Road sign on the wall of Neville Hall, before the Literary and Philosophical building), which says that the route of the Wall went under the building. And on Westgate Rd, in the small **Black Swan courtyard** by a pottery, you'll find some stone foundations unearthed in 1985 by the potter himself, David Fry, that have been interpreted as belonging to a milecastle (though it must be pointed out that it doesn't actually lie where the milecastle around here would have been). Both these 'sights' are marked on the map on pp84-5. However, apart from these two examples, and some of the stones of Castle Keep which were once part of the Wall's fabric, Hadrian's Wall is virtually invisible in Newcastle.

However, if you travel up West Rd, which follows the line of the Wall through the western half of the city, you will find a few more sights with Roman connections. Modest to say the least, they are, nevertheless, worth seeking out if you have an interest in obscure historical remains, and there's something charming about finding links to Hadrian's Wall in the otherwise ordinary residential suburbs of a modern city.

Your chariot for this West Rd side trip should be Stagecoach North East bus No 39 or 40; buy one of the Day Rover passes (see p82) as you'll be hopping on and off several times to view the sites. The bus leaves frequently from in front of Eldon Square (make sure it's heading to Denton, not Wallsend) and goes past St James' Park football stadium and on to the A186 (West Rd).

After 10 minutes or so, and having passed the hospital, look out on your right for West Gate Community College and the TV mast after it. Jump out at the bus stop here (just before the mast) and walk down Weidner Rd (which is beside the bus stop), before taking the first right onto Westholme Gdns, then the first left onto Broombridge Ave. Right beside the first house on the left are the remains of **Benwell**

important part of the whole military set-up in Britain and anybody with a taste for all things Roman should seriously consider a visit. Though it seems a long way on the map, it's fairly straightforward to get to. Take the metro to South Shields, descend to Ocean Rd (not the bus station), turn right and walk for 10 minutes past Asda, cross the roundabout and then take a left up Baring St past Vespasian St, Trajan St, Claudius Court and Arbeia Unisex Hair Studio. The fort lies opposite Hadrian Primary School (note the great use of Roman names round here).

The name *Arbeia* means 'Place of Arabs' after the soldiers from Tigris, in what is now modern-day Iraq, who were garrisoned here in the 4th century. The history of the fort goes back further than this, however, having been built c AD163 under Emperor Marcus Aurelius to keep an eye on the sea and river. That changed in AD208 when Emperor Septimius Severus converted it into a granary and supply base for his troops campaigning in Scotland (see p59). Though Severus was killed in York just three years later and his Scottish assault ended soon after, the fort continued to supply the troops along the Wall for up to two centuries afterwards.

Because of its purpose as a storeroom, granary and unloading bay for imports arriving up the Tyne from overseas, Arbeia doesn't follow the classic

---

Roman Temple, complete with a platform on which a statue of the god Antenociticus once stood, flanked by a couple of replica altars (as with most treasures, the real altars, along with the head and limbs of the statue that were found, are now in Newcastle's Great North Museum: Hancock). Antenociticus himself was probably worshipped by the Vangiones from the upper Rhineland region who lived in the nearby Benwell Fort (see below); as is usual, the soldiers built their temples away from the fort, considering the latter no place for holy sites. The current residents of Broombridge Ave do not, it is believed, still worship at this site.

The next site – a **Vallum crossing** that would have led to the entrance to **Benwell Fort**, of which this is the only bit left above ground – is within easy walking distance; from the main road, take the next left after Weidner Rd, then walk to the bottom end of the noose-shaped cul-de-sac known as Denhill Park. As with all the sites on this road, the Vallum crossing is owned by English Heritage, who provide a fair artist's impression of how it must have looked in its heyday. You can walk around the ruins, but you'll have to knock on the door of No 26 to get the key.

Jump back on a bus and about a mile (1.5km) further west, just before the main intersection with the A1, is a fairly broad and impressive piece of Wall lying serenely beyond the pavement to the left of the road. Halfway along its length is a foundation that gives the whole ruin its name: **Denton Hall Turret**. As is usual with all the forts along the Wall, the turret would have been manned by around ten men. An inscription recovered from the site suggested that it was built by the First Cohort of the Second Legion of Augusta. Presumably, the soldiers who manned the turret would have walked back to their abode at Benwell Fort. But by good fortune there's a bus stop on the other side of the road to take you back into town.

To get to these sights from Hadrian's Wall Path, walk north up Denton Rd (the A191; see Map 5), then turn left at the second roundabout to reach Denton Hall Turret (half a mile/1km), or turn right to reach Denhill Park (1½ miles/2.5km; for Benwell Fort), or Weidner Rd (1½ miles/2.6km; for Benwell Roman Temple).

playing-card layout of your average Roman fort (about which, see box p102). Nevertheless, some great finds have been dug up by archaeologists, who are still painstakingly excavating the site today. Many of these finds can be seen in the reception, including some incredible carved ringstones. The inhumation (burial) room opposite is also enlightening, showing how the Romans interred their dead.

Outside, two Roman buildings have been reconstructed. **West Gate** provides great views over the site, though in all honesty it is probably not an exact replica of how the gate would have looked. Nevertheless, it is impressive, and contains some useful information on the history of the site.

Of more interest, however, are the barracks at the south-eastern corner that offer a telling glimpse into the rudimentary living conditions of the average soldier in South Shields at the time. Walk around the back of the barracks and you'll find the bright murals of the **Commanding Officer's House**, the exact designs of the murals taken from original Roman designs.

Other museums & galleries

Bessie Surtees House (see map p87; 🖳 historicengland.org.uk; Mon-Fri 10am-4pm, closed bank hols; free) sits in the heart of Quayside at 41-44 Sandhill. The name is not strictly correct, for there are in fact *two* merchants' houses here dating back to the 16th and 17th centuries, one of which is a rare example of Jacobean domestic architecture. The name comes from one of the inhabitants, who eloped with John Scott, who later became Lord Chancellor of England. There's not much to see inside, just three rooms, the main one empty save for a few photos of the house in days gone by. The main attraction is, perhaps, the giant fireplace, the exquisitely carved overmantel bearing a date of 1657.

Laing Art Gallery (☎ 0191-278 1611, 🖳 laingartgallery.org.uk, see map p85; Tue-Sat 10am-5pm, Sun 2-5pm; free but donations appreciated and charges made for some exhibitions), on New Bridge St, is the city's oldest gallery, having welcomed visitors for well over a hundred years. The collection includes both contemporary works and paintings from the 18th and 19th centuries.

Discovery Museum (☎ 0191-232 6789, 🖳 discoverymuseum.org.uk; see map p85; Mon-Fri 10am-4pm, Sat & Sun 11am-4pm; free) is the region's biggest free museum (though donation boxes are situated around the museum), housing a wealth of scientific and technological material as well as displays on social history, regimental militaria and costumes. The museum is also home to the Tyne & Wear Archives (🖳 twarchives.org.uk; Tue-Fri 10am-4pm).

Newcastle University's highly regarded **Hatton Gallery** (☎ 0191-208 6059, 🖳 hattongallery.org.uk; see map p84), was undergoing a £3.8 million redevelopment at the time of research, but was due to reopen in September 2017.

ROUTE GUIDE & MAPS 6

Using this guide

The trail guide has been described from east to west and divided into six stages. Though each of these roughly corresponds to a day's walk, do not assume that this is the only way to plan your walk. There are so many places to stay en route that you can pretty much divide up the walk wherever you want.

On p33 are tables to help you plan an itinerary. To provide further help, practical information is presented on the trail maps, including walking times, places to stay, camp and eat, as well as shops where you can buy supplies, taps (for drinking water), phone boxes and public toilets. Further service details are given in the text under the entry for each settlement. See also the colour maps (with profile charts) and the distance chart at the back of the book.

TRAIL MAPS [see map key p222]
Scale and walking times
The trail maps are to a scale of 1:20,000 (1cm = 200m; 3¹/₈ inches = one mile). Walking times are given along the side of each map and the arrow shows the direction to which the time refers. The black triangles indicate the points between which the times have been taken. **See box on walking times below**.

The time-bars are a tool and are not there to judge your walking ability. There are so many variables that affect walking speed, from the weather conditions to how many beers you drank the previous evening. After the first hour or two of walking you will be able to see how your speed relates to the timings on the maps.

Up or down?
The trail is shown as a dotted line. An arrow across the trail indicates the slope; two arrows show that it is steep. Note that the arrow points towards the higher part of the trail. If, for example, you are walking

> ❏ **Important note – walking times**
> Unless otherwise specified, **all times in this book refer only to the time spent walking**. You will need to add 20-30% to allow for rests, photography, checking the map, drinking water etc. When planning the day's hike count on 5-7 hours' actual walking.

from A (at 80m) to B (at 200m) and the trail between the two is short and steep, it would be shown thus: A – – – >> – – – – B. Reversed arrow heads indicate downward gradient.

Accommodation

Accommodation marked on the map is either on or within easy reach of the path. If arranged in advance, many B&B proprietors based a mile or two off the trail will collect walkers from the nearest point on the trail and take them back the next morning.

For **B&B-style accommodation** the number and type of rooms is given after each entry: **S** = single room (one single bed), **T** = twin room (two single beds), **D** = double room (one double bed, or two single beds pushed together), **Tr** = triple room and **Qd** = quad. Note that many of the triple/quad rooms have a double bed and either one/two single beds, or bunk beds, thus in a group of three or four, two people would have to share the double bed, but it also means the room can be used as a double or twin.

Unless stated otherwise, **rates** quoted for B&B-style accommodation are **per person (pp)** based on two people sharing a room for a one-night stay; rates are usually discounted for longer stays. Where a single room **(sgl)** is available the rate for that is quoted if different from the rate per person. The rate for single occupancy **(sgl occ)** of a double/twin may be higher and the per person rate for three/four sharing a triple/quad may be lower. At some places, generally chain hotels, the only option is a **room rate**; this will be the same whether one or two people (or more if permissible) use the room. Unless specified, rates are for bed and breakfast. See p20 for more information on rates. Very few B&Bs or campsites accept **credit/debit cards** but many guesthouses, and nearly all hotels and hostels do.

Rooms either have **en suite** (bath or shower) facilities, or a **private** or **shared** bathroom, or shower room, just outside the bedroom. Most of these have only a shower. In the text ☛ signifies that at least one room has a bathroom with a **bath**, or access to a bath, for those who prefer a relaxed soak at the end of the day.

Also noted is whether the premises have **wi-fi** (WI-FI), if **dogs** (🐾 – see also pp35-6 and pp221-2) are welcome in at least one room (many places have only one room suitable for dogs and accept them only subject to prior arrangement), or at campsites. Some make an additional charge (usually per night but occasionally per stay) while others may require a deposit which is refundable if the dog doesn't make a mess. And finally if **packed lunches** (Ⓛ) can be prepared, again subject to prior arrangement.

Other features

Features are marked on the map when pertinent to navigation. In order to avoid cluttering the maps and making them unusable not all features have been marked each time they occur.

The route guide

WALLSEND TO HEDDON-ON-THE-WALL [MAPS 1-8]

Getting to the start of the walk

There are several ways of getting to the start of the walk. Most people choose to use public transport (see p82) and jump out at Wallsend Metro or the adjacent bus station (which is helpfully signed in Latin – *Raedarum publicarum statio* – someone in charge of signage at the city council clearly has a sense of humour). From there you can walk across the road to the **Asda supermarket** for some last-minute supplies or straight towards the Tyne and Segedunum.

SEGEDUNUM [see Map 1, p105]

(☎ *0191-278 4217;* 🖥 *segedunumromanfort.org.uk; Apr-Oct daily 10am-5pm, Nov to mid Dec & mid Jan to Mar Mon-Fri 10am-3pm, Sat 11am-2pm; adults £5.95, concessions £3.95, children under 16 free, Note: these details may change so check before you visit*)

Nestling adjacent to Swan Hunter shipyard (see box p103), which itself is replete with history, Segedunum is a fantastic introduction to the kind of Wall fort that will become oh-so-familiar as you progress along the trail.

Translating as 'Strong Fort', Segedunum is the last Wall fort heading east; instead of continuing from here to the sea, the Wall took a sharp turn south at this point, heading off from the fort's south-eastern corner through the now-defunct Swan Hunter shipyard and down to the water's edge. You can see a little bit of this Wall by the side of the trail at the very start of the walk, just outside the fence that surrounds Segedunum.

At first it seems strange that the Wall doesn't actually cover the entire breadth of the country. After all, what is the point of building a wall right across an island if you're not going to finish the job, thereby allowing the locals to sneak around one end? But with Arbeia Fort (see pp96-8) guarding the river's mouth from the other side of the Tyne and this fort watching over the land to the east on this side, it's fair to say that little could cross undetected from one side – of either the Tyne or the Wall – to the other. In fact, Segedunum was actually something of an afterthought; originally, the Wall terminated at Pons Aelius (see box p95) and only later did they decide to extend it a further three miles east to Segedunum.

Today, little remains of the original Roman fort which would have held 600 men. The Saxons proved pretty efficient at carting off the masonry for their own building projects, such as Bede's monastery at Jarrow. Newcastle's Great North Museum: Hancock has proved equally efficient at appropriating much of the remainder to fill their display cases (this is, after all, the most excavated of all the Wall forts).

But what makes the fort here so appealing is not so much what the Romans left behind but the way the little that has survived has been presented. From the 35m-high Panorama Tower, which provides great views over the site, to the clear information boards and the reconstructed bath-house, this fort is a good example of how history should be told. And whilst some may complain at the slightly child-centric **galleries**, with their games and quizzes designed to keep young minds interested, many will find it stimulating and useful and the reconstructed cavalry barrack (complete with horse!) gives a fair idea of what living conditions were like on the Wall. Upstairs in the Strong Place Gallery (Strong Place being a translation of Segedunum) is the history of the location of the fort, including exhibits from its time as a coal mine and as part of Swan Hunter shipyard.

Highlights of Segedunum include the aforementioned **Panorama Tower**, where you get a better idea of just how large the fort was (note that the fort

---

❏ The layout of the Wall forts

The fort at Segedunum is pretty typical of the design of all Wall forts along the trail. Often described as '**playing-card shaped**' (ie rectangular with rounded corners), the layout varied little from one to the next. At its centre were the **headquarters (HQ)**, the *Principia*, the heart and brains of the fort. It was here that justice was dispensed, plans formulated, men paid and ceremonies, both secular and religious, performed. Sometimes, as with Segedunum, a **shrine** was housed within this building under which, in a small safe-room, the money to pay the soldiers' wages would be stashed. The **commanding officer's house**, or *praetorium*, where he lived with his family and servants, stood next door, usually to the east of the HQ, while the **hospital** and other public buildings sat to its west. Often you'd find the fort's **granary** here too, one of the most interesting buildings, architecturally, of the whole fort. The granary's sides were buttressed to help the walls withstand the pressure created by all that grain being housed within it, while the floor itself was raised to allow air to circulate, thus preventing the grain at the bottom of the heap from going mouldy. The granary would have had a porch, too, to stop the grain getting wet when it was being unloaded from the carts. There's a particularly good granary, complete with the porch pillars, at Corbridge.

Flanking these buildings to north and south were the barracks. **Cavalry barracks** are distinguishable from the infantry barracks by a recess or ditch hewn into the floor – dug to collect the horse's urine and prevent it from seeping into the cavalry officers' quarters next door. Segedunum has fine examples of these. Usually, three men and three horses would share one of these 'apartments' and there would be about nine apartments to each barrack. **Infantry barracks** were much simpler affairs, housing about five men to a room. At the end of each barrack were the living quarters of the *decurian*, the man in charge of the barrack. The fort at Arbeia has recreated a block of infantry barracks. Scattered amongst these buildings were others, such as the **public latrines**, of which Housesteads has a particularly fine example.

As with Segedunum, the whole fort would often lie on both sides of the Wall, with its northern end extending beyond the Wall's line into 'barbarian' territory. There would usually be more gates on the northern side than the southern side, too, to allow the soldiers to charge out quickly to meet their barbarian foes.

Other buildings associated with the fort would lie outside its walls, including religious buildings such as **temples** (witness the Mithraeum outside Brocolitia, for example), and **public baths** (the ruins at Chesters have a great example of these). A **civilian settlement**, or *vicus*, would often grow up around the Wall, too, peopled with retired soldiers from the fort, their children (who automatically became Roman citizens when their father did), wives (who *didn't*), traders and locals.

originally covered the large paved area to the north of the main road too, which today is outside the official site). The **Roman baths** (closed for essential maintenance work at the time of research) are good, too, though if you've seen other Roman baths you may well be disappointed by the rather plain, undecorated look of this one. There's a reason for this: Roman baths along the Wall, including this one (which would not have stood originally on this spot but outside the fort, near where Ship Inn is today), would have been for the use of soldiers rather than Roman civilians and as such would have been less fancy than the average mosaic-floored *balineum* of popular imagination. Still, the reconstruction has been done as authentically as possible using recreated Roman cement, *opus signinum*, for the floors, and there are frescoes on the walls. Outside, there's a small Roman-style medicinal **herb garden**. One other highlight is the only **stone toilet seat** surviving from Roman Britain.

There is also a *café* here, in the museum building (no ticket required), which opens the same days and hours as the site and sometimes earlier.

❑ **Swan Hunter Shipyard** [see Map 1, p105]

Though not quite as venerable as the nearby Roman ruins of Segedunum, the Swan Hunter Shipyard, with its iconic, multi-coloured cranes puncturing the skyline of north Tyneside, is nevertheless a vital part of the region's history. Unfortunately, it appears that history has come to an end. In 2007, Swan Hunter's boss Jaap Kroes declared shipbuilding to be an industry with no future, and put the yard – and its cranes – up for sale. Sold to North Tyneside Council and One NorthEast in 2009, by 2013 it was being cleared up in preparation for development, with the council unveiling plans in 2015 to turn the 32-acre (13 hectare) site into a centre for the renewable energy, advanced engineering and offshore sectors.

The sale was a huge body blow to both Wallsend and the city of Newcastle as a whole, an area that had suffered from more than its fair share of economic woes through the decades. Though it must be said that on this occasion the decision to close the site permanently wasn't entirely surprising, given its dramatic decline. Between 1993 and 2003 not one new ship was launched from Swan Hunter's yard, and a decision by the Ministry of Defence to hand over the work on an unfinished ship at Swan Hunter to the BAE Systems site at Govan in Glasgow in 2006 resulted in the shipyard being mothballed. Attempts to secure new contracts or change tack and become a breaking business both failed, and the managers were left with no choice but to lay off all but 10 of Swan Hunter's remaining 260 workers.

All of which seems a long way away from the time when Britain led the world in shipbuilding and the Tyne produced a staggering 25% of the world's ships. Many of the world's most famous and innovative vessels were created at Swan Hunter during the 20th century, including the Cunard liner *Mauretania*, a revolutionary steamship launched in 1906 that was, for a time, not only the world's largest ocean liner but also its fastest.

In recent years, however, the stories coming out of the Swan Hunter shipyard tended to be about job cuts and industrial disputes as the yard struggled to make its mark in the new globalised market. Jaap Kroes's decision to invest in the shipyard in 1995 brought a glimmer of hope and for a while, as several refurbishment contracts rolled in, it appeared as if the good times were back once more. But when the *Lyme Bay* was taken to Scotland to be fitted out, it was the first time a ship had left Swan Hunter unfinished, and many then saw the writing on the wall.

104 Wallsend to Heddon-on-the-Wall

The ticket also includes entry to the 20m-long **reconstructed Wall**, which lies outside the site just to the north-west. Less eye-catching, but of greater historical significance, is the 50m-stretch of **Wall foundations** which lies beside it and which was excavated in 2016. On the other side of the reconstructed Wall are the remains of **Wallsend Colliery B pit**, an old colliery shaft which dates from 1781 and which was rediscovered during the Segedunum excavations.

The route

From the entrance to Segedunum, turn right and head down Station Rd, which runs along the back of Segedunum's reception and museum. A path runs east–west above Station Rd; this is the start of the trail. Before you begin, however, don't forget to stamp your passport at the Segedunum reception or, if they're closed, at the box by the rear entrance to the museum or at Asda across the road. (Both Segedunum and Asda also sell the passport, badge and certificate.)

This **15-mile (24km; 4¾-5hrs)** first stage begins by the only remaining piece of the Wall that originally ran down from the fort to the Tyne, and which now stands just over the railings outside the fort grounds. As the easternmost part of the Wall still in existence, this is an appropriate place to begin. Through all of Newcastle, the trail is called **Hadrian's Way** and this is what you'll see on the signs. Heading west, the path you are following was originally an old railway track, an extension of Blyth and Tyne Railway. By the side of the trail are the abutments of old bridges and the ironmongery of various parts of the railway, now finding secondary employment as makeshift stools and benches.

It must be said that, though not without interest, this is not the most auspicious start to a trail. It's not the way the trail leads through the industrial heart of the city that disappoints; if you're in the right frame of mind a short walk through an entirely man-made landscape can be as diverting as any country romp. But hemmed in by warehouses and the backs of housing estates, there's little industry, or indeed anything to see. Unfortunately, one or two hikers have also been subjected to insults and threats from local kids on both this stretch and the one that leads across Denton Dene (see Map 5, p111) and have written to say that they felt threatened in these areas. The abuse, as far as we know, has only ever been verbal and seems to be quite rare, but is unpleasant to hear about nonetheless.

Crossing roads and following the signposts, eventually the path passes a school and a **gas tower** (Map 2), drops away from the railway track and heads down to the water's edge and **Walker Riverside Park** (an appropriate name for a park at the start of a national trail).

From peaceful St Anthony's Point, the path plots a westward course through the smart **St Peter's Marina** and on to the very heart of the city, past such modern Tyneside icons as **BALTIC** and **Gateshead Millennium Bridge** (Map 3) – the first of the city's seven bridges (see box p95). Also look out for seals swimming in this stretch of the Tyne. They have been spotted by hikers close to St Peter's Marina, as well as by the bridge at Wylam. Further on, as you march through the town centre, you'll see Castle Keep (see pp94-5 and map p87) to your right, situated on the site of the Roman fort of Pons Aelius.

(cont'd on p108)

Map 1, Wallend 105

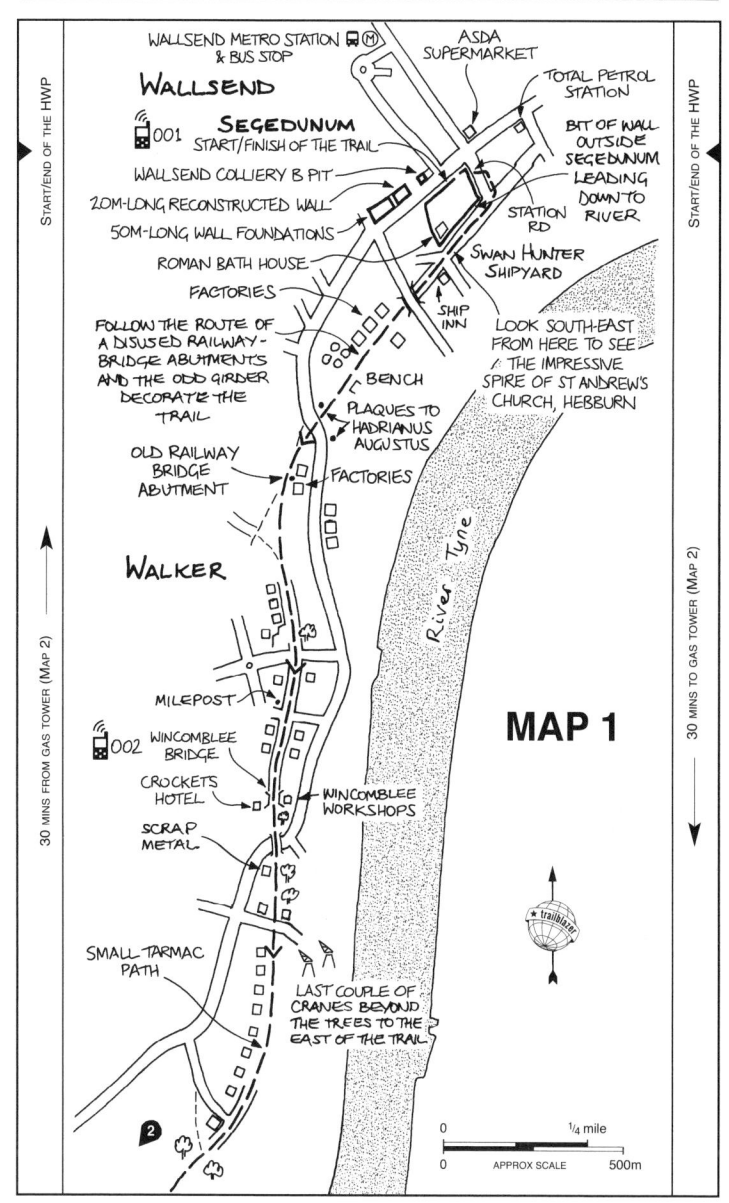

106 Wallsend to Heddon-on-the-Wall

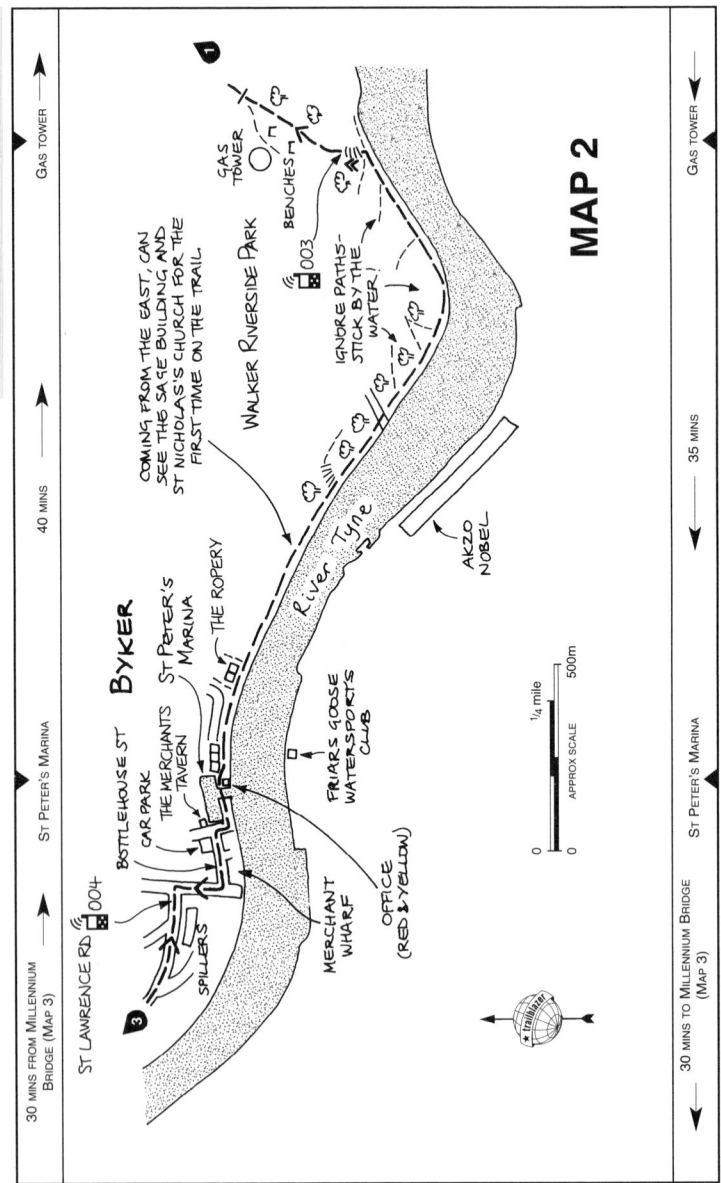

Map 3, Newcastle city centre 107

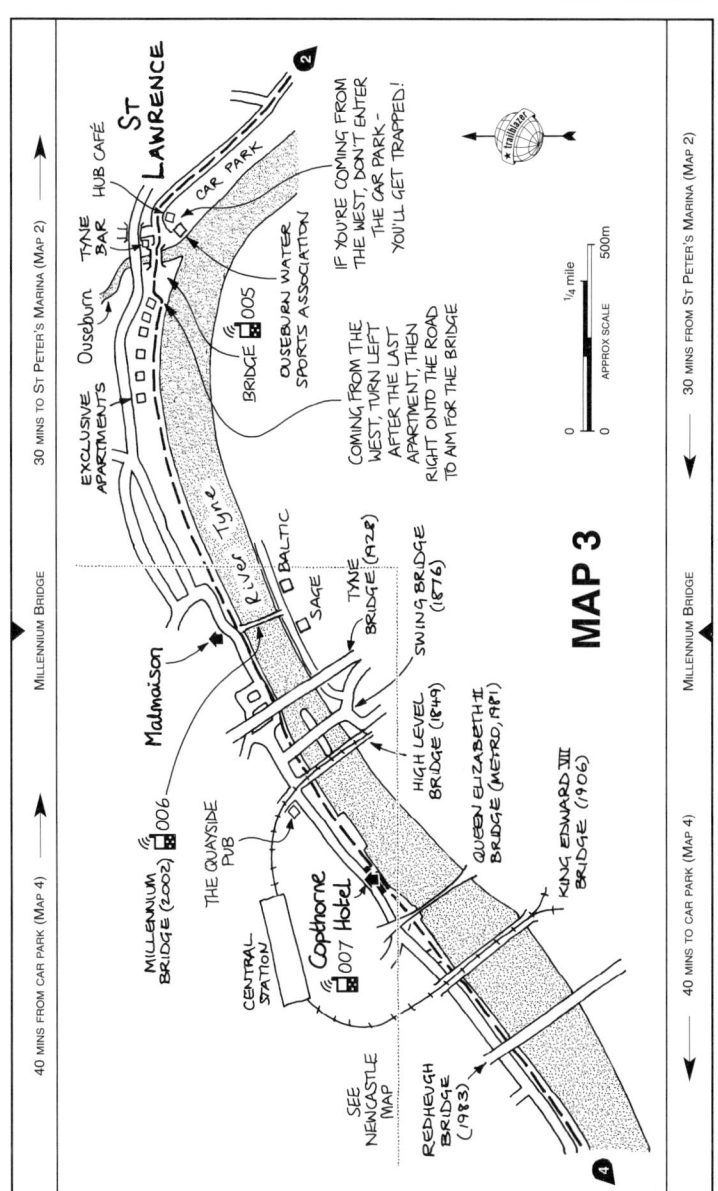

(cont'd from p104) Note how, less than two hours into the walk, you've already encountered two of the Wall's 17 Roman forts. Though the milecastles and turrets were evenly spaced out along the Wall, the forts were not, being built instead at strategic points along it – in this case, to overlook one of the two Wall bridges to cross the Tyne. This bridge would have stood where Swing Bridge now stands though, alas, nothing remains today. After the seventh and final

❏ William Armstrong – the forgotten man of the Industrial Revolution

However high we climb in the pursuit of knowledge we shall still see heights above us, and the more we extend our view, the more conscious we shall be of the immensity which lies beyond. **William Armstrong**

Though something of a local hero, William Armstrong's star has faded when compared to the lustre of his near contemporary, George Stephenson (see box p114). Yet the impact of both men on the history of Newcastle, Britain, and the wider world was equally enormous.

Born in 1810 in Pleasant Row, in the Shieldfield area of Newcastle, William George Armstrong's first calling was as a solicitor, a vocation in which he showed enough talent and ambition to become a partner in a legal practice in the city. Yet throughout this time Armstrong's first love was not the law of man but the immutable laws of science and, in particular, engineering. Indeed, he used to give lectures at Newcastle's Lit and Phil Society on this very subject, and it wasn't long before he was turning his hand to constructing the machines he talked about. His first major project was a hydro-electric generator, which he unveiled to the world in 1842. Switching from hydro-electrics to hydraulics, just four years later Armstrong was persuading a number of wealthy local businessmen to back his plans to develop hydraulic cranes, which would be powered with the assistance of the Whittle Dene Water Company, a firm that he himself had helped to set up a few years previously. (You'll pass Whittledene Reservoir on the trail.) The result of all this endeavour was the Newcastle Cranage company, based at Elswick, which later became known as Armstrong's Factory – as mentioned in the song *Blaydon Races*. The manufacture of cranes became the cornerstone both of his industrial empire and of the Industrial Revolution itself; Isambard Kingdom Brunel was just one of his regular customers.

Yet Armstrong wasn't finished yet; with the advent of the Crimean War he became involved in the development of arms, manufacturing an 18lb breach-loading gun that was sold all over the world. Indeed, such was the popularity of his weapons that *both* sides in the American Civil War were armed with Armstrong's artillery. He also developed an interest in bridges, constructing Newcastle's Swing Bridge and much of London's Tower Bridge.

There were, of course, considerable financial benefits to his success. By 1850 over 300 men were employed in Armstrong's Elswick factory, bringing unprecedented prosperity to the area. (The modern incarnation of his company, Vickers, formerly Vickers Armstrong, still operates in the area and lies just off the path; see Map 4.) The country at large also benefited, with Armstrong gifting his patents to the British government, an ostensibly selfless act which was nevertheless rewarded with a knighthood. His success also enabled him to own most of Jesmond Dene, as well as a magnificent mansion at Cragside. But as was typical of the man, despite the riches, he continued to invent, even though he became less involved in the company that he founded. It comes as no surprise, therefore, to find that Cragside has a place in history as the first house in the world to be lit by hydro-electric power.

Map 4, Elswick 109

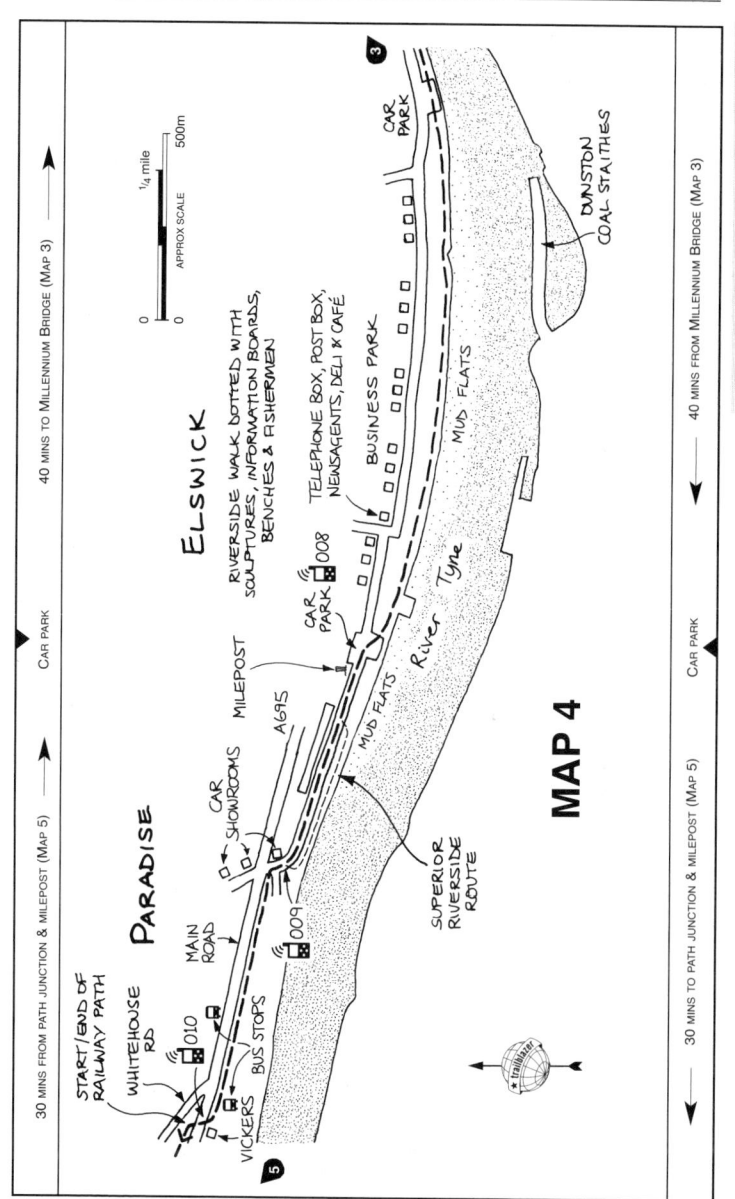

Tyne bridge, **Redheugh**, the trail continues, hugging the river through mile after mile of business parks and industrial estates. This is Armstrong country (see box p108) and his crest can be seen at various points along the trail.

The dominant architectural feature of this section, however, lies across the river on the south bank. These are **Dunston Coal Staithes** (Map 4), which were used to load coal from the collieries onto the colliers – the ships that would transport the cargo south to London and elsewhere.

Negotiating a rather charmless section to cross the A695, you join yet another disused railway-turned-footpath, this one originally running between **Scotswood** (Map 5), Newburn and Wylam. Though located in the midst of a veritable spaghetti-like mix of major traffic arteries, factory showrooms and noisy warehouses, the walk itself is pleasant enough, with the worst industrial excesses hidden behind a screen of trees.

Crossing the A191 to **Denton Dene**, the trail continues to seek out the city's greener elements amidst the noisy urban sprawl, hopping from one green space to the next. Rejoining the disused railway at the end of a cul-de-sac (Ottringham Close), the path finally takes on a more peaceful aspect, though with the suburbs of Lemington and Newburn just a few metres away, you're never far from either civilisation or traffic. Note **Lemington Glass Cone** (Map 6) ahead and to the left of the trail. This marvellous late 18th-century cone-shaped brick chimney derives its name from its former purpose as a furnace for making glass. Almost opposite, the *café* (Mon-Fri 8am-3pm; WI-FI) in **Lemington Centre** (☎ 0191-264 1959, 🖥 www.lemingtoncentre.co.uk) is a nice (and very cheap) little stop serving snacks and lunches. They are extremely welcoming to Hadrian's Wall walkers. Arriva/Stagecoach's 85/685 **bus** calls in at Lemington (see pp46-7).

Crossing the old toll road at **Newburn** you come to *The Boathouse* (☎ 0191-229 0326; food served Mon-Sat 9.30am-6pm, Sun noon-4pm). Look on the wall for the flood markers; the height of the water in 1771 is particularly impressive. The old toll road also marks the unofficial limits of the city, at least as far as Wall walkers are concerned, as you finally leave the hullabaloo of Newcastle behind to enter the delightful **Tyne Riverside Country Park**. It's a lovely way to wind down at the end of the first stage, a pleasant and peaceful riparian stroll with dog-walkers, joggers, butterflies, swans and the first truly mature trees on the trail as company. There's also a **Visitor Centre**, and while its opening hours are limited (generally weekends and school holidays), it shares the building with **toilets** and sinks that have potable water.

Those who don't want this initial stage to end may like to consider calling in at *The Keelman* (Map 6; ☎ 0191-267 1689, 🖥 biglampbrewers.co.uk/keelman-pub), behind the Visitor Centre. It's one of the best pubs on the route; a vast place with real ales, its own micro-brewery, **Big Lamp Brewery**, and **accommodation** (8D in Salmon Cottage/6Tr in Keelman's Lodge, all en suite; ☛; WI-FI; Ⓛ), in two buildings, between them. They charge from £34.25pp (sgl occ £51.50, three sharing £85.50). The pub serves **food** (Sun-Fri noon-9pm, Sat to 9.30pm), including breakfast (Mon-Fri 7-10am, Sat & Sun from 8am; £7.95 full English, £4.95 continental). *(cont'd on p114)*

Map 5, Scotswood 111

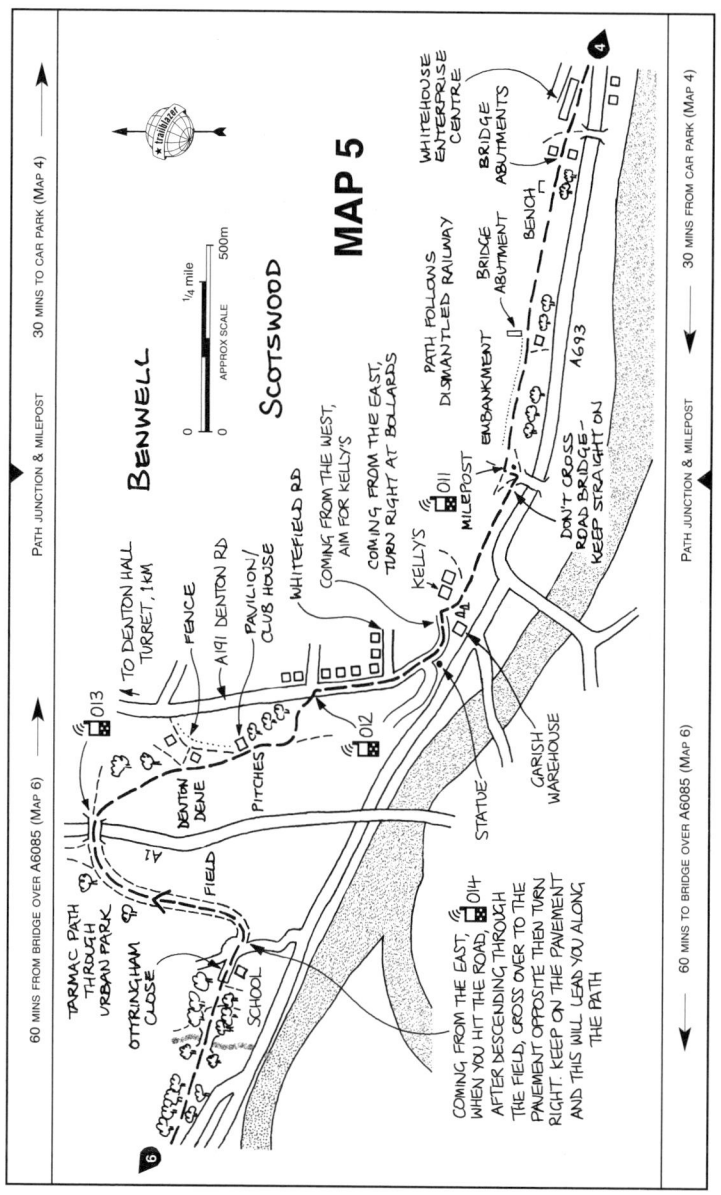

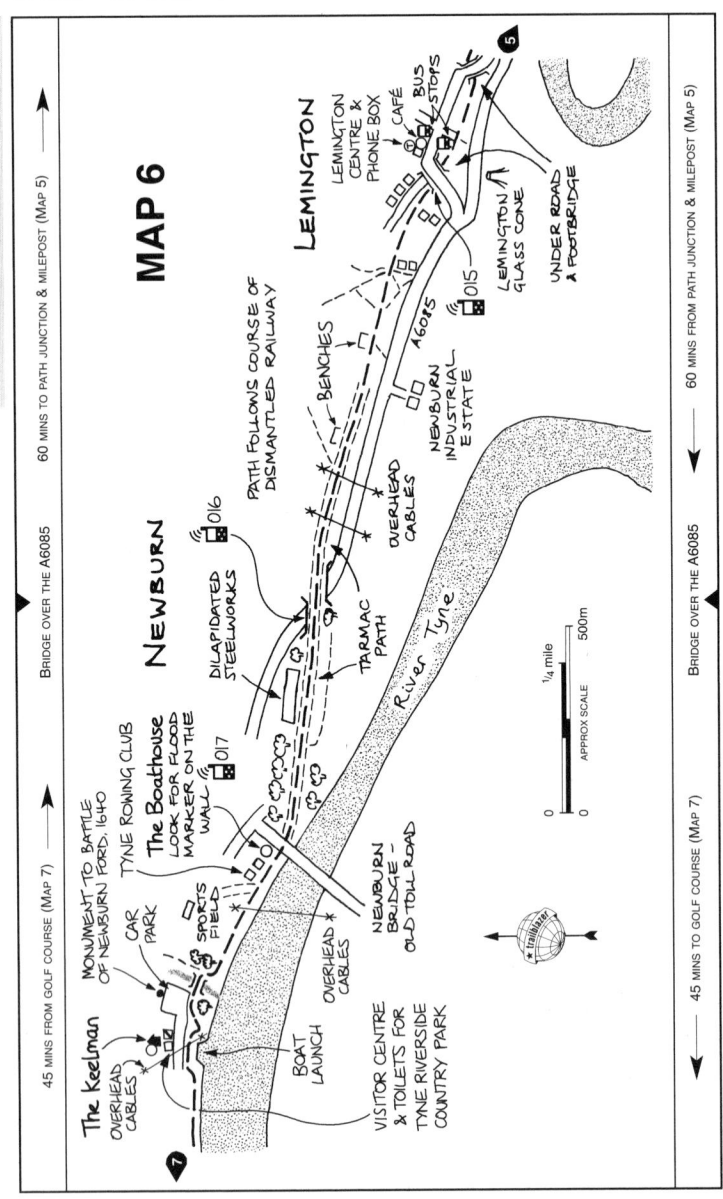

112 Wallsend to Heddon-on-the-Wall

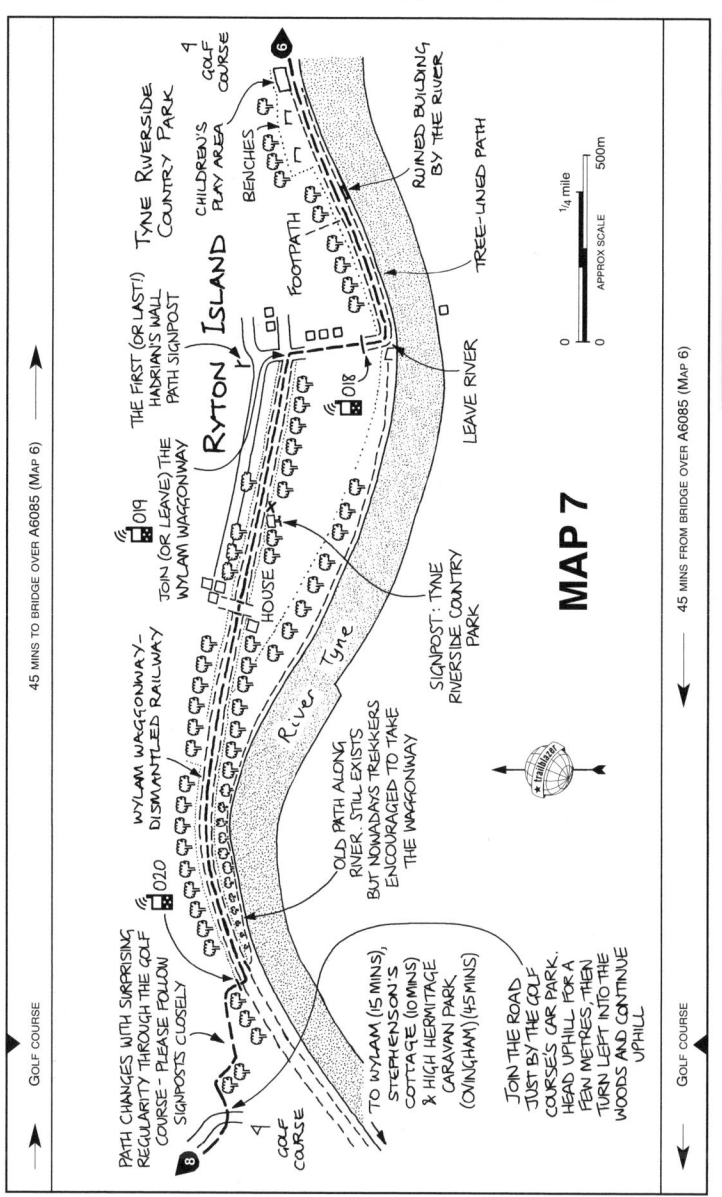

Map 7, Wylam Waggonway 113

(cont'd from p110) Non-residents can also have breakfast here (Mon-Fri from 8am, Sat & Sun from 9am) but this must be booked in advance.

Otherwise, it's onwards and upwards, having forsaken the water's edge to join, briefly, **Wylam Waggonway** (Map 7). Thanks to the popularity of the trail, and the relative paucity of B&B options in Heddon-on-the-Wall, **Wylam**, 15-20 minutes along the Waggonway from the trail, is seeing an increasing number of hikers looking for somewhere to stay on their first (or last) night.

❑ George Stephenson and the Wylam Waggonway

Born (on 9 June 1781) and raised on the eastern fringes of Wylam, right by the old Wylam Waggonway, it was perhaps inevitable that George Stephenson – who, as a child, must have watched the progress of those early horse-drawn waggons passing his house – would somehow be drawn into the industry. Indeed, his very first job was working on the waggonway, where he was hired as a boy to keep a neighbour's herd of cows off the tram road.

Lacking formal education and unable to read or write, Stephenson joined his dad at Killingworth Colliery, though it wasn't long before his fascination for machinery, combined with a single-minded nature and fierce ambition, was leading him in new directions. In 1812 he became enginewright at the colliery and less than a year later Stephenson had persuaded his manager to let him try his hand at building a railway engine. The result was *Blucher*, a slow and clumsy beast (it was said to do no more than 4mph) which nevertheless became the first engine to avoid using cog-and-rack pinions – a breakthrough that thrust Stephenson to the very forefront of steam technology at the relatively tender age of 32.

Sixteen locomotives later and in 1819 Stephenson, his reputation for engine building now unmatched, was asked to construct an eight-mile line from Hetton to Sunderland. It was his – and the world's – first major steam railway project. It was also the task that convinced Stephenson that steam railways, if they were to have a future, needed to be constructed on as level a ground as possible; the hilly terrain that separated Hetton from Sunderland meant that his locomotive could not complete the journey without significant help from fixed hauling engines to help it negotiate the steeper parts, which slowed down the engine's progress considerably.

Further success followed; on 27 September 1825 – a date now known as the Birth of the Railways – his invention, *Locomotion*, carried 450 passengers at 15mph (24km/h) between Darlington and Stockton along his own railway line. Several years later, in 1829, an updated version of *Locomotion*, built with the help of his son Robert and called *Rocket*, won a competition to find the fastest locomotive when it travelled at an average speed of 36mph (58km/h) from Liverpool to Manchester, the line for which Stephenson had become chief engineer. It became his most celebrated achievement and firmly established his reputation as 'Father of the Railways'. With his new-found fortune Stephenson bought Tapton House, a grand Georgian manor near Chesterfield, where he kept busy opening coal mines, ironworks and limestone quarries in the nearby area. It was at Tapton that he died, on 12 August 1848, aged 67.

Stephenson's childhood home (☎ 01661-843276, 🖥 www.nationaltrust.org.uk/george-stephensons-birthplace), at Wylam, is now owned by the National Trust. The white-stone cottage is a simple miner's affair that's been furnished to reflect the typical living arrangements of the late 18th century (when Stephenson was born), with everybody living in the one room. Note that the property will be closed for the whole of 2017. See the website for details.

WYLAM

There are two decent accommodation options in the village, and a campsite nearby, as well as a good place to eat.

There's also a **pharmacy**, a **post office**, a Spar **supermarket** (daily 6am-9pm) with an **ATM** and JA Stobo & Son grocery store.

Wylam has a small **railway station** on the Newcastle to Carlisle line. Go North East's No X84 **bus** service also calls here; see pp46-8 for further details.

For **B&B** there's *Wormald House* (☎ 01661-852529, 🖥 www.wormaldhouse.co.uk; 2D/1T, all en suite; ☻; WI-FI; Ⓛ), the first place you come to as you reach the village from the trail. They have drying facilities and, if prearranged, will pick you up at Heddon and drop you off the next morning. B&B costs from £33.50pp (sgl occ £37).

Further up the hill, *Black Bull* (☎ 01661-853112, 🖥 www.blackbull-wylam.co.uk; 1S/3D/1Tr/1Qd, all en suite; WI-FI; Ⓛ; 🐕) has rooms starting from £22.50pp (sgl £25, sgl occ room rate, £65/85 for three/four sharing. Note that they don't provide breakfast. **Food** (Tue-Fri 4-9pm, Sat noon-9pm, Sun noon-5pm) is served later on, though, but not on Mondays.

At the other end of town, just across the river by the railway station, *Boathouse* (☎ 01661-853431, 🖥 theboathousewylam @live.co.uk; food served daily 11am-'late'; WI-FI; 🐕) is renowned for its award-winning cask ales (it often wins the CAMRA Northumberland Pub of the Year) with some good cheap fodder: Thai food is served noon-6pm and sandwiches, toasties and pies, such as local hand-made pies with mushy peas, all day.

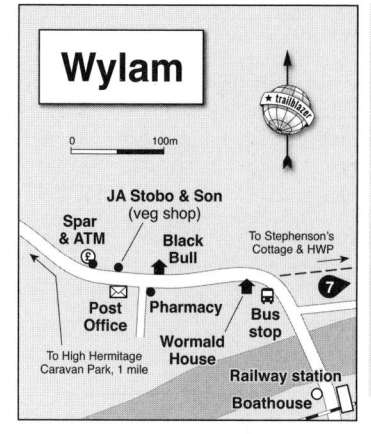

Just over a mile beyond Wylam (walk west along the main road), **camping** is available beside the river at *High Hermitage Caravan Park* (☎ 01661-832250, 🖥 www.highhermitagecaravanpark.co.uk; 🐕; £10pp), in **Ovingham**. It's a bit of a trek from the trail to get here, but it's the only realistic camping option on day one, unless you fancy a 26-mile (42km) hike all the way to East Wallhouses on your first day! The X84 **bus** (see pp46-8) stops in Wylam and Ovingham making staying here a realistic option.

It's a bit of an exhausting schlep to the top of the hill but **Heddon-on-the-Wall** (see p116), with its pubs, accommodation and, best of all, a great chunk of Hadrian's Wall, is a worthy reward at the end of a long but interesting first day. You'll notice over the next few days that the Wall turns up in the unlikeliest of places, and it's no different here: lying parallel to the busy B6528, this portion is, at over 100m, the longest section of *broad* Wall remaining.

As you'll see on the next stage, the Romans soon reduced their building ambitions, for although they still had the foundations for a broad Wall, west of here they built a narrow Wall on top of them. The flat circular platform that's incorporated into the Wall is a kiln that post-dates the Roman era.

HEDDON-ON-THE-WALL [Map 8]

A fine place for a first night, as Heddon-on-the-Wall marks the start of your Wall walk proper and, as if to emphasise that point, there's a **sizeable chunk of Wall** for you to savour, just a minute's walk from the path.

As for Heddon itself, it's not a bad little place; rather quaint in parts. It also has a few services for hikers, including a **tearoom-cum-delicatessen** – the highly rated *Dingle Dell Tearooms* (☎ 01661-854325; Mon-Sat 9am-5pm), serving a range of local cheeses, meat, preserves and pickles, as well as toasties, pies and soups.

The petrol station also acts as a Spar **supermarket** (Mon-Sat 7am-9pm, Sun 8am-9pm) and the local **post office**. There are **ATMs**, both of which charge, in the Spar and in The Swan. Note, some foreign bank cards are not accepted at these ATMs.

There are several **bus** services between Heddon and either Newcastle or Hexham, including Arriva's/Stagecoach's No 685 & 85 services and Go North East's X84 & X85 services; see pp46-8 for details.

Heddon also has a couple of **pubs**. The *Three Tuns* (☎ 01661-852172, 🖳 www.the threetunsheddon.co.uk; **food** served Mon-Sat noon-8pm, Sun noon-4pm; WI-FI; 🐾), on the B6528, is a great old place, and where the spirit of the village now resides. It serves simple but tasty, affordable pub grub. The preferred option for most hikers, though, seems to be *The Swan* (☎ 01661-853161, 🖳 www.vintageinn.co.uk/restaurants/northeast/swan-at-heddon; food served Mon-Sat noon-10pm, Sun to 9.30pm; WI-FI; 🐾 in certain parts only), with some huge meals. They do standard pub fare (mains £10-15) as well as sandwiches and a roast on Sundays.

For **accommodation**, before you even reach the village there's *Heddon Lodge* (☎ 01661-854042 or ☎ 07802-660485, 🖳 www.heddonlodge.co.uk; 1D/1D or T, both en suite/1D with private bathroom; ✎; WI-FI; Ⓛ; 🐾), at 38 Heddon Banks, which has some splendid accommodation (£45-47.50pp, sgl occ £75) surpassed only by the fantastic breakfasts, with ingredients sourced locally and organic where possible.

On the trail itself is the handy, but basic *Hadrian Hideout* (☎ 07786-592634, 🖳 Hadrianhideout@outlook.com; 1T or Tr, en suite), a converted garage that sleeps two people in a bunk bed but there is also a sofa bed for a third person. (£20-22.50pp, sgl occ £30, three sharing £55). There's rudimentary cooking facilities, including a kettle; breakfast is a make-your-own fruit-and-porridge affair, although all the ingredients are provided. Guests can sit on the garden patio and use the owner's home wi-fi if they want.

More comfortable, but about half-a-mile's walk from the trail, is *Hadrian's Barn* (☎ 07944-004601, 🖳 www.hadrians barn.co.uk), a delightful self-contained

---

❑ **Milecastle numbers**

The **milecastles** built along the Wall have each been assigned their own unique figure – whether the milecastles can be seen today or not. The order runs from east to west, so the first milecastle on the Wall (which would have been near Segedunum in Newcastle) is called Milecastle 1, and so on up to Milecastle 80 at Bowness-on-Solway.

In addition to this designation, some of the more famous have been given their own name, such as the Grindon Milecastle (aka Milecastle 34). The Wall's **turrets** also have their own special number, each derived from the milecastle immediately to their east, with the turret closest to that milecastle given the letter A, and the next one to the west labelled B. So, for example, the turret immediately to the west of Milecastle 38 is known as Turret 38A, the next one to the west Turret 38B.

Note that a number of these milecastles were destroyed soon after they were built: when it was decided to move the forts up to the Wall from the Stanegate (see p49), many were built on top of old milecastles or turrets. Cilurnum (Chesters) Fort, for example, was built on Turret 27A and remains of it can still be seen.

Map 8, Heddon-on-the-Wall 117

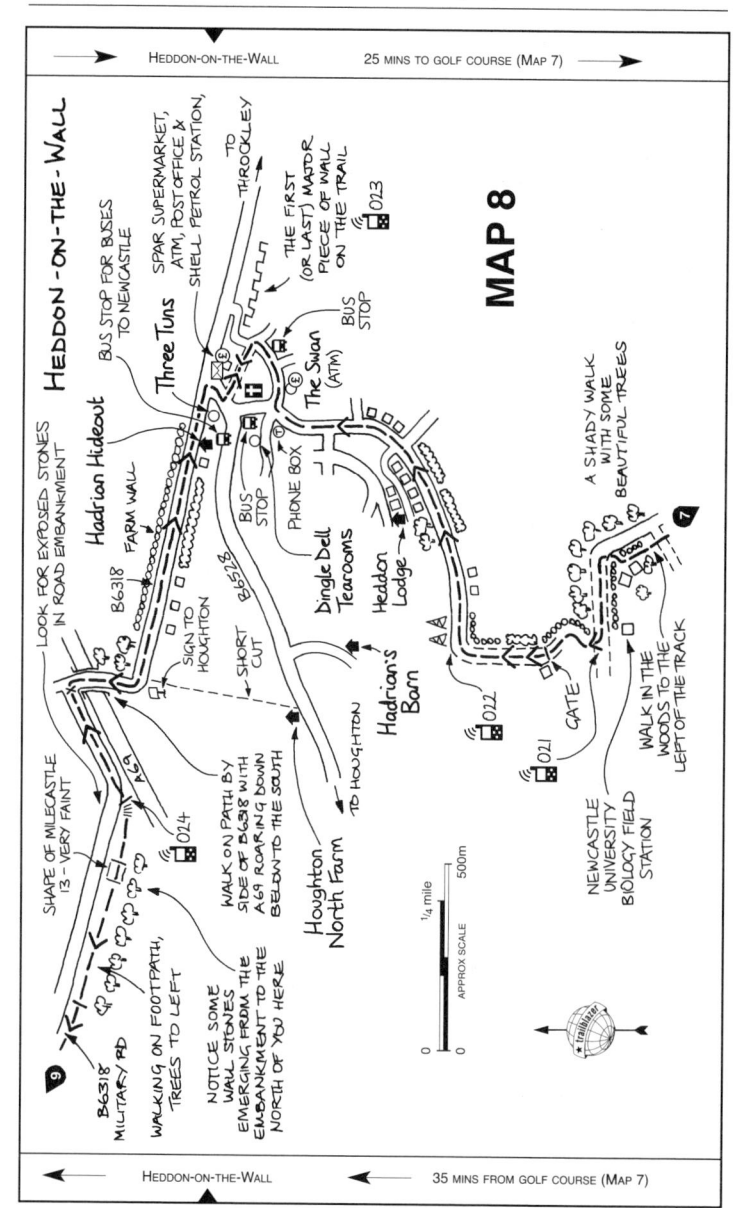

cottage (1T or Qd; WI-FI) with a living area, which has a sofa bed, and a fully equipped kitchen. The rate (£45pp, sgl occ £90, three/four sharing £127/156) includes ingredients to make your own breakfast.

Slightly further along the B6528 is the large hostel-like *Houghton North Farm* (☎ 01661-854364, ☎ 07708 419911, 💻 www.hadrianswallaccommodation.com; 1T/4Qd shared facilities, 1Tr and a room sleeping up to five, both en suite; WI-FI; ⓛ; Mar/Apr-Nov). A cut above your average hostel or bunkhouse. There's also a kitchen and dining area, free internet access, TV lounge and power shower to die for, as well as high standards of comfort and cleanliness. Rates (£28pp, sgl occ £35, £25pp for groups) include a buffet-style continental breakfast.

HEDDON-ON-THE-WALL TO CHOLLERFORD [MAPS 8-16]

Introduction

Anyone glancing at the maps for this **15-mile (24km; 6¾-7hrs)** stage will find their heart sinking and probably conclude that this is a walk to be endured, not enjoyed. Why? Because most of the trail on this stage is owned by Northumberland Highway Department and throughout much of its length this walk is accompanied by one of its most important charges, the thundering B6318. Indeed, based on what the map is telling you, some of you may even decide to take the Corbridge–Hexham–Acomb deviation instead (see pp126-38), and rejoin the official trail again towards the end of the stage St Oswald's Hill Head. But don't be so hasty; this stage is packed with interest. For one thing, though the road is a constant companion, for most of this stage you'll be hiking slightly away from it in fields with livestock and other, wilder creatures of the British countryside such as hares, rabbits and a superb variety of birdlife including crows, lapwings, finches, swallows and, on the waters of Whittledene Reservoir, the great-crested grebe, tufted duck and dunlin. Indeed, there's even a birdhouse on one of the signposts by the reservoir.

Furthermore, permanent presence though it may be, the road is rarely an obtrusive one. (That said, sometimes you'll need to cross or at the very least walk alongside this very straight – and thus very fast – road, and outside Robin Hood Inn there's a memorial to a trekker who was hit by a vehicle on this stage, so you do need to exercise due caution throughout.) Bear in mind that the reason the trail follows the highway in the first place is because it is built right *upon* the Wall: the B6318 is merely the modern and more mundane moniker for the **Military Road**, built on top of the Wall on General Wade's orders in the 18th century to facilitate the rapid movement of his troops across the country in order to ward off incursions by Bonnie Prince Charlie and his followers. And though the Wall itself may not make much of an appearance until after St Oswald's (see p138), this allows its accompanying defences – the Vallum and, on the Wall's (and thus the road's) northern side, the Roman ditch – a chance to bask in the spotlight for a change; and it will be these, and the expansive views beyond, that will be occupying your attention for this stretch.

So, by all means, take the Corbridge–Hexham alternative if you prefer – it's a cracking walk – but not if your only reason for doing so is because you believe the official trail to be a bit duff. It's not. Perhaps best of all would be to take the detour and *then* come back and do the proper trail, or vice versa.

The route

The day begins as it means to continue: on the B6318 which starts behind the Three Tuns. It's not long before the first evidence of the Wall appears: as you enter a field following a diversion to cross the A69, **stones from the Roman Wall** lie where they emerged from the road embankment. Those with eagle eyes may be able to make out the platform outline of Milecastle 13, though it's extremely faint and you shouldn't worry if you can't make it out; there are plenty of better examples of milecastles to come. A few hundred metres further on in the next field are the also-hard-to-distinguish subterranean remains of **Rudchester Fort** (aka Vindobala Fort; Map 9), once heavily pillaged by local farmers and the builders of the Military Road in the 18th century but now lying undisturbed beneath the soil of Rudchester Farm. Now owned by the local county council, there are hopes that this 4½-acre (1.8-hectare) fort will be re-excavated (it was last explored thoroughly in the 1930s) and developed properly one day – though what exactly is left after all these depredations remains to be seen.

The next few miles provide scant evidence that you are following a Wall, though other Roman constructions are evident. **B&B** is available at ***Ironsign*** (☎ 01661-853802, ✉ lowen532@aol.com; 3T, all en suite; ➖; Ⓛ; late Mar-Oct). They charge £37.50pp (sgl occ £55) and, if booked in advance, also do evening meals (served at 6.30pm).

A little beyond Ironsign you cross the road to walk in the **Roman ditch**, the fortification that lay to the north of the Wall. This you follow almost all the way up to **Harlow Hill** (Map 10), a tiny, lonely little settlement whose most noticeable feature is its old church, now converted into a farmyard barn. A few yards up the hill, many of the buildings in the hamlet have been converted into Harlow Hill MXVI (✉ harlowhill-mxvi.co.uk), a series of luxury holiday cottages where a minimum stay of three days is required. The unusual name, by the way, refers to the fact that this was once the site of Milecastle 16 (see box p116 for milecastles).

From here the trail continues in the ditch down to Whittledene Reservoir's **Great Northern Lake**. With Welton Burn feeding this reservoir and Whittle Dene Aqueduct from Hollington Reservoir flowing into Great Southern Lake at the southern end, this series of lakes rarely freezes over even in the depths of winter, and as such attracts birdlife year-round. Indeed, over 190 species of birds, as well as red squirrels and deer, have been spotted on or near the lakes. This gigantic series of reservoirs is more than just a nature reserve, however, for the reservoir pumps 25 million gallons of water a day to the treatment works. With picnic tables, a hide that provides invaluable shelter from the rain, and views opening up north and south, it's a highly disciplined hiker who resists taking a break here. After the reservoir, the path keeps to the north of the road until Robin Hood Inn. *(cont'd on p122)*

❑ **Walk side by side and on healthy grass** In other words don't walk in single file or on worn areas. Protect our heritage!

120 Heddon-on-the-Wall to Chollerford

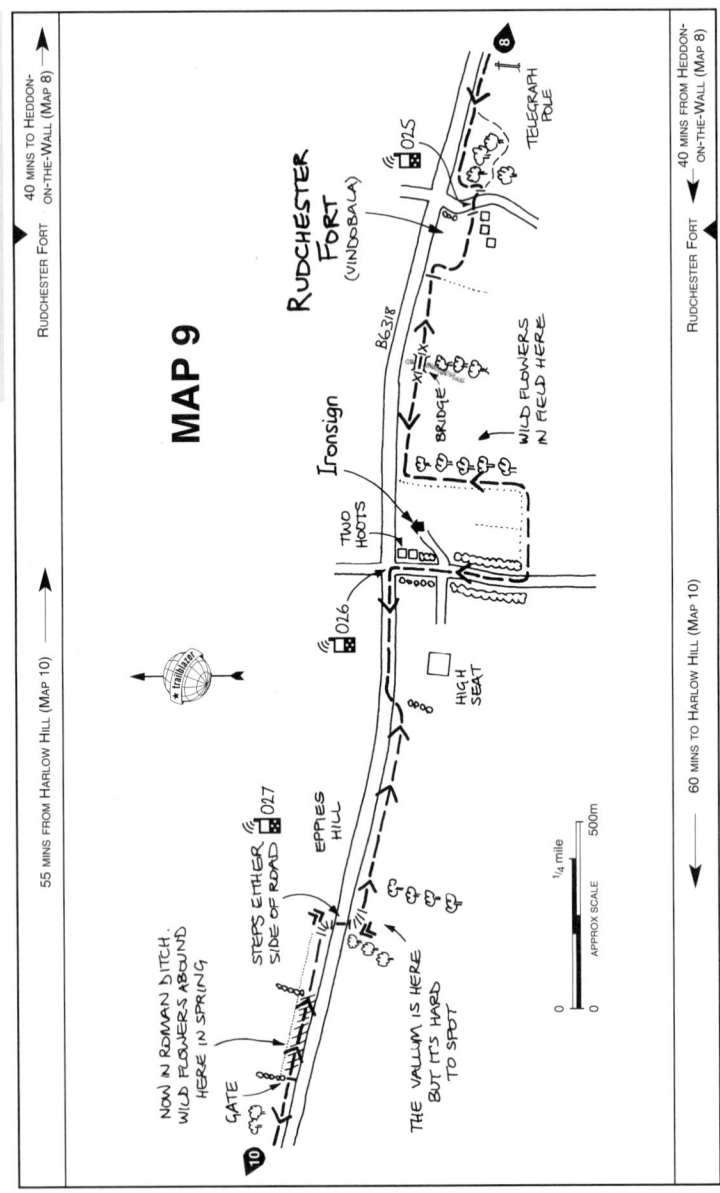

Map 10, Harlow Hill 121

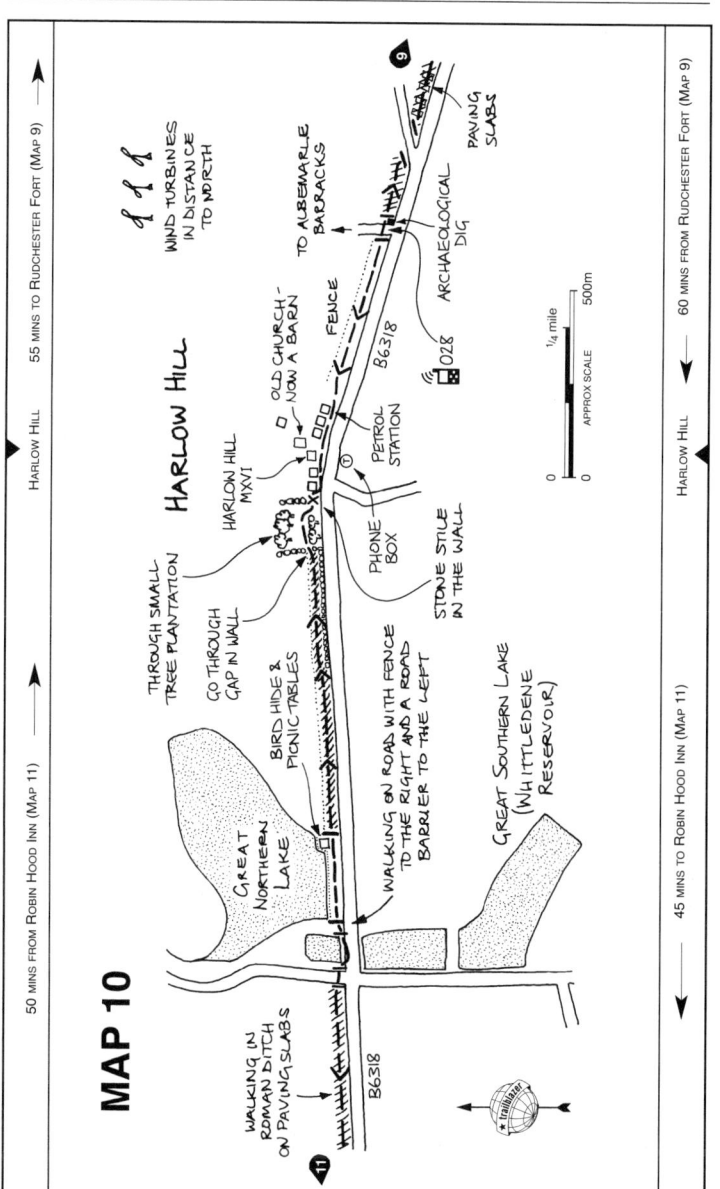

EAST WALLHOUSES (& AROUND)
[Map 11]

Robin Hood Inn (☎ 01434-672549, 🖥 www.robinhoodinn-militaryroad.co.uk; 🐕 bar only; WI-FI), a pub dating back to 1752, is a favourite stop for hikers with some decent **food** (served daily noon-9pm) and a **passport stamping point** (see box p40). **Campers** can pitch a tent at the back; from £15 per tent (Apr-Sep) and, if requested in advance, can have breakfast (£5.95). They also operate a **B&B** (1D/2T, all en suite; ▼; ⓛ; WI-FI) and charge £50-60pp (sgl occ £85).

The only alternative to the pub for food is the nearby *Vallum Farm Tearoom* (☎ 01434-672652, 🖥 www.vallumfarm.co.uk; WI-FI), a very popular, licensed café (summer daily 9am-5pm, winter Mon-Fri 10am-4pm, Sat & Sun to 4.30pm) with a great selection of cakes, breakfasts and lunches. On a hot day their **ice-cream parlour** (Mon-Fri 10am-4.30pm, Sat & Sun to 5pm) is just the ticket, while across the courtyard is their **bakery & patisserie** (same hours), which also does **fish & chips** at weekends (Fri-Sun noon-4pm).

Exactly a mile to the north, and signposted from the trail, is *Matfen High House Farm* (☎ 01661-886192, 🖥 www.highhousefarmbrewery.co.uk), part **tearoom-restaurant** (Sun-Tue 10.30am-5pm, Thur-Sat 10.30am-9pm), part farm and part **brewery**. Booking is recommended for the evenings as the restaurant may be closed for an event. You can find out exactly how beer is made on a tour (by appointment; £6pp) of the brewery, sample some at the Real Ale Bar, then buy a bottle or two to take along the trail with you. Across the yard, the stately *Matfen High House B&B* (☎ 01661-886592, 🖥 struan@struan.enterprise-plc.com; 1D/1T en suite, 1D/1T shared bathroom; ▼; WI-FI; ⓛ; 🐕) dates back to 1735 and charges £37.50-45pp (sgl occ £40-45).

For **camping**, you can either stay in the back garden of Robin Hood Inn, or walk one mile south of the trail to the friendly *Wellhouse Farm Camping & Caravan Park* (☎ 01661-842193, 🖥 www.wellhousefarm.co.uk; 🐕; Apr-Oct), with 45 pitches (£7pp), a spacious toilet and shower block, coin-operated washing machines and dryers, and a good-sized dining room that comes into its own on rainy days. To get here, continue west along the B6318 and, just as the path turns right into fields by East Wallhouses, take the first left (see Map 11). Note, if you're not cooking your own food, you'll have to hike a mile each way to the main road and back to eat at the pub or the tearooms.

Having passed Robin Hood Inn (note that on a Monday this is the last place serving food before you reach Chollerford), tiptoe through the free-range chickens in the next field and skirt around Wallhouses. The trail now travels alongside miles of farmland before eventually arriving at a row of pretty cottages lining the busy road, known as **Halton Shields** (Map 12). Turning left off the road at the end of the hamlet, you come to the next major Roman remain on your walk: the large, soft, curvaceous undulations of the **Vallum** as it burrows its way through the fields south of the trail. The Vallum quickly disappears again, lost beneath the corrugations caused by medieval ploughing and the depredations of an old quarry.

The Wall makes an appearance, however, in the fabric of the 18th-century cottage **Halton Red House** (Map 13; ☎ 01434-672209, 🖥 www.haltonredhousefarm.com; 1D en suite/1T, private shower facilities; WI-FI; May-mid Mar), constructed at least in part from Wall stones; B&B here costs £37.50pp (sgl occ £60). Note that they do not do B&B between mid March and the end of April because that is the lambing season. *(cont'd on p126)*

Map 11, East Wallhouses 123

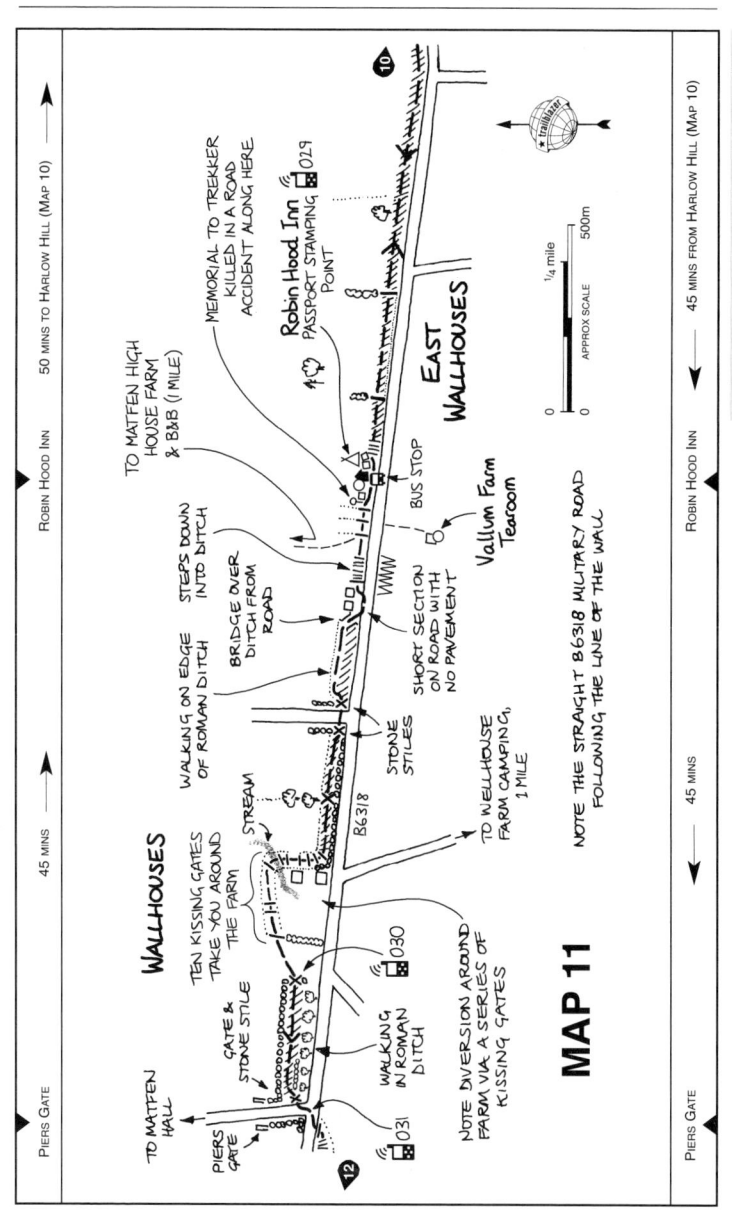

124 Heddon-on-the-Wall to Chollerford

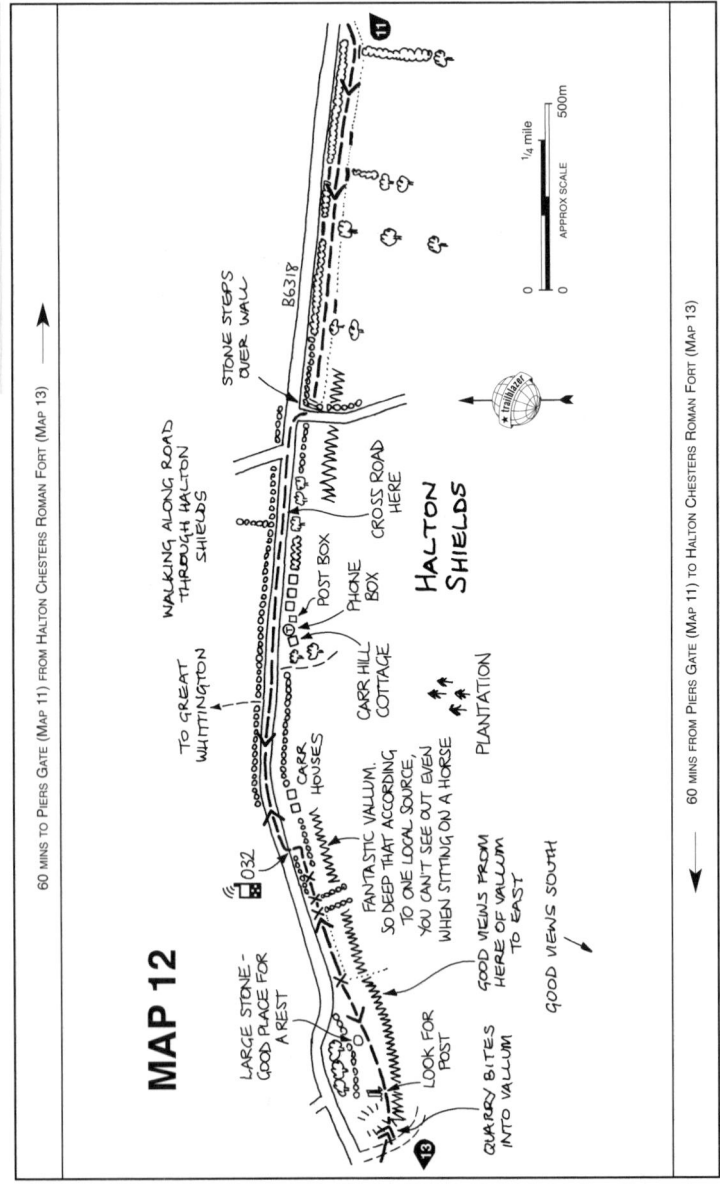

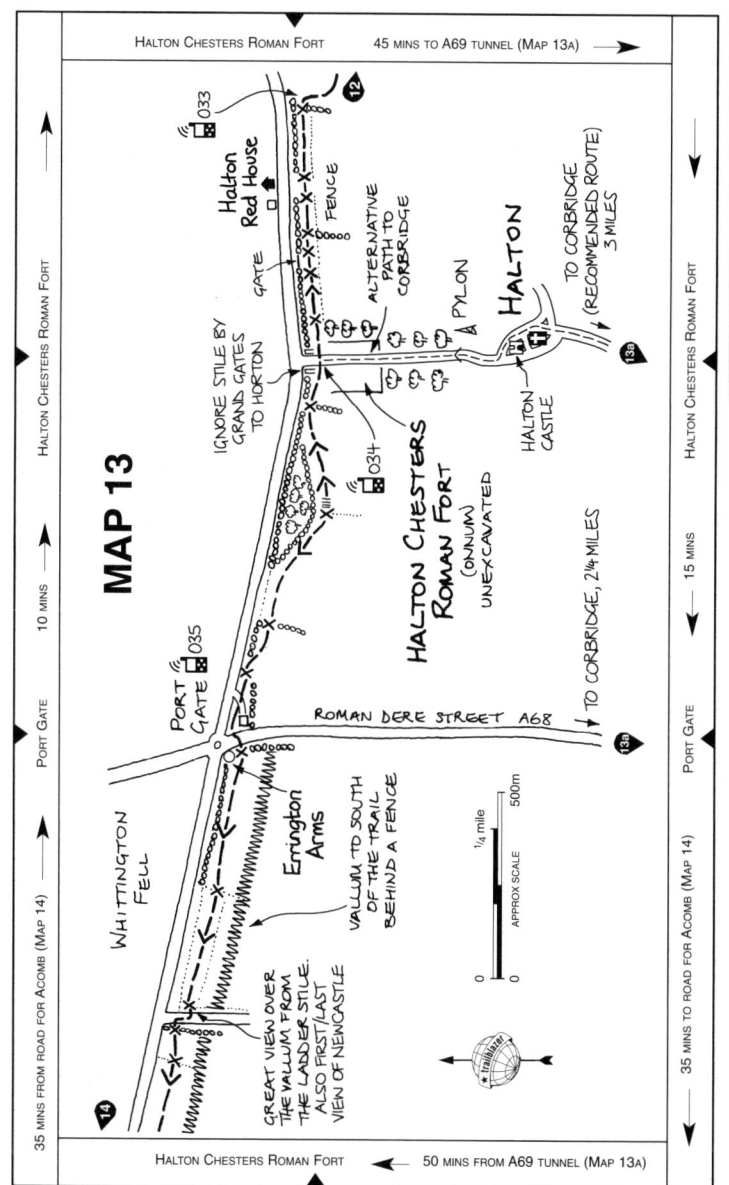

Map 13, Halton Chesters Roman Fort 125

126 Heddon-on-the-Wall to Chollerford

(cont'd from p122) A little further on, more incongruous grassy bumps beckon by the monumental gates of Halton Castle. These mounds in the field are the remains of **Halton Chesters** (also known as Onnum; Map 13), the second unexcavated Roman fort on this stage. As with Rudchester Fort (Vindobala), there's little to get too excited about with everything covered by a layer of turf and the undulations, other than the outline of the fort itself, difficult to distinguish from other, later, bumps.

Those wishing to take the Corbridge–Hexham–Acomb diversion (see below), or who are staying in Corbridge overnight, should head south from here. If staying on the official Hadrian's Wall Path turn to p138.

THE CORBRIDGE–HEXHAM–ACOMB ALTERNATIVE [Maps: 13 p125; 13a; 13b p132; 13c p133; 13d p134; 13e p139; & 15 p141]

This alternative trail (**12 miles/19.5km**; 4½-4¾hrs; Halton Chesters Roman Fort to St Oswald's Hill Head via Corbridge, Hexham and Acomb) has a bit of everything; magnificent stretches of woodland, a riparian stroll along the banks of the Tyne and even a few hills – thus far, for those coming from Newcastle, a rare treat.

The market town of Hexham, with its ancient abbey overlooking the market place, is an unqualified delight, as is the compact town of Corbridge, home to a 17th-century bridge, a pele tower by the church that's made of Roman Wall stones and more pubs than you can shake a Roman spear at. And then, of course, there's the main object of this diversion: the excavated ruins of Corbridge Roman Town (see pp130-1), just 15 minutes west of Corbridge near the banks of the Tyne.

From the Hadrian's Wall Path to Corbridge

There are several places where you can leave the Wall trail and head down to Corbridge. Perhaps the most appropriate, though, is the Roman Dere Street that once ran from the Firth of Forth through the Port Gate (see p138) to Corbridge and on to York. This, after all, was the main thoroughfare running north–south in Roman times. But for aesthetic reasons – not to mention the fact that it's a rather dangerous, pavement-less road in places – it is perhaps more advisable to begin your detour a little way to the east of here, turning off at the grand, tree-lined driveway leading to **Halton Castle** (Map 13). This turn-off is also where the Roman Wall fort of Halton Chesters (Onnum) was once situated.

The path leads left past the castle grounds, where chickens, ducks, horses and a number of over-excitable dogs roam free, and on down the hill along country lanes. Look out for lapwings, buzzards and the ubiquitous rabbits as you go. Eventually you pass under the A69 (Map 13a) where a bridleway leads off right. Follow the directions on the map opposite and on p128 and, all being well, 50 minutes after leaving the main trail you'll arrive in front of Corbridge's old church and pretty market square.

CORBRIDGE [see map p128]

In many ways Corbridge is a typical little English market town; smart, quaint, with a largely medieval centre and plenty of teashops and pubs to keep the floods of visitors that come every summer refreshed. Some find the place a bit twee – every second shop seems to describe itself using the adjectives 'artisan'

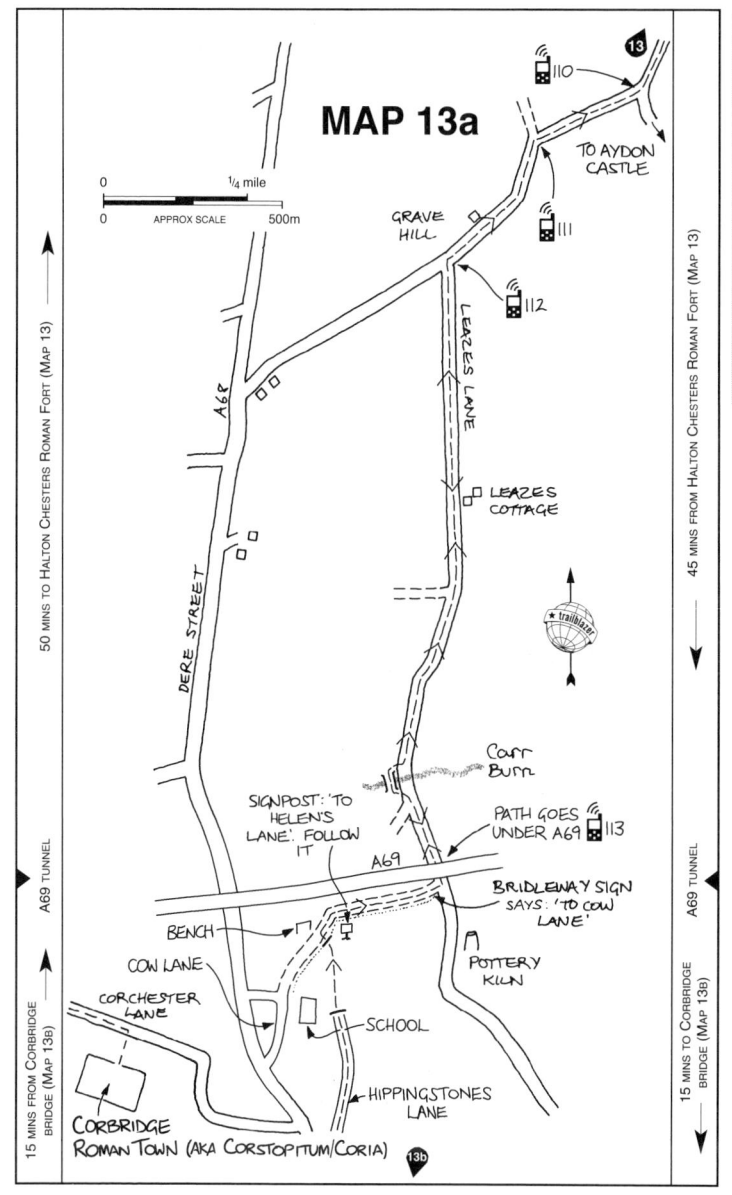

Map 13a, Corbridge–Hexham–Acomb alternative 127

128 Heddon-on-the-Wall to Chollerford (alternative route)

or 'designer' and there are shops called 'Skrumshus' and 'Kute' – but you can't deny that it's pretty and has just about everything a walker could wish for.

In addition to the wonderful Roman Town (see pp130-1), in the centre of Corbridge is Northumberland's finest Anglo-Saxon church, **St Andrew's**, built c AD786. In the churchyard there's a **pele tower** built using Roman stones, while a Roman gateway, which presumably originally stood at Corbridge Roman site, separates the baptistry from the rest of the church. Outside the church on the pavement is the site of the **King's Oven**, the main oven of the village in the 14th century.

Services

The centre of Corbridge is compact; in the main square you'll find the **post office** and **tourist information centre** (☎ 01434-632815, 🖥 www.visitnorthum berland.com/corbridge; Apr-Oct Mon-Sat 10am-1pm & 1.30-4.30pm, Nov-Mar Wed, Fri & Sat 11am-4pm); the staff are happy to do accommodation booking. Another website worth looking at for Corbridge is 🖥 www.thisiscorbridge.co.uk. You'll also find a **Co-op supermarket** (daily 7am-10pm) and a small **Spar supermarket** (Mon-Sat 7am-9pm, Sun 7.30am-8pm). There's a branch of Barclays with an **ATM** and a Lloyds Bank without one.

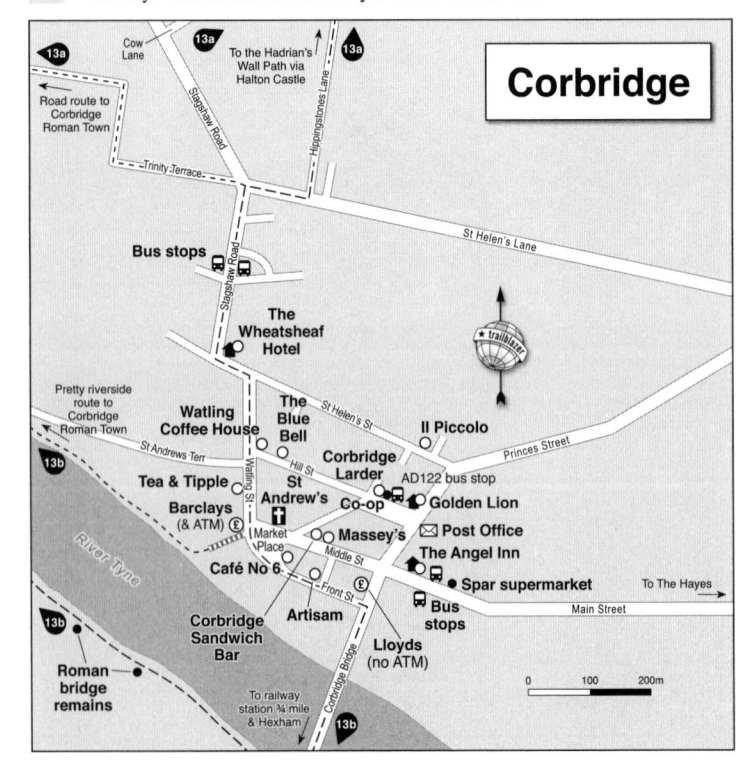

Transport
[See pp46-8] Arriva's/Stagecoach's No 685/85, Go North East's Nos 10 and X84/X85 all stop here. **Train**-wise, there are plenty of services to Hexham – with some continuing on to Carlisle – and to Newcastle. The **railway station** is about three-quarters of a mile south of the river (see Map 13b).

Where to stay
Near Market Place, *The Wheatsheaf Hotel* (☎ 01434-632020, 💻 www.wheatsheafhotelcorbridge.co.uk; 1S/4D/1T, all en suite; ✉; WI-FI; Ⓛ) is more like a smart pub that does food and B&B (£45-50pp, sgl from £54.95, sgl occ room rate). In a similar style, though more down-to-earth, *Golden Lion* (☎ 01434-632216, 💻 thegoldenlioncorbridge.co.uk; 5D/1T all en suite; ✉; WI-FI; Ⓛ) is a surprisingly vast place with a warm welcome and decent food (see Where to eat). B&B costs from £45pp (sgl occ £59.95). Across town from these two, *The Angel Inn* (☎ 01434-632119, 💻 www.theangelofcorbridge.com; 5D/1D or T/1D with bunk beds/apartment with two double bedrooms, all en suite; ✉; WI-FI; Ⓛ), a former coaching inn dating back to 1726, is the smartest place to stay. B&B costs £47.50-125pp (sgl occ £75-190; apartment £250-500); at weekends they prefer bookings of two-night stays.

About 500m east up the hill lies another B&B option: *The Hayes* (☎ 01434-632010, 💻 hayes-corbridge.co.uk; 1S/1Qd with private bathroom, 1Tr/1Qd both en suite; ✉; WI-FI; Ⓛ), a huge country house set in seven acres. They charge £38.50-40pp (sgl £38.50, sgl occ £48.50, three/four sharing £38.50-40pp).

Where to eat and drink
Watling Coffee House (☎ 01434-634425; Mon-Sat 8.30am-4.30pm, Sun 9.30am-4.30pm; WI-FI) is one of the smartest of the many **coffee shops** in Corbridge. A little way south, *Tea & Tipple* (Mon-Sat 9am-5pm, Sun 10.30am-3pm) serves scones and cream teas in the morning, before bringing out the sandwiches and light meals for lunch.

Also around Market Place is the cute *Café No 6* (Mon-Sat 9.30am-4.30pm, Sun 11.30am-4.30pm), the takeaway-only *Corbridge Sandwich Bar* (Mon-Fri 9am-3pm, Sat 10am-3pm), and the very friendly *Massey's* (daily summer 9am-4.30pm, winter 10am-3.30pm), with its great choice of breakfasts (£4-7) and sandwiches (£5) plus filter coffee with free refills!

Close by, the popular *Corbridge Larder* (☎ 01434-632948, 💻 www.corbridgelarder.co.uk; Mon-Sat 9am-5pm, Sun 10am-4pm, winter months Mon-Sat from 9.30am; WI-FI; 🐾) is a good-quality ground-floor deli with a health-conscious café upstairs.

Restaurants include the upmarket Chinese restaurant *Artisam* (☎ 01434-634214, 💻 artisam-corbridge.co.uk; Sun-Thur 6-9.30pm, Fri & Sat noon-2pm & 6-10pm) and the Italian restaurant-café *Il Piccolo* (☎ 01434-634554, 💻 www.ilpiccolo.co.uk; Tue 9.30am-2.30pm, Wed-Sat 9.30am-2.30pm & 6-9pm).

For decent **pub grub**, head to *The Angel Inn* (see Where to stay; Mon-Thur noon-9pm, Fri & Sat to 9.30pm, Sun noon-8pm), *Golden Lion* (see Where to stay; daily noon-9pm; 🐾), *The Wheatsheaf Hotel* (see Where to stay; food served Mon-Sat noon-3pm & 5-8.45pm, Sun noon-3pm) or *The Blue Bell*, which is also your best bet for quality cask ale.

CORBRIDGE ROMAN TOWN [Map 13a, p127]
(☎ *01434-632349*, 🖳 *www.english-heritage.org.uk; Apr-Sep daily 10am-6pm, Oct daily 10am-5pm, Nov-Mar Sat & Sun 10am-4pm (winter days/ hours subject to change, check in advance); adults £6.80, concessions £6.10, children under 16 £4.10, children under 5 & English Heritage members free)*

It is, perhaps, a measure of how much we still have to learn about the Romans in Britain that when the first edition of this book was published, in 2006, this site was known as 'Corstopitum' after what everybody believed was the Roman name for the fortress that originally stood here. However, doubt has recently been cast as to whether this was true, with many experts now believing that the fortress, built to guard what was, at ten piers wide, Britain's largest stone bridge in Roman times, was actually called 'Coria' by the Romans. Proponents of this latter theory point to the Vindolanda postcards (see pp162-3) to back up their assertions. On one of the tablets, commanding officer Julius Verecundus reports that there were 337 soldiers at 'Coris', and this is just one of nine definite references to Coria/Coris on the Vindolanda tablets. But while it is generally accepted now that Coria was the most likely name for this site, it is not universally so, with a dwindling band of archaeologists still preferring the name Corstopitum (even though there is only one contemporary occurrence of this name, in a document known as the *Antonine Itinerary*). As such, English Heritage now officially refers to the site as Corbridge Roman Town.

Regardless of what the original name was, the site's new name is probably more informative. For whilst its origins were undoubtedly as a Roman fortress – indeed it was, for many years, the nerve centre of Roman operations in northern England – the site was rebuilt time and again over the years, each time with modifications to suit its changing function. As such it is one of the most important sites near the Wall for archaeologists have been able to peel back each of these different stages, like layers on an onion, to discover the history of the fort; and bits of each of those layers are visible to the visitor today.

That history is a long and complex one. The first fort, built around AD85 under the governor Agricola, was situated about half a mile west of here and lasted only about 20 years before it was burnt down, to be replaced by a second, made of turf and built on this site, the following year. This, too, lasted fewer than 20 years before being abandoned, as Hadrian began to build his Wall and troops were moved north to new fortresses such as Halton Chesters (Onnum; see p126) that lay along its length. Corbridge was revived again,

---

❏ **The world's first archaeological dig?**
The history of the Roman site at Corbridge didn't abruptly come to an end when the Romans retreated to the Mediterranean. A few Saxon relics have been found to suggest that there was life here after the 5th century. Perhaps the most intriguing part of the fort's history, however, occurred in 1201 when King John undertook an excavation of the ruins in search of treasure. Though he found nothing except 'stones marked with bronze and iron and lead', his hunch was a good one: in 1911, more than 700 years later, 160 coins were found in a bronze jug; one of the largest hoards of Roman coins ever found in Britain. The find now resides in the British Museum. It may have been a fruitless search for John, but it earned him a prize of sorts: his excavation is seen by some as the first recorded archaeological dig in British history.

however, c AD140 under Emperor Antoninus, when it became a supply base for the soldiers fighting his Scottish campaign. Soon after this, c AD180, its function seemed to change again and in place of its strictly military role the fort began to take on the appearance of a town. By the 3rd century it was home to a largely civilian population, though still with a military core, and remained like this until the Romans departed in the 5th century. Thus, while this site probably once had the typical 'playing-card' layout so familiar from the fortresses along the Wall – and, indeed, in many parts still does – there are also ruins from its days as a largely civilian settlement. And it is these that make this place unique amongst today's Wall remains.

The proof of the importance of this fortress to the Romans can be seen merely by looking at a Roman road atlas. Running from the fortress to the north is **Dere Street**, the road the Romans built and would eventually use to launch their campaigns north into what is now Scotland; to the south, across the bridge, the same road continued to York; while running away to the west from here all the way to Carlisle was the **Stanegate**. As such, Corbridge was the transport hub of the region and a major supply town for forts along the Wall.

The Stanegate is still the main thoroughfare through the fort, though now it's at a higher level than the rest of the site thanks to all the resurfacing that went on during its lifetime. A stroll along here will take you past the **granaries** with their underfloor channels, built around AD180 when this site was metamorphosing from a regular fort into a supply base for troops on the Wall; the **fountain** next door which would once have been the centrepiece of the entire site; and the remains of various civilian buildings to the south of the Stanegate.

The original fortress that lay half a mile (1km) west of here (the one that was built under the reign of Agricola and burnt down), was rediscovered only in 1974 during the construction of the Corbridge bypass. You can see some of the things the archaeologists dug up there, as well as the best of their excavations here, in the museum adjacent to reception. Most famously of all, the so-called **Corbridge Hoard** – the contents of an iron-bound leather-covered wooden chest found on-site in 1964 – are now on display; dating from around 138AD, it comprises armour, tools, weaponry, wax writing tablets and papyrus – the essential possessions, one assumes, of your average Roman soldier. You can also see a replica of the famous **Corbridge Lanx** (the original is in the British Museum, London), a silver salver discovered in the 1730s near the riverbank by a young girl out walking.

From the fort, the quickest way back into town is to turn right and head east along pavement-less Corchester Lane. A far more pleasant route, however, is to turn left and, after a short distance, left again. This leads alongside a tributary down to the North Tyne, from where it's a pleasant stroll to the impressive bridge that gave the town its name. Built in 1674, this bridge replaced an Anglo-Saxon one on the same spot that became derelict in the 17th century.

Corbridge to Hexham

The walk to Hexham is pleasant. Beginning with a crossing of the bridge followed by a gentle riverside stroll, the route winds its way up through **Dilston**, home to **Dilston Physic Garden** (Map 13b; 🖥 dilstonphysicgarden.com; mid Apr to mid Oct Wed & Sat 11am-4pm; £4/3 adults/concs), established by a neuroscientist at Newcastle University and containing over 800 plant species that can be used for health and healing. The path continues on up the hill, with

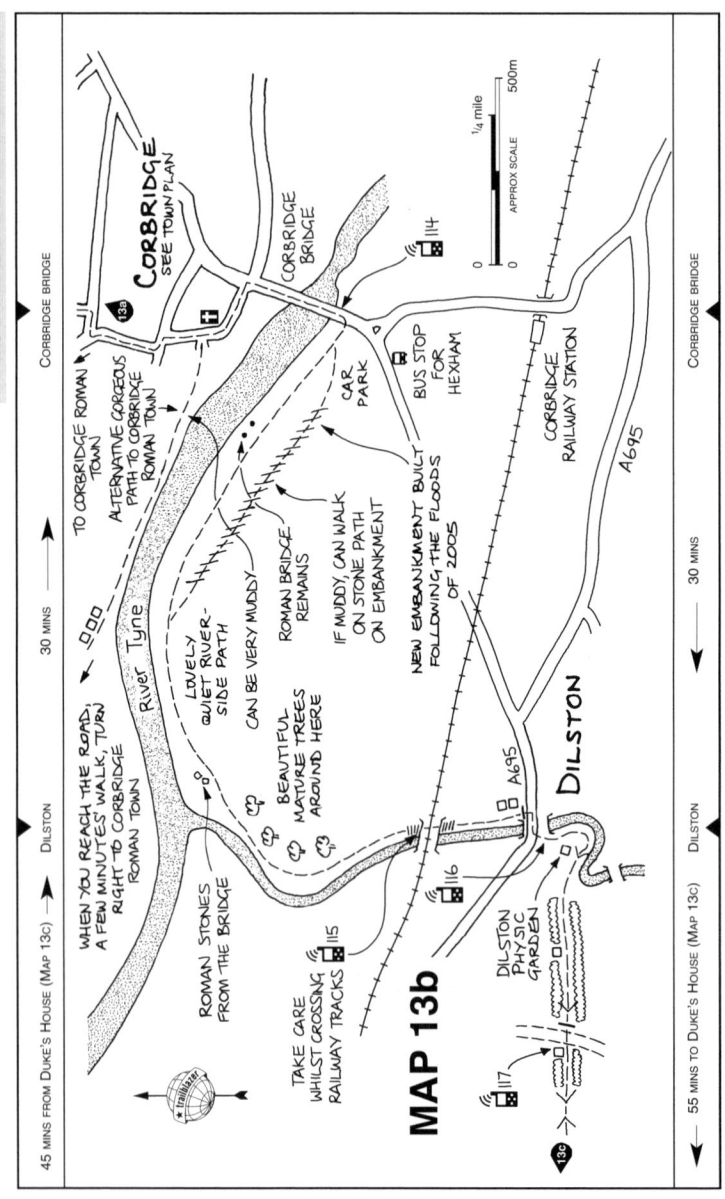

132 Heddon-on-the-Wall to Chollerford (alternative route)

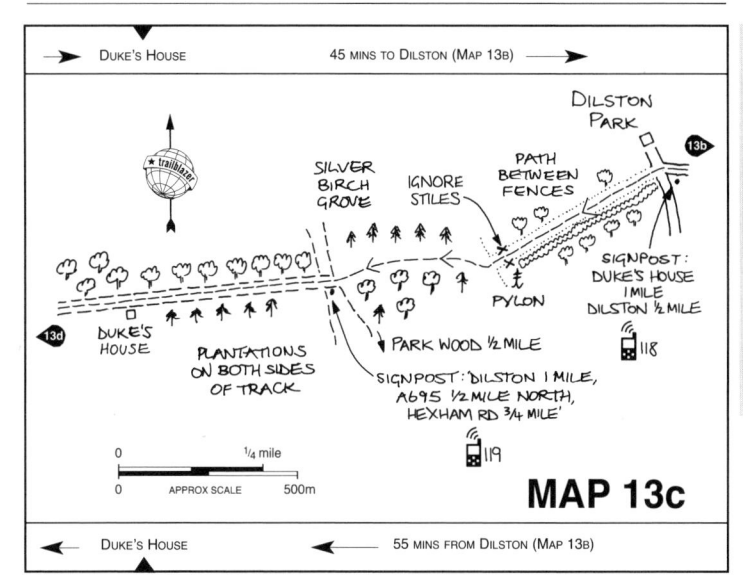

glorious views to the north across the valley towards the stately home of Beaufront (owned by the Errington family, after whom the pub at Port Gate is named; see p138). These views are enveloped in foliage as you enter into pine plantations, the path leading from here to the riot of chimneys and turrets known as **Duke's House** (Map 13c), surrounded on all four sides by some beautiful woodland that plays host to deer, badgers and red squirrels. Plenty of paths lead down from here to Hexham which you'll reach about two hours – plus breaks – after leaving Corbridge.

HEXHAM [See map p135]
The main market town for the district is a quaint and compact little place, the modern façades of shops and cafés concealing, but not obliterating, the medieval character of the town centre.

Pride of place in the heart of town goes to the glorious **Hexham Abbey** (🖳 www.hexhamabbey.org.uk; daily 9.30am-5pm, services permitting; recommended donation £3). The first abbey was built here in AD672, though much of today's construction dates from the 12th century when it was refounded as an Augustinian priory. Following the Dissolution of the Monasteries in 1537 it became the Parish Church of St Andrew, which it still is today. Take your time to explore the Abbey's impressive interior and look out for the large memorial to a 25-year-old Roman standard bearer from the 1st century AD – an original stone carving of which you'll see several casts in various museums, including Chesters and Newcastle's Great North Museum: Hancock.

Across the square from the Abbey, **Old Gaol** (🖳 www.hexhamoldgaol .org.uk; Apr-Sep & last week of Oct Tue-Sat 11am-4.30pm, plus Bank/school

134 Heddon-on-the-Wall to Chollerford (alternative route)

[Map 13d — hand-drawn route map showing Hexham area. Key features labelled on the map:]

- 13e (to Map 13e)
- A69
- HEXHAM BRIDGE
- SMALL ROAD OFF TO LEFT (WEST) BEFORE ROUNDABOUT. TAKE IT!
- TESCO SUPERMARKET
- WAITROSE SUPERMARKET
- RAILWAY STATION
- River Tyne
- AD122 BUS STOP
- The Station Inn
- HEXHAM BUS STATION
- HEXHAM SEE TOWN PLAN
- EASTGATE
- NATIONAL PARK HEADQUARTERS
- GREAT VIEWS TOWARDS HEXHAM
- VIEW TOWARDS MASSIVE EGGER CHIPBOARD FACTORY
- SIGNPOST: 'DUKE'S HOUSE ¾ MILE' — 121
- SCHOOL
- GALLOWSBANK
- FELLSIDE – GOOD VIEWS OVER HEXHAM ABBEY
- HALFMILE WOOD
- HORSE FIELD
- FELLED TREES
- SIGNPOST: 'HEXHAM ½, DILSTON 1½' — 120
- 13c
- **MAP 13d**

Scale: 0 – ¼ mile / 0 – 500m APPROX SCALE

Margin labels: 35 MINS TO ST JOHN LEE CHURCH (MAP 13E) / 25 MINS FROM ST JOHN LEE CHURCH (MAP 13E) / HEXHAM / 25 MINS FROM DUKE'S HOUSE (MAP 13c) / 35 MINS TO DUKE'S HOUSE (MAP 13c)

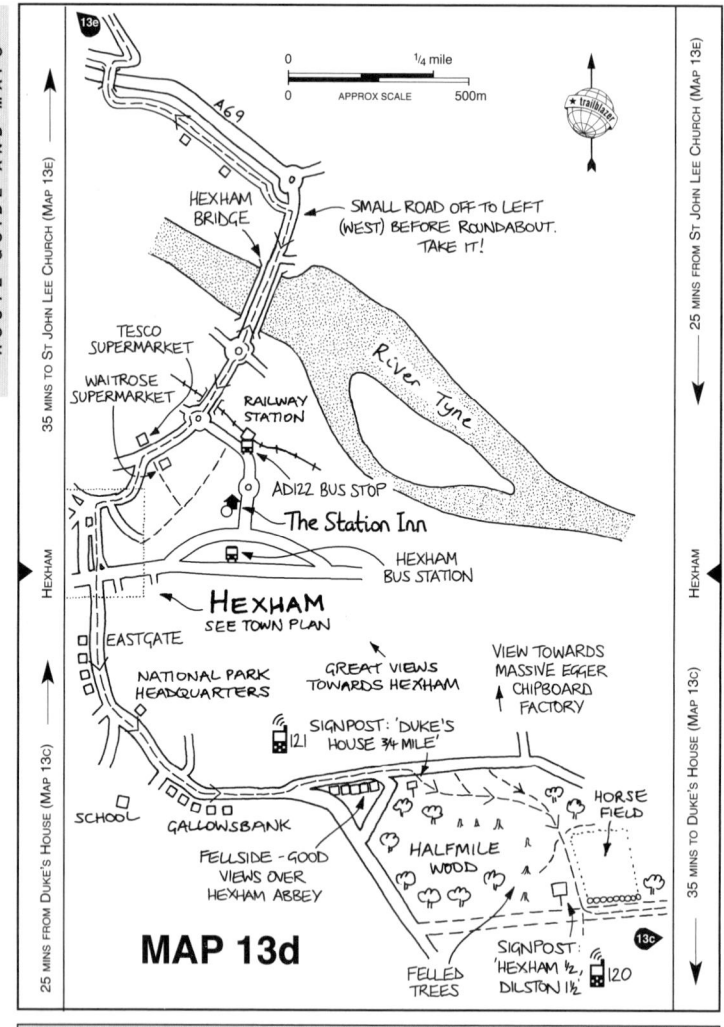

❑ Where to stay: the details
In the descriptions of accommodation in this book: ⬬ means at least one room has a bath; Ⓛ means a packed lunch can be prepared if arranged in advance; 🐾 signifies that dogs are welcome in at least one room but also subject to prior arrangement, an additional charge may also be payable; WI-FI means wi-fi is available. See also p100.

summer holiday Mons; Oct-Nov & Feb-Mar Tue & Sat 11am-4.30pm; £3.95/2.50 adults/children) is England's oldest purpose-built prison; it was built around 1330.

Services

The **tourist information centre** (☎ 01670-620450, 🖳 www.visitnorthumber land.com/hexham; Mon-Sat 9am-5pm) is in Queen's Hall on Beaumont St. It is in the same building as the library and they do accommodation booking (there is a 10% charge for this).

For **wi-fi**, try any of the numerous cafés or pubs in town.

Fore St is very useful for walkers; you'll find **banks/ATMs**, a **post office**, a Boots the **chemist**, and branches of the **trekking shops** Mountain Warehouse and Millets. The road leading out to the railway station has a two large **supermarkets** – Tesco and Waitrose (see Map 13d for both) – opposite each other.

Transport

[See pp46-8] There are plenty of **buses** to and from Hexham. The AD122 bus calls at the bus and railway stations (see Map 13d). Arriva's/Stagecoach's No 685/85 & Go North East's X84, X85, 10, 74 & 680 also pass through.

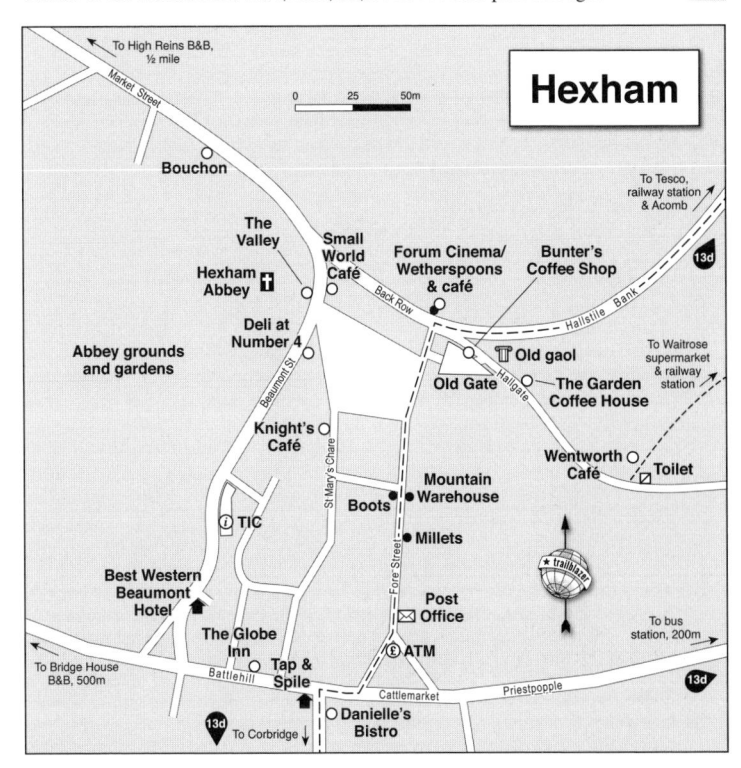

From the nearby **railway station** (see Map 13d, p134) there is a frequent service to both Carlisle (approx 60 mins) and to Newcastle (35-40 mins).

If you need a **taxi** contact Advanced Taxis (☎ 01434-606565, 🖳 www.advancedtaxis.com/hadrians-wall-service),

Where to stay
The most central place offering B&B, and with the added attraction of being a real-ale pub, is *Tap & Spile* (☎ 01434-602039; 1D/1T/1Tr, shared bathroom; ➡; WI-FI; 🐾); it has three very reasonably priced rooms (£27.50pp, sgl occ £35, three sharing £65). *Bridge House B&B* (☎ 01434-609973, 🖳 www.bridgehousehexham.co.uk; 1D en suite/1Tr private bathroom; ➡; WI-FI), a little west of the town centre, has two lovely rooms and a family-friendly welcome; B&B here costs £37.50pp (sgl occ £55, three adults sharing £100).

One mile north-west of the town centre, on Leazes Park, is *High Reins* (☎ 01434-603590, 🖳 www.highreins.co.uk; 3S/1T/2D, all en suite; ➡; WI-FI), a well-established B&B in a large country house and charging from £37.50pp (sgl/sgl occ £40-45).

The Station Inn (Map 13d; ☎ 01434-603155, 🖳 www.stationinnhexham.co.uk; 4S/1D/6T/1Tr/2Qd, all en suite; WI-FI; Ⓛ; 🐾) is a very friendly pub close to the railway station that has a selection of smart but simple rooms (£34.50pp, sgl £39, sgl occ £69, three/four sharing £90) and does decent food.

If you prefer a **hotel**, the family-run *Best Western Beaumont Hotel* (☎ 01434-602331, 🖳 www.bw-beaumonthotel.co.uk; 24D/10T, all en suite; ➡; WI-FI; Ⓛ), has a very convenient location opposite Abbey Gardens and charges from £42.50pp (sgl occ £85-100), but check their website for the best rates. Some rooms can have extra beds for children.

Where to eat and drink
Cafés and tea rooms There are more cafés and tearooms in Hexham than you can shake a cinnamon stick at.

Opposite the Abbey is the excellent *Deli at Number 4* (☎ 01434-608091, 🖳 www.deliatnumber4.co.uk; Mon-Tue & Thur-Sat 9am-5pm, Wed to 4pm, Sun 11am-4pm; WI-FI), with much of its food locally sourced, and a tiny **café** (same hours) upstairs. Nearby is *Small World Cafe* (☎ 01434-606200, 🖳 the smallworldcafe.com; Mon-Sat 9am-5pm; WI-FI), a bright, modern, health-conscious café with quality coffee and teas.

Through the Old Gate, and opposite the Old Gaol, is the cute and friendly tearoom known as *Bunter's Coffee Shop* (daily 9.30am-5pm), while slightly further down the hill, past the Old Goal, you'll find *The Garden Coffee House* (Mon-Sat 9am-4pm; 🐾), with homemade soups and scones, and a back garden that welcomes dogs.

Walk a little further down the hill and you'll eventually reach the good-value, no-frills *Wentworth Café* (Tue-Sat 8.30am-5pm, Sun-Mon 9.30am-4pm), overlooking the car park leading to Waitrose supermarket. For value for money, though, you can't beat *Knight's Café* (daily 8am-3pm), a tiny first-floor café hidden down a back alley and up a steep flight of stairs, where pie and chips will cost you just £3.60, and nothing costs more than a fiver.

Pubs Music-lovers and real-ale drinkers should make a beeline for the pint-sized *Tap & Spile* (see Where to Stay), where they stock a selection of cask ales and have live music some evenings. They don't do food, other than toasties, bar snacks and a curry night on Mondays, but along the same road, *The Globe Inn* does serve pub grub, as well as a good choice of real ales. You can also watch sport on TV here.

On the other side of the town centre, **The Forum** is an Art Deco **cinema** (💻 forumhexham.com) and a *Wetherspoon's pub* (daily 8am-midnight) serving breakfasts as well as good-value meal deals. The cinema also has a licensed, first-floor *café*.

Restaurants For something more substantial, *Danielle's Bistro* (☎ 01434-601122, 💻 www.danielles-bistro.co.uk; Tue-Fri noon-2pm & 6-9pm, Sat 6-9.30pm) is on the way into town from Corbridge; it serves hearty English and Mediterranean dishes and charges around £10.95/15.75 for a two-course lunch/dinner.

There's also a quality Indian restaurant, *The Valley* (☎ 01434-601234, 💻 www.valleyrestaurants.co.uk; Tue-Sun 5.30-10.30pm), right next to the abbey, while a short walk north-west of the centre, at 4-6 Gilesgate, is *Bouchon* (☎ 01434-609943, 💻 www.bouchonbistrot.co.uk; Mon-Sat noon-2pm & 6-9.30pm), a well-renowned, award-winning French bistro that's even made an appearance on television, on Gordon Ramsay's *The F Word*.

Hexham to Acomb

The thrills of walking on this diversion from the Wall don't end at Hexham, though you'd be forgiven for thinking otherwise as you walk on a tarmac bridleway alongside, and then across, the noisy A69. But a minute later you're back in rural splendour, with the venerable **St John Lee Church** (Map 13e) a diverting distraction, followed by a tramp through sheep fields and across a stream and on up to the pant (fountain) at Acomb.

ACOMB [Map 13e, p139]

Acomb is a friendly, attractive place; a string of stone terrace cottages inhabited by unassuming locals and with the **pant** (fountain) at the top of the village's Main St.

There's little to delay those who aren't staying here, save for a small **post office** (Mon, Tue, Thur & Fri 9.30am-12.30pm & 1.30-5.30pm, Wed 9am-1pm, Sat 9am-12.30pm) and no fewer than three pubs, two of which offer **accommodation**.

The first is *The Sun Inn* (☎ 01434-602934, 💻 www.sun-inn-acomb .co.uk; 1T/1D shared facilities, 1T/1D both en suite; ⬤; 🐾; WI-FI; Ⓛ) which charges £35-37.50pp (sgl occ £40-55). They were only serving bar snacks at the time of research, but had plans to reintroduce a proper pub menu.

Down the hill, *The Queen's Arms* (☎ 01434-607857, 💻 queensarms acomb.co.uk; 1S/1D/1T, all en suite; ⬤; 🐾; WI-FI; Ⓛ) also offers B&B (£32.5-37.50pp, sgl occ £45, sgl occ rates on request). The double and twin can be combined to provide a family room. They serve food on Thursday (noon-2pm & 6-9pm) as well as Sunday lunch (noon-3pm; £7.50).

Back at the top of the hill by the pant, *Miner's Arms* (☎ 01434-603909, 💻 www.theminersacomb.com; Mon-Fri 5pm-midnight, Sat & Sun noon to midnight; WI-FI; 🐾 but not in dining area) is a quintessential Northumbrian pub where great local beers are served every night. Hearty traditional **pub grub** (Tue-Fri 5-8pm, Sat noon-8pm, Sun noon-3pm) is available here too.

The other option for food is the long-standing takeaway **chippy** behind The Queen's Arms, called *Sea Chef* (☎ 01434-609370, 🖳 seachef.co.uk; Mon 4.30-9.30pm, Tue-Sat 11.30am-1.30pm & 4.30-9.30pm). It's been in business for 25 years and knocks out top-quality fish & chips (£5.80), plus pizza, burgers, sandwiches and paninis.

The AD122 **bus** stops here as does GNE's No 680; see pp46-8.

Acomb to the Hadrian's Wall Path

From Acomb the path leads north from just above The Sun Inn, round the back of the houses at the top of the village. It continues across a stream and alongside fields of grain and a farmhouse guarded by Highland cattle to the road. At the road, turn right up the hill before taking a right through a **green gate**. Continuing on the path through a sheep field, the path dips at the end to reunite with the B6318 (the Military Road) and the main trail, which you rejoin by the wooden cross in the south-western corner of the site of the Battle of Heavenfield (see below and Map 15 p141).

(cont'd from p126) Continuing west, it's not long before the road and trail join forces for the final push up to **Port Gate** (see Map 13, p125; also spelt Portgate). A modern traffic roundabout at the junction of the A68 and the Military Road, this may not seem the most auspicious place to find evidence of Roman occupation. But the A68 to Corbridge was once the old Roman **Dere Street** that ran between the fort (and indeed further on down to York) all the way north to Scotland; and, as such, Port Gate was one of the few gateways the Romans built into the Wall. When the roundabout was built in the '60s it was deliberately moved a little way to the north so as not to disturb the unexcavated archaeological remains around here.

Reaching the roundabout, a pause at *Errington Arms* (☎ 01434-672250, 🖳 www.erringtonarms.co.uk; pub closed Sun eves and all-day Mon except bank hols; **food** served Tue noon-2.30pm, Wed-Sat noon-2.30pm & 6.30-9pm, Sun noon-4pm; WI-FI; 🐾), named after an important local family, is scribbled into the itineraries of most walkers, and with good reason; the food here is great, with an extensive menu of dishes including plenty of sandwich options (from £5.50). For evenings, try their delicious moussaka (£9.95), or splash out on the chef-special luxury fish pie and mash (£12.95). Note the pub's opening hours are often reduced significantly in the winter.

Fully refreshed, head off from behind Errington Arms through the field, with the **Vallum** a constant and clearly defined companion to your left, before another bout of Roman-ditch walking follows as you cross the road by the outline of **Milecastle 24** (Map 14).

Through fields and woods the trail continues to **St Oswald's Hill Head** (Map 15), with its lovely little church (see box p142) set in a meadow to the north of the trail, just before the site of the **Battle of Heavenfield**.

Those staying in Acomb or Hexham may wish to turn left, south off the trail by the large cross in the corner of Heavenfield to join the route of the Corbridge–Hexham–Acomb diversion (see route above but in reverse). The rest of you (and anyone who is rejoining the path) should continue through the fields and across the road down to Planetrees. *(cont'd on p142)*

Map 13e, Acomb 139

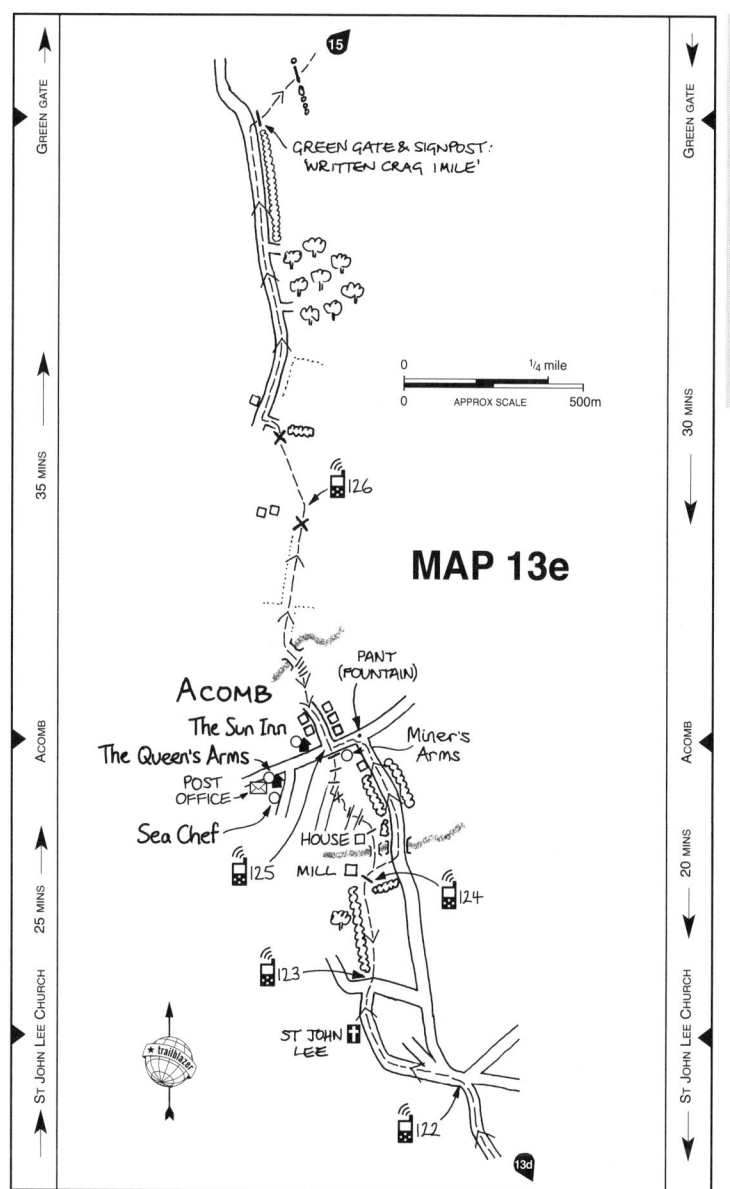

140 Heddon-on-the-Wall to Chollerford

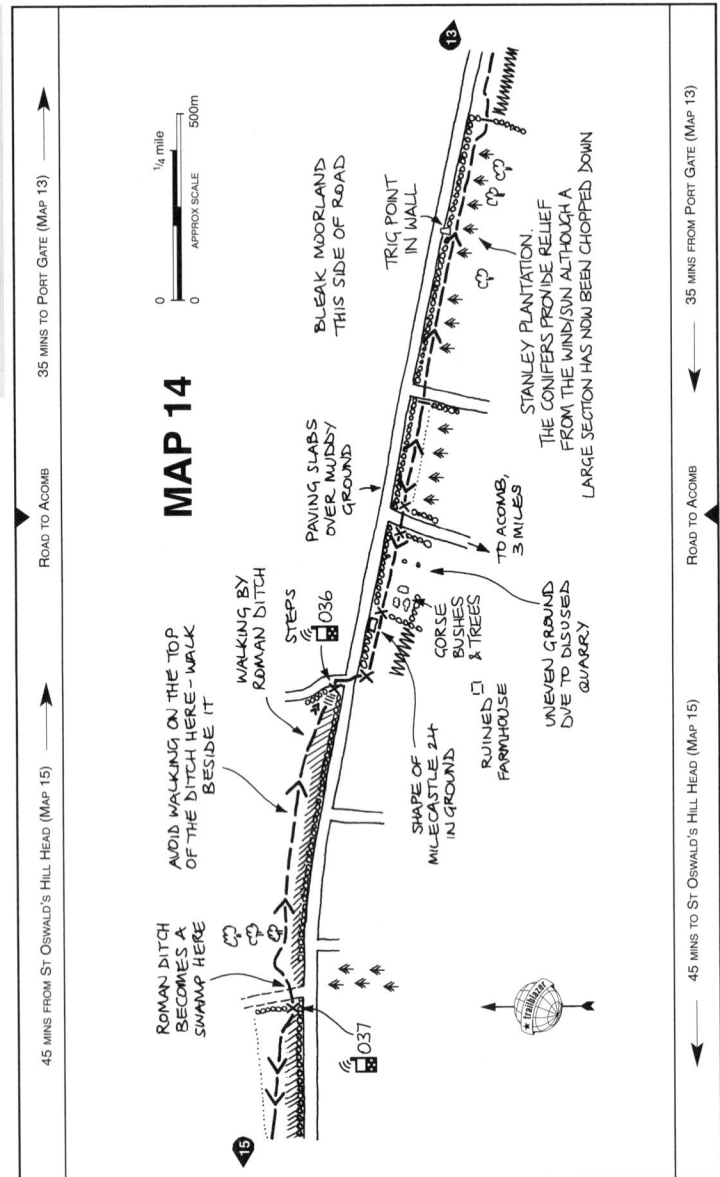

MAP 14

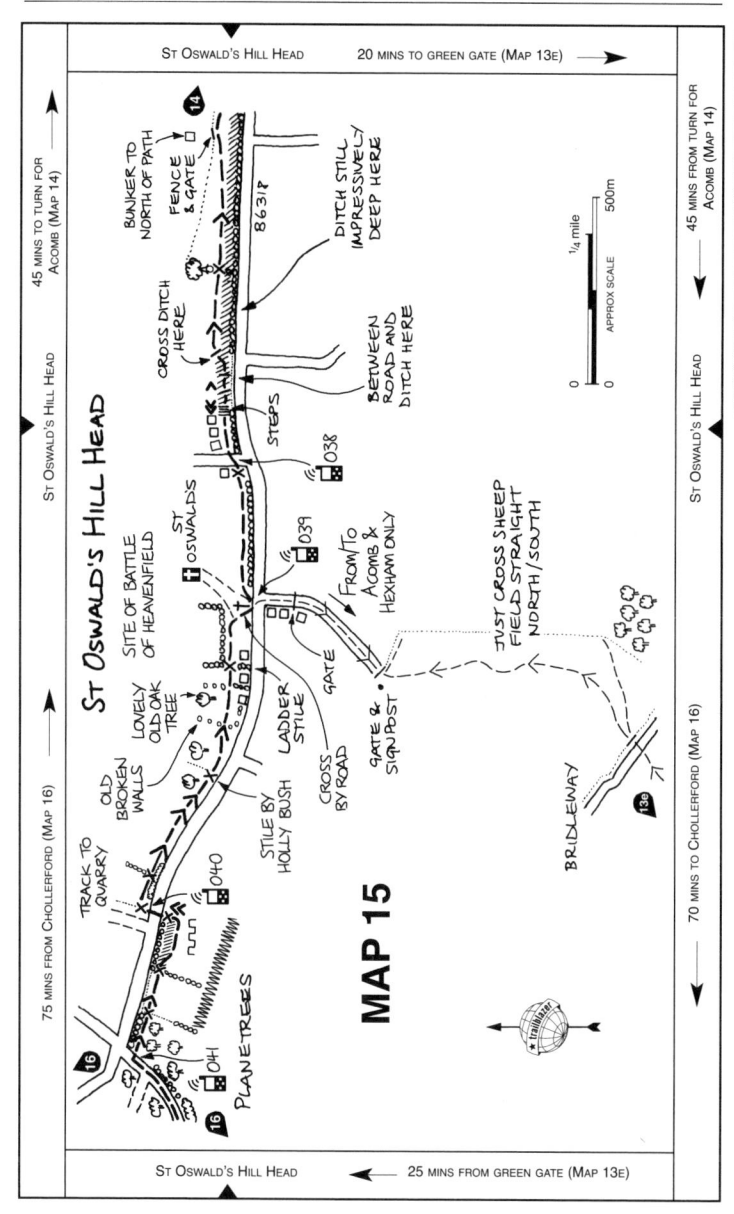

Map 15, St Oswald's Hill Head 141

❏ St Oswald's church
This was built to commemorate the victory of the eponymous saint over his rivals Cadwallon and Penda at the **Battle of Heavenfield**, which took place in the field in which you are probably now standing. In the 7th century St Oswald, who was merely a king at this stage, was the leader of the Angles following the death of Edwin (after whom Edinburgh is named) in AD633. His defeat of the combined forces of Gwynedd and Mercia, though not quite the victory of Christianity over paganism that the Venerable Bede portrays in his *History*, was nevertheless a significant victory for the Anglo-Saxons over the Celts and, as such, an important moment in English history. Incidentally, at the back of the church by the font there's a large **Roman altar**.

The church is also the official end (or start) of **St Oswald's Way** (🖥 www.stoswaldsway.com) which covers 97 miles of beautiful Northumberland countryside and coastline between here and Lindisfarne, linking some of the places associated with St Oswald.

(cont'd from p138) **Planetrees** is the first proper bit of Wall on this entire stage. Its existence is largely due to the efforts of William Hutton, who came across some workmen taking stones from the Wall to be used as raw materials for a new farmhouse. Hutton's entreaties to the local landowner responsible for the desecration, Henry Tulip, ensured that this small fragment survived; though 204m (224 yards) of the Wall did not, having already been pulled down by Tulip's men before Hutton arrived. However, the portion that has survived is interesting: notice how, near the culvert built into the Wall to prevent water from collecting and weakening the foundations, the Wall changes from being a *broad* Wall on broad foundations, as seen at Heddon, to a *narrow* Wall on broad foundations.

A similar pattern can be seen at Brunton Turret (see p144), just a little further on, and suggests that it was around here that the Romans gave up building an all-broad Wall and opted instead for a narrower version that nevertheless still made use of the original broad foundations. But before you get to Brunton Turret there's a rather dull stretch of road-walking that veers towards, and then away from, the village of Wall.

WALL [Map 16]
It is typical of the sometimes perverse nature of this trail that Wall village doesn't actually lie on the Wall.

The village is perhaps of most interest to hikers because of a highly commendable decision by the local parish council to allow a night's **camping** on the village green, free of charge as long as you don't stay for more than 24 hours and leave the place exactly as you found it. There are **toilets** nearby but no other facilities. Nor indeed is there a shop in town. But there is a very good pub-cum-B&B at the southern end of town, about 10 minutes from the trail: *The Hadrian Hotel* (☎ 01434-681232, 🖥 www.hadrianhotel.co.uk; 2D/2T both en suite/2T shared bathroom; ☞; ✖; WI-FI; Ⓛ) is an 18th-century coaching inn that offers **food** (summer daily noon-8.30pm, winter noon-3pm & 6-8.30pm) and has some very comfortable **rooms**, including some with a four-poster bed. B&B costs £40-45pp (sgl occ £50-60).

GNE's 680 **bus** service stops here; see pp46-8 for further details.

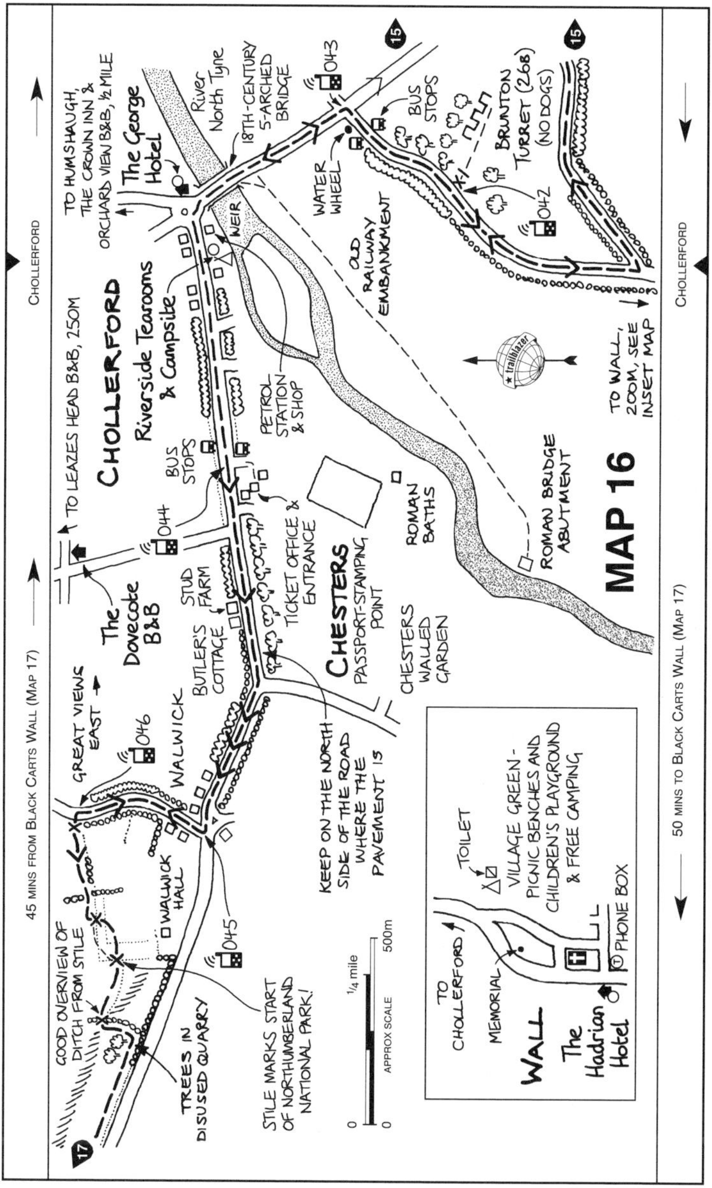

MAP 16
CHOLLERFORD
45 MINS FROM BLACK CARTS WALL (MAP 17)
50 MINS TO BLACK CARTS WALL (MAP 17)
TO HUMSHAUGH, THE CROWN INN & ORCHARD VIEW B&B, ½ MILE
The George Hotel
River North Tyne
18TH-CENTURY 5-ARCHED BRIDGE
043
BUS STOPS
WATER WHEEL
OLD RAILWAY EMBANKMENT
BRUNTON TURRET (26B) (NO DOGS)
042
TO WALL, 200M, SEE INSET MAP
TO LEAZES HEAD B&B, 250M
Riverside Tearooms & Campsite
WEIR
PETROL STATION & SHOP
BUS STOPS
TICKET OFFICE & ENTRANCE
ROMAN BATHS
ROMAN BRIDGE ABUTMENT
044
The Dovecote B&B
STUD FARM
BUTLER'S COTTAGE
CHESTERS
PASSPORT-STAMPING POINT
CHESTERS WALLED GARDEN
GREAT VIEWS EAST
046
WALWICK
KEEP ON THE NORTH SIDE OF THE ROAD WHERE THE PAVEMENT IS
WALWICK HALL
045
GOOD OVERVIEW OF DITCH FROM STILE
TREES IN DISUSED QUARRY
STILE MARKS START OF NORTHUMBERLAND NATIONAL PARK!
APPROX SCALE
0
¼ mile
500m
TO CHOLLERFORD
MEMORIAL
WALL
The Hadrian Hotel
TOILET
VILLAGE GREEN - PICNIC BENCHES AND CHILDREN'S PLAYGROUND & FREE CAMPING
PHONE BOX
trailblazer

Instead of turning left at the junction to Wall, if you keep on the path, by turning right, you'll soon come upon **Brunton Turret** (officially Turret 26B), sitting in a field to the right of the road. Said to be the finest turret extant on the Wall – up to eleven courses high in places – it was excavated by John Clayton in 1876. Note how the Wall is of different widths here, going into the turret at one width and coming out the other side at a narrower gauge. As you may have already seen at Planetrees, this kind of chopping and changing with the width of the Wall continues for several miles, though nobody's really sure why. Possibly it was for economic reasons, or maybe it was because the limestone core they used west of here was stronger than the puddled clay used in the eastern section of the Wall, and thus the Romans decided a thinner Wall would suffice.

Continuing along the road, some hikers may want to check out the remains of the **Roman bridge abutment** on the southern side of the river facing Chesters Fort. It's just over half a mile (1km) off the trail but it's a pleasant walk and you'll be rewarded with a sighting of big fat **phallus** that would make your auntie blush; this is arguably the most impressive example of this Roman symbol of prosperity on the entire trail. The symbol is carved into one of the stones on the abutment's eastern side, just above ground level. Two other piers in the water were also discovered but are visible now only when the water is low. Incidentally, this was the third Roman bridge over the Tyne; the first, of course, being Pons Aelius in Newcastle, and the second at Corbridge.

CHOLLERFORD & HUMSHAUGH
[Map 16, p143]

For those not staying here, **Chollerford** is a bit of a non-event: having crossed the sturdy **18th-century five-arch bridge**, the trail turns immediately left and continues along the road to Chesters, all but bypassing Chollerford and its neighbour, Humshaugh.

Note that there are no ATMs here but there are a few services of interest to trekkers. The petrol station, just over the bridge, has a small **shop** (Mon-Fri 8am-6pm, Sat 9am-5pm, Sun 10am-4pm) selling essentials (bacon, eggs, bread, milk) and next door is *Riverside Tearooms* (☎ 01434-681325; Mon-Fri 9am-4pm, Sat & Sun 10am-4pm). The friendly owners also run *Riverside Campsite* (contact details as for the tearoom; Easter-Oct; 🐕 if on lead) in the field behind, where camping (for walkers only) costs £7pp, including use of the shower/toilet block.

Across the other side of the roundabout is *The George Hotel* (☎ 01434-681611, 🖳 www.coastandcountryhotels.com; 25D/20T/2Qd, all en suite; ▼; 🐕; WI-FI; ⓛ), set in its own landscaped gardens by the North Tyne and boasting its own pool and gym. B&B costs from £60pp (sgl occ full room rate, three/four sharing room rate plus £15pp). Light snacks are served daily noon to 5pm, with the restaurant open daily 6.30-8pm. There's also a bar here, but there's better beer, and better-value food, in the pubs in the nearby villages of Wall and Humshaugh.

Humshaugh is about half a mile north. Just past the church, you'll find *The Crown Inn* (☎ 01434-681231, 🖳 www.crownhumshaugh.co.uk; bar daily noon-11pm, food served Wed-Sun noon-2pm & daily 5.30-8pm; WI-FI; 🐕 beer garden only), with hearty meals and real ale.

About 100 metres past the pub is the community-run **Humshaugh Village Shop** (☎ 01434-681258, 🖥 www.humshaughshop.co.uk; Mon-Fri 7.30am-1pm, Thur also 6-7pm, Sat 7.30am-noon, Sun 9am-noon, bank hols 9-11am) whose volunteers won the Queen's Award for Voluntary Service in 2016. It's only small, but they sell milk, bread, snacks and fruit & veg with a smile.

There's a **B&B** here too at a pleasant place: *Orchard View* (☎ 01434-681658, 🖥 www.northumberlandbedandbreakfast.biz; 1D or T/1Tr, both en suite; ☛; WI-FI; Ⓛ; Mar-Oct) charges from £40pp (sgl occ £70, three sharing £100).

There are two more smart B&Bs just past the entrance to Chesters Fort, and roughly half a mile north of the trail: *The Dovecote* (☎ 01434-681984, 🖥 dovecotehadrianswall.co.uk; 3D in the main house, 1D or T/1D in the dovecote, all en suite; WI-FI; Ⓛ; 🐾) charges £37.50-47.50pp (sgl occ rates on request), while just beyond it, *Leazes Head B&B* (☎ 01434-689014, 🖥 leazeshead.co.uk; 1D en suite, 1D/2T private bathroom facilities; ☛; WI-FI; Ⓛ; Mar-Oct) where B&B costs £37.50-47.50pp (sgl occ £55-80).

Transport-wise, the AD122 **bus** stops outside Chesters Roman fort. See pp46-8 for further information.

CHESTERS [Map 16, p143]
(☎ 01434-681379, 🖥 www.english-heritage.org.uk; Apr-Sep daily 10am-6pm, Oct daily 10am-4pm, Nov-Mar weekends only other than Feb half-term (winter days/hours subject to change, check in advance); adults £6.50, concessions £5.90, children £3.90, English Heritage members free.)

'Jack Bob and self went to Chesters to view the remains of the Roman Fort and Bridge.' Found in the **diary of a militia officer** and dated June 1761, proving that Wall tourism is not a new phenomenon.

In its day, Chesters, or **Cilurnum** (meaning, 'Cauldron Pool') as it would have been known then, was *the* fort in which to be stationed out of all of those on the Wall. Set on a beautiful spot amongst mature trees on a bend in the river, the fort was built to guard the nearby bridge over the North Tyne, covered 5¾ acres, and was inhabited by 500 members of the Roman cavalry – who were better paid than their infantry counterparts and seemed to have enjoyed slightly preferential treatment too. The Asturian cavalry from Spain is the auxiliary force most associated with Chesters.

The fort itself was built c AD130 on land previously occupied by Turret 27A. It was excavated by that one-man preservation society, John Clayton, in the 19th century, undoing the work of his father, Nathaniel Clayton, who had turfed over the fort ruins in order to enjoy a smooth, uninterrupted grassy slope to the River Tyne. John Clayton inherited the estate in 1832, and continued working on this and other Wall fortifications until his death in 1890.

Today's visitors will not only be able to **stamp their passports** (see box p40) at reception (or on the wall by the entrance when it's closed) but will also be able to enjoy the beautiful, traditional-style **museum** that Clayton established – full of dusty glass cases filled with some fascinating finds – as well as the ruins themselves. Top billing goes to the fort's **baths**, the highest of all the Roman ruins on the entire trail and located, as is usual, outside the fort itself, in this instance down the hill near the river.

These ruins give a really good idea of how the baths would have looked in their heyday, and how the water was channelled around and heated. Incidentally, during an early excavation of the baths in the 19th century, no fewer than 33 bodies, together with the remains of two horses and a dog, were discovered interred in the bathhouse. Curiously, their whereabouts is something of a mystery today, though at the time it was speculated that they dated back to the Saxon period. From the scattered remains beside the baths you can also make out how the Wall itself would have travelled across the bridge, up to the fort (some Wall remains abutting the fort can be seen), right through the spot where the large country house (Clayton's old home) now stands, and beyond into the hills.

CHOLLERFORD TO STEEL RIGG (FOR ONCE BREWED)
[Maps 16-23]

Introduction
Perhaps the most thrilling section of the entire walk, this is a **13-mile (21km; 5¼-6½hrs)** stage to be savoured. Encompassing the best-preserved fort on the Wall, the finest views, the most complete sections of the Wall, the northernmost point of the trail and some fabulous if slightly exhausting walking, this is a day for superlatives. So bring plenty of food and water with you (there's nowhere to stock up between Chesters and Housesteads apart from a seasonal café van at Brocolitia car park), bucketloads of stamina, and make sure your camera's fully charged – you'll be snapping photos all day.

The route
Despite the thrills to come, the day begins in a rather mundane fashion, with a bit of road walking along the by now all-too-familiar B6318 – the Military Road. Climbing up the hill, the path takes an unexpected right-hand turn at the

---

❏ **Northumberland National Park and the Dark Sky Park**
Walking along the trail from the east, when you cross the stile around the back of Walwick Hall, you are actually also crossing a boundary into Britain's most northerly national park. Covering 1048sq km (404.6 sq miles), or about a quarter of the entire county after which it is named, Northumberland National park stretches from Hadrian's Wall all the way up to the Scottish border; indeed, if you were to continue from the stile by Walwick Hall (see Map 16, p143) along the Hadrian's Wall Path, you'll find you won't actually leave the park until near Thirlwall Castle, almost 20 miles (32km) later.

The park is famous not only for what it has – including several rare species such as black grouse, pipistrelle bats, water voles and bog orchids – but also, beautifully, for what it lacks. The absence of any significant light pollution here means that visitors to the park are able to witness some of the clearest views of the night sky anywhere in the country. Indeed, such is the area's reputation in this respect that in 2013 the International Dark-Sky Association (the leading international organisation combating light pollution worldwide) awarded Dark Sky Park status to the entire area of Northumberland National Park and the adjacent Kielder Water and Forest Park, thus making it the largest protected Dark Sky Park in the whole of Europe. In giving the award the Association described the park as 'a wild and remote place that demonstrates an ability to conserve the dark skies above and a commitment to providing opportunities for the public to enjoy them'. The award was not only deserved but necessary, conferring as it does 'protection' on the clarity of the night sky, with controls in place to prevent light pollution from nearby sources.

tiny village of **Walwick** before heading around the back of a farm, then following the line of General Wade's highway. You enter **Northumberland National Park** at a stile here.

Soon after crossing the first possible turn-off for Green Carts Farm (see below) you come to the day's first treat: a cracking bit of Wall known as **Black Carts** that slopes ahead up the hill, has its own **turret** (No 29A) and is even joined, along its length, by the distinctive 'V' of the **Wall ditch**. (Incidentally, the grand house you can see to the north is Chipchase Castle, a medieval tower house with Jacobean and later additions.)

Green Carts Farm (Map 17; ☎ 01434-681320, 🖳 www.greencarts.co.uk) is about half a mile from the path and is, for many hikers, the best **campsite** (adult/child £5/2.50 inc use of shower/toilet facilities, coin-operated laundry facilities, electric hook up £3 extra) on the whole trail; super friendly, and with a super location in a huge grassy field with wonderful countryside views. They also offer **B&B** (3T/1D, all en suite; ➷; 🐾; WI-FI; 🅛; from £35pp, £50 sgl occ), a well-equipped **bunkhouse** (2 x 4-bed rooms; £25/20pp with/without breakfast, sgl occ rates on request; 🐾) with its own kitchen, toilets and shower, and a basic but delightful **camping barn** (sleeps 14; WI-FI; £12pp, bedding £3, breakfast £5) with some cooking facilities (kettle, toaster) and an old TV. Solo hikers can rent single bunks in the camping barn. The bunkhouse, though, is rented out per room, rather than per bed. If requested in advance, you can also get a takeaway cooked breakfast (£7), packed lunches (£6) and evening meals (from £12), or else you can order meals from the local Indian takeaway (ask the owners for a menu). Another rare bonus for a campsite is that the owners are usually able to accept cards for payment (as long as the wi-fi's working). If you are staying here it's quicker to take the first road to the right after passing turret 29A.

Eventually the Wall disappears but that's not the end of the Roman masonry on this part. At **Limestone Corner**, where the Wall and trail take a turn to the south-west, you'll find some large boulders lying in the Wall ditch that clearly display evidence of having been worked on by workmen – and specifically Roman workmen. The rock here is whinstone, a super-hard basalt stone, and it appears the Romans soon realised that trying to hack through this rock was pointless; so they left the blocks where they were and moved on. This is one theory, anyway, and it's interesting that the ditch does stop here (though it's worth noting that the Vallum continues unbroken on the other side of the road). Perhaps of more interest, Limestone Corner is the northernmost point of the trail – thus the Wall here would have been the northernmost point of the entire Roman Empire. Continue along the trail and, just before crossing the road you come to a turn-off for Hallbarns (off Map 18, around a mile from the trail – look for the signpost on the trail pointing north); *Hallbarns* (☎ 01434-681419, 🖳 www.hallbarns-simonburn.co.uk; 1T/2Qd en suite, 1T private facilities; ➷; 🐾 sleep in stable; WI-FI; 🅛), a pleasant **B&B** (£30-40pp, sgl occ £40-60, three/four sharing rates on request) with drying facilities. They can also provide an evening meal if booked in advance. *(cont'd on p150)*

148 Chollerford to Steel Rigg (for Once Brewed)

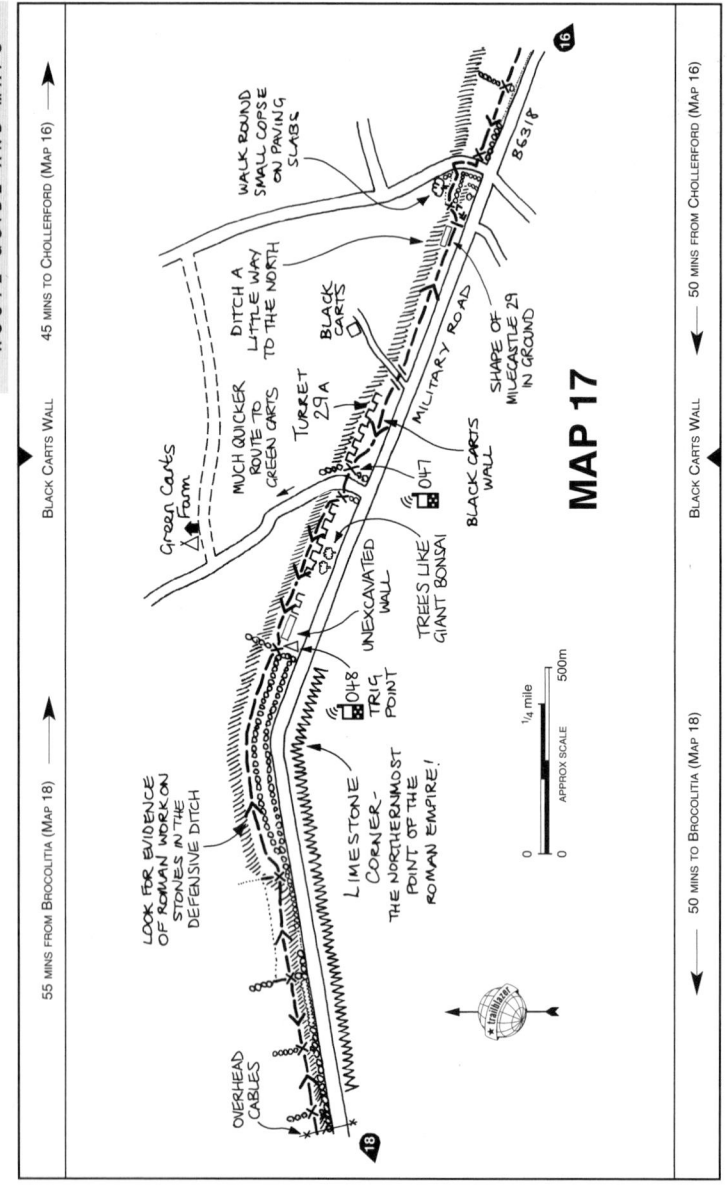

Map 18, Brocolitia Roman Fort 149

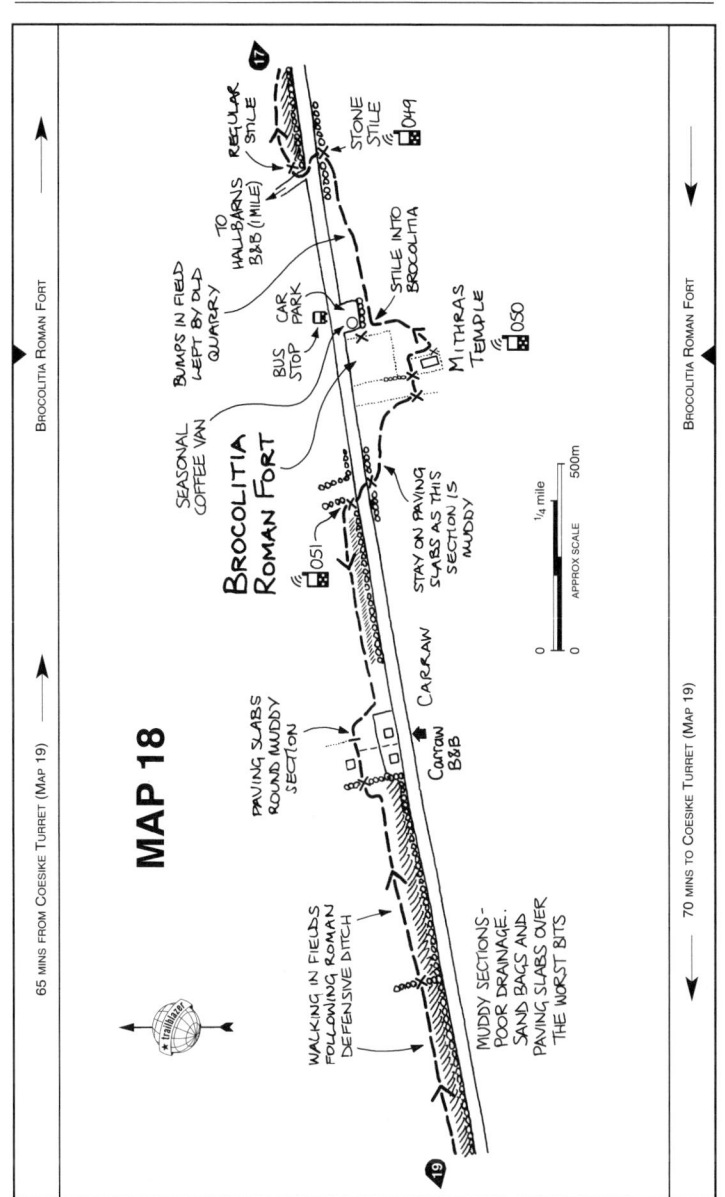

(cont'd from p147) The next piece of Roman architecture lies across the road from the turn off to Hallbarns. **Brocolitia Fort** (aka Carrawburgh, pronounced 'Carrawbruff'; Map 18) remains unexcavated. It is, however, an unusual fort, clearly built some time after the Wall, for Brocolitia actually lies over the infilled Vallum. It was around this site in 1876 that John Clayton opened up Coventina's Well and discovered 13,487 coins (4 gold, 184 silver and the rest bronze) which would have been tossed into the water for good luck – just as we throw money into wishing wells today. Three hundred of these coins commemorated the pacification of northern Britain following disturbances in AD155; Britannia, who may be found on the back of some 50p coins looking regal and serene, appears slumped and forlorn on these Roman coins.

In addition to the money, Clayton also found carved stones, altars, jars, pearls, brooches and incense burners – the religious stuff having been deliberately placed here for safe keeping following the Theodosian Edict banning pagan temples in AD391 (see box pp152-3). Much of this can be seen at Chesters Museum (see pp145-6). Coventina, by the way, was a local goddess associated with water; as you may have already seen at the temple to Antenociticus in Newcastle (see box pp96-7), the Roman Empire was largely tolerant of other religions and beliefs and even assimilated certain local gods into their pantheon, in much the same way that Hinduism has done with both Christianity and Buddhism.

Though Brocolitia is once more underground, the nearby **Mithras Temple** (see box pp152-3) is open to both the skies and the public, though the altars are mere copies of the originals now housed in Newcastle's Great North Museum: Hancock. The temple was rediscovered by John Gillam in 1949 when a particularly dry summer 'shrank' the surrounding peat to reveal the stones. Mithraism was one of the more popular religions on the Wall and two other Mithraeums, at Carrawburgh and Rudchester, have been unearthed.

During high season, lucky hikers will sometimes find Corbridge Coffee Company's **coffee van** (☎ 07855-301918) parked in the car park at Brocolitia. They serve tea, snacks and good strong coffee – just the ticket for this rather exposed, sometimes windswept stretch.

Returning to the **Roman ditch** on the northern side of the road, the trail continues through **Northumberland National Park**. *Carraw B&B* (☎ 01434-689857, 🖥 www.carraw.co.uk; 5D/3D or T/1Tr, all en suite; 🐾; WI-FI; 🅛) is a high-quality place (£42.50-55pp, sgl occ £67.50-95, three sharing £150) on the main road right next to the trail. They have very comfortable rooms – four in the Farmhouse, five in the Lodge – and while not serving dinner as such they do offer a 'Carraw supper', namely a bowl of homemade soup and a ploughman's platter (£12.50) served at 6.30pm. They are also licensed to sell alcohol.

Continuing on the trail alongside the ditch, where the B6318 drifts to the left, there's a ladder stile in the wall. Though tempting to cross here onto the road, those staying in **Grindon** should continue on the trail past **Milecastle 33** (Map 19) and then climb onto the road at the next **ladder stile**, where there's a brief reunion with the Military Road. Turn right and, on the junction with the road down to Grindon you'll come to the wonderful **B&B** that is the *Old*

Map 19, Grindon Milecastle 151

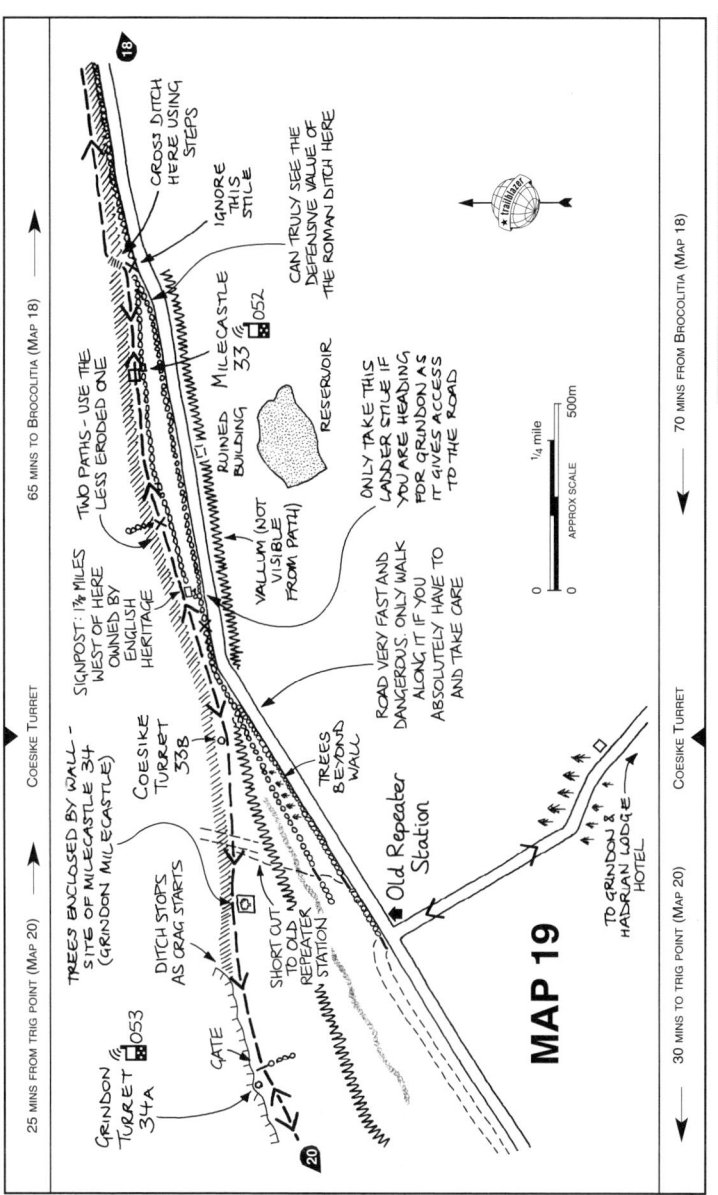

Repeater Station (Map 19; ☎ 01434-688668, 🖳 www.hadrians-wall-bedand breakfast.co.uk; 1S/1D/1T, 1 bunk-bed room sleeps 4, all en suite; WI-FI; 🐕) which charges £35-40pp (sgl/sgl occ £65) and £99/119 for a family/four adults sharing the bunk-bed room including breakfast. A lovely converted stone-and-

❏ THE MYSTERY RELIGION OF MITHRAISM

Much has contributed to the relative lack of modern-day understanding of Mithraism, a mysterious religion centred around the worship of the god Mithras, and practised throughout the Roman Empire from about the 1st to the 4th century AD. The distant era in which it enjoyed its greatest popularity is clearly a factor, as is the secrecy with which it was practised and the attempts that various people made down the centuries to suppress it. Another factor is that much of the written information we do have for the faith comes not from its adherents – the secrecy surrounding the faith was both strict and all-encompassing – but from its detractors, such as the early Church fathers; people whom, it must be remembered, were probably not the most reliable of sources. However, although the followers themselves were silent about their faith, their iconography, by comparison, speaks volumes; and this iconography, found in every Mithraeum (Mithraic temple) throughout the Roman Empire, including those discovered at Hadrian's Wall, has taught us most of what we know about this clandestine religion.

The origins of the faith are still uncertain, with one school of thought believing it to be Persian, dating back as far as 1400BC, while another suggests it was a near-contemporary of Christianity. Plutarch mentions it in 67BC, while the earliest physical remains date from the 1st century AD. Whatever its genesis, we do know that the Mithraic faith quickly gathered a huge following. One of the likely reasons for this popularity was its adoption as the unofficial faith of Roman soldiers. Though originally appealing to slaves and freedmen, the Mithraic emphasis on truth, honour, bravery and discipline would have appealed to the Roman army who would probably have proselytised the faith wherever they were stationed.

Mithraism enjoyed its heyday in the 2nd century AD; by the 5th century it had all but disappeared. The first blow came with the *sole* accession of Theodosius to the imperial throne in AD392 (prior to this he had ruled with two other 'emperors'). The last emperor of a united Roman Empire (following his demise the split between the empire's western and eastern halves, which first appeared at the beginning of the 4th century AD, became permanent), Theodosius was also the first emperor to make Christianity the official religion and went out of his way to promote his chosen faith, issuing edicts and encouraging Christian subjects to attack pagan buildings. One edict in particular, issued in AD391 before he became sole ruler, banned the worship of pagan gods, and many Mithraic temples were destroyed at this time.

The Mithraic organisation
The faith was a complicated one. Its followers were organised into a strict **hierarchy** of seven grades, or levels. An initiate new to the faith would have been known as a *Corax*, or 'Raven', the first and lowest level in the Mithraic hierarchy. At the other end of the spectrum was the rank of '*Pater*', or 'Father', the seventh and highest level. Their clothes, such as the colour of their tunic or the mask they wore at Mithraic rituals, indicated which rank they belonged to.

Rising through the ranks was no easy matter. Near to many Mithraic temples, including Carrawburgh, an 'ordeal' pit has been found, with a bench very close to what would have been a large fire. It is assumed that followers would have undergone some sort of physical trial by fire, cold or fasting in order to climb to the next level.

slate building that makes extensive use of eco-technology (including boreholes, biowaste systems, solar panels and the like), this one-man operation is run by the affable, laconic Les, a man never less than generous with his teapot, and a great cook to boot. Call in advance if you want an evening meal (they are

The Mithraic beliefs: one theory

As a reward for rising through the ranks, the faithful were given revelations into the secrets and mysteries of the faith. According to their beliefs, the god Mithras was born either from the living rock or from a tree. An early life filled with pain and hardship culminated in the **defeat and slaughter of the primeval bull**. This killing allowed the life force of the bull to be released for the benefit of humanity: plants and herbs came from the bull's body, while wine came from the bull's blood and all livestock came from the slayed bull's semen. This victory over the primeval bull, known as the **tauroctony**, would have been depicted in every Mithraeum and each time the same few characters appear in the picture, namely a dog, scorpion, snake and raven, as well as Mithras's torchbearers, Cautes and Cautopates.

As for the Mithraeum itself, it would originally have been quite a dark and gloomy place. Indeed, the temples were usually constructed underground in order to simulate the cave in which Mithras was supposed to have killed the primeval bull. Entering via a door in the south-west corner, a worshipper would have first found himself in a small antechamber with a bench and what would have been a large fire, originally the ordeal pit. Beyond a wickerwork screen at the end lay the nave, with benches arranged along the side to allow the faithful to recline when partaking of ritual meals. Four small altars lay at the end of these benches. It is estimated that the average temple would have been able to hold between 30 and 50 men.

Mithraic beliefs: an alternative theory

For 70 years or so, this interpretation of Mithraism was held to be the definitive one. There was, however, one small problem. The whole reason it was believed that Mithraism came from the east is because the name 'Mithras' is the Latin form of the Iranian god Mithra; that, and the fact that the Roman authors themselves believed it to have come from Persia. But if Mithraism did have its origins in Persia and the Indian subcontinent, why have there never been any discoveries of Mithraism in Iran or any parallels in the folklore and mythologies of that region?

Thus, recently, a new interpretation has been suggested. This postulates that the depiction of Mithras slaying the bull, with the dog, raven, snake and scorpion as onlookers, and the torchbearers, Cautes and Cautopates, in attendance, is in fact a symbolic depiction of the cosmos, with the *dramatis personae* symbols of the zodiac. For example, the dog is in fact a representation of the constellation Canis Minor, and Cautes and Cautopates are the sun and moon respectively.

In this theory, therefore, the reason these temples were 'built' underground is because this subterranean chamber represents the night sky. This new theory may sound far-fetched at first but gathers credence when we look at the remains of Mithraea on the Wall. In particular, at Housesteads, there is one depiction of Mithras emerging from what has been called a Cosmic Egg – a depiction of the cosmos in an oval frame. Could it be that this singular sculpture, found in a remote fort in a far-flung corner of Rome's conquered territories, holds the key to our understanding of this empire-wide faith?

licensed too) or accommodation out of the main season. **Internet access** (charity donation welcome) is available all day (including to non-residents), and Les will even sometimes let you **camp** in the garden if he's full and you're stuck. A repeater station, by the way, was a building located roughly halfway between telephone exchanges and was where the signals on telephone cables were amplified to compensate for the loss of electricity which made speech fainter and led to a loss of clarity. Just over a mile (1.6km) further south, down on North Rd, *Hadrian Lodge Hotel* (off Map 19; ☎ 01434-684867, 🖳 www.hadrianlodge.co.uk; 3D/2T/1D or T/1Tr/two rooms sleeping up to five people, all en suite; ➡; 🐾; WI-FI; Ⓛ; Mar-Nov), which despite the name is in fact a B&B, is a comfy and rather smart place that offers free lifts to and from the Wall, has its own **bar** and offers **evening meals** (but subject to prior arrangement). B&B costs £37-45pp (sgl occ £56-63, three to five people sharing £106-156).

Those not staying in Grindon should continue along the line of the Wall where you will find that the trail leaves the road for good to aim for the comprehensive remains of **Turret 33B**, known as **Coesike Turret**. It then heads up towards the small copse surrounded by a wall that marks the site of **Milecastle 34 (Grindon Milecastle)**. The next turret, **Grindon Turret** or, more prosaically, **Turret 34A**, hides behind the next wall. Both it and Coesike Turret – indeed, maybe all the turrets on the Wall – were probably abandoned less than a century after they were built, before the end of the 2nd century AD, as the Wall forts were established. But unlike the others, after the Romans had gone both these turrets had *shielings* (herdsmen's huts) built into their remains, from which we get the name Sewingshields. Note how the ditch ends abruptly shortly after Grindon Milecastle. The reason for this becomes clear once you notice the area's topography, for it is here that the crags start; crags that form a natural barrier, thus make the digging of a defensive ditch entirely unnecessary.

More Roman delights await beyond **Sewing Shields Farm** (Map 20) at the crest of the hill. This is a **fine stretch of Wall** and begins at the end of the woods that shelter the farm. To the south of the trail the land slopes away gently down to the Military Road but to the north a 200ft (about 60 metres) drop awaits those who cross the Wall. These are **Sewingshields Crags**, a wild and rugged land that, perhaps unsurprisingly, has become the setting of a number of myths and legends, many concerning those stalwarts of British folktales, King Arthur and his knights. Sewingshields Castle, which used to stand at the foot of the crags, was also used by Walter Scott as the setting for his story *Harold the Dauntless*. Whatever the truth or otherwise of the stories surrounding Sewingshields, there's no doubt that the Romans clearly saw no need to construct a defensive ditch to the north of the Wall here. Coming to **Milecastle 35**, you see that, with such a large drop to the north, there's no northern gate here either, presumably for the same reason. Note, too, that the Vallum is now quite a way south of the Wall, where the ground is less stony.

❏ **Walk side by side and on healthy grass** In other words don't walk in single file or on worn areas. Protect our heritage!

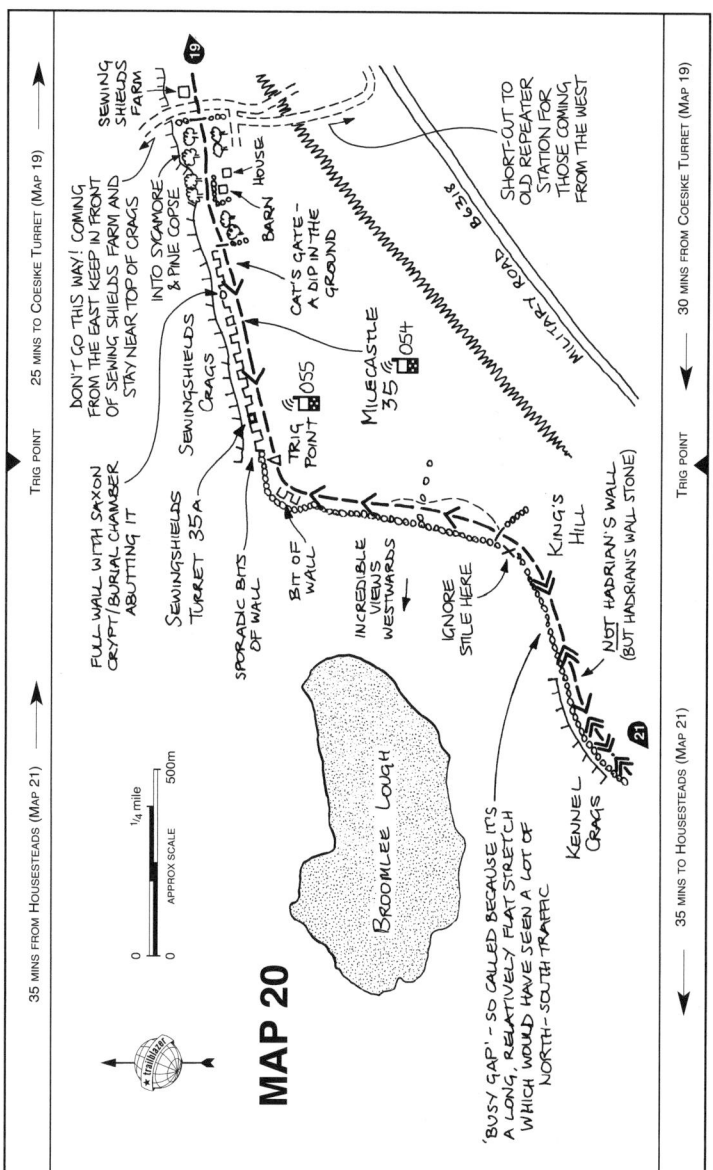

Map 20, Sewingshields Crags 155

156 Chollerford to Steel Rigg (for Once Brewed)

For many people, this is the start of the most splendid part of the trail, with great views, wonderful walking and a really fine, extensive piece of Wall. Though the Wall proper stops at the top of the hill, just past the **trig point**, it is replaced by something more modern and only slightly less attractive which leads all the way to Housesteads Fort, the Wall's finest.

Those not wishing to visit Housesteads should enter the grounds then turn right through **Knag Burn Gate** (Map 21). This was another Roman gateway through the Wall, similar in that respect to Port Gate which many of you will have passed on the previous stage. This gate, however, was introduced into the Wall only in the 4th century AD, presumably to allow the considerable number of locals who lived around the fort to move between the northern and southern sides of the Wall with greater ease. The trail continues north of the Wall, until the far side of Housesteads is reached.

Those who *do* wish to visit the fort, however, should continue to the south of the Wall to the ticket office, near the fort's south-west corner. Note that this office is a **passport stamping station**. They also sell hot drinks, snacks and sandwiches but have no seating (save for a couple of plastic chairs in the museum, and a bench outside the ticket office). The **toilets** here are in a Portaloo only. For proper toilets, saunter downhill to the car park, where there's another gift shop with a slightly larger selection of drinks and snacks and some more outdoor seating. The AD122 **bus** calls in at the car park here; see pp46-8 for further information.

HOUSESTEADS [Map 21]
(☎ *01434-344363*, 🖥 *www.english-heritage.org.uk* or 🖥 *www.nationaltrust .org.uk; Easter-Sep daily 10am-6pm, Oct 10am-5pm, Nov-Easter 10am-4pm, winter days/hours subject to change, check in advance; adults £7, concessions £6.20, children £4.10, English Heritage & National Trust members free)*
'The grandest station in the whole line – in some stations the antiquary feeds upon shells, but here upon kernels' **William Hutton**, 1802 (see pp60-1)

This quote pretty much sums up Housesteads. For if you visit only one fort on the Wall, make it this one. Housesteads is the one place where you can really get a feel for how a Roman fort would have looked. Where the ruins of most other sites are rather fragmentary and barely break the surface of the earth, here the walls in places run to six courses or more – up to 10ft (almost 3m) high – with only the roof apparently missing to complete the structure. For this, as usual, considerable thanks must go to John Clayton, who bought the site in 1838 to protect and excavate it.

By positioning yourself up near the Wall at the top of the hill near the North Gate, you get a great overview of the fort as well as some incomparable views north and south, which is presumably why the Romans built it here in the first place. Known to them as **Vercovicium**, Housesteads was constructed around AD122, making it one of the first to be built along the Wall, and housed around 800 men on its five acres. The First Cohort of Tungrians from Belgium is the auxiliary unit most associated with Housesteads, having been based here in the 3rd and 4th centuries AD.

Map 21, Housesteads 157

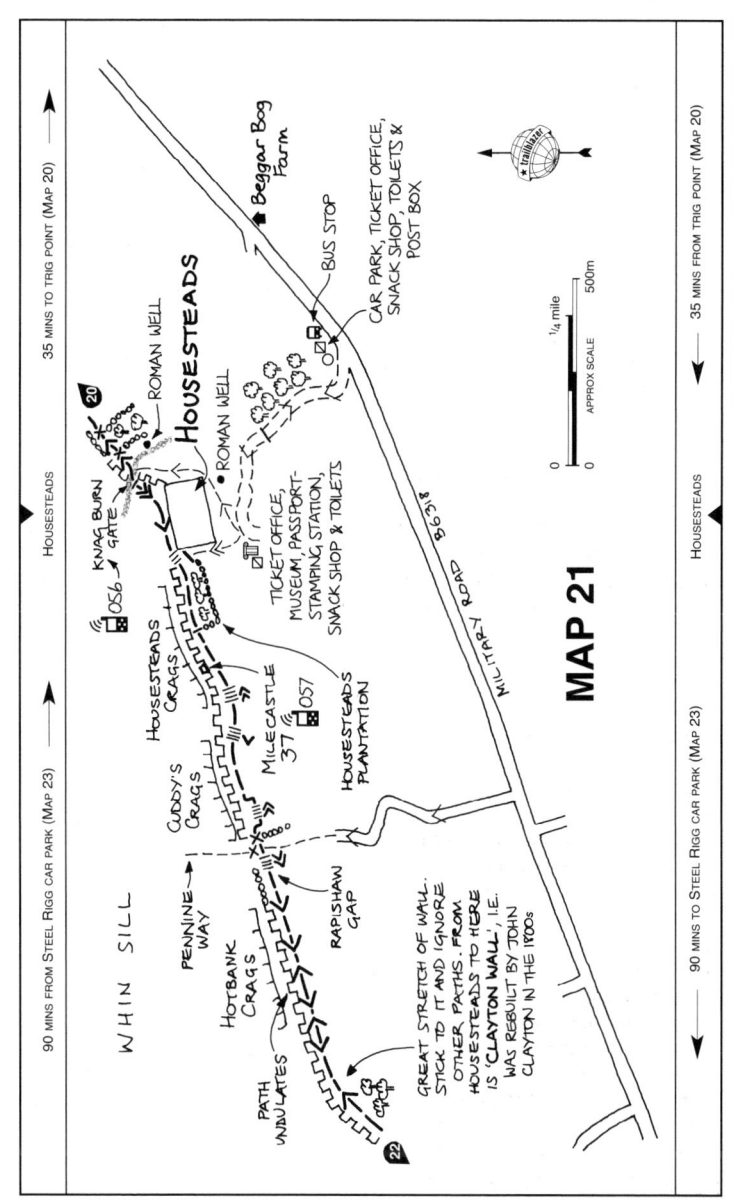

While the fort has the usual playing-card shape, its layout is not entirely typical. For one thing, you'll notice as you approach the fort from the trail that the *whole* of Housesteads lies south of the Wall, unlike Chesters, Segedunum and other sites which protrude north beyond the line of the Wall. Furthermore, Housesteads is elongated west–east (with the **Military Way** forming its central axis), where the longest axis of other forts runs north–south. The central core of the fort is familiar, with the **headquarters** at the centre and the Commander's House or **praetorium** next door. However, on this occasion, the latter lies to the south of the HQ, not to the east as is more typical, probably because the whole fort lies on a ridge and slope. As is usual, the **granaries** and the **hospital** lie nearby, with the near-complete ruins of the **latrines** in the south-eastern corner of the fort. To the south, in the extensive civilian settlement outside the fort walls stands the **Murder House**, so-called because the skeleton of a man with a knife stuck between his ribs was discovered during excavations.

West of here lies the revamped **museum**, where, via the medium of scale models, film, Roman finds and CGI recreations of Roman buildings, you get a good idea of what the place may have looked like 2000 years ago.

For those who have had enough for the day ***Beggar Bog Farm*** (Map 21; ☎ 01434-344652, 🖳 www.beggarbog.co.uk; 1D/1T, both en suite; 🐕 allowed in a separate building; Ⓛ; Mar-Nov) lies a few hundred metres east of the turn-off to the fort on the Military Road. A traditional stone-built farmhouse offering **B&B** (£37.50pp, sgl occ full room rate) in a separate self-contained annexe, Beggar Bog is a smart and friendly place with great breakfasts surpassed only by the view from its elevated position up towards Housesteads and along the Military Road. Evening meals subject to prior arrangement.

The final section of this stage is no less breathtaking. Indeed, this is the finest section of Wall, known as the 'Clayton Wall' after the archaeologist John Clayton who bought and rebuilt this section. You can tell a bit of Clayton Wall as opposed to regular, unreconstructed Roman Wall because Clayton's method of rebuilding differed from the original Roman style, with no mortar and a turf top. This includes the section of Wall immediately after Housesteads that leads through the wooded Housesteads Plantation. The National Trust owns the Wall for three miles west of Housesteads; it owns the fort too, though the day-to-day maintenance of it remains in the hands of English Heritage. Don't forget to occasionally walk up to the Wall to savour the magical views stretching away to the north. This is Northumberland's version of the Lake District, with Bromlee Lough (Map 20) immediately to the north, Greenlee Lough to its west and Crag Lough (Map 22) further along the trail.

Continuing your climb, you pass **Milecastle 37**, one of the best preserved and perhaps the most important on the Wall. It was excavated by Clayton in 1853. Note the start of an archway over the north gate, from which the experts were able to extrapolate the height of the arch and from this the height of the milecastle. (Why a north gate was deemed necessary here but not at Milecastle 35 – see p154 – is unclear, for they both have steep drops to the north.) You can also see holes in the floor by the southern entrance – postholes for the wooden door. This whole ridge that you are walking across is called the **Whin Sill**, while

Map 22, Sycamore Gap (& Vindolanda) 159

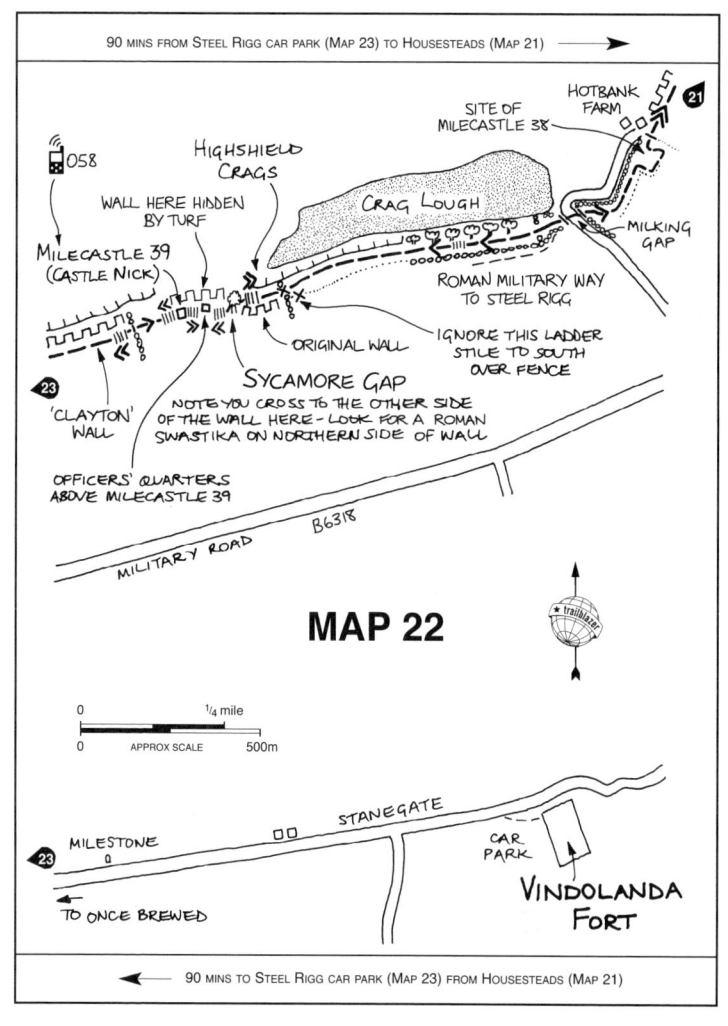

the section you are on now is known locally as **Cuddy's Crags**, after St Cuthbert. Continuing along the top of the crags, eventually the path drops down to **Hotbank Farm** (Map 22), owned by the National Trust and built by the **site of Milecastle 38**. (The trail circumvents this milecastle to avoid further damage to the site; it was this stretch of Wall that suffered so much from the group of bankers who walked on it in 2004, see p63). It was near here that part of an inscribed stone was found that stated the second legion built this milecastle under the governorship of Aulus Platorius Nepos. As Aulus was governor during Hadrian's time, it provided archaeologists with almost irrefutable proof that this was Hadrian's Wall and not, as had previously been believed, Severus's (see box p51).

Beyond the farm the trail now dodges through a gate to head along the north side of the line of the Wall, then goes through a pleasant wood with **Crag Lough** glittering in the sunlight below. The path then follows a familiar pattern, rising and falling with the undulations of the land. This includes a drop to the iconic **Sycamore Gap**, named after the solitary tree growing in the dip, which gained fame when it featured alongside Kevin Costner in the film *Robin Hood*.

Following the gap, there's a climb up past the remains of some **officers' quarters**, unique on the Wall, and **Milecastle 39** to **Peel Crags** (Map 23), before the path falls again to Peel Gap and the very steep **Cat Stairs** via the remains of a turret. Curiously, this is an extra turret, ie a third turret in the mile between milecastles 39 and 40 where normally there would only be two. Presumably it was built to watch over Peel Gap, which is all but invisible from the two turrets on either side. The first road for almost six miles (9.6km) runs through the gap and **Steel Rigg car park** lies hidden away behind trees at the top of the hill. If you didn't join the road down to Once Brewed via the shortcut round the back of Peel Bothy (see Map 23), you can do so from here.

ONCE BREWED [Map 23]

A popular overnight spot with Wall walkers, Once Brewed is tiny, but nevertheless boasts a decent pub, an excellent campsite and, by the time you read this, a state-of-the-art visitor centre and brand-new YHA hostel. It also sports a curious name ... and a legend: according to the story, General Wade, he of Military Road fame and bane of Bonnie Prince Charlie, once stayed at an inn here and, unhappy with the quality of the beer, ordered it to be brewed again. Hence the name – or at least that's how one story has it.

Though still a building site at the time of research, the former Northumberland National Park visitor centre and the old YHA hostel were due to reopen in the latter half of 2017, as part of a £14.2 million lottery-funded project that would see them transformed into the country's first **National Landscape Discovery Centre** (🖥 www.northumberlandnationalpark.org.uk/sill), aka The Sill. The idea is for the centre to help open up the area's rich history and fabulous landscape to families, children and people with disabilities who might otherwise not have the confidence or the ability to explore the region. Its modern, all-glass design will include a fully accessible 'living roof' with sweeping views of the surrounding countryside and the Wall. There'll be a large café, an all-singing-and-dancing tourist information centre, exhibition spaces, and a new improved 86-bed YHA hostel, *YHA The Sill at Hadrian's Wall* (🖥 www.yha.org.uk/hostel/sill-hadrians-wall; 8 x 2-, 3 x 3-, 8 x 4-bed rooms, all en suite, 8 x 4-bed room separate facilities; WI-FI). The hostel will be licensed and meals will be provided. The 3-bed rooms have a double bed. There will be a shop, self-catering and laundry facilities, a drying room and 24hr access. At the time of writing the rates and opening details had not been finalised; for further details contact the YHA (see p19), or visit the website.

Those not staying at the YHA could try to get one of the smart rooms at the local pub, just a couple of hundred metres down the road: *Twice Brewed Inn* (☎ 01434-344534, 🖥 www.twicebrewedinn.co.uk; 10T/7D/1D or T/1Qd, all en suite; 🛏; WI-FI; 🅛; 🐾), whilst not *quite* so accommodating as to rebrew your beer, still does its best to please, and provides many a happy

Map 23, Once Brewed

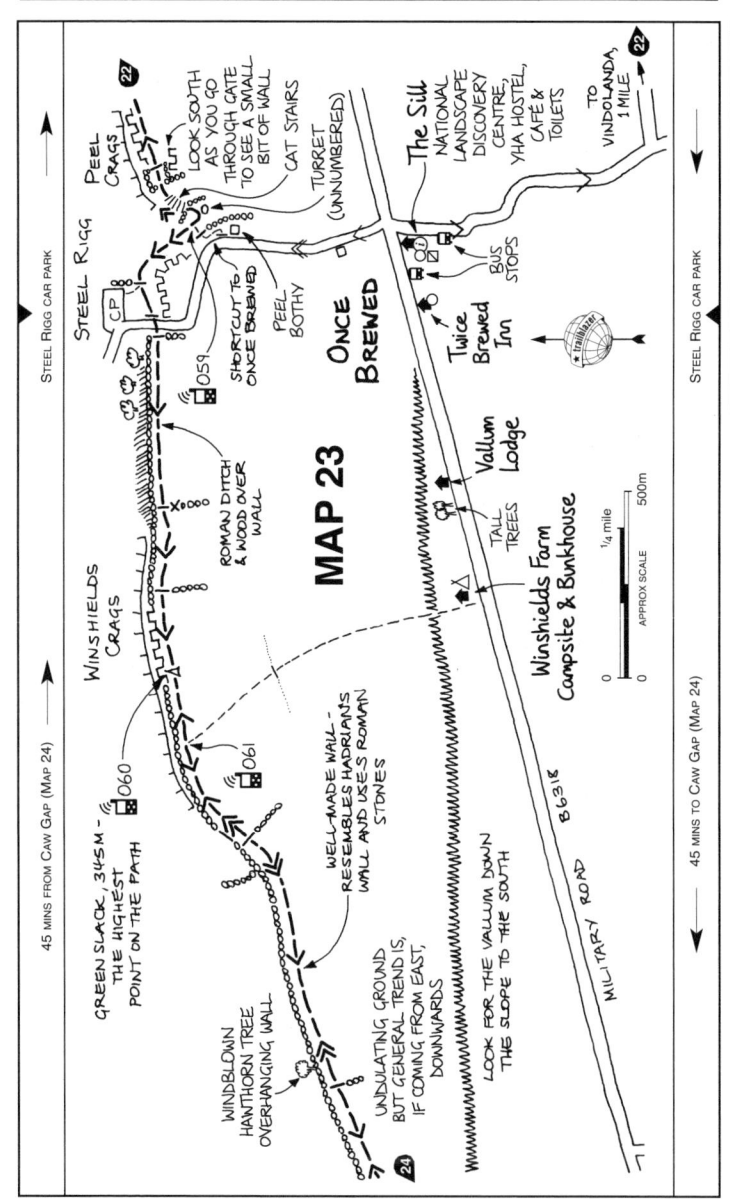

hiker with a meal, a pint, and a bed for the night. B&B here costs £42.50pp (sgl occ £67.50, three/four sharing £100). They serve good-quality pub **food** (summer Mon-Sat noon-9pm, Sun noon-8pm; mains £11-14) and a decent selection of real ales.

Other B&B accommodation in the area includes **Vallum Lodge** (☎ 01434-344248, 🖳 www.vallum-lodge.co.uk; 2D/5D or T, all en suite; ☛; WI-FI; Ⓛ; mid Mar-Oct), which charges £45pp (sgl occ room rate). One of the doubles can have another bed for a child. They also have a so-called 'snug'; a double with its own kitchen/living room that costs £55pp (sgl occ room rate). A short walk further west is the excellent

Winshields Farm Campsite (☎ 01434-344243, 🖳 www.winshields.co.uk; Apr-Oct), with **camping** (£9pp; 🐕), and four **bunkhouses** (£12pp) sleeping four, eight, ten and twelve people. There are shower/toilet facilities, as you'd expect, but also a drying room, a small shop and a nice little **café** (daily Apr-Oct 7am till about 5pm; Ⓛ) in the farmhouse, offering cooked breakfasts (7-9am) and packed lunches. A path from the back of the farmhouse leads directly to the trail.

The **AD122 bus** calls in at the National Park Visitor Centre; see pp46-8 for details. If in need of a **taxi**, call Sprouls Taxis (☎ 01434-321064, or ☎ 07712-321064).

VINDOLANDA [Map 22, p159]
(☎ 01434-344277, 🖳 www.vindolanda.com; daily Apr-Sep 10am-6pm, Oct 10am-5pm, mid Feb-Mar 10am-5pm, Nov-mid Feb check website for details. Entry to Vindolanda costs £7 for adults, concessions £6, children £4.25, family £20; a joint-saver ticket with entrance to Carvoran Roman Army Museum, see p171, costs £11/10/6/32; 10% discount for English Heritage members)

According to a panel of experts at the British Museum, the artefacts found at the fort at Vindolanda are collectively the single most important historic find on these shores, beating such treasures as the Anglo-Saxon hoard at the Sutton Hoo burial, the Roman Mildenhall Treasure and the Lewis Chessmen.

Upon first arriving at Vindolanda, you may well wonder what all the fuss is about. Sure the 1½-mile (2km) walk or bus ride (see above) from Once Brewed is nice enough, with a Roman milepost along the road and some decent views of Sycamore Gap. But once through the gates there's none of the spectacular, near-complete ruins found at Housesteads.

Here at Vindolanda the remains rise only just above foundation level. What's more, the only impressive structures on the site are the modern mock-ups of Hadrian's Wall – one in timber-and-turf and one in stone – that overlook the ongoing archaeological work from the south.

Nevertheless, as those experts at the British Museum tell us, this is *the* most important site along the whole of the Wall. Indeed, it's *the* most important site in Roman Britain, and when the excavation is finally finished – a job that, according to some estimates, could take at least another hundred years – it could even turn out to be the most important Roman site in *the entire world*. And the reason why can be seen in the **museum** at the rear of the site. For thanks to a fortunate combination of silt and water in the soil at Vindolanda, an incredible array of artefacts has been uncovered here, preserved in the earth, providing us with a hitherto unrivalled glimpse into the everyday life of the Roman Empire. Most famously, this is where, in 1973, Robin Birley (having bought the Vindolanda site back in 1929; his old home now houses the museum) discovered the so-called **Roman postcards** (aka Vindolanda postcards) – paper-thin, postcard-sized wooden writing tablets used by the Romans for everything from official reports to birthday invitations, and from school homework to love letters. Many of the 1900 or so tablets that have so far been discovered are now in the care of the British Museum, though the museum in Vindolanda has some of them on loan and examples of some of the best, too, including a letter from a concerned mother promising to send her son more underwear to protect him from the bitter British winter and the icy northern wind that blows up the toga at certain times of the year. Then we have a misquote from Virgil's *Aeneid* written in a schoolchild's hand, after which somebody else – presumably the teacher – has written 'seg', short for *segnis* or 'sloppy work'. There's also the tablet with the famous reference to the 'Britunculli', or 'wretched Britons'. Humdrum, mundane and everyday, these tablets nevertheless add much colour to our understanding of life in the Roman Empire.

In 2012 Professor Birley's son Andrew discovered more of the aqueduct and piping system – used to supply the site with fresh water during Roman times – that had been first discovered by his father 80 years before. They also found the original spring which would have fed the whole system.

Plenty of other objects amaze as well. Take the beautifully intricate leather sandals, for example, discarded casually by the inhabitants into a ditch when broken but immaculately preserved to this day. There are also keys, cutlery, pottery, weapons and even fragments of glass with a gladiatorial scene painted upon them, in colours that are still as vibrant today as they must have been nearly 2000 years ago. Overall, the museum at Vindolanda is a fascinating, absorbing, mind-boggling collection that will ruin your planned schedule for the day. But it also brings home just what life on the Wall during the Roman era was like more than any other attraction on the walk. Don't miss it, or it will haunt you for the rest of your walk.

The **AD122 bus** calls here; see pp46-8 for further information.

STEEL RIGG TO BANKS [Maps 23-30]

Introduction

While this **12½-mile (20km; 6-6¼hrs)** stage may not be quite as spectacular as the previous one, it is arguably the most interesting. It's also something of a redletter day, for it is on this stage that you climb to the highest point of the entire trail. It is on this stage, too, that you cross from Northumberland into Cumbria and the scenery changes from the windswept moors and crags that provided the previous stage's backdrop to the more gentle, rolling, cultivated landscape of England's far north-west. You also cross the watershed on this stage, so that by the end of it any river you encounter from now on flows west to the Irish Sea, not east to the North Sea as had previously been the case.

The limestone runs out on this stage, too, at Banks where the Red Rock Fault splits the country. Moreover, to the west of Gilsland, at Willowford Bridge, the Wall was originally made of turf (possibly because of the lack of limestone) and rebuilt in stone only later. Also at Willowford, the broad foundations that have held up the Wall so far are reduced; from now on it is narrow

---

❑ **Walk side by side and on healthy grass** In other words where possible don't walk in single file or on worn areas in order to protect the fragile earth.

164 Steel Rigg to Banks

wall on *narrow* foundations. And, at the River Irthing, the remains of the third Roman bridge on your walk can be seen; a bridge which once would have carried both the Wall and the Military Way. Quite a stage indeed. And that's before any mention has been made of all the turrets, forts and milecastles – and even, uniquely, a Roman watchtower – that are encountered along the way.

One word of warning, however, before you set off: though this stage ends in Banks, there is just one B&B-cum-campsite there. As such, be prepared to have to stay somewhere before Banks – for example at Greenhead (see p172) or Gilsland (p176) – or to attempt a longer walk to Walton (p184). Off the trail there are some more B&Bs at Haltwhistle (pp167-8) which provide further options.

The route

The day's first treat lies just a 10-minute walk from Steel Rigg car park. This is **Green Slack** (Map 23) on Winshields Crags, and at 345m is the highest point on the trail, with a decent section of Roman Wall leading up to it. Whilst the rest of the stage is only slightly less exhausting than the relentless up-and-down rollercoaster ride of the previous stage, it is at least some comfort that, for the rest of the trip, there'll be more downhill than uphill!

If you feel like taking a breather while you're up here, according to scientists there's no better place in England to take it: the lichen that grows on Winshields Crags requires extremely pure air and, apart from Dartmoor, this is

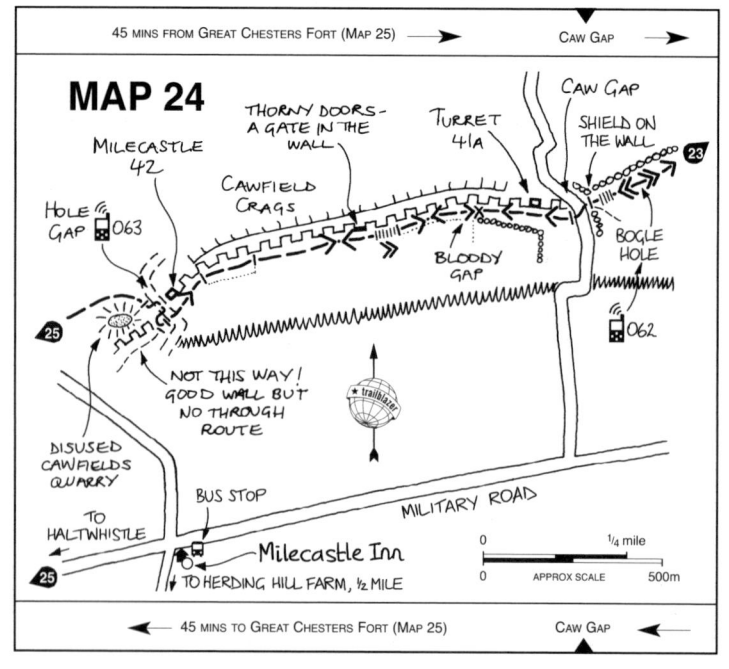

Map 25, Great Chesters Fort 165

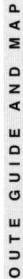

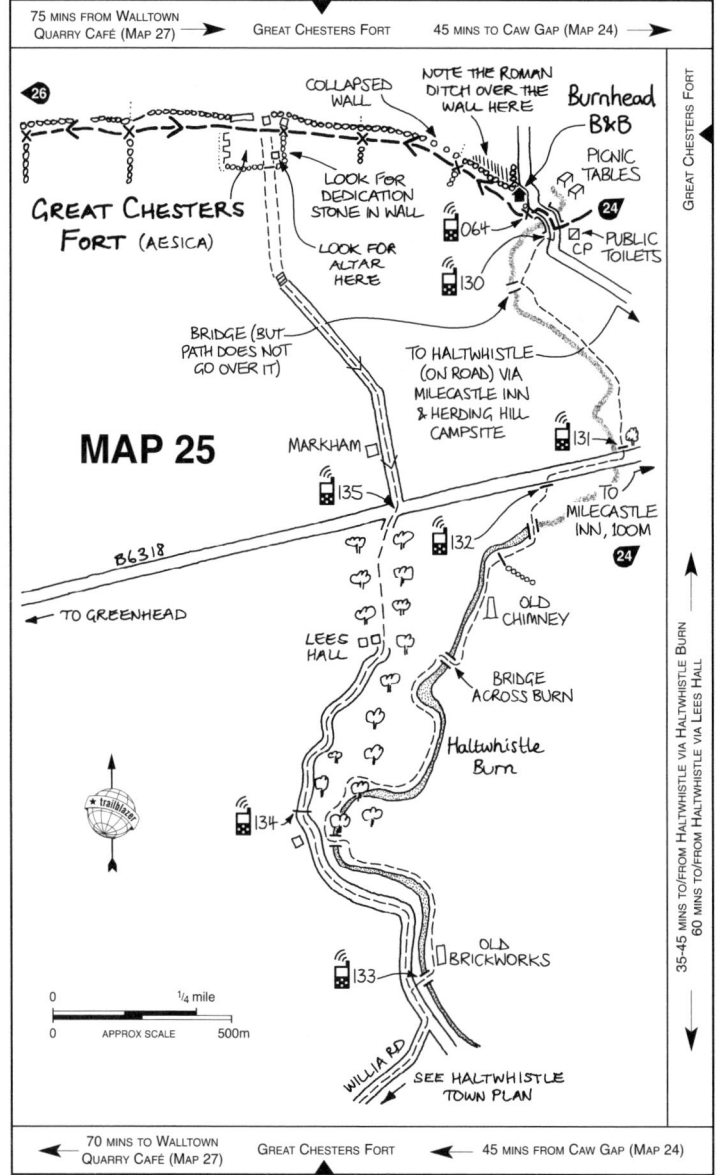

the only place in the entire country where the air is clean enough for this lichen to thrive. The trail varies little for the next two miles (3km) or so as you ride the crest of the crags, following the undulations through wild territory uninhabited since Roman times. The names printed on the maps – Bogle Hole, Caw Gap, Bloody Gap, Thorny Doors – only serve to add to the sense that you're in a land of folklore and myth.

After **Caw Gap** (Map 24) the Wall continues unbroken for over half a mile (1km). Look out for the swastika etched by the Romans into one of the Wall stones – another symbol of prosperity – on the way to **Milecastle 42**, which originally had an entrance in the north Wall until, presumably, the builders saw the steep drop beneath, realised such a door was unnecessary and blocked it up. The trail then rounds the flooded, disused quarry at **Cawfields**. Next to the quarry is a car park (Map 25), a toilet block and a few picnic tables.

Those heading to Haltwhistle should not cross over the bridge but instead head on the path to the south of the Burn. Alternatively, you can wait until you hit Great Chesters fort, just a short walk further on, and take the path down to Haltwhistle from there. For either path, see Map 25 and the route below.

Walking to and from Haltwhistle (1hr) [Map 25, p165]

The path down to Haltwhistle, particularly if taking the trail that shadows Haltwhistle Burn, is both easy and lovely. Furthermore, you actually hike in woods under the shade of trees for much of the path – a stark contrast to the more exposed, wind-blasted walking along much of the Wall.

To get to the Burn trail, leave the Hadrian's Wall Path at the road bridge just after the car park by **Cawfields Quarry** (Map 24), taking the path that runs south of the Burn. The path heads towards a small bridge in the middle of a field *but doesn't take it*! Instead, you bend leftwards and continue to follow, roughly, the course of the Burn until it hits the B6318.

If in need of a hot meal or a pint, turn left when you meet the road to ***Milecastle Inn*** (Map 24; ☎ 01434-321372, 🖥 www.milecastle-inn.co.uk; **food** served daily noon-2.30pm & 6-8.30pm, but not on Sunday evening in the winter; WI-FI) with a menu of standard pub fare augmented by some really good 'rural' dishes such as pheasant slow cooked in cider and bacon. Note, however, that dogs are not allowed.

Continue for 10 minutes or so along Shield Hill (the road running south from Milecastle Inn) and you come to ***Herding Hill Farm*** (off Map 24; ☎ 01434-320175, 🖥 www.herdinghillfarm.co.uk; 🐾 apart from in belle tents; WI-FI), a very well equipped **campsite** with three **tipis** (each sleeps 4; with woodburning stove; £70 plus additional adult £20, Apr/May-Sep), 17 **wooden wigwams** (sleep 2-5; minimum 2-night stay; £68-98; hot tub £30) and four **belle tents** (each sleeps 4; £85; Apr/May-Sep), as well as **pitches** for ordinary tents (£12pp plus £4.40-5 per extra person; Mar/Apr-Oct). They also have a small **shop** (open summer one hour at each end of the day) with camping essentials plus beer and wine, and offer homemade pizza for campers (Easter to Oct at weekends). Check the website for details of when the site is closed. The AD122 **bus** service (see pp46-8) calls both here and at Milecastle Inn.

If you just want to head straight down to Haltwhistle and rejoin the trail, stride a little way west along the road, and take a left to follow the footpath which passes a weir, heads through a gate in a stone wall then follows the path as it meanders into the woods that shroud the Burn. The trail continues sedately down before finally ending up at the **Old Brickworks** on the outskirts of Haltwhistle.

For the **return journey**, rather than taking the same path back you can follow Willia Rd all the way to its termination at a gate, which you should go through and head towards **Lees Hall**. Crossing the B6318 once more, you go north down the slope past Markham House, then up towards Great Chesters Fort, which you arrive at behind the old Roman altar.

HALTWHISTLE

Though not on the trail itself, Haltwhistle is an important place for hikers. Good bus and train connections (Haltwhistle is on the Newcastle–Carlisle line), a variety of accommodation, plenty of shops, restaurants and tearooms and a location almost exactly halfway along the Wall (one of the hotels on the main street is even called The Centre of Britain) ensures that many a Wall walker calls in for the night.

It's also a particularly historic town, with bastle (see p217) houses lined up along Main St and an even earlier Pele Tower now forming part of the Centre of Britain Hotel. These buildings were, of course, built as defensive fortifications during the long-running skirmishes between the English and the Scots, a time when much of the border region was considered bandit country. Such was the fear and enmity between both sides that a plaque in Market Square recounts the sad tale of a young local girl who had attempted to run away and marry a Scot. Her reward for this act of 'treason' was to be the last person executed in Market Sq – along with her fiancé – in 1597.

Today Haltwhistle is a genteel sort of place with a pretty main street and a plethora of tearooms and eateries, many of which display notices saying that 'Walkers are welcome here' – a nice touch.

Services

The **tourist information centre** (☎ 01434 321863; Mon-Fri 10am-1pm & 1.30-4.30pm, Sat 10am-1pm), in the **library**, is perhaps the office most dedicated to the Hadrian's Wall Path. Staff will do accommodation booking (see box p43). The library (same hours) has free **wi-fi**, and you can use their computer terminals to access the **internet** for free (max 2hrs per day per person) as long as you are a member of the library (it's free to join).

For a quirky introduction to the history of the village, look in Market Square for the free-to-use, foot-pump-operated audio recording for tourists.

There is a Barclays Bank with **ATM** on Main St and another outside the **post office** (Mon-Sat 9am-5.30pm), while a little further up you'll find a self-service **launderette** (daily 8am-6.30pm; £4 for a load plus £1 for 20 mins in the dryer), a rarity on this walk. Down from the post office, on the opposite side, there's a Boots the **chemist** (Mon-Fri 9am-6pm, Sat to 1pm).

For **provisions**, there's a Co-op (daily 7am-10pm) on the main street and a large Sainsbury's (Mon-Fri 8am-10pm, Sat 7.30am-10pm, Sun 10am-4pm) just to the north of Main St behind the shops; Sainsbury's has an **ATM** and there is a path to it between Lucky Palace and Ocean Fish & Chips.

Transport

[See pp46-8] The AD122 **bus** stops at Market Sq and at the railway station. Arriva's/Stagecoach's No 685 and GNE's No 185 also call in Haltwhistle.

There are **trains** approximately every hour to Newcastle (journey time 50-60 mins) and Carlisle (just over 30 mins).

Where to stay

Ashcroft (☎ 01434-320213, 🖳 www.ashcroftguesthouse.co.uk; 4D/3T/1Tr/1Qd, all en suite; ☛; WI-FI; 🅛), a former vicarage on Lanty's Lonnen, is a lovely place with some award-winning terraced gardens. The rooms are full of features – one double has a four-poster bed; another has its own wood-decked terrace – and the quad is a two-bedroomed apartment suite with lounge, kitchen and private entrance. They charge £47-52pp (sgl occ £72-90, three/four sharing £47-50pp).

Manor House Inn (☎ 01434-322588, 🖳 www.manorhouseinnhaltwhistle.co.uk; 5T/1D, all en suite; ➖; WI-FI; Ⓛ; 🐾) is a friendly pub with basic but neat and tidy rooms above it. B&B costs £35pp (sgl occ £40).

Just across the road – but a few steps up in terms of quality – *Centre of Britain Hotel* (☎ 01434-322422, 🖳 www.centreofbritain.co.uk; 5T/6D/1Qd, all en suite; ➖; 🐾; WI-FI; Ⓛ), part-housed in the 15th-century Pele Tower, is the pick of the hotels on Main St. One room also has pull-out beds for children and two rooms have their own sauna. Rates are £36-56pp (sgl occ £60-81, three/four sharing £115/138).

Further east on Main St, *Grey Bull* (☎ 01434-321991, 🖳 www.greybullhotel.co.uk; 3D/2T/1Qd, all en suite; WI-FI; Ⓛ; 🐾 but not in dining room; mid Feb-mid Dec) is a friendly place sporting comfortable rooms (£37.50pp, sgl occ £60, three/four sharing £35pp) with a modern finish.

In the centre of things, *Hall Meadows* (☎ 01434-321021, 🖳 www.accommodationinhaltwhistle.co.uk; 1T/1D both en suite, 1S/1D private bathroom; ➖; Ⓛ; WI-FI; Mar-Oct) is a very attractive late 19th-century building covered with creepers that looks slightly out of place on Main St. B&B costs £35pp (sgl/sgl occ £35-50). If both the single and double are booked the bathroom is shared.

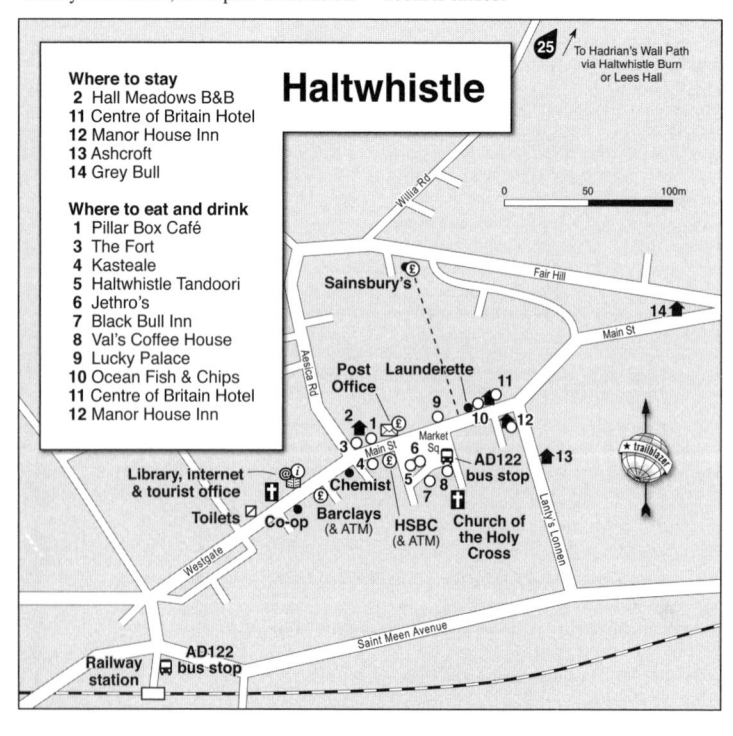

Haltwhistle

Where to stay
2 Hall Meadows B&B
11 Centre of Britain Hotel
12 Manor House Inn
13 Ashcroft
14 Grey Bull

Where to eat and drink
1 Pillar Box Café
3 The Fort
4 Kasteale
5 Haltwhistle Tandoori
6 Jethro's
7 Black Bull Inn
8 Val's Coffee House
9 Lucky Palace
10 Ocean Fish & Chips
11 Centre of Britain Hotel
12 Manor House Inn

Where to eat and drink

One of the main reasons for dropping down off the path to visit Haltwhistle is the quality (and quantity) of eateries here. Cafés abound.

Kasteale (☎ 01434-394121, ☐ www.kasteale.co.uk; summer Mon-Sat 9am-5pm, Sun noon-4pm, winter days/hours variable; 🐕; WI-FI) is a lovely little café-cum-bakery-cum-deli serving mainly home-baked goods using organic and locally produced ingredients. Their sandwiches, wraps and paninis (takeaway £3-3.50, eat in from £4.95) are great for packed lunches, and their organic teas and fresh coffees cost just £1.50 for takeaway (eat in £1.60-2.30).

Another popular café, right on Market Sq, is *Val's Coffee House* (☎ 01434-321370; summer Mon-Sat 8am-4.30pm, Sun 9am-4.30pm, winter hours variable; 🐕; WI-FI) with good-value breakfasts and light lunches and a few tables overlooking the pretty church behind. Also on Market Sq, *Jethro's* (Mon-Sat 8am-3pm, Sun 9am-1.30pm) is a friendly sandwich deli with some seating out back, overlooking the historic Black Bull Inn. Sandwiches and jacket potatoes cost £2.50-3.

Next to the post office is the quirkily named but down-to-earth *Pillar Box Cafe* (Mon-Sat 9am-4pm), a cheap, no-frills place that's popular with Haltwhistle's older locals.

Café by day, Indian restaurant by night, *The Fort* (☎ 01434-322220; summer daily café 9am-3.30pm, winter closed Wed; restaurant daily 6-10.30pm) is an unusual place that's also very affordable and popular with the locals.

Haltwhistle Tandoori (☎ 01434-321388; daily 6-11pm) also serves Indian food, but is takeaway only. Other takeaway outlets include *Ocean Fish & Chips* (Mon-Sat 11.30am-1.30pm & 5-9pm), and the Chinese *Lucky Palace* (☎ 01434-322330; Tue-Sun 5-11pm).

There are a few options for **pub food** too, the stand-out choice being the historic *Black Bull Inn* (☎ 01434-320463; food served Mon-Fri 5.30-8pm, Sat 12.30-2.30pm & 5.30-8pm, Sun 12.30-3pm; 🐕; WI-FI), a traditional, cosy, dog-friendly timber-and-horse-brass sort of place; a real ale pub with pub-grub mains that won't break the bank. You could also try *Manor House Inn* (see Where to stay; food served daily noon-2.30pm & 6-9pm; 🐕 bar only inside), which is also dog-friendly and has a beer garden, or the more expensive, but good quality *Centre of Britain* (see Where to stay; daily 6.30-9pm) where a three-course meal in the evening costs £21.50.

To continue on Hadrian's Wall Path and reach Great Chesters Fort, cross the bridge and climb over the nearby farm wall. The attractive farmhouse, which was built in 1830 using Roman stones, is home to *Burnhead B&B* (Map 25; ☎ 01434-320841, ☐ www.burnheadbedandbreakfast.co.uk; 2T, both en suite; WI-FI; ⓛ), which charges £40pp (sgl occ £40-50).

Soon afterwards, round the back of a neighbouring farm, lies the buried remains of **Great Chesters Fort** (not to be confused with Chesters Fort in Chollerford, see pp145-6), known to the Romans as **Aesica**. It is known that the Dalmatae from the Yugoslav mountains were garrisoned here during Hadrian's reign and later the Hamii from Syria, who were famous archers.

❑ **Where to stay: the details**
In the descriptions of accommodation in this book: ▼ means at least one room has a bath; ⓛ means a packed lunch can be prepared if arranged in advance; 🐕 signifies that dogs are welcome in at least one room but also subject to prior arrangement, an additional charge may also be payable; WI-FI means wi-fi is available. See also p100.

There have been some important finds at Great Chesters. For example, one of the few tombstones of a legionary soldier (as opposed to an auxiliary) was found here. Archaeologists also found evidence of an aqueduct that once supplied the fort – bringing water from the head of Haltwhistle Burn, some six miles away. What's more, before the fort, which was built to guard Caw Gap, this farmyard was the home of Milecastle 43. This is yet further evidence that the Wall and its accompanying defences were built in two stages, with the decision to move the forts up to the Wall taken only after the Wall itself and its accompanying milecastles and turrets had already been built; see p50 for details. Indeed, where Haltwhistle Burn crosses the Stanegate the remains of an early Roman fort have been discovered – presumably the one that was abandoned when Aesica was built, its garrison moved to the new premises.

Alas, there's little remaining of small, three-acre (1.2-hectare) Aesica except for some outer walls and an **altar** to the east of its south gate; heavily eroded, it is nevertheless the only original altar remaining in situ on the Wall and still inspires many a hiker to leave a small fiscal donation on its top, presumably for luck. The path to Haltwhistle leaves from near the altar, heading down the slopes.

Back on the trail, leave the wood (Map 26) to the west of the fort, making sure you check out the gatepost on the right as you descend from the stile – large and cylindrical, it was clearly once a **Roman milestone**. The only other sign of Roman construction is the defensive ditch which appears intermittently along this section; the Wall itself disappears from the top of the ridge, while the Vallum lies some way to the south.

Dropping steeply down past **Turret 44B** (King Arthur's Turret), the trail continues along **Walltown Crags** to the excellently preserved **Turret 45A** (Map 27) and the start of an impressive section of Wall – believed to be one of the few remaining parts of the Wall that hasn't undergone any 19th-century restoration – which is ended abruptly by a regular farm wall that leads south down to **Walltown Quarry**. Once a working quarry, the land around here is now a country park and plays host to a variety of ducks and other birdlife.

At the far end of the quarry is **Walltown Quarry Country Park Information & Shop** (Easter to end Oct daily 9.30am-5pm), which sells hot

---

❏ **The Elizabethan wall that never was**

Much of the period between the departure of the Romans and the ordination of the Wall as a UNESCO World Heritage Site was characterised by the practice of border reiving, where gangs would attack their rivals and neighbours to raid, rustle and rape.

While these days this 'hidden history' of the Wall receives scant attention, there is no doubt that at the time the problem was a serious one; serious enough for a protection racket to be established and a new word, 'blackmail', to be coined (see box p204). Indeed, the raiding reached such a height in Elizabethan times that in 1587 a proposal was made to revive and rebuild the Wall in order to keep some semblance of order. If that wasn't practical, the proposal declared, a new wall, constructed on similar lines to the Roman version, should be built, with *sconses* (castles) at every mile. Unfortunately, the cost was estimated to be a prohibitive £30,000 and was never taken up.

Map 26, Walltown Crags

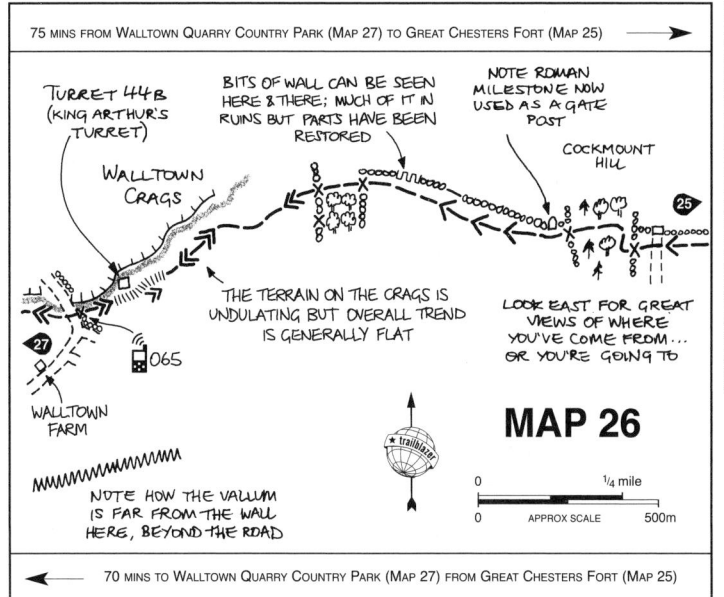

[Map 26: Hand-drawn trail map showing Walltown Crags area. 75 mins from Walltown Quarry Country Park (Map 27) to Great Chesters Fort (Map 25). Features labelled include: Turret 44B (King Arthur's Turret), Walltown Crags, Cockmount Hill, Walltown Farm. Notes on the map: "Bits of wall can be seen here & there; much of it in ruins but parts have been restored"; "Note Roman milestone now used as a gate post"; "The terrain on the crags is undulating but overall trend is generally flat"; "Look east for great views of where you've come from... or you're going to"; "Note how the Vallum is far from the Wall here, beyond the road". 70 mins to Walltown Quarry Country Park (Map 27) from Great Chesters Fort (Map 25).]

drinks, snacks, ice-creams and Wall-related souvenirs. The picnic benches outside are pleasant places to hang out and soak up the sun. If the weather's less than perfect, you may want to head instead to the nearby ***tearoom*** at the **Roman Army Museum** (☎ 016977-47485, 💻 www.vindolanda.com; daily Apr-Sep 10am-6pm, mid Feb-Mar & Oct 10am-5pm, Nov-Feb check website for details; adult £5.75, concessions £5, children £3.25, family £16; see Vindolanda, pp162-3, for details of combined entry tickets). Features here include a 3D film of a visualisation of the top of the wall from here to Vindolanda and additional exhibits about life in the Roman army. The museum is situated by the site of the Roman fort, Magna ('Rocks') at **Carvoran**.

The fort lay to the south of the Vallum by the Stanegate so, presumably, was not a Wall fort, despite its proximity to the Wall. The museum itself has a reasonable collection, though it comes a distant second compared to its sister museum at Vindolanda (see pp162-3). It does, however, have a wonderful **video** featuring a bird's-eye view of the Wall, including computer-generated reconstructions of how the Wall must have looked almost 2000 years ago.

The Roman Army Museum is a stop for the AD122 **bus** and GNE's No 185 also calls in here on its way between Haltwhistle and Gilsland. See pp46-8 for further information.

As you continue on the trail, the long-absent Vallum once again becomes your companion as you stroll down to the bridge. Just before the bridge you'll reach *Holmhead* (Map 27; ☎ 016977-47402, 🖥 bandb-hadrianswall.co.uk; Mar-Oct), a popular place with a delightful location. Almost directly in the shadow of the enigmatic Thirlwall Castle, right on the line of the Wall, and actually *built* from Hadrian's Wall stones (which, with delicious irony, were nicked from Thirlwall Castle which had nicked them from the Wall in the first place) this fabulous farmhouse, surrounded on two sides by pretty streams, provides accommodation for all budgets. As well as **B&B** (2D/2T, all en suite; WI-FI; 🅛; £35-40pp, sgl occ £60), there are two **camping barns** (£13.50pp plus £3.50 to hire a sleeping bag) which sleep six people each and which have a kitchenette with hob, microwave, fridge and toaster as well as decent shower/toilet facilities. The owners also allow hikers to **camp** (£10 per tent) in their small back garden. Camping facilities are limited, though, to a picnic table in the garden, and a small outhouse with toilet and shower combined.

Holmhead also possesses its very own Roman inscription. Inside the conservatory, engraved on a brick beside the kitchen door, are the words: *Civitas Dumnoni*, commemorating the work of a tribe from Devonshire which was drafted up here for Wall construction and repairs. It's quite a rare inscription, for the Wall was built almost entirely by regular Roman troops and manned by auxiliaries from Spain, Bavaria etc; the British rarely got a look in, so why these troops were asked to undertake work on the Wall here is unknown.

As for the 14th-century **Thirlwall Castle**, Thirlwall means 'Gap in the Wall' in the local dialect and the castle was built in a gap in the Wall where it was crossed by the Tipalt Burn. A typically strong, defensible home, Thirlwall was built to protect the owners from the cross-border reiving raids (see box p204) that were rife at this time.

The Thirlwall family (they adopted the name of the local area when they bought the land for the castle) had made their fortune in military campaigns in France. It is one thing to earn a fortune, however, and quite another to keep it, particularly in this part of the world in the 14th century. Hence the extravagant fortifications to their family home, built using whatever material lay close at hand – which, of course, meant the Wall. The castle lasted for 300 years before the family moved to Hexham and the castle was sold to the Earl of Carlisle for £4000. Already in possession of one large country pile, the earl was interested only in Thirlwall's land and allowed the castle to fall into disrepair and, eventually, ruin. There's little to see today except the shell of the keep but it remains an atmospheric and charmingly dilapidated place.

Opposite the castle, a path leads alongside a stream to a railway, where you have a choice: to head south for Greenhead, or to continue along the main trail to Gilsland. For Greenhead, turn left before the railway, and walk over the bridge.

GREENHEAD [Map 27]

Though small, Greenhead is well-known to Wall walkers thanks to its proximity to the trail and its facilities: there's a school, a church, a café, a hostel and a pub with accommodation.

GNE's No 185 **bus** stops by the hotel/village hall and if you walk to the road end (A69), a few minutes away, you can catch Arriva's/Stagecoach's No 685 service. See pp46-8 for further information.

Map 27, Greenhead 173

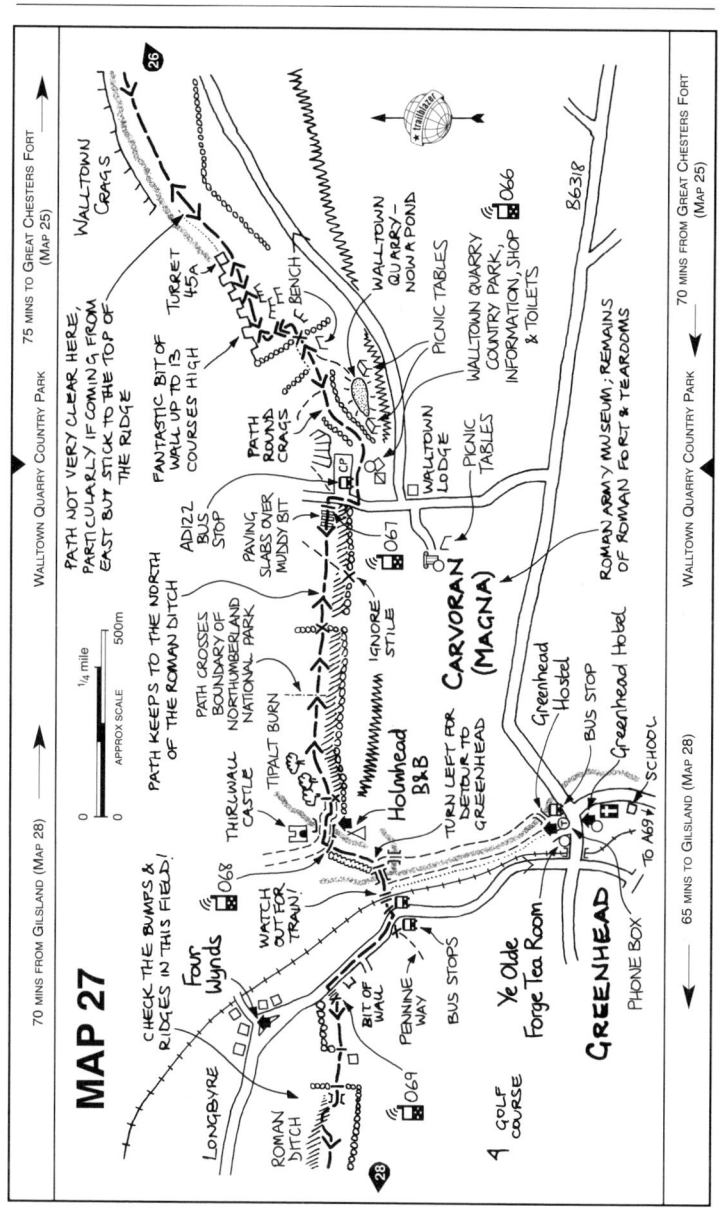

Greenhead Hotel (☎ 016977-47411, 🖥 www.greenheadhotelandhostel.co.uk; 2D or T/2Tr, all en suite; 🐕; WI-FI downstairs; (L)) is a pub with rooms (£40-50pp, sgl occ £50, three sharing £100-110) and a restaurant, and is the focus of the village. **Food** is served daily (noon-8.30pm).

Under the same ownership is *Greenhead Hostel* (contact details above; 4 x 6-bed rooms, 2 x 8-bed rooms; (L)), housed in a converted Methodist church, dating from 1885. They charge £17.50pp, or £85/100 for a whole 6-bed/8-bed room. Separate toilet/shower facilities for men and women. Breakfast (£2.50-10) is available if booked by the night before.

The only alternative to the pub for food is *Ye Old Forge Tea Room* (daily 10am-4pm), a bright, airy café with large windows and a good choice of teas, coffee, cakes and fresh fruit as well as sandwiches, soups and jacket potatoes. They also have a small selection of emergency hiking supplies (socks, plasters, maps etc).

Back on the main trail at the railway line, continue straight on to the main road where, turning right and then left, you pass a decent chunk of Wall that's been shored up to allow the B6318 to bisect it. For **B&B** stay on the road (turning right down the slip road) to reach the very welcoming *Four Wynds Guest House* (☎ 016977-47972, 🖥 www.four-wynds-guest-house.co.uk), situated in the quiet hamlet of **Longbyre**. Guests stay in two self-contained lodges (D or T; both en suite; WI-FI; (L); 🐕; Feb-Oct) in the garden; and breakfast is served in the conservatory in the house. A laundry and drying service is available (charge may apply), and the owners have a 'roam and stay' service, whereby they will drop you off and pick you up at further sections of the Wall if you use their B&B as a base for two or more days. Their rates are from £34pp (sgl occ £48).

The path follows the line of the Wall past the undulations of the Vallum, Military Way and the Wall itself. Continuing to Gap Farm (named after the Tyne Gap which runs nearby and which marks the watershed of Britain), you soon arrive at the large, friendly village of Gilsland.

GILSLAND [Map 28]

Gilsland is an important place on the walk. It is here that you reach the border between Northumberland and Cumbria; Gilsland is actually still in Northumberland but is the last place that is. Here, too, you cross the watershed and the Red Rock Fault.

Despite its relatively large size, Gilsland is a quiet place. The post office (and therefore the village's only shop) is now run on a pop-up basis by volunteers. However, Gilsland does still have a lovely tearoom, a decent pub, a great bunk/camping barn nearby and one bus service calls here. Oh, and some of the most impressive Roman ruins on the whole trail too, for it's here that you will find **Poltross Burn Milecastle** (No 48), one of the most important on the Wall. In excellent nick, the ruins include a series of steps in their north-east corner; by estimating their direction, archaeologists were able to determine the height of the walkway on the Wall at 12ft (3.66m). It is also, alas, one of the last Roman milecastles, providing further evidence that you are leaving the wild, windswept lands of Northumberland behind to enter the more rural, cosy scenery of Cumbria, where the land has been ploughed and cultivated for centuries, destroying much of the Wall in the process.

Services

The outreach 'pop-up' **post office** (Tue 1-4pm, Thur & Fri 9.30am-12.30pm) has cash-withdrawal facilities and sells a very limited supply of drinks and snacks. There's also an **ATM** at Gilsland Hall Hotel (see Where to Stay).

Go North East's No 185 **bus** service (see pp46-8) stops by Bridge Inn.

Map 28, Gilsland 175

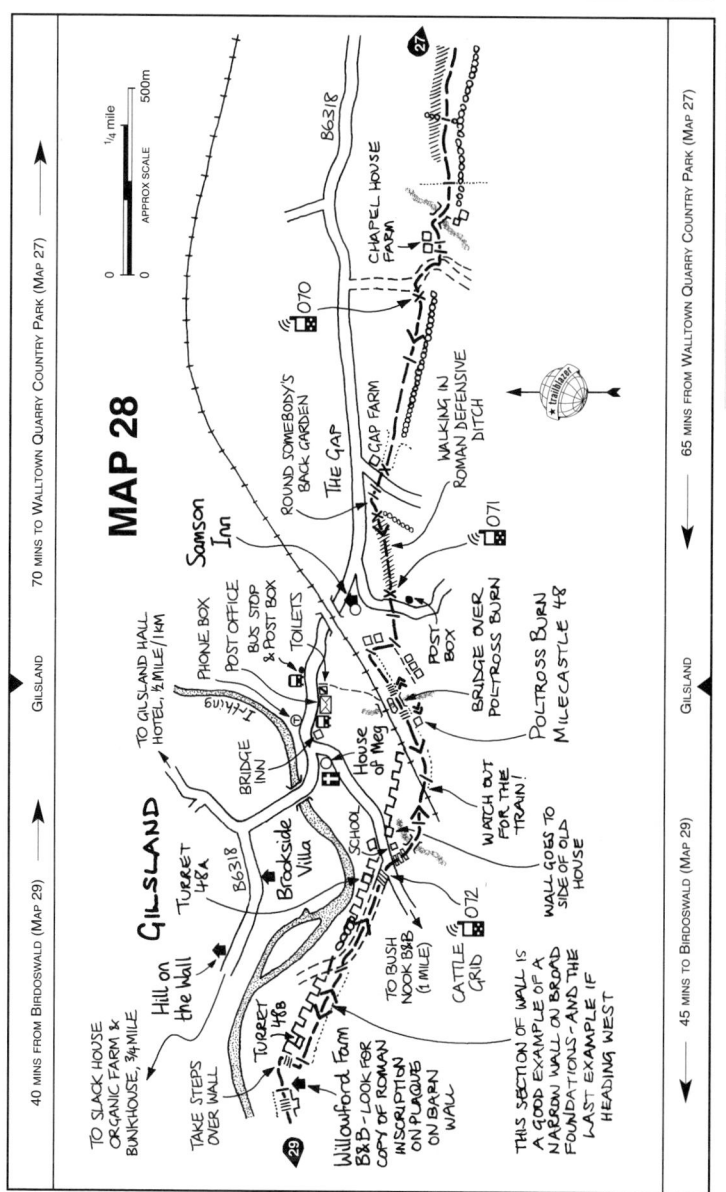

Where to stay

Samson Inn (☎ 016977-47880, 🖥 thesamson.co.uk; 2D/2T, all en suite; WI-FI; ⓛ) is a real-ale pub that also offers food (see Where to eat) and **B&B** (£25-45pp, sgl occ £30-70), in a building next door.

Its owners also run the excellent ***Willowford Farm*** (☎ 016977-47962, 🖥 willowford.co.uk; 5D or T, all en suite; 🐾; WI-FI; ⓛ; 🐕; Feb/Mar-Oct/Nov) which stands at the other end of the village, right on the Wall. The rooms (which, before their conversion, were a milking parlour, cart house, grain store and two pig holes!) are incredibly cosy with underfloor heating, sheep wool insulation and digital radios. With a lovely free-range and (mostly) organic breakfast in the morning and a whacking great bit of Wall right outside, this is a great place. They charge £44-50pp (sgl occ £68-100). It's also possible – though can't be promised – that they'll give you a lift to the pub if they're free.

Not too far away, ***Brookside Villa*** (☎ 016977-47300, 🖥 www.brooksidevilla.com; 3D or T/2Qd, all en suite; 🐾; WI-FI; ⓛ; 🐕) also offers good-quality accommodation plus evening meals if arranged in advance. They are fully licensed too. They charge £45pp (sgl occ £60, three/four sharing £40pp); their 'trail walkers package' includes B&B, packed lunch and dinner for £69pp. They also have a laundry service and drying room.

Nearby, ***Hill on the Wall*** (☎ 016977-47214, 🖥 www.hillonthewall.co.uk; 1D/1T both en suite, 1T private bathroom; 🐾; WI-FI; ⓛ; Mar-Oct) is an award-winning B&B housed in a fortified 16th-century house, or bastle (see p217). It's a beautiful place – perhaps the best-looking accommodation on the entire trail – with wonderful old furniture including a large pine table hewn from the wood of a 17th-century mill. They charge £45pp (sgl occ £65).

A little north out of town but very much part of its history, ***Gilsland Hall Hotel*** (off Map 28; ☎ 016977-47203, 🖥 www.gilslandhall.uk; 13S/30D/40T/1Tr/1Qd/one room sleeping five, all en suite; 🐾; WI-FI in public areas only; ⓛ; 🐕) dates back to the 1740s, when it was called The Shaw's Hotel, and was a popular spa resort during the 19th and 20th centuries. The remains of the original Spa Well, and Victorian swimming pool can be found within the 140-acre grounds. B&B rates here are £48pp (sgl occ rates on request, three/four/five sharing £48pp).

Even further out west of town, past Hill on the Wall B&B (although perhaps best reached from Birdoswald, which stares it in the eye across the valley), ***Slack House Organic Farm*** (off Maps 28 & 29; ☎ 016977-47351, 🖥 slackhousefarm.co.uk; 🐕 if no-one else is staying) is a former B&B turned **bunkhouse** that's deservedly been receiving great reviews since opening in 2012. Run by the friendly and knowledgeable Diane, a former teacher, and her husband, this independent farmhouse hostel is immaculate and features a wood burner in the downstairs lounge area, an adjacent kitchen area, as well as laundry and drying facilities. For accommodation, there's a 5-bed bunk room, a 6-bed camping loft (with extra airbeds if needed) and a 3-bed family room. It's £15 per bed in any of the rooms (sole use of 5-bed room £60, family room £45, 10-bed dorm £90). The small **café** was closed at the time of research (the owners were looking for a new manager), but they were still providing pre-booked meals for guests. The **farm shop** (Mon-Fri and most Sun 10.30am-5pm) was still open, though, selling the cheeses that they make on site at the Birdoswald Dairy, along with other organic farm produce. It's about 20 minutes' walk from the main trail.

Also about a mile south from the trail, ***Bush Nook*** (off Map 28; ☎ 016977-47194, 🖥 www.bushnook.co.uk; 1S/4D/3T, room sleeping up to five, all en suite; WI-FI; ⓛ; 🐕) is an 18th-century stone-built former farm constructed, at least in part, from Hadrian's Wall stone (though as the genial owner rightly points out, try to find a building that isn't made of Hadrian's Wall stone around here!). The rooms are beautifully furnished; most have open-beamed ceilings and part-exposed brickwork, and there's a delightful conservatory and even a hot tub. B&B here costs £45-50pp (sgl occ £70, three/four/five sharing rates on request).

Gilsland 177

They also have a self-catering apartment (1D; £55pp, sgl occ rates on request), and are licensed and serve food (£15-20 per head); meals need to be arranged in advance, though. To reach Bush Nook, turn left upon hitting the road after Poltross Burn Milecastle, and another left at the next junction.

Where to eat and drink

For **food** during the day, your best bet is the delightful, and very friendly **House of Meg** (☎ 016977-47777, 🖳 www.houseofmeg.co.uk; Easter-Oct Mon-Fri 7.30am-4.30pm, Sat 8am-4.30pm, Sun 10am-4pm, rest of year Mon & Wed closed in afternoon; WI-FI), a smart little café serving extremely tasty baguettes and sandwiches, great coffee and a few homemade cakes. They also stock a limited supply of groceries. The name of the café is derived from a character from Walter Scott's *Waverley*, which was set around here.

For dinner, **Samson Inn** (see Where to stay; daily noon-2.30pm & 6-8.30pm; 🐕) is a gastro-pub that maintains a good bar. The food is great with an excellent selection of vegetarian dishes; mains cost around £10-15.

Galloways Bar (food daily noon-2pm & 6-8pm), at Gilsland Hall Hotel (see Where to Stay), is open to anyone; food is always available in the coffee bar even when Galloways Bar isn't serving food.

From Poltross Burn Milecastle 48, the trail crosses the train tracks to a field where a rather remarkable sight awaits: an extensive and well-preserved piece of Roman Wall clearly going into, and under, the dilapidated (but still occupied) old house. This, it can be assumed, was the Romanway Guest House (aka the Old Vicarage), mentioned by Hunter Davies (see p42) and others, which used to have two Roman altars on its porch. Unfortunately, they don't accept guests these days, and the Wall is out of bounds.

Across the road you rejoin the Wall, again a decent chunk, this one leading from one farmhouse on the outskirts of Gilsland to another in the middle of a field. This Wall section has its own turrets too – Nos **48A** and **48B** – the latter near Willowford Farm (see opposite). Look back from the second turret to the first and, given that the Romans built their turrets at equal intervals between their milecastles, you get an idea of what one-third of a Roman mile looked like – and thus can imagine roughly what one Roman mile looked like.

Negotiating the various gates and barriers of the second farmhouse (check out the 'Roman-style' plaque stuck to the side of the barn wall), the trail – and Wall – continues down to River Irthing and the **Willowford Bridge** foundations, where the Wall and Military Way once crossed the river (Map 29). Note how the river has changed its course down the centuries, for this abutment would once have been on the riverbank. There were a number of bridges at this spot, the first being built around the same time as the Wall in AD122-8. The latest, **Irthing Bridge**, one of the most beautiful on the trail, is made of weathered steel and lies just a few metres away.

The Willowford crossing also holds quite an important place in the history of the Wall. It was here that the stone Wall, which the Romans started to construct in Newcastle and extended westwards, finally met up with the turf Wall from Bowness-on-Solway. In other words, this was the last section of Wall to have been built; once they'd done this bit and joined the two sections together, their ambition to build a barrier across Britain had been realised. Any construction done after this – moving the forts up to the Wall, for example, or converting the turf Wall into a stone one – were mere refinements carried out when their infrastructure improved and allowed them to transport limestone this far west. It was also here that the broad Wall foundations ran out. Presumably, by the time the stone wall to the west of the Irthing was being constructed, to replace the original turf and timber one, the Romans had settled on a narrow Wall so built narrow foundations to suit it.

After the bridge, it's a bit of a schlep up to **Milecastle 49**, followed by a lengthy section of Wall leading up to Birdoswald. Don't be in too much of a hurry to get there: there are estimated to be half a dozen or so engravings on this section of the Wall. Two of the best known include a dedication stone, just over halfway between the milecastle and the fort (look for the large brown stone near the top of the Wall) and, best of all, a great phallic symbol near Birdoswald itself. To find the latter, look for where a 'modern' stone wall hits Hadrian's Wall at a 90° angle on its northern side, not long before you enter into Birdoswald itself. You'll notice that at this point there is a hole in the foot of the Wall – presumably a culvert to allow the water to drain properly. Facing this hole, look to the left of it and a few metres away you'll see a second, smaller hole in the foot of the Wall. Almost directly above this, at about chest height, is the symbol. Incidentally, it was to the west of Milecastle 49 that the Wall was originally made of turf, and was only converted to stone much later.

If you are not visiting **Birdoswald Fort** remember to **stamp your passport** before you continue on.

BIRDOSWALD [Map 29]
(☎ *016977-47602*, 🖥 *www.english-heritage.org.uk; Apr-Sep daily 10am-5.30pm, Oct 10am-5pm, Nov-mid Feb Sat & Sun 10am-4pm only, all week in Feb half-term, but check opening days/hours in advance of visit; adults £6.10, concessions £5.50, children £3.70; English Heritage members free*)

The Roman name for Birdoswald was **Banna**, meaning 'Spur' and the fort does indeed sit on a spur above the River Irthing. It's a lovely position up here, with views in every direction best appreciated, perhaps, from the picnic area set up at the southern end of the fort. Unfortunately, the ruins themselves fail to live up to their setting. But no matter, for the beauty of Birdoswald lies mainly in the details. There are the carvings on the Wall leading up to Birdoswald, as mentioned above; the pleasant **farmhouse** which dominates the site, with Roman stones clearly visible in the fabric of its walls which actually date back to the early 17th century; the remains of a **granary**, the only extensive set of ruins that have thus far been excavated in this fort that once held a thousand soldiers; and the **excavated Roman gates**, one of which, on the east side, is among the best preserved on the Wall, with the *voussoir* (arch stone) and the impost stone (the stone that supported the arch) still extant.

The **museum** is one of the smartest, too, and deals not only with the Roman occupation of the site but with the location's entire history. There is also a **café** (same hours) here, as well as a souvenir **shop** and **toilets**.

Perhaps the most remarkable discoveries, however, were the 19 or so religious altars, all but one dedicated to Jupiter, that were found in the same area

Map 29, Birdoswald

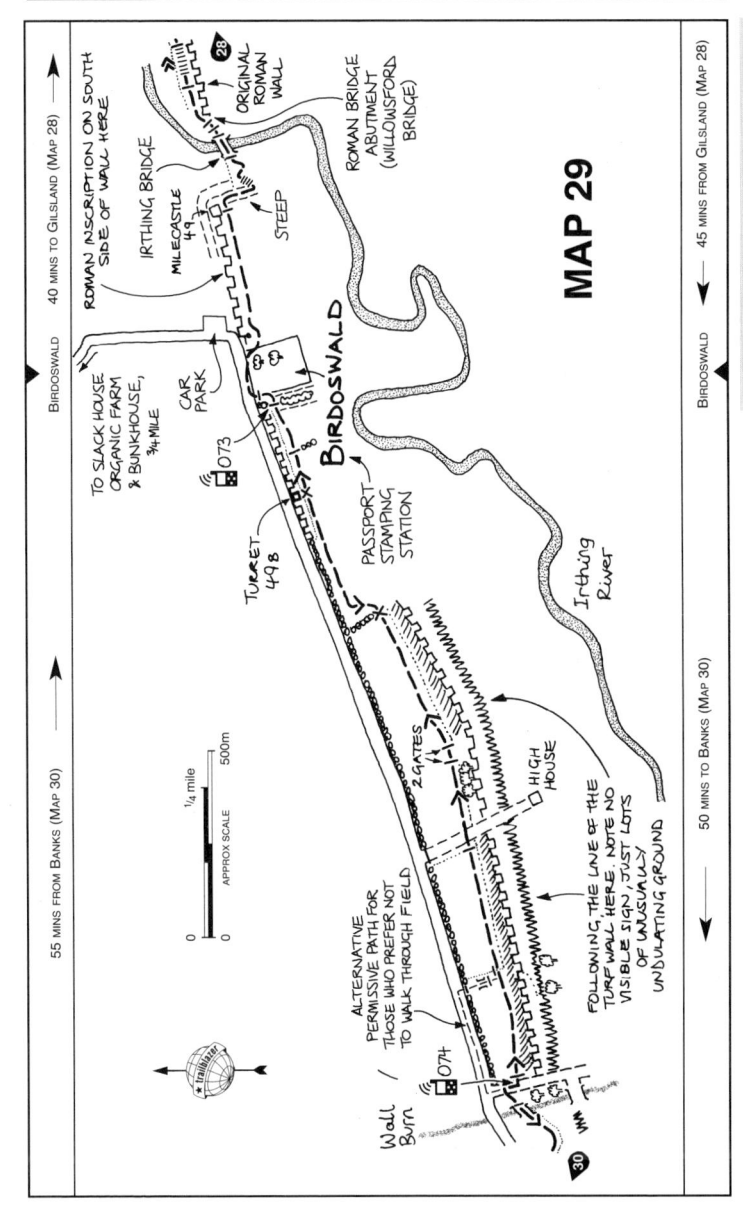

to the east of the fort. The theory is that these altars were deliberately buried there as part of some elaborate ritual, possibly on Jupiter's day on January 1 after the annual parade. (The only altar not dedicated to Jupiter was dedicated instead to the Cumbrian war god, Codicus.)

After Birdoswald, the Wall continues for a little longer until the trail deserts both it and the road to follow what appears to be either the line of the Vallum or the ditch, a clear topographical feature for the next few miles. But it's a little more complicated than that. Remember, west of the Irthing the Wall was originally built of turf and these clear, steep undulations in the earth are the remnants of this, the turf Wall (the only obvious turf section left on the entire trail), which would later be replaced by stone. What you are actually following for the next couple of fields is, immediately to your left, the ditch and the Vallum, with the two separated by the remains of the turf Wall. But note how the turf Wall is *not* on the same line as the later stone Wall you followed from Birdoswald, which is down near the road.

There's one other point of interest about this stretch: neither the stone nor the turf Wall have particularly good views to the north, unlike the Wall of the previous two stages which followed the tops of ridges and crags. Why this is the case is unclear, though a popular theory is that the local Brigante tribe in this area were more trouble than the Caledones to the north, so the Romans decided to locate the Wall with good views to the south rather than north.

The turf Wall peters out altogether as you progress down the hill past Turret 50B (which is actually not on the trail). After crossing over the farm track and **Wall Burn** the path has been rerouted away from the Vallum, though it rejoins it briefly for a short stretch through woodland (Map 30), where you can buy **drinks and snacks** from Matthew's Honesty Box, before forsaking it once more to reunite with the stone Wall.

Passing **Piper Sike Turret** (No 51A), the trail continues on or near the road to **Pike Hill Signal Tower** – the only signal tower on the Wall. A pre-Hadrian construction, the tower was possibly built for the Roman campaigns in Scotland under Agricola, where other such towers have been found, to give early warning of any movements by the Caledones. As these campaigns came to an end and the Wall was built, the tower was integrated into the Wall defences. Note how the Wall kinks to incorporate the tower – proof that the tower came first. The ruined remains of the tower's structure only rise a few feet above the ground these days, but the views from here, as you'd expect from a signal tower, are pretty good.

BANKS [Map 30]

A semi-circular huddle of houses, there's not much to Banks at all, though there is a post box, telephone box, and a **B&B** called ***Quarryside*** (☎ 01697-72538, 🖳 www.quarryside.co.uk; 1D en suite, 1T/1D share bathroom; ☕; 🐕; WI-FI; Ⓛ) on the west side of the semi-circle. They charge £32.50-35pp (sgl occ £40-45). Lifts to and from the local pub may be available by prior arrangement. They also have a **campsite** (25 pitches; £5pp) with toilet and washing-up facilities, but no showers. If there is space, campers can have breakfast (£7).

If you happen to be here on a Wednesday the BR3 **bus service** calls here; see pp46-8.

Map 30, Banks 181

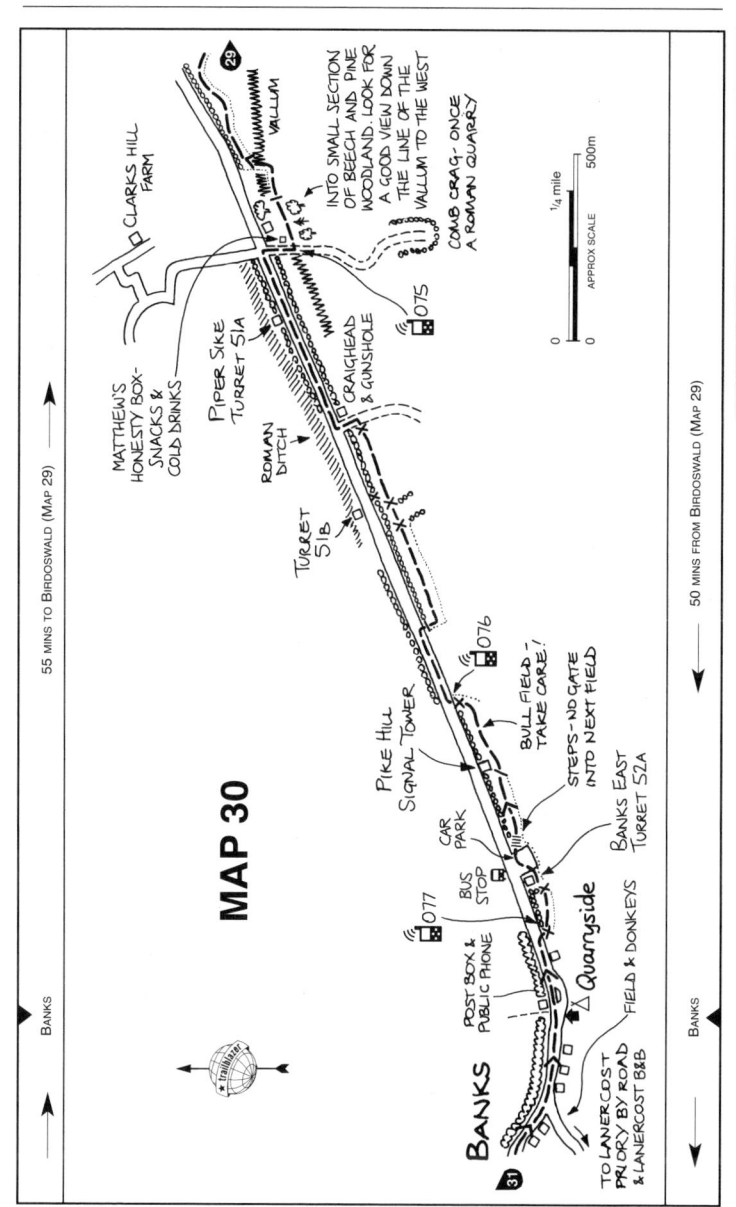

BANKS TO CARLISLE [MAPS 30-38]

Introduction

Prepare yourself to say a tearful goodbye to the last remnants of the Wall itself. By the time you reach Walton on this stage there is pretty much nothing left save for the odd trace of Vallum and ditch. The depredations of man on this side of the Pennines have served to destroy the Wall completely; odd, considering that Newcastle, the largest of all settlements on the route, still manages to muster two or three remaining sections of its own (see pp96-8 and box pp96-7). But though central Carlisle has much olde-worlde charm, there is nothing left of Roman Britain outside the museums, save for some stones, the remnants of an old Roman bridge that were dredged up from the bottom of the River Eden.

Do not despair, though, for the walking is no less pleasant on this **14½-mile (23.3km; 6-6¼hrs)** stage for its lack of Wall sightings, and the scenery, in places at least, is superb. And occasionally, just occasionally, you do get proof that the trail is still following the line of the Wall and its associated defences.

The route

The various pieces of Wall on this stage occur quite early on. The first is **Hare Hill** (Map 31), just 10 minutes or so of road walking from Banks. Once thought to be the highest remaining piece of Wall left on the trail, it is now widely believed to be little more than a 19th-century reconstruction that used original Roman stones. That's not to dismiss it altogether, however, for if you walk around the side of the Wall facing away from the road you should be able to find, at approximately head height, a small Roman inscription indicating that Primus Pilus, a senior centurion of the First Cohort, built it. In fact, this stone was taken from a site called Moneyholes, some distance to the west.

❏ **Lanercost Priory** [Map 31]

The enchanting Lanercost Priory (☎ 01697-73030, 🖳 www.english-heritage.org.uk; Apr-Sep daily 10am-6pm, Nov-Mar weekends only 10am-4pm; adults £4.10, concessions £3.70, children £2.50, English Heritage members free; contact them to check the winter opening days/times before visiting; see also 🖳 www.lanercostpriory.org.uk) was founded in 1166 by Sir Robert de Vaux and built, like so much else round here, from masonry taken from the Wall; masonry which has been combined with the local sandstone. The mortally ill Edward I (see p208) rested here for five months as he headed north to fight the Scots. A wealth of Roman stones and remains are housed within, including one of the 19 altars found at Birdoswald.

There's also a wonderful **B&B** in the grounds at **Abbey Farm**: *Lanercost* (☎ 016977-42589, 🖳 www.lanercostbedandbreakfast.co.uk; 4D or T, all en suite; ➡; 🐾; WI-FI; Ⓛ) is an award-winning place with four lovely rooms, superior breakfasts, a large open fire and walls that are once again made from pilfered Wall stone. B&B costs £46.50-49pp (sgl occ £83-88); evening meals (£25 for three courses) are also available, as is freshly ground coffee, quality loose-leaf tea, and some seriously good wine (they are fully licensed and also have real ale on tap). Nearby is the excellent ***Lanercost Tearoom*** (☎ 016977-41267, 🖳 www.lanercosttearoom.co.uk; daily 9.30am-5pm; WI-FI; 🐾) and also a **Hadrian's Wall Visitor Centre** (same hours).

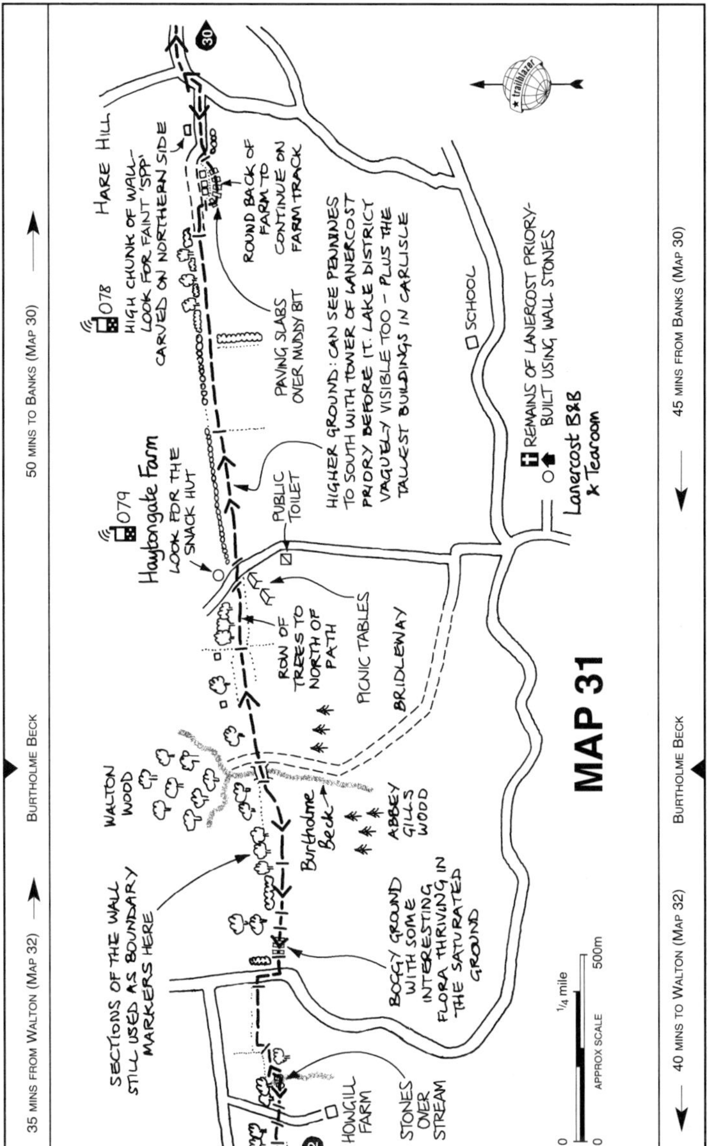
MAP 31
35 mins from Walton (Map 32)
50 mins to Banks (Map 30)
Burtholme Beck
40 mins to Walton (Map 32)
45 mins from Banks (Map 30)
30
32
Hare Hill
078
High chunk of wall – look for faint 'SPP' carved on northern side
Round back of farm to continue on farm track
Paving slabs over muddy bit
079
Haytongate Farm
Look for the snack hut
Public toilet
Higher ground: can see Pennines to south with tower of Lanercost Priory before it. Lake District vaguely visible too – plus the tallest buildings in Carlisle
School
Remains of Lanercost Priory – built using wall stones
Lanercost B&B & Tearoom
Row of trees to north of path
Picnic tables
Bridleway
Walton Wood
Burtholme Beck
Abbey Gills Wood
Sections of the wall still used as boundary markers here
Boggy ground with some interesting flora thriving in the saturated ground
Howgill Farm
Stones over stream
0
1/4 mile
0
500m
Approx scale

The next feature on the Wall is Haytongate Farm where a '**snack hut**' (daily 7am-11pm) sits by the path. As with all such huts – and you'll find many on the Cumbrian side of the trail – the owners are relying on your honesty to pay for anything you consume; please don't betray their trust. The hut also sells some neat Hadrian's Wall themed T-shirts. About 150m along the driveway there's also a public **toilet**.

Having crossed Burtholme Beck, beneath the trees on your right you'll see an original piece of Wall, unaltered and unreconstructed, save for some restoration work that was carefully carried out on it in 2014. This is the last serious bit of the Wall left on the entire trail for those heading west; or at least the last section of the Wall that's *visible*, for there is one more major piece of Roman masonry just before the village of Walton, itself reached by a delightfully pleasant stroll through fields, across bridges and along roads. The Roman ruins in this case were once the abutment to a bridge and lie just above where the 'modern' **Dovecote Bridge** (Map 32) sits today. Unfortunately, being made of sandstone, the abutment and the Wall which once led up to it have since been backfilled to prevent them eroding away completely, though you can find a description of them in Hunter Davies's travelogue *A Walk along the Wall* (see p42).

The path used to follow the line of this Wall to the river (a tributary of the Irthing) but for the past decade walkers have been encouraged to take what they say is a 'temporary' diversion along the road. However, it would appear that this has become a permanent path and the prettier, riparian option is now, alas, closed to the public.

WALTON [Map 32]

With a lovely café, two great little bunkhouses and some back-garden camping with magical views of the Pennines, the tiny village of Walton is a great place for Wall walkers to rest up. There's an old church with **phone** and **postbox** opposite, beyond which you'll find *The Reading Room* (☎ 07867-868763; Easter-end Oct daily 10am-4pm, rest of year days and hours vary so contact them; WI-FI; 🐾), a very friendly café with super food and they are happy to refill water bottles for walkers.

Walton has a very limited **bus** service, with the BR2 service calling here on Thursday only; see pp46-8.

Right on the trail, and in the heart of the village, *Florries on the Wall* (☎ 016977-41704, 🖥 florriesonthewall.co.uk) is an extremely welcoming, family-friendly **bunkhouse** (2 x 4-bed room, 1 x 6-bed room, private room sleeping 4/5, all en suite; 🐾; WI-FI; ⓛ; Mar-Oct) with simple but spotless rooms. Rates (£23-25pp, sgl occ from £55) include bedding and a tasty breakfast; the owners can rustle up evening meals (including booze) if requested in advance.

Low Rigg Farm (☎ 016977-3233, 🖥 www.lowriggfarm.co.uk; 1T/1D shared facilities, 1Qd en suite; 🐾; WI-FI; ⓛ; Apr-Sep), a 5-minute walk beyond the café, is a 125-acre (5-hectare) working dairy farm which makes its own bread and preserves and uses them as ingredients for breakfast. The views across to the Pennines are gorgeous – as, indeed, are the multitude of cats and chickens that roam around the courtyard. They charge £30-45pp (sgl occ from £50, three/four sharing £36pp).

Sandysike (Map 32; ☎ 016977-2330, 🖥 sandysike@talk21.com) is a working farm with a gorgeous Georgian farmhouse. The owners allow **camping** (£6pp inc excellent shower facilities; 🐾) in their well-sheltered, flower-filled back garden, which has fantastic views over the Pennines and the north-eastern edge of the Lake District. There's also a charming 8-bed

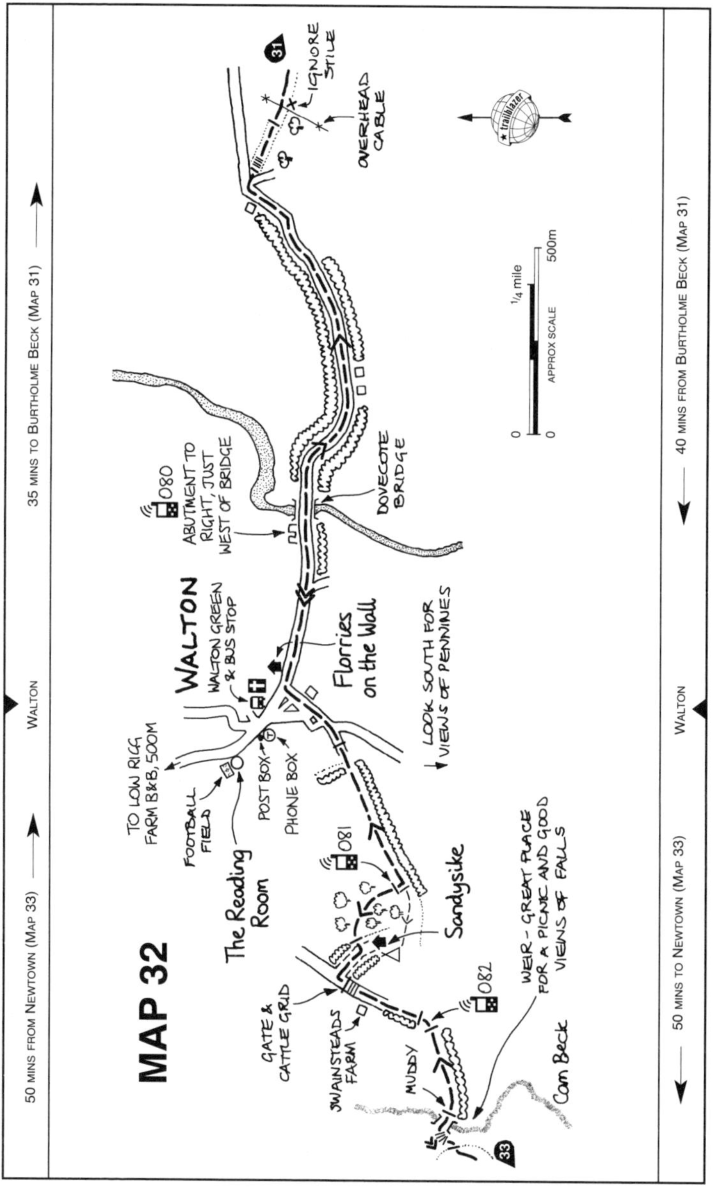
MAP 32
50 mins from Newtown (Map 33)
Walton
35 mins to Burtholme Beck (Map 31)
50 mins to Newtown (Map 33)
Walton
40 mins from Burtholme Beck (Map 31)
31
IGNORE STILE
OVERHEAD CABLE
trailblazer
0
1/4 mile
0
APPROX SCALE
500m
080
ABUTMENT TO RIGHT, JUST WEST OF BRIDGE
DOVECOTE BRIDGE
WALTON
WALTON GREEN & BUS STOP
Florries on the Wall
LOOK SOUTH FOR VIEWS OF PENNINES
TO LOW RIGG FARM B&B, 500M
FOOTBALL FIELD
POST BOX
PHONE BOX
The Reading Room
081
Sandysike
082
WEIR - GREAT PLACE FOR A PICNIC AND GOOD VIEWS OF FALLS
GATE & CATTLE GRID
SWAINSTEADS FARM
MUDDY
Cam Beck
33

bunkhouse (☎ 077256 45929, 🖳 diccon sutcliffe@hotmail.com; £15pp, bedding hire £5pp) with kitchen and shower facilities, which campers can use too.

If arranged in advance campers, and those staying in the bunkhouse, can order breakfast (continental from £4.50, full English £8), and evening meals can also be provided. Debit/credit cards are accepted (as long as the wi-fi's working). Overall, a cracking place.

From Walton, the trail drops through more farmyards following, approximately, the line of the Roman ditch. Crossing a small stream, the path climbs through woods to Sandysike (see p184). From here the path follows the farm track, taking a first left through the cow field before the farm buildings (there should be a signpost there), then drops again to a bridge over a second, slightly larger stream with a series of little waterfalls: this is **Cam Beck**. A 3¾-acre (1.5-hectare) Roman fort, **Castlesteads** (Map 33), lies just a few hundred metres to the south. Unfortunately it's out of bounds. Unusually, **Camboglanna** (as the Romans knew it; the name means 'Crooked Glen') lay between the Wall and the Vallum and not actually on the Wall. At different times it was garrisoned by troops from Spain, Gaul and Tungria. In his book, *A Walk along the Wall*, Hunter Davies (see p42) mentions visiting the house that now occupies the site and finding Roman altars lying around in the summerhouse.

One more stream and a whole patchwork of fields are crossed as you make your way towards Carlisle, a city whose highest buildings start to appear on the horizon as you progress westwards. Before long you reach **Newtown**, home to ***Orchard House Bed and Breakfast*** (☎ 016977-42637, 🖳 www.orchardhouse bednb.co.uk; 1D en suite, 1D/1T share bathroom if both rooms booked; ⬛; WI-FI; ⓛ), which charges £35-37.50pp (sgl occ £52.50). Just beyond the crossroads is another honesty-box **snack hut**, in the front garden of a kind local. They even have a picnic table for walkers to rest up at – just be sure to buy something if you use it. Newtown is a stop on the infrequent BR1, BR2 & BR3 **bus services**; see pp46-8 for details.

Turn left onto the A6071, Longtown Rd, to reach **Brampton**, 2½ miles to the south-east.

BRAMPTON

Brampton's a lovely little market town sitting snugly in the Irthing Valley, reasonably convenient for the trail and with virtually every second building either a pub, hotel or tearoom. Granted a Market Charter in 1252, the main market day is Wednesday. The main sight is **St Martin's Church** (🖳 www.stmartinsbrampton.org.uk; usually open during the day), the only church designed by architect Philip Webb, with some wonderful stained-glass windows by his fellow pre-Raphaelite Edward Burne-Jones. There's also a **statue of Emperor Hadrian** on the approach into town.

Services
The **tourist information centre** (TIC; ☎ 016977-3433; Mar-Apr & Sep-Oct Mon-Sat 10am-4pm, May-Aug 10am-5pm, Nov-Feb to 3pm) is housed in the cute, octagonal clocktower known as Moot Hall, built in 1817 and located at the eastern end of Front St, the main street in the town. They will book accommodation (see box p43), and they have one computer terminal which can be used for **internet** access. You can also get online at the **library** (Mon, Thur & Fri 2-5pm, Wed 10am-noon & 2-5pm, Sat 10am-1pm). Most of the cafés and pubs

have free **wi-fi**. There's a Co-op **supermarket** (daily 7am-10pm) behind Market Place, with a Spar (Mon-Sat 7am-10pm, Sun 8am-10pm) across the road from the TIC. Just a couple of doors down is H Jobson **pharmacy** (Mon, Wed, Fri 9am-6pm, Tue & Thur to 5.30pm, Sat to 3pm) and next door is a **bank** (HSBC) with **ATM** (with a Barclays a little further down on the opposite side). Next door to HSBC is the **post office** (Mon-Fri 9am-5.30pm, Sat to 12.30pm).

Transport
[See pp46-8] Arriva's/Stagecoach's No 685 **bus** calls in here as well as the limited BR2 and BR3 services. Note that, while Brampton does boast a **railway station** on the main Newcastle-to-Carlisle line, it's 1½ miles east of town. A branch line connecting the station with the town centre closed in 1923, and is now a pleasant, if less convenient public footpath.

Where to stay
Oakwood Park (☎ 016977-2436, 🖳 www.oakwoodparkhotel.co.uk; 1S/1D/2T/1Tr, all en suite; ✆; WI-FI; Ⓛ; Mar-Nov), Longtown Rd, is a sumptuous Victorian house set in 10 acres of grounds about a mile north of town on the way to the Wall.

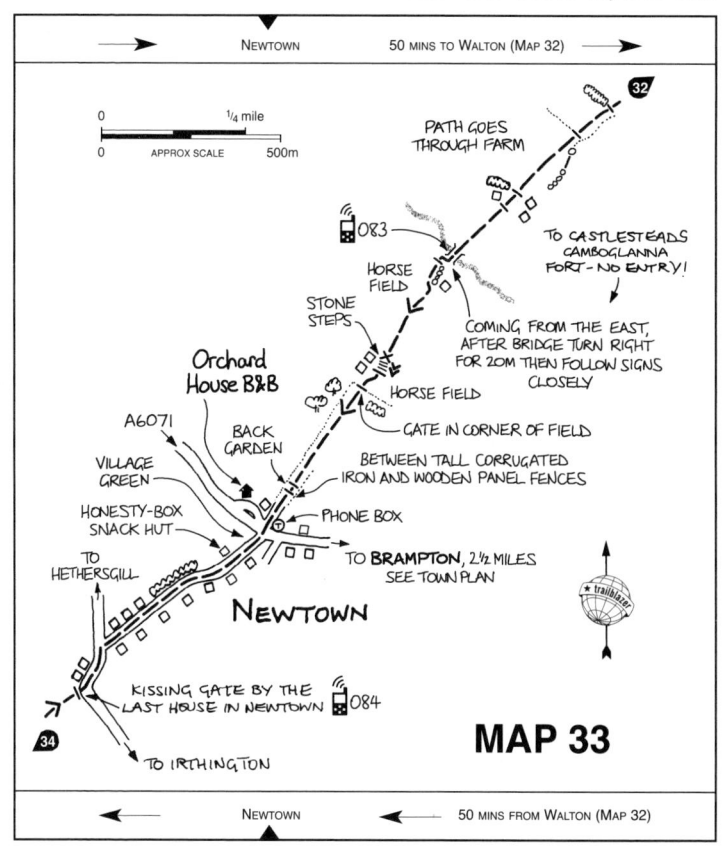

MAP 33

188 Banks to Carlisle

Brampton

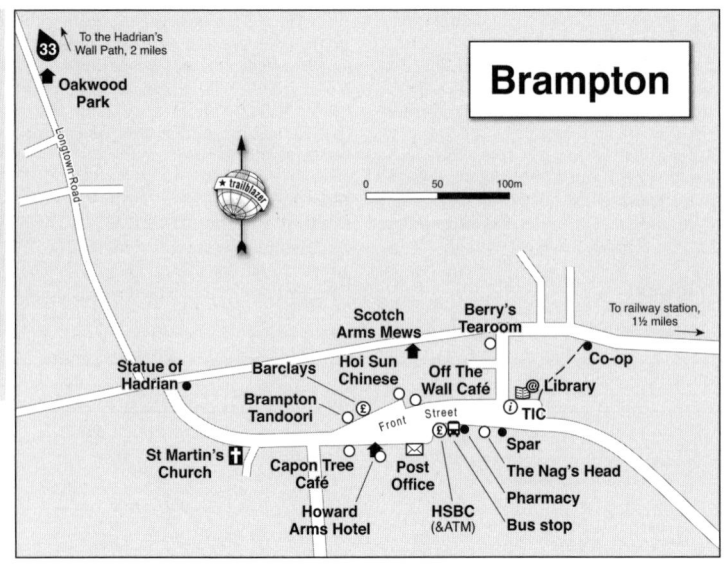

(Map showing: To the Hadrian's Wall Path, 2 miles; Oakwood Park; Longtown Road; Statue of Hadrian; St Martin's Church; Barclays; Brampton Tandoori; Capon Tree Café; Howard Arms Hotel; Scotch Arms Mews; Hoi Sun Chinese; Front Street; Post Office; HSBC (&ATM); Berry's Tearoom; Off The Wall Café; Library; TIC; Spar; The Nag's Head; Pharmacy; Bus stop; Co-op; To railway station, 1½ miles)

Full of class and character, it's a wonderful place to stay. B&B costs £35pp (sgl/sgl occ £38, three sharing £75); afternoon teas and evening meals (except on Sundays) can be arranged with prior notice.

More central, *Scotch Arms Mews* (☎ 016977-41409, 🖳 www.thescotcharms mews.co.uk; 3S/7D or T, all en suite; ✆; WI-FI; ⓛ) is a former pub turned B&B (£44.50pp, sgl £50-59, sgl occ £69) with stylish rooms, a guest lounge, laundry facilities and a drying room. The rate includes a continental breakfast.

Nearby, *Howard Arms Hotel* (☎ 016977-42758, 🖳 www.thehowardarms brampton.com; 1S/7D/2T, all en suite; ✆; 🐾; WI-FI) is a pub that has a selection of B&B rooms (from £39.50pp, sgl/sgl occ from £45) and does food (see Where to eat).

Where to eat and drink

Brampton's longest-running café, *Capon Tree Café* (☎ 016977-3649; Mon-Sat 9.15am-4.30pm; 🐾), does good-value home-cooked fare such as soups, quiches and scones and is still very popular.

Close by, *Off The Wall Cafe* (☎ 016977-41600, 🖳 coffeecogs.wordpress .com; Mon-Fri 8.30am-5pm, Sat 8.30am-4pm; WI-FI; 🐾) is a lovely, family-run business, serving homemade cakes, scones and soups, plus freshly prepared sandwiches, toasties and paninis. They also exhibit the work of local artists.

Just round the corner is *Berry's Tearoom* (☎ 016974-51732; Mon-Sat 9am-4.30pm; WI-FI), another very friendly café, much loved for its 'freak shakes'; devilishly creamy fruit-filled milk-shakes served in huge jam-jar-type jugs. Don't worry; they do healthy food too.

The best place for pub grub is probably *The Nag's Head* (☎ 016977-42548, 🖳 www.thenagsheadbrampton.com; WI-FI; 🐾), a traditional real-ale pub with good-value food (served Feb-Dec daily noon-3pm & 5-9pm, rest of year 5-9pm). They welcome walkers and have a selection of baguettes (from £4.95) as well as main meals (£6.95-7.95).

Howard Arms Hotel (see Where to stay; daily Mon-Sat noon-3pm & 5-9pm,

Sun noon-8pm) also does pub food and is a decent place for an evening meal.

Takeaways in Brampton include ***Brampton Tandoori*** (☎ 016977-2600/1; Sun-Fri 6-10.30pm, Sat 4-10.30pm) and ***Hoi Sun Chinese*** (☎ 016977-2090; Tue-Thur 4.30-10.30pm, Fri-Sun 4.30-11pm).

From Newtown, follow both the Vallum and ditch. A short-cut tree-lined path leads from the grassy track off north to Laversdale (off Map 34), home to the pleasant little ***Stonewalls Campsite*** (☎ 01228-573666), where a pitch costs £5pp; shower (£2) and toilet facilities are available and they have a neat little shed-cum-kitchen where you can make your own tea-and-toast breakfast (an honesty box is provided). If you don't want to cook your own food in the evening, Hoi Sun Chinese in Brampton (see above) delivers this far out but you'll need to pay extra for this service.

The trail eventually meets up with a road at Oldwall and the 17th-century Old Wall Cottage as well as a bus stop (the limited BR1, BR2 & BR3 **bus** services operate from Laversdale; see pp46-8 for details); if you are planning to stay in Laversdale and missed the short-cut path turn right onto the road here; it's a 15- to 20-minute walk.

Shortly after this you'll reach Bleatarn Farm, behind which is ***Bleatarn Farm Caravan & Campsite*** (☎ 07795-490579; 🐾; mid Mar to mid Nov), a small campsite with portacabin showers and toilets. They charge £10 for up to two people in a tent.

Just after Bleatarn Farm you'll pass Stall on the Wall, another honesty-box **snack stall**, before you reach Blea ('blue') Tarn itself – with Carlisle Airport hidden away to the south – on a slightly raised, arrow-straight path. This is actually both the Roman Military Way and the base of the Wall that you are walking upon. The minor road that follows also marks out the course of the Wall, though you leave it after half a mile (1km) or so to join a *clarty* (the local word for muddy) bridleway, Sandy Lane (Map 35), down to **Crosby-on-Eden**. Here, again, the Romans intrude on the modern world: the road you join at Crosby is actually part of the Stanegate. Just before the road is a long-established **refreshment stall** with hot and cold drinks and snacks. Don't forget to use the honesty box! The same people run ***Crosby Camping*** (☎ 01228-573000; 🐾; £7.50pp), a tiny campsite on the front lawn of High Crosby Farm. A shower and toilet are available.

CROSBY-ON-EDEN (LOW CROSBY)
[Map 35 p191 & Map 36 p192]

A village split into two parts, **Crosby-on-Eden** lies an hour or two from Carlisle on the trail and thus is a perfect place to take the weight off your feet, get yourself a drink and gird your loins for that final push into the city. As with many of the minor villages encountered in this western half of the walk, Crosby is built around, and consists of little more than, the main road. It's here you'll find **St John's Church**, on the way into Low Crosby village, erected in 1864 on the site of a much older edifice. Along the main road in **Low Crosby**, you'll find The Stag Inn (Map 36; ☎ 01228-573210), which was just about to be taken over by new owners at the time of research. This 17th-century inn had for many years been a hugely popular place with Wall walkers, but was forced to close following serious

190 Banks to Carlisle

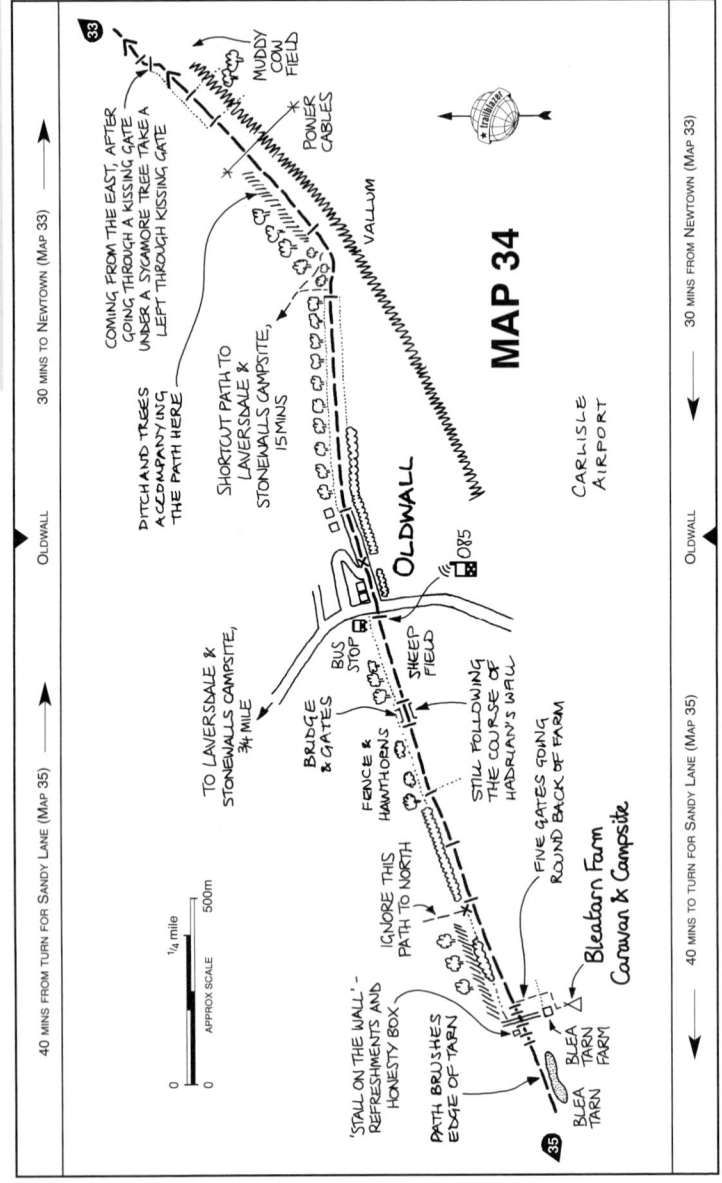

Map 35, Crosby-on-Eden 191

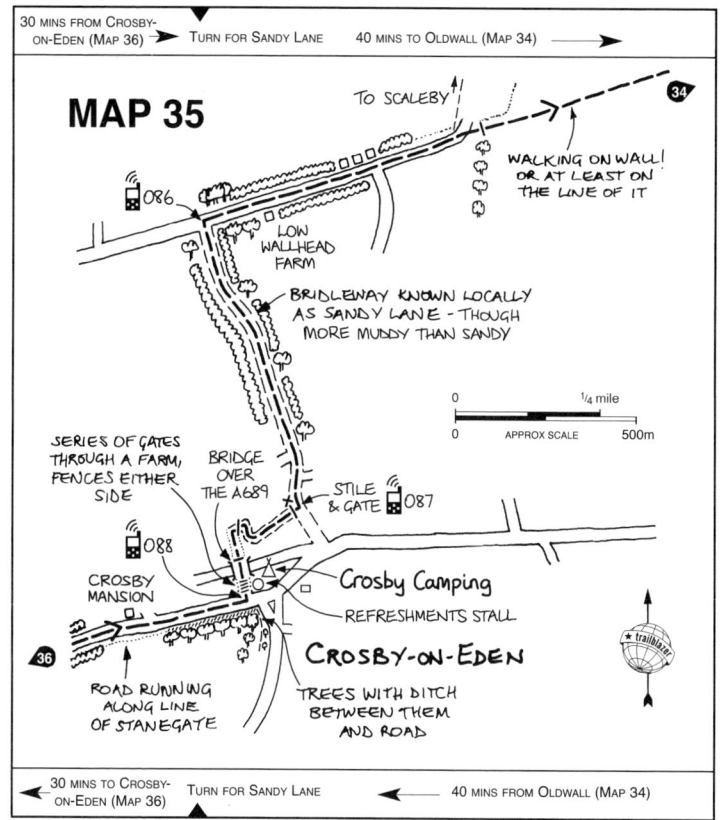

MAP 35

- 30 MINS FROM CROSBY-ON-EDEN (MAP 36) → TURN FOR SANDY LANE — 40 MINS TO OLDWALL (MAP 34) →
- TO SCALEBY
- WALKING ON WALL! OR AT LEAST ON THE LINE OF IT
- 086
- LOW WALLHEAD FARM
- BRIDLEWAY KNOWN LOCALLY AS SANDY LANE – THOUGH MORE MUDDY THAN SANDY
- SERIES OF GATES THROUGH A FARM, FENCES EITHER SIDE
- BRIDGE OVER THE A689
- STILE & GATE 087
- 088
- CROSBY MANSION
- Crosby Camping
- REFRESHMENTS STALL
- CROSBY-ON-EDEN
- ROAD RUNNING ALONG LINE OF STANEGATE
- TREES WITH DITCH BETWEEN THEM AND ROAD
- 36
- ← 30 MINS TO CROSBY-ON-EDEN (MAP 36)   TURN FOR SANDY LANE   ← 40 MINS FROM OLDWALL (MAP 34)

flood damage in December 2015. Let's hope the new owners continue with its long-held tradition for good-quality real ale and fine pub grub.

About half an hour outside Crosby, but only five minutes from the path, *Park Broom Lodge* (off Map 36; ☎ 01228-573696, ☐ www.parkbroomlodge.co.uk; 2S/3D/2T/1Tr/2Qd, all en suite; ●; 🐾; WI-FI; Ⓛ) is a comfortable B&B (from £35pp, sgl £50, sgl occ £55, three/four sharing £30pp) and licensed **restaurant** (daily noon-9pm) lying on the busy A689.

Transport-wise, the only **bus** service to call here now is BR1 and that only operates on Tuesday and Friday. See pp46-8 for more information.

From Crosby-on-Eden, you now forsake the line of the Wall altogether to indulge, as you did on the first stage from Newcastle, in a little bit of riverside strolling. It's a pleasant walk, curtailed by a diversion to Linstock to cross the M6.

192 Banks to Carlisle

MAP 36

START OF BRIDLEWAY → 25 MINS → CROSBY-ON-EDEN →

CROSBY-ON-EDEN (LOW CROSBY)

PHONE BOX, POST BOX, SCHOOL, ST JOHN'S
THE STAG INN
GREEN LANE
BUS STOP — 35

A PROLIFERATION OF WILD FLOWERS CROWD IN ON BOTH SIDES AS THE RIVER AND PATH SEPARATE

BIG PORTICOED HOUSE — 089

TO PARK BROOM LODGE HOTEL & RESTAURANT (4-5 MINS)

POWER LINES

PATH UNCLEAR — JUST FOLLOW RIVER

PATH FOLLOWS TOP OF EMBANKMENT BY THE RIVER

37

SHED

River Eden

MUDDY BRIDLEWAY — 090

0 — 1/4 mile
0 — APPROX SCALE — 500m

← START OF BRIDLEWAY ← 25 MINS ← CROSBY-ON-EDEN ←

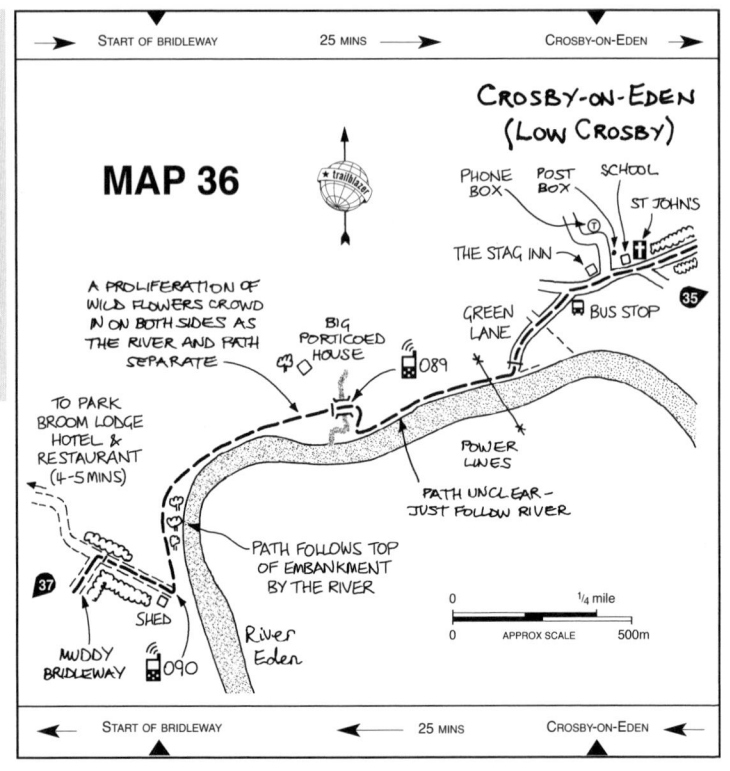

The **remains of Linstock Castle** (Map 37), an old fortified house and pele tower now incorporated into a modern farm, lies to the right of the trail as you enter the village. After the M6 another lengthy piece of road-walking follows before the trail joins a cycle route, separated from the road by a hedge.

This cycle route takes you round the back of **Rickerby** (Map 38), an entire village that, with all its towers and turrets, resembles one enormous Victorian folly. There's even a tower to the north of the trail in a field often planted with oilseed-rape. This eccentric architecture was the work of the eccentrically named George Head Head (1795-1876). Crossing a pleasant park at the end of Rickerby, the trail traverses an **iron bridge** and continues past a school and golf course and then follows the water's edge to **Sands**

❏ **Walk side by side and on healthy grass** In other words where possible don't walk in single file or on worn areas in order to protect the fragile earth.

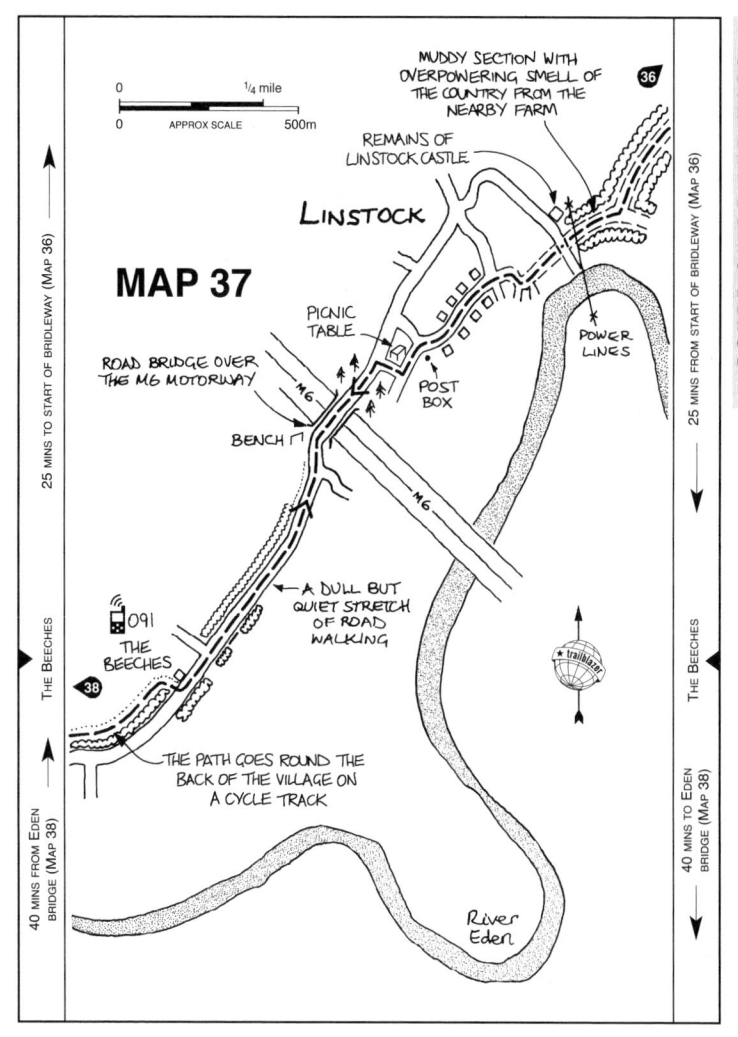

Sports Centre which has a *café* (Mon, Tue, Thur & Fri 9am-6pm, Wed 9am-9.45pm, Sat 9am-5pm, Sun 10am-5pm) and a **passport-stamping point** (see box p40). You can turn left here to head into Carlisle, although the official diversion through the city (see p194) sees you turn left through **Bitts Park**, after you cross underneath Eden Bridge.

❏ The 2015 Carlisle floods
The devastation from the flooding caused by Storm Desmond on December 5, 2015, has had long-lasting effects on Carlisle and Hadrian's Wall Path. Record-breaking rainfall levels caused rivers to burst their banks; roads were blocked, bridges collapsed and many homes had to be evacuated. In total across the UK 3500 properties were flooded and 2000 of them were in Carlisle alone. No wonder then that parts of Hadrian's Wall Path, which follows the River Eden as it skirts its way around Carlisle, were also heavily affected. At the time of research, much of the river bank that had collapsed in 2015 had yet to be repaired so a significant temporary diversion, leading hikers through the city instead of along the river, was still in place. The original route wasn't expected to be reinstated for some time, so the chances are you'll still have to follow the diversion by the time you read this.

Carlisle floods diversion
The diversion doesn't add much, if any, extra mileage to the walk (if anything, it's slightly shorter than the stretch it replaces), but it is far less appealing than the original riverside stroll, leading you, as it does, through parts of the city's uninspiring suburbs. It is signposted, although sometimes only with a small acorn sticker on a lamppost, so keep your eyes peeled.

After walking underneath Eden Bridge (see Carlisle city map), diversion signs direct you left through **Bitts Park**, and out onto **Castle Way**. Walk past the castle (keeping the castle to your right), cross over the railway line, and keep walking straight on until you pass the large Sainsbury's supermarket and then the McVitie's factory, both on your right. Turn right after the McVitie's factory, along Port Rd, which becomes Newtown Rd, then after about half a mile, turn right down **Coledale Meadows** (a diversion sticker shows the way, but it's easy to miss).

Once in Coledale Meadows, bear left down a pathway marked '**Engine Lonning**' (once a bustling rail yard, now a small nature reserve), then take the left fork in the path and walk through the wood. Once you reach the river, turn left, and you'll find yourself back on the main trail (see Map 39).

CARLISLE
Though it cannot compare in scale with Newcastle, the trail's other Wall city, Carlisle, is a pleasant place to visit, with a fair amount to see and do and a compactness and modesty that means it never feels intimidating or overwhelming. It has in the last few years also become very keen to celebrate its Roman connections and as you walk along the path you'll see several pillars emblazoned with the word 'Luguvalium' – the name of the original Roman fort at Carlisle – dotted throughout Bitts Park.

There is a distinct lack of any significant Roman ruins within the city boundaries today, save a small huddle of 90 or so stones lying to the north of the trail in Bitts Park that were dredged up from the Eden and which were, apparently, the remains of an old Roman Bridge. There are also, inevitably, Roman stones in the fabric of Carlisle Castle and an archaeological dig at the castle in 2010 discovered over 80,000 Roman artefacts! But there are very few Roman ruins left in situ; the most extensive example you'll find is the sunken shrine in the grounds of Tullie House Museum (see p200) – a museum which is an essential port of call in Carlisle for anyone interested in the Romans and their Wall.

Map 38, outskirts of Carlisle 195

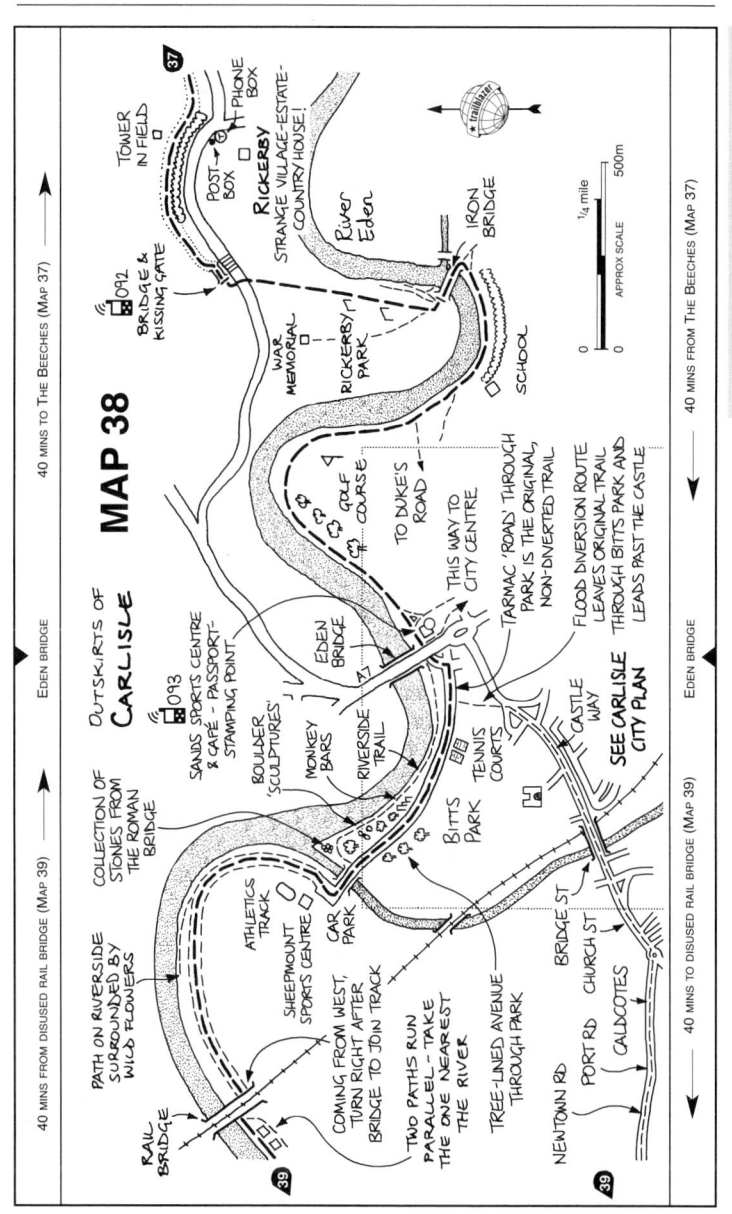

The lack of any significant Roman remains is remarkable when one considers two salient facts: first, that when St Cuthbert visited the city in AD685 he was taken to see a 'remarkable' Roman fountain (see box below), and second, that 2000 years ago this city was the headquarters for the whole Wall and the home of two forts, one of which was the largest of them all. Uxelodunum, commonly known as Stanwix after the suburb that exists today in this location on the north side of the Eden, measured 9.3 acres (3.72 hectares) in total and was garrisoned by the 1000-strong Ala Petriana cavalry – said to be the largest body of calvary stationed anywhere in the entire empire!

Stanwix was not the first fort in town, however. That was Luguvalium, stretching from Botchergate (near the railway station) to the Castle – covering pretty much the whole of the city centre. This first fort was built around AD72 by governor Cerialis to defend the Stanegate. (There is some evidence that Agricola had a turf fort here around AD80.) Despite the presence of Stanwix, built around 50 years later when the Wall was constructed, Luguvalium (the name is derived from the sun god, Lug) continued to be used until the 4th century or so, although it filled a role that was less military and more civic as time went on.

The local tribe, the Carvetii, saw the presence of such a large garrison not as a threat but an opportunity, and began trading with the Romans and inhabiting the land near Luguvalium Fort. This continued until the Carvetii's settlement became their unofficial capital – and Carlisle was born (though the name, Caerluel, is a post-Roman invention meaning 'Castle of Luel'), rising to provincial capital status by the end of the 4th century.

But despite such rich Roman history, there are few sights in Carlisle that demand your time (apart from the essential and absorbing Tullie House Museum, and perhaps a visit to the Castle, see p201), which leaves you free to enjoy the city's shops, restaurants, cafés and bars, of which there are plenty.

Services

The focus of the city centre is Market Cross, the cobbled pedestrian-only junction where you'll find the Old Town Hall, now home to the **tourist information centre** (TIC; ☎ 01228-598596, 🖳 www.discover carlisle.co.uk; Mon-Sat Mar-June & Sep-Oct Mon-Sat 9.30am-5pm, July-Aug to 5.30pm, Sun May-Aug 10.30am-4pm, Nov-Feb Mon-Sat 10am-4pm, bank hol Mons 1.30am-4pm). They sell a few Wall-related souvenirs here and can book accommodation (£4 charge).

There are **banks** and **ATMs** dotted around the city centre, especially on English St, where you'll also find the **post office** (Mon-Sat 9am-5.30pm) inside a branch of WH Smith.

For **internet access**, try Cyber Café (Mon-Sat 10am-6pm; £1/15 mins, £3/1hr) on Warwick Rd, or use the free wi-fi at any of the cafés or pubs in town.

There's a Boots **pharmacy** on English St. Those looking for **hiking gear** should head to Cotswolds on English St.

For a **supermarket**, Tesco Metro is near the station, or else there's a huge Sainsbury's on Church St, a few hundred

---

❏ **The Wall's first tourist?**
According to the Venerable Bede, in AD685 St Cuthbert came to Carlisle to visit an English queen staying in a nunnery in town. Whilst there, Cuthbert was taken by the citizens of Carlisle to look at the town walls and the 'remarkable fountain, formerly built by the Romans'. Thus, with this brief mention by Bede, Cuthbert becomes the first recorded tourist to visit the Wall. The 'remarkable fountain', incidentally, has never been found, though in the 1930s a building was excavated with a fountain in its central courtyard, which dated back to AD78 and the reign of Vespasian. Could this be the fountain Cuthbert was shown?

Carlisle 197

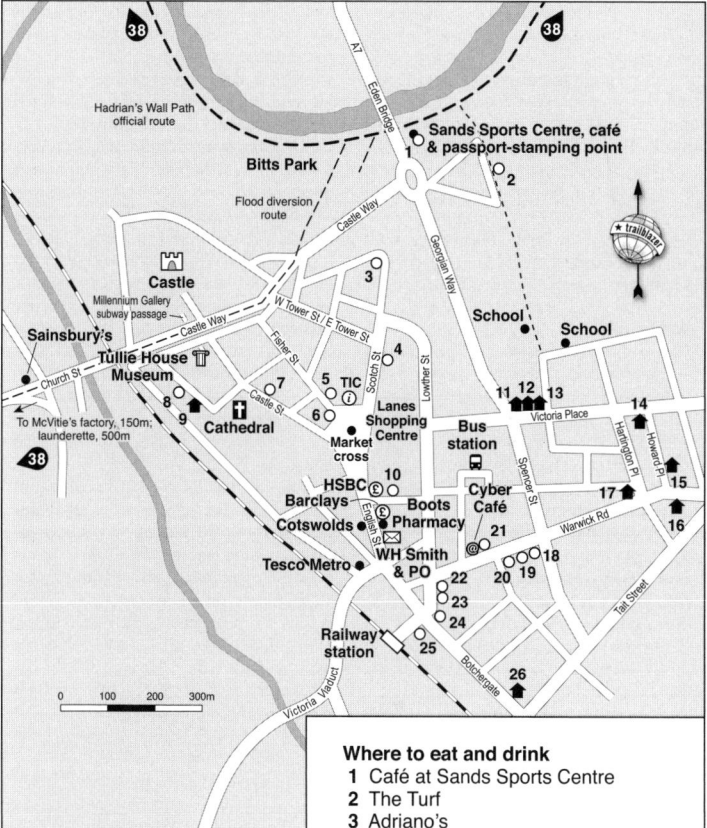

Carlisle

Where to stay
9 Carlisle City Hostel
11 Brooklyn House
12 Cartref
13 Ashleigh House
14 Abberly House
15 Langleigh Guest House
16 Howard Lodge Guest House
17 Cornerways Guest House
26 Ibis Hotel

Where to eat and drink
1 Café at Sands Sports Centre
2 The Turf
3 Adriano's
4 Mama's Fish Restaurant
5 King's Head
6 Franco's
7 The Chimes Café
8 Foxes
10 John Watt & Son
18 Alexandros & Alexandros Greek Deli
19 Davids
20 La Mocha
21 Yummy's
22 Pizza Bravo
23 La Mezzaluna
24 Home & Away
25 Pancho's

metres west of the castle, which you'll pass if you're taking the Carlisle floods diversion (see p194).

The nearest **laundrette** to the city centre is Polyclean Centre (☎ 01228-521513; Mon-Sat 9am-4pm, to 5.30pm on Wed, Sun 9am-3pm) on Wigton Rd; walk past the Sainsbury's on Church St, then go straight on up the hill at the small roundabout and it's on your right after 300 metres.

You can get your **Hadrian's Wall Passport stamped** at Sands Sports Centre (see Where to eat), by Eden Bridge.

Transport
[See pp46-8] Though Wall walkers usually turn off the trail into the city at Eden Bridge, those arriving by public transport will alight either at the **bus station** on Lonsdale St, home to both local and National Express buses (see p45), or at the **railway station**, just to the south of the city centre off Botchergate.

Arriva's/Stagecoach's No 685 is a very useful **bus** service, but perhaps of most interest is Stagecoach's No 93/93A service to Bowness-on-Solway. The limited BR1 & BR2 services also stop in Carlisle.

Train services run hourly to Newcastle via Brampton, Haltwhistle, Hexham and Corbridge.

If you need a **taxi** try City Taxis (☎ 01228-520000).

Where to stay
Finding somewhere to stay in Carlisle is not as easy as it should be. B&Bs are relatively plentiful but often book up quickly, there's only one hostel, and the nearest campsite is in Beaumont (see p205).

The one hostel is *Carlisle City Hostel* (☎ 01228-545637, or ☎ 07914-720821, 🖳 carlislecityhostel.com; 2 x 6-bed dorms shared facilities, 2Qd, one en suite; WI-FI), at 36 Abbey St, an independently run hostel with a great location, overlooking the back of Tullie House Museum, and just a stone's throw from both the cathedral and the castle. Both quad rooms have a double bed and a bunk bed. They charge £19 per dorm bed (private room sgl occ £40, two/three/four adults sharing £50/66/74)

and a light breakfast is included. There are also self-catering facilities and they provide a laundry service (£6).

For a **B&B**, the first area to look is Victoria Place, just a 5-minute walk from Eden Bridge and the trail, where three listed buildings stand next to each other: *Cartref* (☎ 01228-522077, 🖳 www.cartref guesthouse.co.uk; 1S/1D/4Tr, all en suite; 🐾; WI-FI; (L)), at No 44, is perhaps the smartest of these, a large and attractively furnished place. The owners work really hard to make this place as comfy as possible – each room comes equipped with a foot spa – and they succeed. The rates (£35-40pp, sgl £30-70, sgl occ £50-80, three sharing £75-100) don't include their award-winning breakfast, but it only costs £5pp.

Next door, at No 46, *Ashleigh House* (☎ 01228-521631, 🖳 www.ashleighbedand breakfast.co.uk; 2S/4D/1T/2Tr, all en suite; WI-FI; (L)) is one of the more established places in town; they charge £35pp (sgl £40, sgl occ rates on request, three sharing £100). On the other side of Cartref, at No 42, is *Brooklyn House* (☎ 01228-590002, 🖳 www.brooklynhousecarlisle.co.uk; 2S/ 1D or T/2Tr/2Qd, all en suite, 1S private bathroom; ✉; WI-FI; (L)) where B&B costs from £35pp (sgl £40, sgl occ £50, three/four sharing £25-30pp).

Nearby, on the corner of Victoria Place and Howard Place, is *Abberley House* (☎ 01228-521645, 🖳 www.abberleyhouse.co .uk; 1S/5D/2T, all en suite; WI-FI), a large Victorian house with a warm welcome; B&B costs from £35pp (sgl £35, sgl occ £40). Two of the doubles can have an extra bed for a child.

Down Howard Place itself, at No 6, *Langleigh Guest House* (☎ 01228-530440, 🖳 www.langleighhouse.co.uk; 2S/4Tr/1Qd all en suite, 1Tr private bathroom; ✉; WI-FI; (L)) has huge, immaculate rooms and is run by a trained chef, so the breakfasts should be decent. They will provide an evening meal if requested at least 24hrs in advance. They charge from £36.50pp (sgl £43, sgl occ £65, three/four sharing rates on request).

At the southern end of Howard Place, at 90 Warwick Rd, *Howard Lodge Guest*

House (☎ 01228-529842, 🖥 www.howard-lodge.co.uk; 2S/1D/1T/2Tr, all but two en suite; WI-FI; ⓒ; 🐾) prides itself on its large breakfasts. B&B costs from £32.50pp (sgl from £35, sgl occ rates on request, three sharing from £90).

Further down Warwick Rd, at No 107, *Cornerways Guest House* (☎ 01228-521733, 🖥 www.cornerwaysbandb.co.uk; 4S/1D/3T/2Tr, most en suite, some shared facilities; WI-FI; ⓒ) has new owners who plan to refurbish the previously uninspiring rooms. They charge £30-40pp (sgl £40-45, sgl occ £60-70, three sharing £90).

Down in Botchergate, the road running south from near the station, are several larger hotels. They include *Ibis Hotel* (☎ 01228-518000, 🖥 www.ibishotel.com; 65D/15T/17Tr, all en suite; 🐾; WI-FI), a depressingly ugly place on the outside but comfortable inside. Rack rates are £74-100 for a room, but you can get discounts through their website, sometimes getting a room for less than £50. Breakfast (£8.95pp) costs extra.

Where to eat and drink

Unlike the accommodation situation, you'll have no trouble finding food in the city.

Cafés & teahouses Cafés abound, but the best of the lot in terms of the quality of its teas and coffees is *John Watt & Son* (☎ 01228-521545, 🖥 www.johnwattandson.co.uk; Mon-Thur 8.30am-4.30pm, Fri & Sat 8am-4.30pm, Sun 10am-3.30pm), a coffee-roaster's and tea-blender's extraordinaire that was first established in Carlisle in 1865. The aroma of freshly ground coffee beans envelopes you as soon as you walk in the door and they have single-origin coffees and loose-leaf teas from all over the world. The food is excellent too, and unlike the tea and coffee, sourced locally (within a 30-mile/50km radius) wherever possible. Breakfasts (£3.50-6.95) are served until 11.30am. Lunches (£3.95-6.95) include homemade soups, sandwiches and salads. You can also buy tea, coffee and other related items from their small **shop** (Mon-Sat to 5pm, Sun to 4pm) by the entrance.

Another café that stands out from the crowd is *Foxes* (☎ 01228-491836, 🖥 www.foxescafelounge.co.uk; Mon-Fri 8am-4.30pm, Sat 10am-4.30pm; WI-FI), a more trendy, slightly quirky affair, that doubles as a lounge-bar some evenings. Again the coffee is good, and they serve craft beer too, including some from their own small brewery. They have occasional live music and film evenings here too, but during the day, it's just a cool, laid-back café serving good drinks and tasty food (pancakes, bagels, soups, sandwiches and burgers) in generous portions. Nearby, *The Chimes Café* (☎ 01228-590727; Mon-Sat 8.30am-4pm, Sun 11am-3pm) is a simple, friendly place where you can get an all-day full-English breakfast, including a cup of tea or coffee, for just £4.50. They have a good-value sandwich menu too.

Another great-value café is the pocket-sized *La Mocha* (Mon-Fri 7.30am-4.30pm, Sat 8am-3pm), down by the railway station area. They do a large selection of sandwiches, rolls and baguettes (£1.70-2.40), plus jacket potatoes (£1.70-2.60) and teas and coffees (£1.20-1.95). Nearby, is *Alexandros Greek Deli* (☎ 01228-592227, 🖥 www.thegreek.co.uk; Mon-Fri 9.30am-5pm, Sat 10am-5pm), attached to a Greek restaurant (see Pubs & restaurants) of the same name, and the perfect place to pick up an espresso and some Mediterranean-flavoured lunch-box fillers.

Back up on the trail, by Eden Bridge, **Sands Sports Centre** has a family-friendly *café-restaurant* (Mon-Fri 9am-6pm, Sat 9am-5pm, Sun 10am-4pm) where you can get sandwiches (£2.70) and baguettes (£3.60) as well as proper meals (£7-8). There's also an attached bar.

Pubs & restaurants One of the first eateries you'll see as you walk into town from Eden Bridge is *The Turf* (☎ 01228-515367; food served daily 11am-10pm), one of the Hungry Horse chain offering basic but filling, good-value pub fare and with lots of special deals (eg curry and a pint for £5 on Wednesdays).

For a more traditional pub, try *King's Head* (food served Mon-Sat noon-3pm), near the TIC. It's been selling cask ales to thirsty punters since 1904 and also serves food at lunchtime.

For fish & chips, you'll do hard to beat *Mama's Fish Restaurant* (Mon-Sat 11am-6pm, Sun 11am-4pm), a super-friendly, down-to-earth chippy that has a sit-down café-restaurant area too. You can get fish & chips here for as little as £4.50, but they also do steak pie, chip butties, burgers and jacket potatoes.

For more upmarket dining there's *Davids* (☎ 01228-523578, 🖥 www.davidsrestaurant.co.uk; Tue-Sat noon-3.30pm & 6-9pm), a cracking little place on Warwick Rd, which serves much quality British cuisine and sources much of its food locally. The menu changes regularly, but rarely disappoints. Evening mains cost around £20, while the lunch-time set menus are £16.95 for two courses and £21.95 for three. Just a few doors down, *Alexandros* (see Cafés; Mon 5.30-9.30pm, Tue-Fri noon-2pm & 5.30-9.30pm, Sat noon-2pm & 6-10pm) is a wonderfully authentic Greek eatery. If you're unaccustomed to ordering Greek dishes, try their lunchtime mini-meze (£13.50pp, minimum two people), though don't be fooled by the term 'mini'– it's enormous. Evening mains cost £11-15.

There are several good Italian places in town including *Franco's* (☎ 01228-512305, 🖥 www.francoscarlisle.com; Mon-Fri 11.30am-2.30pm & 5.30-10pm, Sat 11.30am-10.30pm, Sun noon-2.30pm & 6-9pm) near Market Cross, behind the TIC; this is Carlisle's oldest Italian restaurant having been founded here in 1974. Pizza or pasta dishes cost £8-10, although you'll pay more for main-course meat dishes. They also run *Adriano's* (yes, it is named after Hadrian; ☎ 01228-599007, 🖥 ristoranteadriano.co.uk; Tue-Sat 11.30am-1.30pm & 5.30-9.30pm, Mon to 9pm, Sun 5.30-9pm), a slightly cheaper Italian option on Rickergate.

For something much more affordable, although far less classy, head down to the railway station to *Pancho's* (Tue-Sun 9am-late), a Mexican diner and salsa bar with good-value burgers, wraps and tapas, and dirt-cheap breakfasts (£3-6; until noon).

Takeaways The railway station area is the best place to go for takeaways. You'll find plenty of places with late opening hours including *Home & Away* (☎ 01228-512615; Sun-Thur 11am-midnight, Fri & Sat 11am-3am), a chippie with some seating on bar stools; *Pizza Bravo* (☎ 01228-558844; daily 4pm to 'late') near the centre of The Crescent, which does kebabs as well as pizzas; and, next door, *La Mezzaluna* (☎ 01228-534472, 🖥 www.lamezzalunacarlisle.co.uk; Mon & Wed-Sat 10am-10pm, Sun 11am-9pm), an Italian restaurant which also offers a take-out service.

Not too far away, *Yummy's* (☎ 01228-598800; daily 5pm-midnight) does Chinese takeaway.

What to see and do

The only must-see Wall-related sight is housed in one of Carlisle's most historic buildings, the Jacobean **Tullie House Museum** (☎ 01228-618718, 🖥 www.tulliehouse.co.uk; Apr-Oct Mon-Sat 10am-5pm, Sun 11am-5pm, Nov-Mar Mon-Sat 10am-4pm, Sun noon-4pm; £7.70/5.50/free adults/concs/children aged 18 and under) on Castle St. As interesting as the 16th-century townhouse that forms part of the museum (and for which it is named) may be, the main reason for calling in is the chance to see their £1.36 million Roman Frontier Gallery. Opened in 2011, it's a wonderful run-through of the Roman story in this area and includes many interactive exhibits and some gorgeous items from belt buckles to brooches, tombstones to trinkets. One display recreates a murder case; the victim, possessing severe injuries to the skull, was found covered with rubbish at the bottom of an old well within the city of Carlisle. Younger visitors should enjoy creating their own Roman avatar and dressing up in the Roman costumes the museum provides.

The rest of the museum shouldn't be ignored though, with absorbing displays on the reivers (see box p204) and in another Roman section, a fantastic reconstruction of the wood-and-turf version of Hadrian's Wall that really gives you a good idea of how imposing and formidable a barrier it was. They also have a sunken Roman shrine in the grounds of the house – for a long time the only Roman ruins discovered in situ in the city.

From Tullie House a subway passage – called the Millennium Gallery – leads under the main road to Carlisle's other main attraction: its large **castle** (☎ 01228-591922, 🖳 www.english-heritage.org.uk/visit/places/carlisle-castle; varied opening times but usually daily 10am-4 or 5pm, Nov-Mar Sat & Sun 10am-4pm except for school holiday periods; £6.40/5.80/3.80 adults/concs/children; free for English Heritage members). A castle was originally built on this site by William Rufus in 1092, though that earth-and-timber construction was replaced in 1122 under orders of Henry I by the impressive and imposing stone structure you see today.

CARLISLE TO BOWNESS-ON-SOLWAY [MAPS 38-45]

Introduction

This is an unusual end to the walk. There are no ruins, neither of Wall nor fort, and only occasional glimpses of Vallum and ditch. There are no moors either, nor crags, nor even really any gradients worth moaning about. Nevertheless, there are some delights in store on this **14-mile (22.5km; 4¾-5hrs)** stage, including a couple of cute villages, some great views over the River Eden to Scotland and a stroll through an Area of Outstanding Natural Beauty; and if the weather holds, the walk is both a peaceful, gentle pleasure and the perfect way to finish and reflect upon the epic journey you've just undertaken. Note, that the start of this stage is affected by the Carlisle floods diversion (see p194).

There are a couple of mysteries surrounding this last stage. The first is why the Wall dodges around so much? In all, it changes direction 34 times over the 14 miles between Carlisle and Bowness. By comparison, on the way into Carlisle there were just 19 changes in 17 miles. One theory, and it's the only one we have at the moment, is that 2000 years ago the Eden, which the Wall roughly follows on this last leg, was itself full of kinks and changes in direction. (It is interesting to note, too, that the Vallum strays from the line of the Wall after

---

❏ **High tide in the Solway Estuary**
For the final section (Carlisle to Bowness-on-Solway) it's worth checking beforehand to see when the high tides occur in the Solway Estuary. Parts of the trail between Burgh-by-Sands and Drumburgh (Maps 42 & 43) are sometimes flooded during very high tides. To be sure of a dry passage, it's worth avoiding walking on this stretch an hour either side of the high-tide point.

You can find out when high-tide times are in a number of ways: many B&Bs and hostels have a **booklet** of tide times; there are **noticeboards** at Bowness-on-Solway and Dykesfield (where the trail floods; see Map 42) with the times printed on; or you can check on the internet. Visit the website 🖳 easytide.ukho.gov.uk, then click on Predict then Area, choose 1-4 for Europe, then England in Country/regions and then look down the list and choose Silloth. Alternatively check 🖳 www.tidetimes.org.uk/silloth-tide-times. If walking during British Summer Time (late Mar to late Oct) you will need to add two hours to the high-tide times given (one hour in winter) as Silloth, while the nearest port to the trail, is not located on the path.

leaving Carlisle – again nobody is entirely sure why.) The other mystery, of course, is why there are so few ruins, especially considering that this stage was bookended by the two largest Roman forts on the entire Wall (see box below) with three more along its route. The trail can't be blamed on this occasion.

❏ Where has the Wall gone?
One of the most noticeable aspects of the walk from Carlisle to Bowness on Solway is the lack of any concrete evidence (or more accurately, facing-stone-on-rubble-and-puddled-clay-or-limestone-mortar evidence) of the actual Wall on this stretch of the trail. Indeed, one can say that the Wall pretty much vanishes *before* Carlisle too, with the last solid evidence of the Wall if heading west being the bridge abutment before Walton – which has now been turfed over for its own protection too, so even here the Wall, while extant, remains hidden. Thus, for a distance of some 26 miles (42km), which equates to almost the entire last third of the route, walkers have to make do without any visible evidence of the main reason why the trail exists in the first place!

This is even more curious considering that this stage was bookended by the two largest Roman forts on the entire Wall (with Carlisle's Stanwix being the largest, Bowness the second) with a third fort at Burgh-by-Sands and a fourth at Drumburgh. Indeed, Carlisle was the headquarters of the entire frontier, with not one but two forts located within the boundaries of the modern city (see p196). Logic would therefore suggest that this would have been the most populated and heavily fortified part of the Wall – which you would have thought would yield the greatest amount of evidence that the Romans were here.

So why then, is there such little evidence of Hadrian's greatest architectural achievement on this westernmost stretch of the trail? Well, part of the answer can be found in the churches passed on this stage. St Mary's at Beaumont, St Michael's at Burgh-by-Sands and St Martin's at Bowness are all clearly built with Roman masonry, the very fabric of the churches made up from bits of the Wall (indeed, at Beaumont the church's exterior wall is said to include a 'building stone' inscribed by the 5th cohort of the 20th legion; the stone is in the left-hand wall as you head up the hill). One can also point to the marshes on the way to Bowness, where no evidence of a Wall has ever been found between Milecastles 73 (at Dykesfield) and 76 (at Drumburgh). That's not to say that the Wall wasn't built on the marshes – as the old archaeological adage goes, absence of evidence is *not* the same as evidence of absence. But there is, possibly, a case to be made that the Wall builders decided that the mud and sand of the Solway would be defence enough and thus never bothered to construct a Wall here.

Nevertheless, despite the lack of the Wall itself, there are some charming little Roman 'curios' that provide some sort of proof that they were here; the two Roman altars, for example, at the front of Drumburgh Castle. And some of the best artefacts currently in the new Roman Gallery at Carlisle's Tullie Museum are also from the west of the city, including a tiny figure of Mars found on the site of Aballava Fort in Burgh-by-Sands; a rough sandstone head of the goddess Minerva with her classical Corinthian helmet, found at Kirkandrews-on-Eden; and a small stone altar dedicated to the Goddess Latis, deity of the pool and found in Kirkbampton. There is also said to be a fragment of an altar dedicated to Hercules at Cross Farm in Burgh, which sits above the stable door. All of which, of course, amount to very little – but with archaeologists claiming that only about 5% of the Wall has been properly studied, there's hope that plenty more will emerge from this western end of the trail in due course.

Carlisle to Bowness-on-Solway 203

Unlike at Newcastle – where the trail deliberately deviates from the line of the Wall to provide walkers with a more pleasant experience as they make their way through the city – one look at an archaeological map of the Wall proves that the route continues to follow, as faithfully as the modern landscape and the current laws on rights-of-way allow, the line of Rome's northernmost frontier. And the bridge stones in Carlisle, the various churches along the way that have been built from Roman masonry as well as the odd altar that now finds secondary employment as a lintel decoration or garden ornament are all proof that the trail has not forsaken its duty and continues to adhere, as closely as it can, to the line of the Wall.

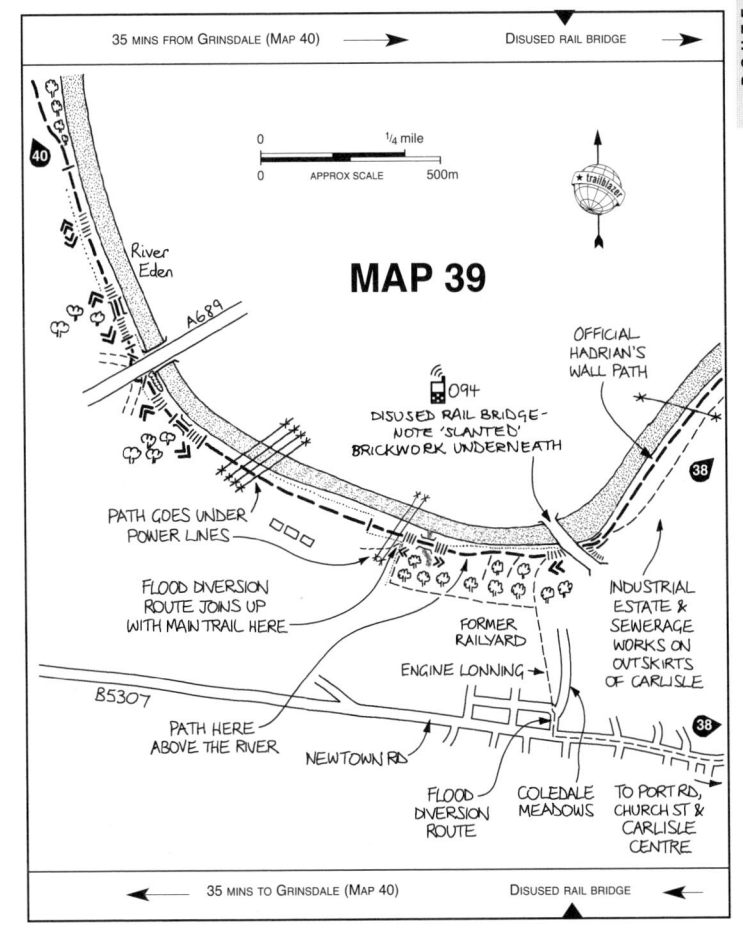

MAP 39

35 MINS FROM GRINSDALE (MAP 40) → DISUSED RAIL BRIDGE →

River Eden

A689

094 DISUSED RAIL BRIDGE – NOTE 'SLANTED' BRICKWORK UNDERNEATH

OFFICIAL HADRIAN'S WALL PATH

PATH GOES UNDER POWER LINES

FLOOD DIVERSION ROUTE JOINS UP WITH MAIN TRAIL HERE

FORMER RAILYARD

ENGINE LONNING

INDUSTRIAL ESTATE & SEWERAGE WORKS ON OUTSKIRTS OF CARLISLE

B5307

PATH HERE ABOVE THE RIVER

NEWTOWN RD

FLOOD DIVERSION ROUTE

COLEDALE MEADOWS

TO PORT RD, CHURCH ST & CARLISLE CENTRE

← 35 MINS TO GRINSDALE (MAP 40) DISUSED RAIL BRIDGE ←

❑ The reivers

The Middle Ages, particularly the 300 years or so between the War of Scottish Independence c1315 and the Union of the Crown in 1603, was a tempestuous and bloody time for the Wall region. The almost constant warring between Scotland and England meant that those poor souls who chose to live in the borderlands between the two were subject to frequent harassment by one side or another. Their crops were regularly destroyed or appropriated by the troops and their livestock slaughtered to feed the army. As a result, many locals chose to engage in sheep and cattle rustling, a practice known as **reiving**, in order to eke out a living and ensure their survival.

Such was the ubiquity of this practice that reiving eventually became a way of life and one that local borderers regarded as a profession rather than a crime. Nor was it merely English families raiding Scottish ones and vice versa, for often they stole from their fellow compatriots. Nor, for that matter, was reiving confined merely to the destitute and desperate – local nobles condoned and occasionally even indulged in the practice themselves, as did the Wardens of the Marches, the very people who were supposed to be upholding the rule of law in the region!

As the reiving continued through the generations, various strange (or so it seems to us now) laws were put in place to try to regulate the situation. For example, a victim of a reive had two courses of action open to him. The first was to file a complaint with the warden who would then be compelled to investigate. Or, and this was by far the more common choice, the victim could raise a raiding party of his own and pursue the reivers himself. It became enshrined in Border Law that anybody encountering this counter-raid was compelled to ride along with them and offer such help as they could, or else stand accused of being complicit in the original raid. If this counter-attack caught the reivers within 24 hours they could fight to retrieve their livestock. If, however, the 24 hours passed without any encounter with the thieves, the reivers could keep their booty. Eventually, to try to combat the worst excesses of reiving, the two countries decided to set up armies, known as Borderers, as a first line of defence against raiding parties from across the border. Heavily armed, the Borderers were recruited from local families and travelled on horseback, using their intimate knowledge of the local area to launch guerrilla attacks on local reiving parties.

The whole phenomenon of reiving effectively ended with the accession of James VI of Scotland to the English throne. His attempts to unify the two countries included appropriating the land of reiver families, the introduction of a ban on weapons and a drive to arrest and execute notorious reivers. There was even talk of rebuilding Hadrian's Wall to limit and control cross-border movement. Whereas before the reivers could raid in one country then cross into another for safety, with the two countries unified no such safe haven existed and the reivers could be pursued relentlessly. The construction of the Military Road in the mid-18th century also helped the authorities police the region more efficiently.

But though the phenomenon of reiving no longer exists, echoes of this troubled period in the region's history can still be heard. The terms 'kidnapping' (a favourite pastime of the reivers), 'blackmail' (originally protection money paid to the reivers, as opposed to legitimate rent paid to a landowner which was called 'greenmail') and 'bereaved' (which originally meant to lose a loved one by the hand of the reivers) are all words that come from this period. And the remnants of some imposing fortifications built by well-to-do families to protect themselves from reivers can still be seen today; bastle houses (see p217), such as Drumburgh Castle in the village of the same name; pele towers, such as the ones at Burgh-by-Sands, Linstock, or Corbridge; and even larger fortifications such as the wonderful Thirlwall Castle.

The route

The stage begins where the last one left off, with a stroll beside the Eden through the outskirts of Carlisle, although note that the Carlisle Floods Diversion (p194) will take you away from the river for the first couple of miles. Eventually the trail forsakes the river near the village of **Grinsdale** (Map 40) which has little save for a wooden box with drinks and snacks and an honesty box (with CCTV to make sure you remain honest!). Note that although the river is the dominant feature, the trail still follows the line of the Wall where it can, invisible though it is. Proof of this is in the reappearance of the Vallum, the dip in the field to your left as you cross the little **Sourmilk footbridge** (where a sandstone head of Minerva, goddess of wisdom and warfare, was found in the 19th century; it's now in Carlisle's Tullie Museum (p206).

You soon reach **Beaumont** and its church, situated at the top of the 'beautiful mountain' that gives the village its name and which is now reached via a seemingly-permanent diversion following a landslip that swept away part of the path. Unsurprisingly, the church is largely built with stones from the Wall and is in fact the only church on the whole route that lies directly on the line of the Wall. Stagecoach's No 93/93A **bus** service calls here; see pp46-8.

If you take a left at the junction near the church instead of a right you'll end up at *Roman Wall Lodges* (☎ 07784-736423, 🖥 www.hadrians-wall-accommodation.co.uk; WI-FI; ◐; 🐾), a small, friendly, well-equipped **campsite** (£5pp) with two smart wooden '**wigwams**' (sleep 4; £40 for walkers), one of which is en suite (£50 for walkers) in a small field by the quiet roadside. The owners are very amiable and can conjure up a cooked breakfast if requested. The communal facilities are great here. A large wood cabin houses two bathrooms (one of which has a bath tub), a dining room (plates and cutlery provided), a reading room (with a fine selection of books to browse), a drying room and a wood-decked terrace; all of which makes things so much more manageable for campers caught out in the rain. The campsite also has the advantage of being a stone's throw from one of the best pubs on the whole trail: *Drover's Rest* (☎ 01228-576141; food served Mon-Sat noon-2pm & 5-9pm, Sun noon-2pm & 5-7.30pm; WI-FI; 🐾) at **Monkhill** (Maps 40 & 41) is an award-winning real-ale pub with a good selection of well-priced pub grub (mains £8-10), including a number of curries. It's the beers that are the main focus, though; they rotate the real-ale selection so frequently that they keep a tally on the wall of the pub (between Aug 2013 and Sep 2016 they served 500 different ales!), and if you're not sure which brew to sample, try their three-beer flight; three third-pint glasses of three ales of your choice for a bargain £3.30.

BURGH-BY-SANDS   [Map 41, p207]

Burgh-by-Sands (pronounced 'Bruff-by-Sands') is the largest settlement on this final stage, albeit little more than a village that stretches out along the road. The 13th-century **St Michael's Church** is the main focus for Romanophiles; its walls largely made from Wall stones and its location at the centre of what was once a five-acre (two-hectare) Roman fort. This was **Aballava**, garrisoned for much of its history by auxiliary troops of Moors from North Africa.   *(cont'd on p208)*

206 Carlisle to Bowness-on-Solway

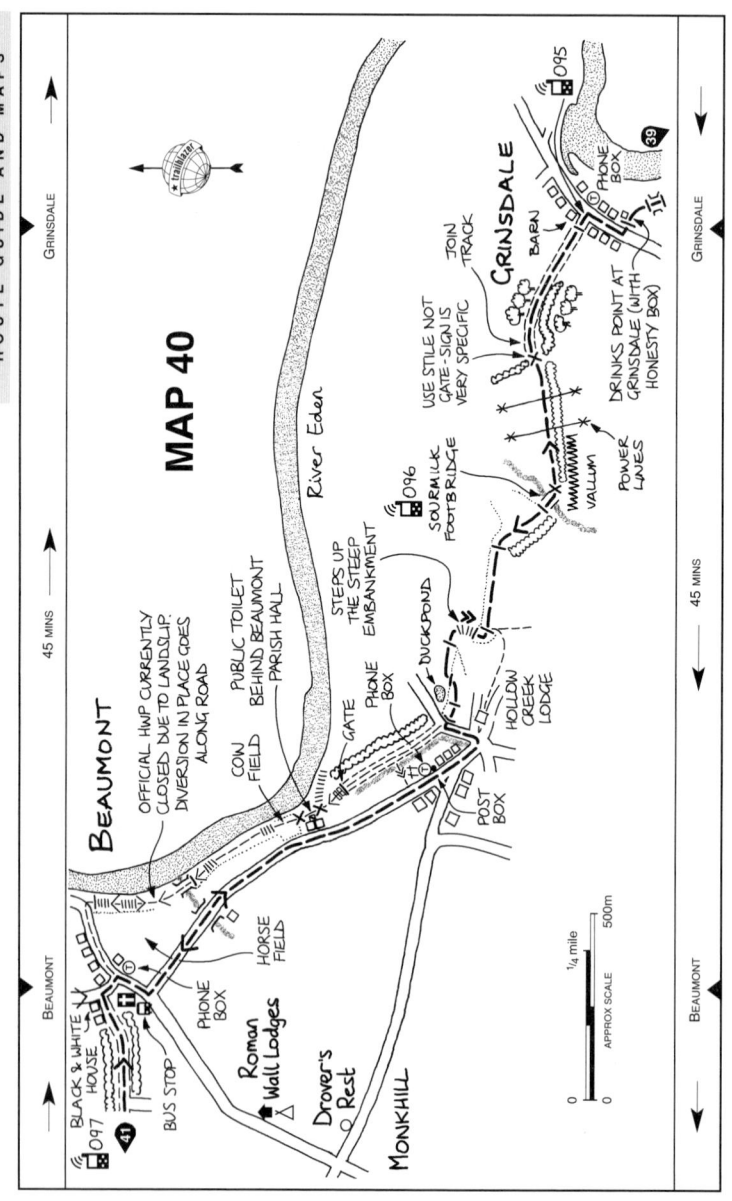

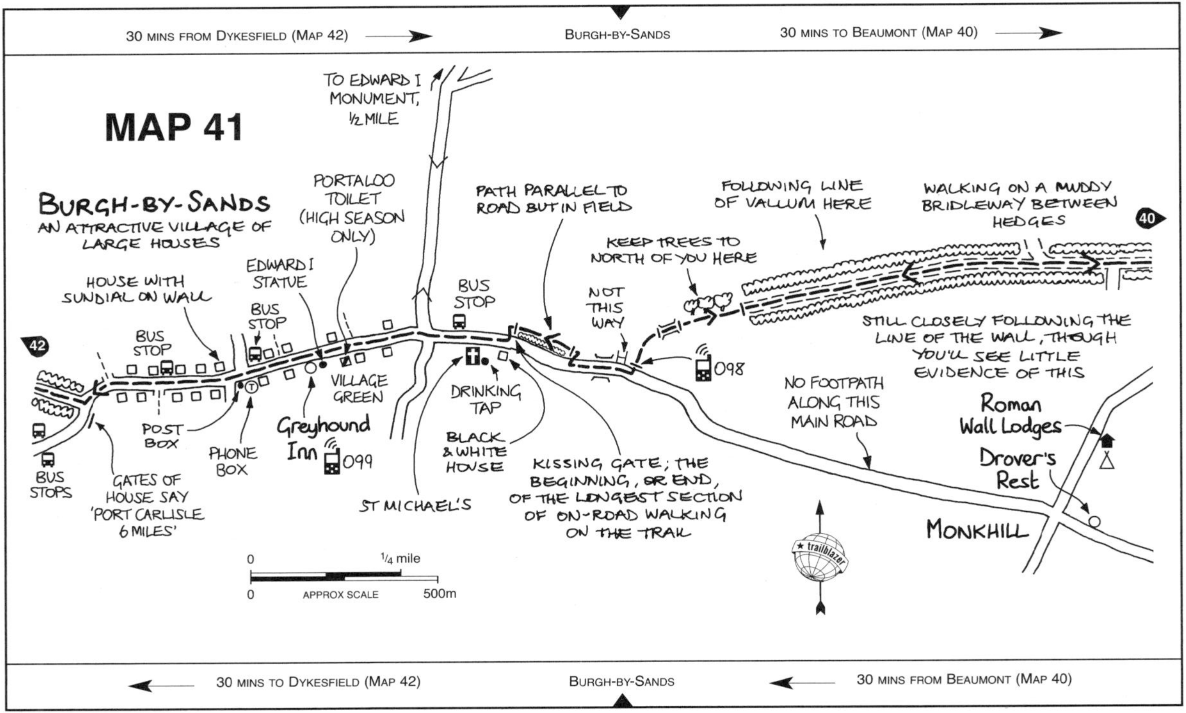
30 mins from Dykesfield (Map 42)
Burgh-by-Sands
30 mins to Beaumont (Map 40)
MAP 41
TO EDWARD I MONUMENT, ½ MILE
BURGH-BY-SANDS
AN ATTRACTIVE VILLAGE OF LARGE HOUSES
PORTALOO TOILET (HIGH SEASON ONLY)
PATH PARALLEL TO ROAD BUT IN FIELD
FOLLOWING LINE OF VALLUM HERE
WALKING ON A MUDDY BRIDLEWAY BETWEEN HEDGES
40
KEEP TREES TO NORTH OF YOU HERE
EDWARD I STATUE
HOUSE WITH SUNDIAL ON WALL
BUS STOP
BUS STOP
BUS STOP
NOT THIS WAY
STILL CLOSELY FOLLOWING THE LINE OF THE WALL, THOUGH YOU'LL SEE LITTLE EVIDENCE OF THIS
42
098
VILLAGE GREEN
DRINKING TAP
NO FOOTPATH ALONG THIS MAIN ROAD
Roman Wall Lodges
Drover's Rest
POST BOX
PHONE BOX
Greyhound Inn
099
BLACK & WHITE HOUSE
BUS STOPS
GATES OF HOUSE SAY 'PORT CARLISLE 6 MILES'
ST MICHAEL'S
KISSING GATE; THE BEGINNING, OR END, OF THE LONGEST SECTION OF ON-ROAD WALKING ON THE TRAIL
MONKHILL
trailblazer
0
¼ mile
0
APPROX SCALE
500m
30 mins to Dykesfield (Map 42)
Burgh-by-Sands
30 mins from Beaumont (Map 40)

208 Carlisle to Bowness-on-Solway

(cont'd from p205) Comparatively little is known of Aballava, though we do know that the bathhouse (which, as is typical, would have been outside the fort) was located where the vicarage is today, and excavations have revealed a number of Roman artefacts, including glassware and metalwork, and in 1928 a section of Wall foundations was uncovered in the graveyard. Today, some stone slabs line the churchyard path and recount the history of the village for visitors. There's more evidence of Roman occupation within the church itself, where the face of a pagan god can clearly be discerned on the east wall of the chancel behind the altar, emerging from the blank plaster that covers the rest of the wall. Presumably the builders of the church weren't fussy about which Roman stones they used, hence the pagan face. Isn't it curious how it hasn't been removed, especially as, when the faithful face the altar and bow, they are also bowing to this pagan god? At the opposite end of the aisle, note how the church tower has no exterior door and only tiny slit windows, presumably because it was once a pele tower used to protect the locals against raiders.

Statue of Edward I

There's a **drinking tap** outside the east wall of the church.

Virtually opposite the church, a road leads up to the **Edward I monument**, marking the spot where the so-called Hammer of the Scots died from dysentery while waiting to cross the Solway Firth on 7 July 1307. The king's body lay in state in the church before being buried in Westminster Abbey. There's also an impressive **statue of Edward** outside The Greyhound Inn in Burgh, which was erected on the 700th anniversary of the same event.

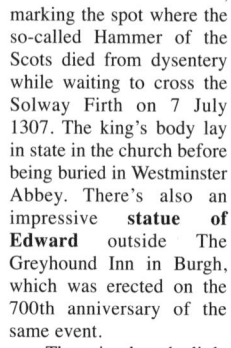

There is, though, little reason to dally in Burgh, except perhaps to call in at ***Greyhound Inn*** (☎ 01228-576579, 🖥 thegreyhound inn-burgh.co.uk; food served mid Apr to Dec Mon-Fri noon-2pm & 5.30-8pm, Sat & Sun to 3pm & 5.30-8pm, Jan-mid Apr no food on Mon or Tue; WI-FI; 🐕), a very welcoming village local that serves tea and coffee from 11am and is happy to refill water bottles for walkers.

Stagecoach's Nos 93/93A **buses** stop here en route to Bowness or Carlisle; see pp46-8 for further information.

After Burgh, the path continues along the road. It also still follows the line of the Vallum, though the only suggestion that this is the case is the name of one of the houses – 'Vallum House' – along the way.

Continuing your tarmac travails, you come next to **Dykesfield** (Map 42) and on, over the cattle grid, to the area of the trail that is liable to flooding at certain times of the year; see box p201. It's also one of the most interminable stretches, a wearying trek over flat terrain with a floodbank blocking your views to the south and the wind whipping off the shore to chill your marrow from the north. Stagecoach's 93/93A **bus** service (see pp46-8) stops here if you need a break, but if the weather's fair and the traffic's minimal it can be quite pleasant, with herons swooping above the sunbathing cows. You can vary the walk slightly by walking atop the embankment to the south of the road – one of the last vestiges of the old railway that ran through here to Port Carlisle – where at least

Map 42, Boustead Hill 209

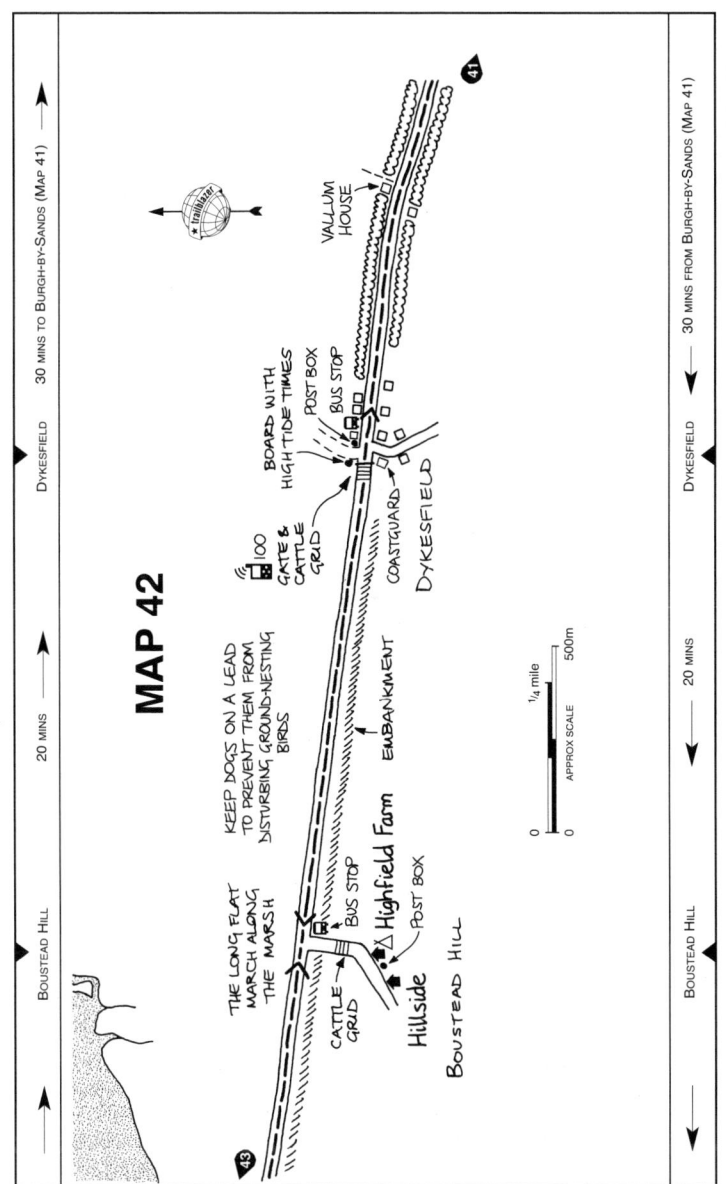

210 Carlisle to Bowness-on-Solway

you can get a better view of Skiddaw and the Lake District peaks to the south (though watch your step as the embankment is precarious in places).

Eventually you reach, on your left, a road leading to the small hamlet of Boustead Hill. Stagecoach's No 93/93A **bus** service calls here; see pp46-8 for further details.

BOUSTEAD HILL [Map 42, p209]

Most people whizz through this last section from Carlisle to Bowness, hurrying along to make sure they arrive at the end of the trail to catch the last bus back. But those who take their time are rewarded with some very pleasant accommodation, good food and lovely people; and Boustead Hill, at approximately halfway between Carlisle and the end of the walk, is a logical place to stop. True, it's little more than a row of rather grand houses, amongst which are two **B&Bs**. But the accommodation, the people and the views across the marshes to the estuary are reason enough to stop for a night.

Hillside (☎ 01228-576398, 🖳 www.hadrianswalkbnb.co.uk; 1T/1D shared facilities; ☛; 🐾; WI-FI; Apr-Oct) is a welcoming place. As well as two B&B rooms (£30pp, sgl occ £35), they also have a **bunk barn** (open all year; sleeps about 12) with its own spacious kitchen-cum-living room (including microwave, crockery, cutlery and gas cooker), shower and toilet; they charge £12pp. The owner is typical of the sort of person you meet at this end of the trail – chatty, friendly, and helpful in a very unfussy way. Breakfasts (£4-5) are also available to guests of the barn if requested in advance. The wi-fi is excellent too, and the showers in the bunkhouse are wonderfully hot and powerful.

The other B&B, just down the hill and the first you come to, is *Highfield Farm* (☎ 01228-576060, ☎ 07976-170538, 🖳 www.highfield-holidays.co.uk; 1D or T en suite/1D or Tr with a spa bath; ☛; WI-FI; Ⓛ; Mar-end Oct), a smarter affair that's good value when considering the quality of the accommodation (£35pp, sgl occ £70, three sharing £90). The double room has a sofa bed so can sleep a third person. They are happy to take guests to and from the pub, but there is a £5 charge. They even have their own family of barn owls living on their 300 acres of land and a **campsite** (🐾 if on leads; Mar-end Oct) out back charging from £10 per pitch, including use of showers, hot and cold water and kitchen facilities. If arranged in advance breakfast (£7) is available for campers.

It's worth mentioning here, as you continue your yomp along the marsh, that there has never been any evidence of the Wall, nor milecastles nor turrets, uncovered on this stretch. Of course, just because nothing has been found yet that doesn't mean there isn't anything to find, but Wall pilgrims will have to wait until the hamlet of **Drumburgh** on the other side – which had both a milecastle, No 76, and a fort, **Congabata** – to find more archaeological nourishment to feed their obsession.

DRUMBURGH [Map 43]

Drumburgh ('Drumbruff'), an unassuming little farming community, resides where once a small Roman fort stood. This fort was known as Congabata or Concavata, built to watch over the salt flats nearby.

Today the hamlet's highlight is **Drumburgh Castle**, on the left as you enter, a bastle (see p217) house built in 1307 to provide protection against reivers (see box p204). The livestock would be housed on the ground floor, with the family living upstairs. Note the heraldic crest above the door, the griffins perched on the roof and not one but two Roman altars out front.

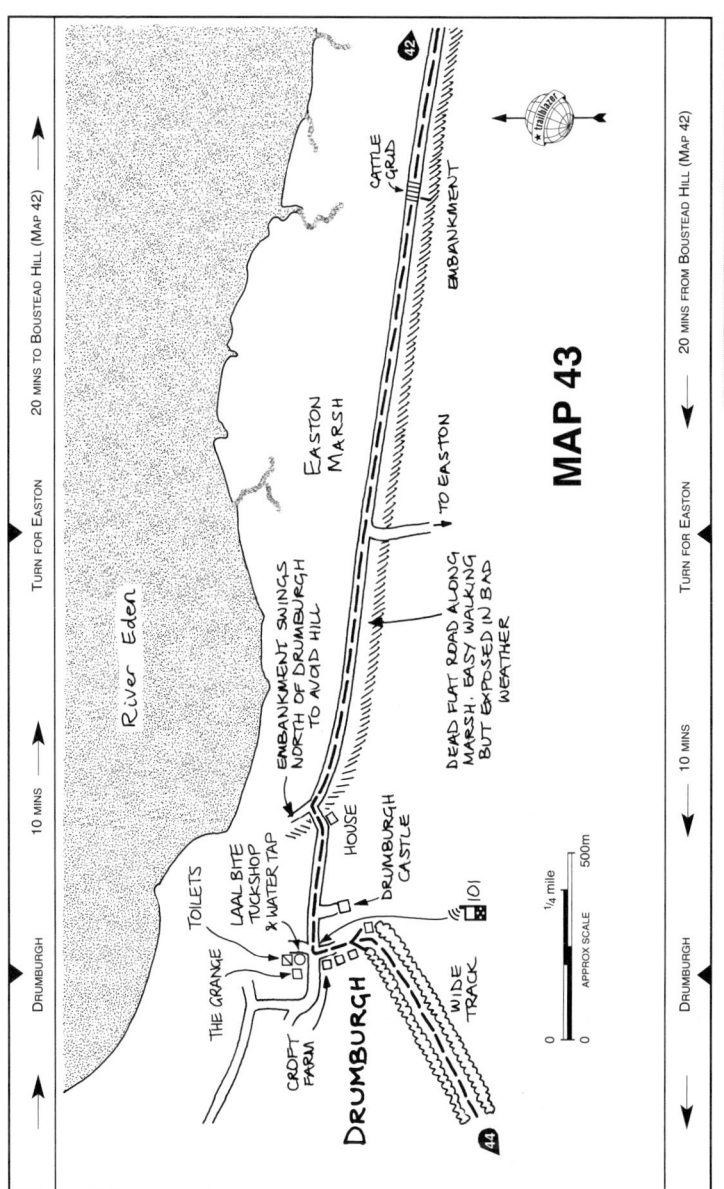

Map 43, Drumburgh 211

Drumburgh has little else to interest walkers except a **serve-yourself tuckshop** called, *Laal Bite* (Easter to Oct daily 8am-6pm) at The Grange, opposite where the trail turns left off the road. They sell ice-creams and chocolate bars and have a hot-drinks machine, a tap for refilling water bottles, and a toilet, as well as a picnic table and a bench in the shade of a couple of apple trees outside. Laal Bite, incidentally, translates as *Little Stand*, a 'stand' being a position allocated to a fisherman from where he can fish and which are traditionally given names by the locals.

Stagecoach's No 93/93A **bus** service calls here; see pp46-8 for further details.

From Drumburgh the trail takes a deviation away from the road to pass through a few farms, emerging eventually at **Glasson**.

GLASSON [Map 44]

For walkers, the appeal of Glasson starts and ends with *Highland Laddie Inn* (☎ 016973-51839, 🖥 highlandladdieinnglasson.co.uk; food served Mon-Sat noon-2.30pm & 6-8.45pm, Sun noon-2pm & 6-8.45pm; ☛; WI-FI; Ⓛ; 🐾), a quiet pub with good-value **food** (mains £8-9) and two **rooms** (1D/1T, shared facilities) where B&B costs £25pp (sgl occ £30). Conveniently, they have now also opened a **grocery shop** (Mon-Sat 8am-8pm, Sun 8-10.30am) next to the pub.

Stagecoach **Bus** No 93/93A stops here; see pp46-8 for further information.

Opposite Highland Laddie Inn, a bridleway heads off north-west, following the line of the Vallum (though you'll have trouble spotting any evidence of this), past Cottage & Glendale Holiday Park. Camping is not allowed here, but it does have a handy, well-stocked **shop** (Sun-Thur 8.30am-3pm, Fri & Sat 8.30am-6pm), the last shop on the trail. Soon after this, it's back towards the shoreline, emerging back onto the road at the end of Port Carlisle.

PORT CARLISLE [Map 45, p215]

The path chooses to ignore Port Carlisle, preferring to hug the shore and turn onto the road only at the end of the village, one of the more interesting on this stage. For one thing, at one time there were big plans for Port Carlisle, with both a railway line and a canal terminating here – both of which followed the line of the Wall. Stephenson's *Rocket* actually travelled along the line in 1829, and indeed it was hoped that the village would become a major port for goods to and from Scotland and Ireland. However, factors conspired against Port Carlisle and the railway line shut after 100 years of use, while the canal was abandoned after 30 years.

Thereafter, Port Carlisle slipped back into the sleepy backwaters of the British Isles. Today, you can see the remains of the lock and port, and you cross the last vestiges of the canal on the walk. Look out across the water too and, just a few metres away, are the remains of the harbour walls.

Today the village is home to the Port Carlisle Bowls Club, which has a **water tap** on the wall of its clubhouse that you can use, and a pub, *Hope and Anchor* (☎ 016973-51460; 🐾 front bar only; WI-FI), which serves real ale and **food** (Mar-Oct Mon-Sat noon-2.15pm & 6-8.30pm, Sun noon-2pm, Oct-Mar no food on Mon or Tue).

Less than a quarter of a mile up the road at Kirkland House Farm, the basic *Chapel Side Campsite* (☎ 016973-51400) has pitches for £5pp (though there's no hot water, just cold showers; 🐾). Should the weather be particularly inclement or you just fancy something a little more comfy, they've also converted their milking parlour into a **camping barn**, equipped with a simple bench (with thin mattresses) around

Map 44, Glasson 213

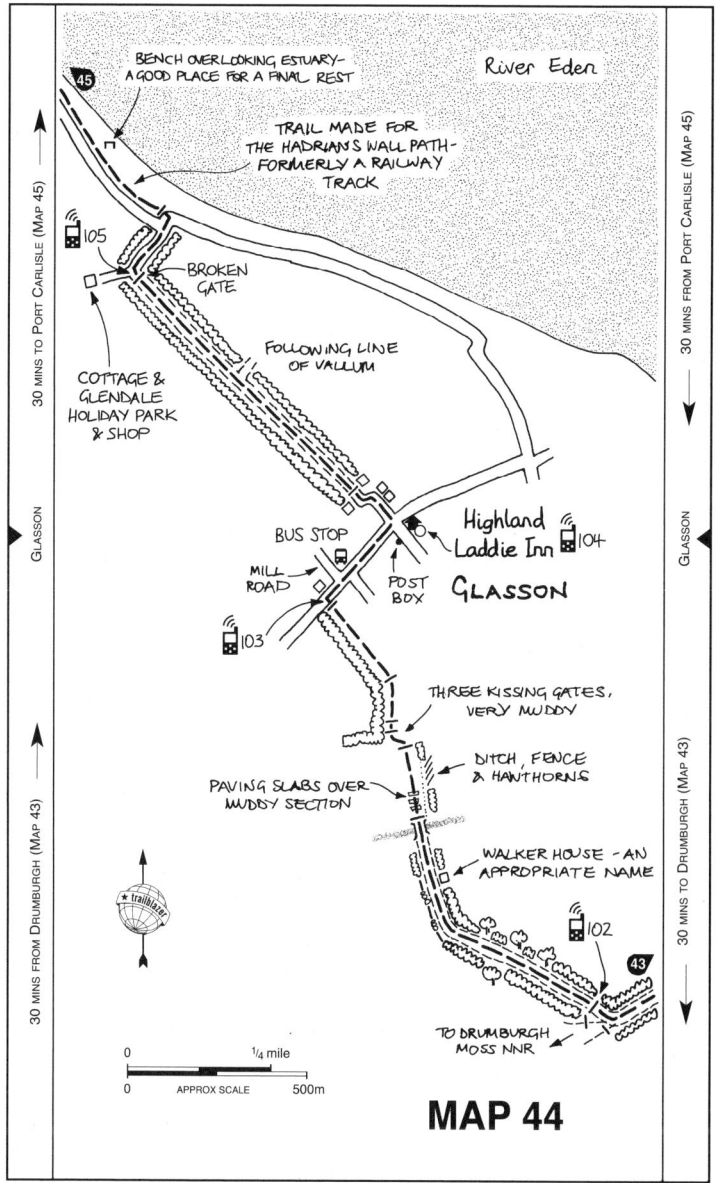

214 Carlisle to Bowness-on-Solway

the walls on which to sleep, a hot shower, small kitchen with kettle, toaster and two-ring stove; rates are £10pp per night. The chapel itself has **kitchen facilities** – sink, kettle, microwave, electric hob, plus tea, coffee and packet soups – which are open to the public and free to use with a donation.

Hesket House, the last house in the village, was formerly the Steam Packet Inn and above the door is a small grey stone **altar**, distinctly Roman, set into the brickwork. It fits in rather well.

Stagecoach **Bus** No 93/93A calls in Port Carlisle; see pp46-8 for details.

From Port Carlisle it's an uneventful 20-minute stroll along the coastal road to Bowness, the trill of the oystercatcher a welcome accompaniment. At Bowness you can get a pint, food, accommodation, and hopefully a bus back to Carlisle. As you enter the village the trail takes a sudden and unexpected turn to the right, between two houses and towards the coast, where a small shelter on **Banks Promenade** marks the end of the trail. In the shelter you'll find the final **passport stamp**, some Roman-style mosaic flooring depicting local birdlife and, most importantly, a seat to rest upon. Cue celebratory cheers, high-fives and group hugs. You've done it; you've walked Hadrian's Wall Path.

BOWNESS-ON-SOLWAY [Map 45]

Bowness is a lovely, peaceful place to finish the walk. In fact, it's almost eerily quiet. Most hikers turn straight round and head for home, via Carlisle, but there are a couple of places to stay, most notably the very welcoming Wallsend Guest House.

The name Bowness comes from the bow-shaped corner of the *ness*, or peninsula here. As the last place where the Solway is fordable, it is understandable why the Romans decided to finish their Wall here, and a large 7-acre (2.8-hectare) fort was built where the village now stands. This was **Maia**, the second largest fort on the Wall (indeed, 'Maia' can be translated as 'Larger'). Originally, the Wall was supposed to continue a little way beyond the fort at Bowness, for the Romans were wary that the Caledones and Irish could sneak by the Wall and land on Cumbria's west coast. However, the Romans soon decided to build a series of towers on that coastline instead, including one at Maryport – now known as the Western Sea Defences.

Today, there's very little evidence of the Romans, though there is an old Roman altar above a blocked-up byre door. (To find it, having emerged onto the main street in Bowness, turn right and, after passing a turn-off to the left there's a low barn or 'byre', followed by a taller one; here you'll see the outline of a blocked-up door with a clear Roman altar above it.) There are also some purloined stones from the Wall in the fabric of the village's striking Norman church, St Michael's, which stands on the site of the fort. Yet the destruction of the Wall around here seems to be quite a recent event: in 1801 there were said to be 500 yards (about 450 metres) of Wall just outside the village.

In the absence of much in the way of Wall or fort remains it's fair to say that Bowness is a little lacking in tourist attractions, though the church has a couple of bells inside at the back behind the font which were stolen from villages across the Solway in the 17th century – yet another manifestation of the antipathy that simmered for centuries between neighbours in this part of the world. It is apparently a tradition for every new vicar across the water to formally ask the parish for the bells back.

Services

Visiting Bowness requires a bit of forward planning. There's no ATM for one thing, although the pub and at least one of the B&Bs takes cards. And there are no shops, post offices or public telephones. Also, the transport links are few and seldom (see Transport).

Map 45, Bowness-on-Solway 215

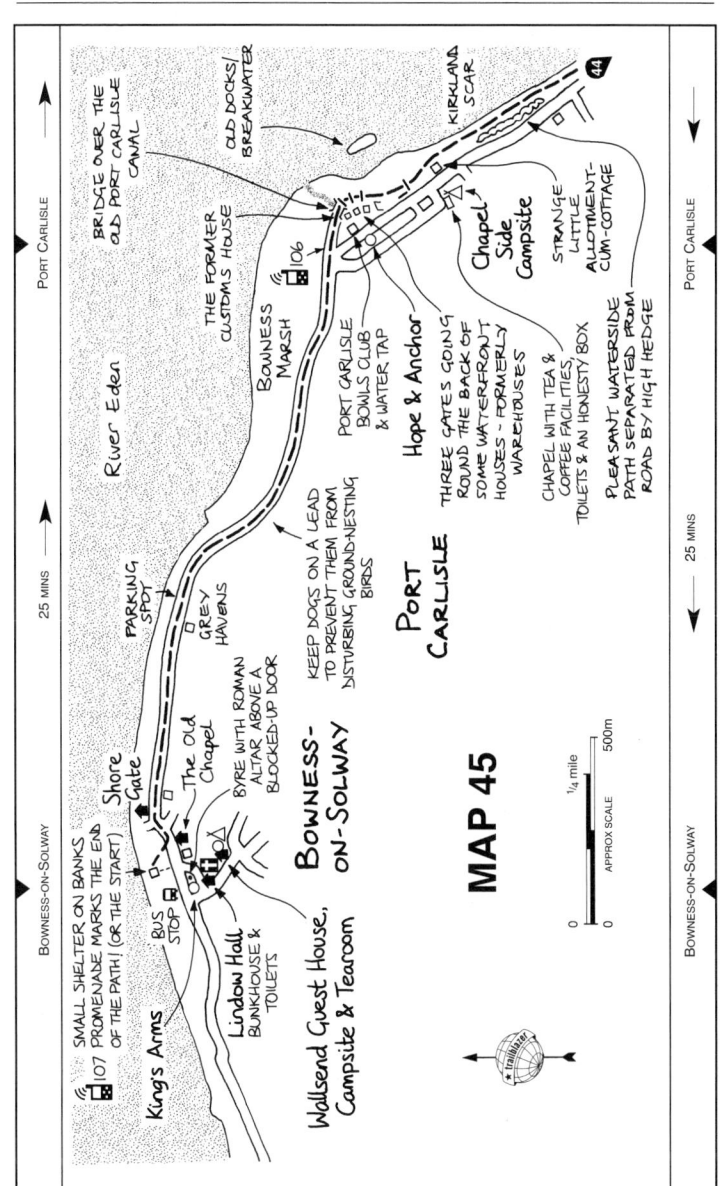

Wallsend Tearoom (see Where to eat) is the place to buy **Hadrian's Wall passports** (£5) if you're starting your walk here, or **completion certificates** (£2.50), if this is the end of your walk. They also sell a few Hadrian's Wall souvenirs; T-shirts and the like.

There are public **toilets** inside Lindow Hall.

Transport
[See pp46-8] To get back to Carlisle is tricky. From Monday to Saturday there's Stagecoach's **bus** No 93/93A which calls in at the bus stop opposite the King's Arms. The bus times are liable to change so it is essential to check them in advance, but at the time of writing they were: 7.34am, 10.12am, 1.37pm, 5.14pm and 6.58pm. It takes about 40 minutes to reach Carlisle.

If it's a Sunday or a Bank Holiday, there's no public transport, so you'll be forced to take a **private taxi** – expect to pay about £30 for a trip to Carlisle; try C&P Taxis (☎ 01228-535425), or P&J Taxis (☎ 07979-922819).

Where to stay
Wallsend Guest House (☎ 016973-51055, 🖳 www.wallsend.net; 1S/2D/1T/1Tr, all en suite; ✉; WI-FI; ⓛ; 🐾) is the smartest and most established **B&B** (£45pp, sgl £60, sgl occ £75, three sharing £100) in town, and is housed in a lovely building, the Old Rectory, at the western end of the village just below the church. They also have a fabulous **campsite** in a back field, with four **wigwams** (luxury en suite twin cabins; 🐾; WI-FI) for £37.50pp (sgl occ £75) and space for pitching **tents** (£10pp); there is a communal toilet and shower block for campers. They can do breakfasts for campers from 9am (ie when the B&B people have left the dining room); a continental breakfast costs £5 but they are also happy just to do a cup of tea. Note, they can accept payment by card here.

Also providing good-quality B&B is *Shore Gate* (☎ 016973-51308, 🖳 www .shoregatehouse.co.uk; 3D or T/1Tr, all en suite; WI-FI; ⓛ), right at the beginning of the village and with sumptuous views of the estuary; rates here are from £42.50pp (sgl occ £60, three sharing £105).

A few paces up the road, *The Old Chapel* (☎ 016973-51126, 🖳 www.old chapelbownessonsolway.com; 2S/1T private bathroom, 1Qd en suite; ✉; 🐾; WI-FI; ⓛ) is a lovingly converted sandstone Wesleyan chapel from 1872 that lies on the trail. Guests also have access to a modern kitchen area complete with cooker, microwave, fridge – and washing machine. B&B costs £35pp (whatever room you are in) and includes a cooked or continental breakfast.

There's also **bunkhouse** accommodation at *Lindow Hall* (☎ 016973-52487 or ☎ 01228-576157, 🖳 www.lindowhall.org.uk; 16 beds, £12pp), just up from the church. Lottery funding was used to convert the old reading room upstairs into a simple, but spacious bunkhouse. There can be separate male and female shower facilities; rates include use of the kitchen and dining area. Continental breakfast costs an extra £5. Bedding isn't provided, but can be rented for an extra £4. Note, you cannot just turn up and stay here. You must book in advance through their website or by phone.

Where to eat and drink
The most pleasant place to eat is *Wallsend Tearoom* (see Where to Stay; Wallsend Guest House; Easter-Sep daily 10am-4pm), especially if the weather's fine enough to eat outside. They do soups, sandwiches and fantastic homemade cakes, as well as afternoon tea and scones.

For a proper evening meal, head to *King's Arms* (☎ 016973-51426, 🖳 www .kingsarmsbowness.co.uk; bar only all day in summer but from 3.30pm in winter; food served Mar-Oct daily noon-8.30pm, Nov-Mar Mon-Fri 5-8pm, Sat & Sun noon-2pm & 5-8pm), which serves generous portions, and does a cracking pint of cider. On the outside wall they have a map showing where the original Roman fort would have stood, with the pub lying almost at its heart.

APPENDIX A: GLOSSARY

Antonine Wall Turf wall built to the north of Hadrian's construction by his successor, Antoninus Pius

Bastle house A fortified house built during the Middle Ages in the border region to protect the owner and his family from bandits

Brigantes The main tribe whose land was crossed by the Wall

Caledones The collective name for the tribes living north of the Wall

Gask Frontier The first border separating the conquered lands in the south from the 'Barbarians' in the north. Established by Domitian (AD81-96), it was also built to watch over the glens but moved further south when troops were required elsewhere in the empire

> ### ❏ Norse words
> Squashed between the Saxons and the Scots, the area of the Borders and the Lake District has kept many Norse words that you'll find today in the local place names. Amongst them:
>
> | Norse | Meaning |
> | --- | --- |
> | fell | upper slope of hill |
> | beck/burn | stream |
> | haugh | flat land beside river |
> | holm | island in river |
> | hope | sheltered valley |
> | moss | peat bog |

Milecastle A series of 'mini-castles' spaced 1000 paces apart (or one Roman mile) along the entire length of the Wall. Built to house troops, each could hold an estimated 32 men

Military Road Now the B6318, the Military Road was an 18th-century thoroughfare built on the orders of General Wade to thwart further attacks from Bonnie Prince Charlie

Military Way A Roman thoroughfare built around AD160 between the Stanegate and the Wall, often along the northern earthwork of the Vallum (which had by then been largely decommissioned)

Pele tower A square defensive tower built by wealthier families in the 16th century in the border counties of England and Scotland to defend themselves against the trepidations of reivers. The layout would typically follow the same design, with a storeroom on the ground floor, from which a staircase would lead upstairs to the living quarters. On the roof the family would light a beacon to summon help during a raid

Reivers Bandits and cattle rustlers during the Middle Ages

Stanegate The east–west road that ran between the Roman settlements of Carlisle and Corbridge which was one of the major reasons for the construction of the Wall

Trig points Small concrete pillars erected in the 1930s to aid surveying

Turret Stone observation posts, 161 in total, spaced evenly along the Wall to watch for movements to the north of the Wall

Vallum Roman earthwork, consisting of a deep ditch running between two high mud or earth walls, that ran to the south of and parallel to the Wall

> ### ❏ Haaf netting
> If you're lucky, when visiting Bowness you may come across the strange sight of half-a-dozen men standing chest-deep in the waters of the Solway holding large nets secured to wooden frames. This practice, known as haaf netting, is the traditional means of fishing in the estuary. The practice is believed to have come from the Vikings in around the 10th century AD, and indeed the very word 'haaf' comes from the Norse word for channel. The haaf net itself is a wooden frame, or 'beam', 5.5m long which is said to be the length of an old Viking oar without the blade. The net is then suspended from this beam, and the fishermen, usually in groups of half a dozen or so, form a line across the channel to catch any fish, usually sea trout and Atlantic salmon, that pass their way.

APPENDIX B: GPS WAYPOINTS

Each GPS waypoint listed was taken on the route at the reference number marked on the map as below. This list of GPS waypoints as well as instructions on how to interpret an OS grid reference can be found on the Trailblazer website: 🖥 www.trailblazer-guides.com (click on GPS waypoints).

MAP	WAYPOINT	OS GRID REF	DESCRIPTION
1	001	N54 59.313 W1 31.846	Segedunum
1	002	N54 58.431 W1 32.376	Wincomblee Bridge
2	003	N54 57.722 W1 32.737	Top of steps
2	004	N54 58.017 W1 34.658	St Lawrence Rd
3	005	N54 58.280 W1 35.370	Bridge over Ouseburn
3	006	N54 58.215 W1 35.993	Gateshead Millennium Bridge
3	007	N54 57.965 W1 36.755	Copthorne Hotel
4	008	N54 57.731 W1 39.035	Car park
4	009	N54 57.831 W1 39.372	Riverside path joins road
4	010	N54 57.927 W1 39.866	Cross A695
5	011	N54 58.130 W1 41.204	Milepost
5	012	N54 58.364 W1 41.571	Path leaves road for Denton Dene
5	013	N54 58.611 W1 41.886	Bridge across A1
5	014	N54 58.459 W1 42.143	Join road (Ottringham Close)
6	015	N54 58.613 W1 42.902	Path goes under bridge
6	016	N54 58.807 W1 43.962	Over A6085 at Newburn
6	017	N54 58.900 W1 44.649	The Boathouse
7	018	N54 58.884 W1 45.938	Gate at Ryton Island
7	019	N54 59.013 W1 45.985	Join (or leave) Wylam waggonway
7	020	N54 59.067 W1 47.485	Leave (or join) Wylam waggonway
8	021	N54 59.273 W1 48.207	Turn right off track by a stone wall
8	022	N54 59.463 W1 48.213	Track bends right (E)
8	023	N54 59.815 W1 47.322	First (or last) major piece of Roman wall on the trail
8	024	N55 00.005 W1 48.629	Path leaves road at gate
9	025	N55 00.094 W1 49.482	Cross road by Rudchester
9	026	N55 00.217 W1 50.375	Join B6318 by Two Hoots
9	027	N55 00.284 W1 50.989	Cross B6318; steps either side of road
10	028	N55 00.468 W1 52.160	Cross road to Albemarle Barracks
11	029	N55 00.590 W1 55.415	Robin Hood Inn
11	030	N55 00.680 W1 56.604	Stile leads into Roman ditch
11	031	N55 00.692 W1 56.977	Cross B6318
12	032	N55 00.745 W1 59.128	Leave road by wall
13	033	N55 00.670 W1 59.764	Stile by B6318
13	034	N55 00.642 W2 00.355	Path to Corbridge
13	035	N55 00.767 W2 01.232	Port Gate

Corbridge–Hexham–Acomb alternative

13a	*110*	*N55 00.122 W2 00.375*	*Bear right at junction*
13a	*111*	*N55 00.050 W2 00.647*	*Stay on road*
13a	*112*	*N54 59.882 W2 00.870*	*Join Leazes Lane*
13a	*113*	*N54 59.023 W2 00.885*	*Path goes under A695*
13b	*114*	*N54 58.276 W2 01.174*	*Join path by Rivery Tyne*
13b	*115*	*N54 58.141 W2 02.416*	*Cross railway tracks by bridge; take care*

GPS waypoints 219

MAP	WAYPOINT	OS GRID REF	DESCRIPTION

Corbridge–Hexham–Acomb alternative (cont'd)

MAP	WAYPOINT	OS GRID REF	DESCRIPTION
13b	116	N54 58.001 W2 02.422	*Take path off A695 after crossing bridge*
13b	117	N54 57.952 W2 02.657	*Cross track*
13c	118	N54 57.940 W2 03.090	*Signpost to Duke's House & Dilston*
13c	119	N54 57.785 W2 03.897	*Signpost to Dilston, A695 & Hexham Rd*
13d	120	N54 57.730 W2 04.803	*Signpost to Hexham and Dilston*
13d	121	N54 57.911 W2 05.273	*Signpost to Duke's House ¾ mile*
13e	122	N54 59.103 W2 06.098	*Junction of roads below Acomb*
13e	123	N54 59.230 W2 06.327	*Leave road*
13e	124	N54 59.369 W2 06.350	*Gate by mill*
13e	125	N54 59.582 W2 06.452	*Acomb; turn right (by The Sun Inn)*
13e	126	N54 59.939 W2 06.515	*Bear left after crossing a stile*

Main route

MAP	WAYPOINT	OS GRID REF	DESCRIPTION
14	036	N55 01.091 W2 03.854	Stile leads to steps
14	037	N55 01.161 W2 04.591	Cross stile after crossing track
15	038	N55 01.153 W2 05.742	Cross road
15	039	N55 01.155 W2 06.050	Path to Acomb
15	040	N55 01.259 W2 06.669	Cross road by track to quarry
15	041	N55 01.335 W2 07.151	Join road at end of wood
16	042	N55 01.420 W2 07.605	Path to Brunton Turret
16	043	N55 01.564 W2 07.459	Join road to Chollerford
16	044	N55 01.723 W2 08.297	Chesters entrance
16	045	N55 01.763 W2 09.203	Turn right off road to Walwick
16	046	N55 01.946 W2 09.159	Leave road at stile; enter farm
17	047	N55 02.182 W2 11.043	Cross track to Green Carts Farm
17	048	N55 02.301 W2 11.558	Trig point
18	049	N55 02.183 W2 12.857	Stone stile to Brocolitia
18	050	N55 02.034 W2 13.366	Mithras Temple
18	051	N55 02.122 W2 13.624	Cross road and cross stile
19	052	N55 01.861 W2 15.978	Milecastle 33
19	053	N55 01.685 W2 17.660	Grindon Turret 34a
20	054	N55 01.540 W2 18.395	Milecastle 35
20	055	N55 01.474 W2 18.844	Trig point
21	056	N55 00.880 W2 19.715	Knag Burn Gate
22	057	N55 00.731 W2 20.258	Milecastle 37
22	058	N55 00.229 W2 22.528	Milecastle 39 (Castle Nick)
23	059	N55 00.092 W2 23.281	Gates after descent from Peel Crags
23	060	N55 00.120 W2 24.282	Green Slack (trig point)
23	061	N55 00.099 W2 24.433	Path to Winshields Farm
24	062	N54 59.809 W2 25.522	Bogle Hole
24	063	N54 59.629 W2 26.819	Hole Gap
25	064	N54 59.585 W2 27.117	Stile by Burnhead B&B

Walking to and from Haltwhistle

MAP	WAYPOINT	OS GRID REF	DESCRIPTION
25	130	N54 59.585 W2 27.117	*Gate onto road by bridge over Haltwhistle Burn*
25	131	N54 59.262 W2 26.959	*Gate onto B6318*
25	132	N54 59.232 W2 27.119	*Gate off B6318*
25	133	N54 58.645 W2 27.501	*Bridge by Old Brickworks*
25	134	N54 58.769 W2 27.746	*Gate across Willia Rd*
25	135	N54 59.179 W2 27.516	*Cross B6318*

Appendix B: GPS waypoints

MAP	WAYPOINT	OS GRID REF	DESCRIPTION
Main route			
26	065	N54 59.598 W2 30.057	Stile onto track to Walltown Farm
27	066	N54 59.205 W2 31.163	Walltown Country Park Information & Shop
27	067	N54 59.268 W2 31.223	Leave road and join path to the north of the Roman ditch
27	068	N54 59.301 W2 32.050	Gate opposite Thirlwall Castle
27	069	N54 59.281 W2 32.353	Path leaves road; cross stile
28	070	N54 59.325 W2 33.365	Leave track at stile
28	071	N54 59.368 W2 34.156	Cross stile onto road leading to Samson Inn
28	072	N54 59.375 W2 34.720	Cross cattle grid near Turret 48A
29	073	N54 59.375 W2 36.245	Gate at Birdoswald
29	074	N54 59.007 W2 37.901	Gate onto farm track
30	075	N54 58.845 W2 38.486	Join track to Comb Crag
30	076	N54 58.604 W2 39.602	Leave road at stile near Pike Hill Signal Tower
30	077	N54 58.468 W2 40.171	Cross stile and go back onto road
31	078	N54 58.462 W2 40.952	High chunk of wall with faint 'SPP' carved on northern side
31	079	N54 58.392 W2 41.942	Haytongate Farm
32	080	N54 58.296 W2 44.435	Abutment just west of bridge
32	081	N54 58.146 W2 45.362	Gate into woods
32	082	N54 58.118 W2 45.651	Gate heading into second field
33	083	N54 57.812 W2 46.431	Bridge over a stream
33	084	N54 57.219 W2 47.361	Kissing gate by last house in Newton
34	085	N54 56.805 W2 48.853	Gate by bus stop at Oldwall
35	086	N54 56.334 W2 51.308	Join bridleway known as Sandy Lane
35	087	N54 55.901 W2 51.053	Stile and gate off Sandy Lane
35	088	N54 55.755 W2 51.169	Join road after series of gates
36	089	N54 55.452 W2 52.510	Bridge over stream
36	090	N54 55.194 W2 52.922	Turn away from River Eden
37	091	N54 54.395 W2 54.431	Path off road by The Beeches
38	092	N54 54.273 W2 55.208	Bridge and kissing gate
38	093	N54 54.007 W2 56.091	Sands Sports Centre
39	094	N54 53.946 W2 57.775	Go under disused rail bridge over Eden
40	095	N54 54.752 W2 59.179	Path leaves road at Grinsdale
40	096	N54 54.806 W2 59.883	Cross Sourmilk Footbridge
40	097	N54 55.491 W3 01.121	Black and white house
41	098	N54 55.287 W3 02.522	Gate leads to road
41	099	N54 55.301 W3 03.413	Greyhound Inn
42	100	N54 55.351 W3 05.013	Gate and cattle grid at Dykesfield
43	101	N54 55.639 W3 08.904	Turn left at crossroads in Drumburgh
44	102	N54 55.346 W3 09.452	Gate across track
44	103	N54 55.932 W3 10.198	Path joins road at Glasson
44	104	N54 56.052 W3 10.045	Junction by Highland Laddie Inn
44	105	N54 56.397 W3 10.708	Entry to Glendale Holiday Park
45	106	N54 56.983 W3 11.317	Port Carlisle; path joins main road to Bowness-on-Solway
45	107	N54 57.240 W3 12.773	Small shelter on Banks Promenade marks the end (or the start) of the path

APPENDIX C: TAKING A DOG

[See also pp35-6] As noted on pp35-6, the Hadrian's Wall Path is not that dog-friendly. Much of the land through which the path passes is grazed by livestock and dogs must be kept on a lead. However, if you're sure your dog can cope with (and will enjoy) walking 12 miles or more a day for several days in a row, you need to start preparing accordingly. The best starting point is to study the village and town facilities table on pp30-1 and the advice below.

Looking after your dog
To begin with, you need to make sure that your own dog is fully **inoculated** against the usual doggy illnesses, and also up to date with regard to **worm pills** (eg Drontal) and **flea preventatives** such as Frontline – they are, after all, following in the pawprints of many a dog before them, some of whom may well have left fleas or other parasites on the trail that now lie in wait for their next meal to arrive. **Pet insurance** is also a very good idea; if you've already got insurance, do check that it will cover a trip such as this. On the subject of looking after your dog's health, perhaps the most important implement you can take with you is the **plastic tick remover**, available from vets for a couple of quid. These help you to remove the tick safely (ie without leaving its head behind buried under the dog's skin).

Being in unfamiliar territory also makes it more likely that you and your dog could become separated. For this reason, make sure your dog has a **tag with your contact details on it** (a mobile phone number would be best if you are carrying one with you).

When to keep your dog on a lead
- **Near the crags** It's a sad fact that more than one dog has perished after falling over the edge of the crags. It usually occurs when they are chasing rabbits (which know where the edge of the cliffs is and are able, unlike your poor pooch, to stop in time).
- **When crossing farmland**, particularly in the lambing season (around May) when your dog can scare the sheep, causing them to lose their young. Farmers are allowed by law to shoot at and kill any dogs that they consider are worrying their sheep. During lambing, most farmers would prefer it if you didn't bring your dog at all. It is also **compulsory to keep your dog on a lead through National Trust land**. The exception to the dogs on leads rule is if your dog is being attacked by cows. A few years ago there were three deaths in the UK caused by walkers being trampled as they tried to rescue their dogs from the attentions of cattle. The advice in this instance is to let go of the lead, head speedily to a position of safety (usually the other side of the field gate or stile) and call your dog to you.
- **Around ground-nesting birds** It's important to keep your dog under control when crossing an area where certain species of birds nest on the ground. Most dogs love foraging around in the woods but make sure you have permission to do so; some woods are used as 'nurseries' for game birds and dogs are only allowed through them if they are on a lead.

What to pack
- **Food/water bowl** Foldable cloth bowls are popular with trekkers, being light and taking up little room in the rucksack. You can also get a water-bottle-and-bowl combination, where the bottle folds into a 'trough' from which the dog can drink.
- **Lead and collar** An extendable one is probably preferable for this sort of trip. Make sure both lead and collar are in good condition – you don't want either to snap on the trail, or you may end up carrying your dog through sheep fields until a replacement can be found.
- **Medication** You'll know if you need to bring any lotions or potions.
- **Bedding** A simple blanket may suffice, or more if you aren't carrying your own luggage.
- **A favourite toy** Helps prevent your dog from pining for the entire trek.
- **Food/water** Remember to bring treats as well as regular food to keep up mutt morale.
- **Corkscrew stake** Available from camping or pet shops, this will help you to keep your dog secure in one place while you set up camp/doze.   ● **Poo bags** Essential.
- **Hygiene wipes** For cleaning your dog after it's rolled in stuff. ● **Tick remover** See p221.

222 Appendix C: Taking a dog

● **Raingear** It can rain a lot! ● **Old towels** For drying your dog after the deluge.

When it comes to packing, it's a good idea to leave an exterior pocket of your rucksack devoted to your dog's kit. Some dogs even sport their own 'doggy rucksack', so they can carry their own food, water, poo etc – which certainly reduces the burden on their owner.

Cleaning up after your dog
Dog excrement should be cleaned up to ensure it is not left to decorate the boots of others. In towns, villages and particularly in fields where animals graze or which will be cut for silage, hay etc, you must pick up and bag the excrement.

Staying with your dog
In this guide we have used the symbol 🐕 to denote where a hotel, pub or B&B welcomes dogs. However, this always needs to be arranged in advance and some places make an additional charge while others may require a deposit which is refundable if the dog doesn't make a mess. Hostels do not permit them unless they are an assistance (guide) dog; smaller campsites tend to accept them, but some of the larger holiday parks do not. In some cases dogs need to sleep in a separate building. When it comes to eating, most landlords allow dogs in at least a section of their pubs, though few restaurants do. Always ask first and ensure your dog doesn't run around the pub but is secured to your table or a radiator.

Map key

Symbol	Meaning	Symbol	Meaning	Symbol	Meaning
			Library/bookstore	●	Other
♠	Where to stay		Internet	CP	Car park
O	Where to eat and drink		Museum/gallery		Bus station
△	Campsite		Church/cathedral		Bus stop
✉	Post Office		Telephone		Rail line & station
£	Bank/ATM		Public toilet		Park
i	Tourist Information	□	Building	082	GPS waypoint
	Walking Track		Gate		Stream
	Minor Track		Bridge		River
	4WD Track		Fence		Forest / Wood
	Road		Stone Wall		Boggy Ground
	Steps		Hedge		Hadrian's Wall
	Slope		Water		Vallum
	Steep Slope		Sand		Ditch
	Stile		Stones	43	Map Continuation

INDEX

Page references in **bold** type refer to map

Aballava (fort) **53**, 205, 208
access 67-8
accidents 69
accommodation 17-21, 100
  booking 20
  booking services 26, 43
Acomb 137-8, **139**
adders 75
Aesica (fort) **53, 165**, 169
Agricola 49, 56, 130-1, 180, 196
annual events 14
Antenociticus, Temple 97
Antonine Wall 54, 217
Antoninus Pius, Emperor 54, 130-1
Arbeia (fort) 96-8, 101
Areas of Outstanding Natural Beauty (AONBs) 9, 71, 201
Armstrong, William 108
ATMs 24, 30, 39

Backpackers Club 43
baggage carriers 26, 36
bank holidays 24
Banks 180, **181**
banks 24, 30
Banna **53**, 178
Beaumont 205, **206**,
bed and breakfasts (B&Bs) 19-20, 29, 31, 33
Bede, Venerable 52, 196
Benwell Fort **53**, 97
Benwell Temple 96-7
Berm 52
Birdoswald **53**, 178, **179**
birds 75-7
Black Carts 147, **148**
blisters 70
Bloody Gap **164**, 166
Boadicea 56
Bogle Hole **164**, 166
books 41-3
boots 37
Boudicca, Queen 56
Boustead Hill **209**, 210
Bowness-on-Solway **53**, 214, **215**, 216

Brampton 186-9, **187**, **188**
Brampton Old Church **53**
breweries 23
Brigantes 52, 54, 59, 180
British Summer Time (BST) 25
Brocolitia (fort) **53, 149**, 150
Bromlee Lough **155**, 158
Brunton Turret **143**, 144
budgeting 29
bunkhouses 19, 29, 31
Burgh-by-Sands **53**, 205, **207**, 208
bus services 46-8
  AD122 Rover ticket 48
business hours 24

Caledones 49, 52, 56, 180
Camboglanna **53**, 186, **187**
Camden, William 60
campaigning organisations 72
camping and campsites 18, 29, 31, 33, 34
camping barns 19, 29, 31, 33
camping gear 39
Carlisle **53**, 194, **195**, 196-201, **197**
Carlisle Castle **197**, 201
Carrawburgh (fort) **53, 149**, 150
Carvetii 59, 196
Carvoran **53**, 171, **173**
cash machines *see* ATMs
Castle Nick **157**
Castlesteads **53**, 185-6
Cat Stairs 160, **161**
cattle 221
Caw Gap **164**, 166
Cawfields Quarry **164**, 166
chequebooks 25, 39
Chesterholm **53**
Chesters (fort) **53**, 116, **143**, 145-6
Chollerford **143**, 144-5
Chollerford Bridge **53**
Cilurnum (fort) **53**, 116, **143**, 145-6

Claudius, Emperor 55
Clayton, John 61, 144-5, 150, 158
Clayton Wall **157**, 158, **159**
climate 13-15
clothing 38
coaches: to Britain 45
  within Britain 48
Code of Respect, Hadrian's Wall 64-5
Coesike Turret (33B) **151**, 154
Collingwood Bruce, John 61
Comb Crag **181**
compasses 39, 68
Concavata (fort) **53**, 210
Condercum **53**
conservation 71-2
  organisations 72
construction of wall 50-2
Corbridge 126-9, **128**, **132**
Corbridge Lanx 131
Corbridge Roman Town **53**, **127**, 130-1, **132**
Coria 130
Corstopitum *see* Corbridge Roman Town
costs 29
Countryside and Rights of Way Act 67
Countryside Code 67
Coventina's Well 150
cows 221
Crag Lough 158, **159**
cream teas 21
credit cards 25, 39
Crosby-on-Eden 189, **191**
cross-section (wall) **50**
Cuddy's Crags **157**, 159
currency 24
Cuthbert, St 196

Davies, Hunter 42, 177, 184, 186
daylight hours 15
debit cards 24, 25, 39
Denton Dene 104, **111**
Denton Hall Turret 97, **111**

224 Index

Dere Street **53**, **125**, 126, **127**, 131, **138**
difficulty of walk 10-12
digital mapping 41
Dilston 131, **132**
direction of walk 35
ditches, Roman 52, 119
documents 25, 39
dogs 35-6, 64, 221-22
Domitian, Emperor 49, 56
drinking water 23
drinks 21-3
driving: to Britain 45
within Britain 48
Drumburgh **53**, 210-12, **211**
Drumburgh Castle 210, **211**
Dunston Coal Staithes **109**, 110
duration of walk 12
DVDs 44
Dykesfield 208, **209**

earthworks *see* Vallum
East Wallhouses 122, **123**
eating places 21-2, 31
economic impact of walking 64-5
Elswick 108, **109**
emergency services 25
emergency signal 69
English Heritage 40, 43, 72, 97
environmental impact of walking 65-8
equipment 36-44
erosion of wall 63
essential items 39
European Health Insurance Cards (EHICs) 24
events 14
exchange rates 24

ferry services 45
festivals 14
first-aid kit 38-9, 68
fish 75
Flavian Policy 57
flights 45
flora and fauna 73-80
field guides 43-4
flowers 79-80
food 21-2, 68
food stores 31

footwear 37

Gask Frontier 49, 56, 217
Gillam, John 150
Gilsland 174-7, **175**
Glasson 212, **213**
government agencies and schemes 71-3
GPS 17, 41, 218-20
waypoints 218-20
Great Chesters (fort) **53**, **165**, 169-70
Green Slack **161**, 164
Greenhead 172-4, **173**
Greenlee Lough 158
Greenwich Mean Time (GMT) 25
Grindon 150, **151**
Grindon Milecastle 116, **151**, 154
Grindon Turret (34A) **151**, 154
Grinsdale 205, **206**
group walking tours 28
guesthouses 20, 29
guided walking tours 28

haaf netting 217
Hadrian, Emperor 43, 50-1, 57
Hadrian's Wall Code of Respect 63, 64-5
Hadrian's Wall Country bus 48
Hadrian's Wall Country rail line 48
Hadrian's Wall Path Passport 40
Hadrian's Way 104
Halton Chesters (fort) **53**, **125**, 126
Halton Shields 122, **124**
Haltwhistle 166-9, **168**
Hare Hill 182, **183**
Harlow Hill 119, **121**
hazards 68-9
heat exhaustion 70
heatstroke 70
Heavenfield, Battle of 138, **141**, 142
Heddon-on-the-Wall 116, **117**, 118
Hexham 133-7, **134-5**

Hexham Abbey 60, 133, **135**
highlights 13
historical background 49-62
Romans in Britain 55-7, 58-9
construction of Wall 50-2
improvements 52-4
post-Hadrian 54, 58-9
after Roman times 60-2
historical websites 41-2
Hodgson, John 51, 61
Hole Gap **164**
Horsley, Rev John 60
hostels 19, 29, 31, 33
hotels 20
Housesteads (fort) **53**, 54, 156, **157**, 158
Humshaugh **143**, 144-5
Hutton, William 60-1, 142, 156
hyperthermia 70
hypothermia 70

inns 20; *see also* pubs
international distress signal 69
internet access 26
Irthing Bridge 177, **179**
itineraries 30-4

Julius Caesar 55

King Arthur's Turret (44B) 170, **171**
Knag Burn Gate 156, **157**

lambing 221
Lanercost Priory 182, **183**
Laversdale 189, **190**
Lemington Glass Cone 110, **112**
Limestone Corner 147, **148**
Linstock Castle 192, **193**
litter 64-6
local businesses 65
local transport 46-8
Long Distance Walkers' Association 43
Low Crosby 189, 191, **191-2**
Luguvalium (fort) **53**, 196

Index 225

Maia (fort) **53**, 214
Magna (fort) **53**, 171, **173**
mammals 73-5
map scale 99
map keys 222
maps 40-1
　Wall in Roman times **53**
milecastles 52, 116, 217
Milecastle 13: **117**, 119
Milecastle 16: 119
Milecastle 24: 138, **140**
Milecastle 33: 150, **151**
Milecastle 34: **151**, 154
Milecastle 35: 154, **155**
Milecastle 37: **157**, 158
Milecastle 38: 159, **159**
Milecastle 39: **159**, 160
Milecastle 42: **164**, 166
Milecastle 43: 170
Milecastle 48: **175**, 177
Milecastle 49: 178, **179**
Military Road 60, 68, 118, 146, 217
Military Way 58, 158, 217
minimum impact walking 63-8
Mithraism 152-3
Mithras Temple **149**, 150, 152-3
mobile phones 25, 39, 41
money 24-5, 39
Monkhill 205, **206-7**
museums and galleries
　Birdoswald 178, **179**, 180
　Carlisle: Tullie House 194, **197**, 200
　Carvoran: Roman Army Museum 171, **173**
　Chesters **143**, 145-6
　Housesteads 156, **157**, 158
　Newcastle
　　BALTIC Centre for Contemporary Art **85**, 96, **107**
　　Bessie Surtees House **87**, 98
　　Discovery Museum **85**, 98
　　Great North Museum: Hancock **84**, 94
　　Hatton Gallery **84**, 98

museums and galleries
　Newcastle (*cont'd*)
　　Laing Art Gallery **85**, 98
　　Vindolanda **159**, **161**, 162-3

national holidays 24
National Nature Reserves (NNRs) 71-2
national parks 71
national transport 44-8
National Trust 25, 40, 72
Natural England 71-3
Nero, Emperor 56
Nether Denton **53**
Newburn 110, **112**
Newcastle **53**, 81-98, **84-5**, **87**, **88**, **107**
　accommodation 83-9
　airport 45, 82
　Arbeia 96-8, 101
　BALTIC Centre for Contemporary Art **85**, 96, **107**
　Benwell Temple 96-7
　Bessie Surtees House **87**, 98
　bus tours 94
　Castle Keep (Castle Garth) **87**, 94-5
　Chinatown **85**, 91
　city maps **84-5**, **87**, **88**
　Discovery Museum **85**, 98
　eating out 89-93
　entertainment 93-4
　Great North Museum: Hancock **84**, 94
　Laing Art Gallery **85**, 98
　public transport 44-8, 81, 82
　Pons Aelius **53**, 95, 104
　Sage, The **85**, 96, **107**
　St James' Park football stadium **84**, 94
　services 83
　sights 94-8
　Swan Hunter 103
　tourist information 83
　Tyne bridges 95, **107**
　West Road Roman ruins 96-7

Newtown 186, **187**
Norse words 217
Northumberland National Park 146, 147
Northumberland Dark Sky Park 71, 146

Oldwall 189, **190**
Once Brewed 160, **161**, 162
online information 41, 42
Onnum (fort) **53**, **125**, 126
outdoor equipment shops 26
outdoor safety 68-70
Ovingham 33, 34, **113**, 115

passport stamping stations 40
Peel Crags 160, **161**
pele towers 128, 217
Pennine Way **173**
pharmacies 26
Pike Hill Signal Tower 180, **181**
Piper Sike Turret (51A) 180, **181**
Planetrees **141**, 142
Poltross Burn Milecastle **175**, 177
Pons Aelius **53**, 95, 104
Port Carlisle 212, 214, **215**
Port Gate **53**, **125**, 138
post offices 24, 30
public holidays 14, 24
public transport 44-8, **47**
pubs 21-3

rail services *see* trains
rainfall 15
Ramblers' 43
rates of exchange 24
real ales 23
reivers 170, 204, 217
reptiles 75
Rickerby 192, **195**
right to roam 67
Roman bridges 95, 104, **128**, **143**, 144, 164, 177, **179**, 194
Roman coins 130, 150
Roman ditches 52
Roman miles 58
Roman milestones 168, **169**

Roman Military Way 58, 158, 217
Romans in Britain 55-9
Royal Society for the Protection of Birds (RSPB) 72
rucksacks 36-7
Rudchester Fort **53**, 119, **120**

safety 68-70
Scotswood 110, **111**
school holiday periods 24
seasons 13-15
self catering 22
Segedunum (fort) 52, **53**, 101-4, **105**
self-guided holidays 26-8
Severus, Emperor 51, 59
Sewingshields Castle 154
Sewingshields Crags 154, **155**
Sewingshields Turret (35A) **155**
Sites of Special Scientific Interest (SSSIs) 72
smoking 25
snakes 75
Solway Marshes/Estuary 71, 72, 201
Sourmilk Footbridge 205, **206**
Spartianus 50, 51
Special Areas of Conservation (SACs) 72
St Antony's Point 104
St John Lee Church 137, **139**
St Oswald's Church **141**, 142
St Oswald's Hill Head 138, **141**
St Oswald's Way 142
St Peter's Marina 104, **106**
Stanegate 49, 56, 57, 58, 131
Stanwix (fort) **53**, 196
Steel Rigg 160, **161**
Stephenson, George 114
sunburn 70
Swan Hunter shipyard 103
Sycamore Gap **159**, 160

telephones 25
 see also mobile phones
temperature chart 15
Theodosian Edict 150
Thirlwall Castle 172, **173**
Thorny Doors **164**, 166
tides, Solway 201
torches 39, 69
tourist information centres 30, 43
town facilities 30-1
trail information, online 42
trail map key 222
trail maps 99-100
trains: to Britain 45
 within Britain 44, 45, 47, 48
Trajan, Emperor 49, 50, 56, 57
travel insurance 24
trees 77-9
Tulip, Henry 142
turrets 52, 116, 217
Turret 26B 142, **143**
Turret 27A 116, 145
Turret 29A 147, **148**
Turret 33B **151**, 154
Turret 34A **151**, 154
Turret 35A 155
Turret 41A **164**
Turret 44B 170, **171**
Turret 45A 170, **173**
Turret 48A **175**, 177
Turret 48B **175**, 177
Turret 49B **179**
Turret 50B 180
Turret 51A 180, **181**
Turret 51B **181**
Turret 52A **181**
Tyne Riverside Country Park 110, **113**

UNESCO 7, 62, 63
Uxelodunum (fort) **53**, 196

vallum 50, 52, 54, 58, 59, 97
Vercovicium (fort) **53**, 156
Vespasian, Emperor 56
village facilities 30-1
Vindobala (fort) **53**, 119, **120**

Vindolanda (fort) **53**, **159**, **161**, 162-3
Vindolanda postcards 37, 43, 130, 162-3
visitor centres 43

Wade, General 60, 118, 160
Walker Riverside Park 104, **106**
walkers' organisations 43
walking companies 26-8
walking poles/sticks 39
walking seasons 13-15
walking times 99
Wall (village) 142, **143**
wall forts 52, **53**, 54, 61, 102
 see also name of fort
Wallhouses 122, **123**
Wallsend **53**, 101-4, **105**
Walltown Crags 170, **171**, **173**
Walltown Quarry 170, **173**
Walton 184, **185**, 186
water 23, 39, 68
waymarks 17
waypoints *see* GPS
weather 13-15
weather forecasts 69
websites 42-3
weights and measures 25
Whin Sill **157**, 158
Winshields Crags **161**, 164
whistles 39, 69
Whittledene Reservoir 119, **121**
wi-fi 26
wild camping 18, 34, 67
wildlife 66, 73-7
Wildlife Trusts 72
Willowford Bridge **53**, 177, **179**
World Heritage Sites 62, 63
Wylam **113**, 114, 115, **115**
Wylam Waggonway **113**, 114

Youth Hostel Association 19

TRAILBLAZER TITLE LIST

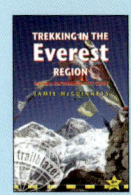

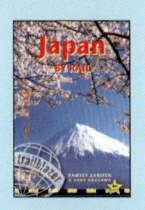

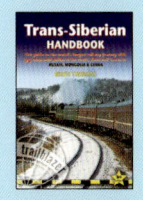

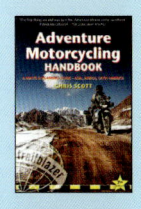

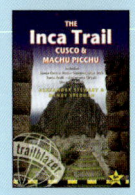

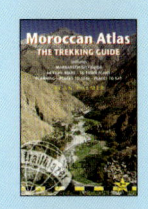

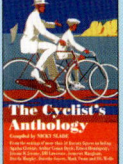

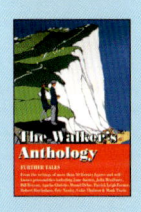

Adventure Cycle-Touring Handbook
Adventure Motorcycling Handbook
Australia by Rail
Azerbaijan
Cleveland Way (British Walking Guide) – due 2018
Coast to Coast (British Walking Guide)
Cornwall Coast Path (British Walking Guide)
Cotswold Way (British Walking Guide)
The Cyclist's Anthology
Dales Way (British Walking Guide)
Dorset & Sth Devon Coast Path (British Walking Gde)
Exmoor & Nth Devon Coast Path (British Walking Gde)
Great Glen Way (British Walking Guide)
Hadrian's Wall Path (British Walking Guide)
Himalaya by Bike – a route and planning guide
Inca Trail, Cusco & Machu Picchu
Japan by Rail
Kilimanjaro – the trekking guide (includes Mt Meru)
Moroccan Atlas – The Trekking Guide
Morocco Overland (4WD/motorcycle/mountainbike)
Nepal Trekking & The Great Himalaya Trail
New Zealand – The Great Walks
North Downs Way (British Walking Guide) – due 2018
Offa's Dyke Path (British Walking Guide)
Overlanders' Handbook – worldwide driving guide
Peddars Way & Norfolk Coast Path (British Walking Gde)
Pembrokeshire Coast Path (British Walking Guide)
Pennine Way (British Walking Guide)
Peru's Cordilleras Blanca & Huayhuash – Hiking/Biking
The Railway Anthology
The Ridgeway (British Walking Guide)
Sahara Overland – a route and planning guide
Scottish Highlands – Hillwalking Guide
Siberian BAM Guide – rail, rivers & road
The Silk Roads – a route and planning guide
Sinai – the trekking guide
South Downs Way (British Walking Guide)
Thames Path (British Walking Guide)
Tour du Mont Blanc
Trans-Canada Rail Guide
Trans-Siberian Handbook
Trekking in the Everest Region
The Walker's Anthology
The Walker's Anthology – further tales
The Walker's Haute Route – Mont Blanc to Matterhorn
West Highland Way (British Walking Guide)

For more information about Trailblazer and our
expanding range of guides, for guidebook updates or
for credit card mail order sales visit our website:

www.trailblazer-guides.com

TRAILBLAZER'S LONG-DISTANCE PATH (LDP) WALKING GUIDES

We've applied to destinations which are closer to home Trailblazer's proven formula for publishing definitive practical route guides for adventurous travellers. Britain's network of long-distance trails enables the walker to explore some of the finest landscapes in the country's best walking areas. These are guides that are user-friendly, practical, informative and environmentally sensitive.

● **Unique mapping features** In many walking guidebooks the reader has to read a route description then try to relate it to the map. Our guides are much easier to use because walking directions, tricky junctions, places to stay and eat, points of interest and walking times are all written onto the maps themselves in the places to which they apply. With their uncluttered clarity, these are not general-purpose maps but fully edited maps drawn by walkers for walkers.

● **Largest-scale walking maps** At a scale of just under 1:20,000 (8cm or 3 1/8 inches to one mile) the maps in these guides are bigger than even the most detailed British walking maps currently available in the shops.

● **Not just a trail guide – includes where to stay, where to eat and public transport** Our guidebooks cover the complete walking experience, not just the route. Accommodation options for all budgets are provided (pubs, hotels, B&Bs, campsites, bunkhouses, hostels) as well as places to eat. Detailed public transport information for all access points to each trail means that there are itineraries for all walkers, for hiking the entire route as well as for day or weekend walks.

Coast to Coast *Henry Stedman*, 7th edition, £11.99
ISBN 978-1-905864-74-4, 268pp, 110 maps, 40 colour photos

Cornwall Coast Path (SW Coast Path Pt 2) *Stedman & Newton*, 5th edition, £11.99
ISBN 978-1-905864-71-3, 3526pp, 142 maps, 40 colour photos

Cotswold Way *Tricia & Bob Hayne* 3rd edition, £11.99
ISBN 978-1-905864-70-6, 204pp, 53 maps, 40 colour photos

Dales Way *Henry Stedman* 1st edition, £11.99
ISBN 978-1-905864-78-2, 176pp, 45 maps, 40 colour photos

Dorset & South Devon (SW Coast Path Pt 3) *Stedman & Newton*, 1st edition, £11.99
ISBN 978-1-905864-45-4, 336pp, 88 maps, 40 colour photos

Exmoor & North Devon (SW Coast Path Pt 1) *Stedman & Newton*, 2nd edition, £11.99
ISBN 978-1-905864-86-7, 192pp, 68 maps, 40 colour photos

Great Glen Way *Jim Manthorpe*, 1st edition, £11.99
ISBN 978-1-905864-80-5, 192pp, 55 maps, 40 colour photos

Hadrian's Wall Path *Henry Stedman*, 5th edition, £11.99
ISBN 978-1-905864-85-0, 224pp, 60 maps, 40 colour photos

Offa's Dyke Path *Keith Carter*, 4th edition, £11.99
ISBN 978-1-905864-65-2, 240pp, 98 maps, 40 colour photos

Peddars Way & Norfolk Coast Path *Alexander Stewart*, £11.99
ISBN 978-1-905864-28-7, 192pp, 54 maps, 40 colour photos

Pembrokeshire Coast Path *Jim Manthorpe*, 5th edition, £11.99
ISBN 978-1-905864-84-3, 236pp, 96 maps, 40 colour photos

Pennine Way *Stuart Greig*, 4th edition, £11.99
ISBN 978-1-905864-61-4, 272pp, 138 maps, 40 colour photos

The Ridgeway *Nick Hill*, 4th edition, £11.99
ISBN 978-1-905864-79-9, 208pp, 53 maps, 40 colour photos

South Downs Way *Jim Manthorpe*, 5th edition, £11.99
ISBN 978-1-905864-66-9, 192pp, 60 maps, 40 colour photos

Thames Path *Joel Newton*, 1st edition, £11.99
ISBN 978-1-905864-64-5, 256pp, 99 maps, 40 colour photos

West Highland Way *Charlie Loram*, 6th edition, £11.99
ISBN 978-1-905864-76-8, 208pp, 60 maps, 40 colour photos

'The same attention to detail that distinguishes its other guides has been brought to bear here'.
THE SUNDAY TIMES

IN PREPARATION FOR PUBLICATION IN 2018
Cleveland Way
ISBN 978-1-905864-91-1

North Downs Way
ISBN 978-1-905864-90-4

TRAILBLAZER
British Walking Guides
SEE p227 FOR FULL TITLE LIST
Dales Way
Pembrokeshire Coast Path
Great Glen Way
Exmoor & North Devon Coast Path
Cornwall Coast Path
The Ridgeway
Orkney
Thurso
Stornoway
Scottish Highlands Hillwalking Guide
Inverness
Skye
Great Glen Way
Aberdeen
Fort William
SCOTLAND
Mull
West Highland Way
Edinburgh
Milngavie
Glasgow
Berwick upon Tweed
Kirk Yetholm
Arran
Pennine Way
Hadrian's Wall Path
N. IRELAND
Bowness-on-Solway
Carlisle
Wallsend
Newcastle upon Tyne
Belfast
Coast to Coast
St Bees
Robin Hood's Bay
Bowness-on-Windermere
Filey
Helmsley
Dales Way
Cleveland Way
Isle of Man
Ilkley
York
REP. OF IRELAND
Leeds
Hull
Pennine Way
Peddars Way & Norfolk Coast Path
Dublin
IRISH SEA
Liverpool
Prestatyn
Manchester
Edale
Lincoln
Anglesey
Bangor
Crewe
Nottingham
Cromer
Norwich
ENGLAND
Offa's Dyke Path
Birmingham
Cotswold Way
Cambridge
Knettishall Heath
Cardigan
Chipping Campden
The Ridgeway
WALES
Pembrokeshire Coast Path
Amroth
Kemble
Ivinghoe Beacon
Chepstow
London
Thames Path
Cardiff
Bristol
Bath
Overton Hill
Canterbury
Exmoor & N Devon Coast Path
Winchester
Farnham
Dover
Minehead
Salisbury
North Downs Way
Bude
Portsmouth
Eastbourne
Brighton
Exeter
Poole
Cornwall Coast Path
South Downs Way
Plymouth
Isle of Wight
Dorset & S Devon Coast Path
0 50 100km
0 25 50 miles
Isles of Scilly
ENGLISH CHANNEL

Maps 38-45
Carlisle to Bowness-on-Solway
14 miles/22.5km – 4¾-5hrs
NOTE: Add 20-30% to these times to allow for stops

Map area

- **Barclose**
- **Walby**
- **Todhills**
- **Rockcliffe**
- **Harker**
- MAP 36
- MAP 41 — **Beaumont**
- Burgh-by-Sands
- MAP 40 — **Monkhill**
- **Grinsdale**
- **Houghton**
- MAP 37 — **Linstock**
- MAP 38
- **Moorhouse**
- *Go under A689*
- MAP 39
- *Flood diversion route*
- **CARLISLE**
- **Little Orton**
- **Great Orton**
- **Scotby**

Elevation profile

Burgh-by-Sands	Beaumont	Grinsdale	Go under A689	Carlisle
7 – 6	5	4 – 3	2	1 – 0 miles

300m / 250 / 200 / 150 / 100

Overview

Bowness-on-Solway — **Carlisle** — **Wallsend**

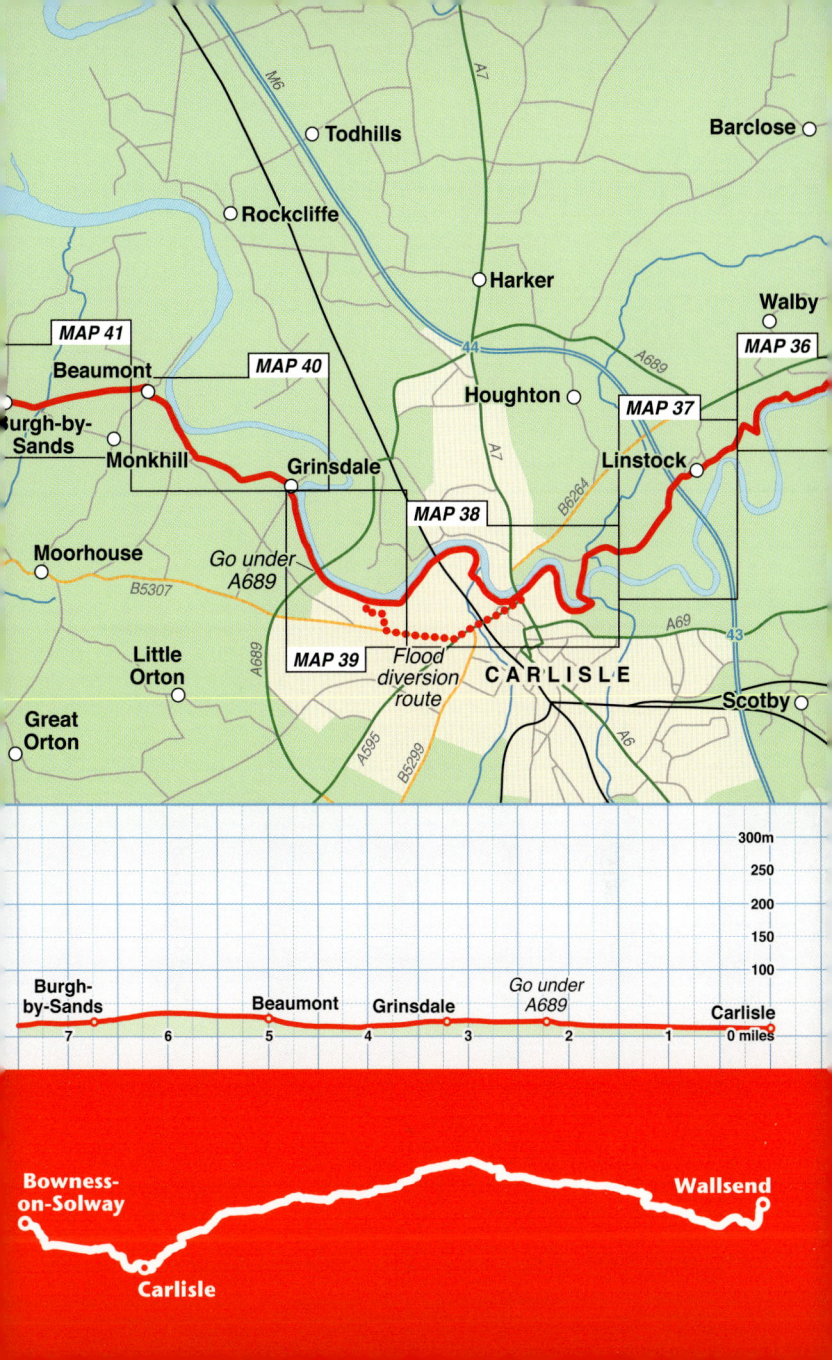

Maps 30-38
Banks to Carlisle
14½ miles/23.3km – 6-6¼hrs

NOTE: Add 20-30% to these times to allow for stops

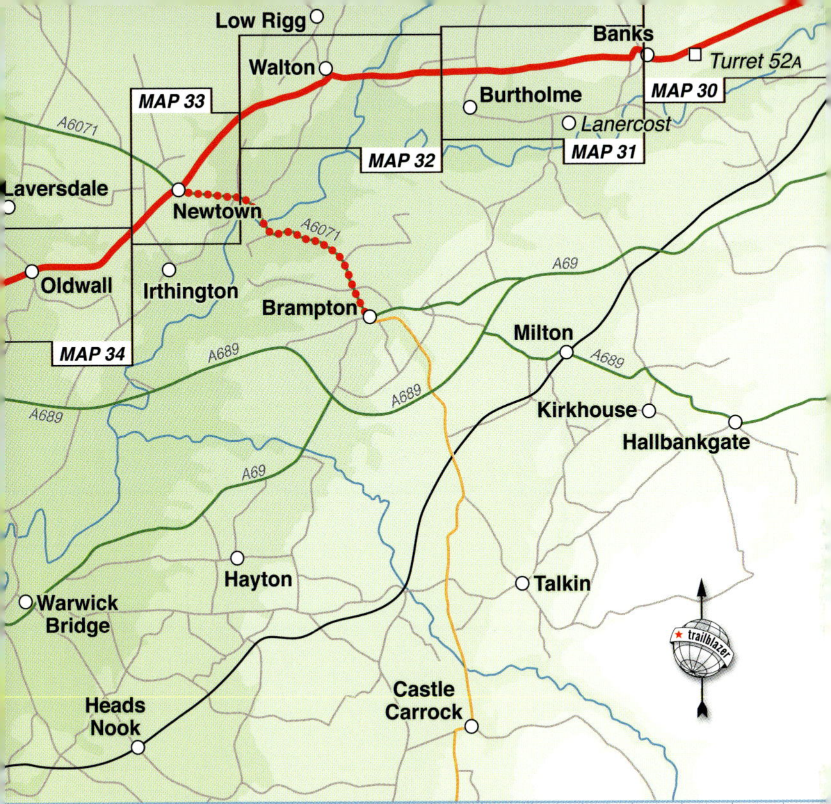
Low Rigg
Banks
Turret 52A
Walton
MAP 33
Burtholme
MAP 30
Lanercost
A6071
MAP 32
MAP 31
Laversdale
Newtown
A6071
Oldwall
Irthington
A69
Brampton
Milton
MAP 34
A689
A689
A689
Kirkhouse
A689
Hallbankgate
A69
Hayton
Talkin
Warwick Bridge
trailblazer
Castle Carrock
Heads Nook

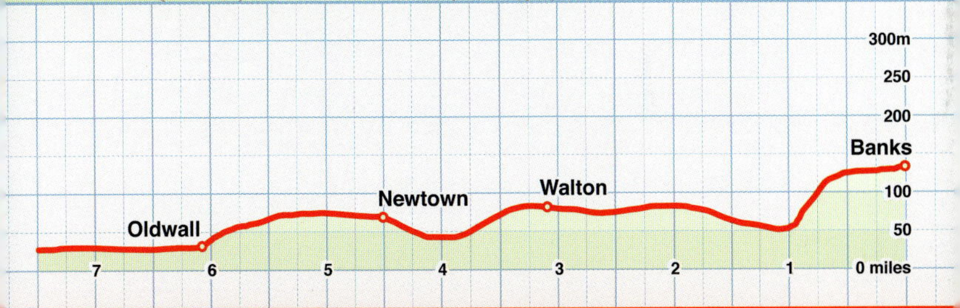
300m
250
200
Banks
150
100
50
0 miles
Oldwall
Newtown
Walton
7
6
5
4
3
2
1

Bowness-on-Solway
Carlisle
Banks
Wallsend

Maps 23-30
Steel Rigg to Banks
12½ miles/20km – 6-6¼hrs
NOTE: Add 20-30% to these times to allow for stops

MAP 20
MAP 21
MAP 22
MAP 23
MAP 24
MAP 25
MAP 26

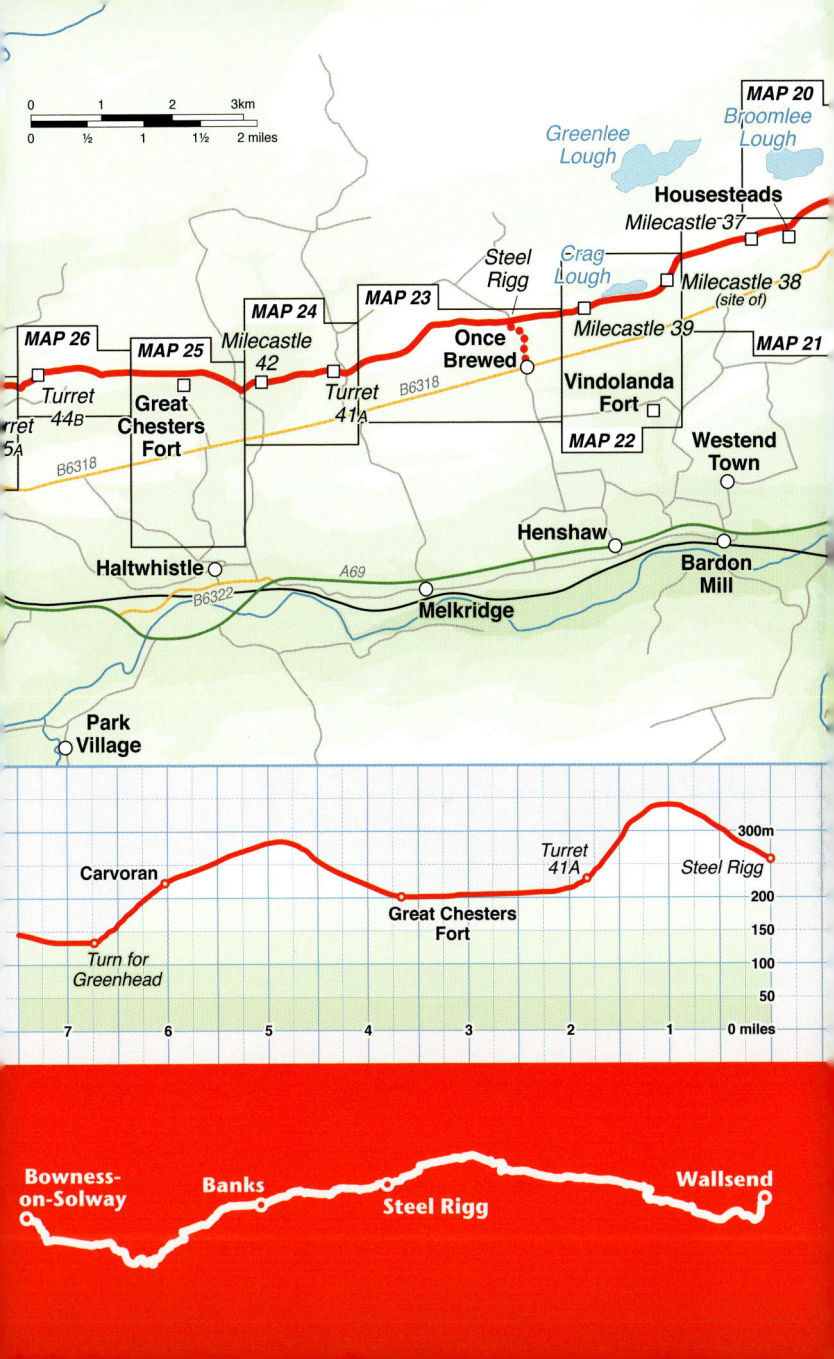

Greenlee Lough
Broomlee Lough
Housesteads
Milecastle 37
Crag Lough
Milecastle 38 (site of)
Steel Rigg
Once Brewed
Milecastle 39
Vindolanda Fort
Milecastle 42
Turret 41A
Great Chesters Fort
Turret 44B
Turret 45A

Westend Town
Henshaw
Bardon Mill
Haltwhistle
Melkridge
Park Village

B6318
A69
B6322

7	6	5	4	3	2	1	0 miles

Carvoran — Turn for Greenhead — Great Chesters Fort — Turret 41A — Steel Rigg

300m
200
150
100
50

Bowness-on-Solway — **Banks** — **Steel Rigg** — **Wallsend**

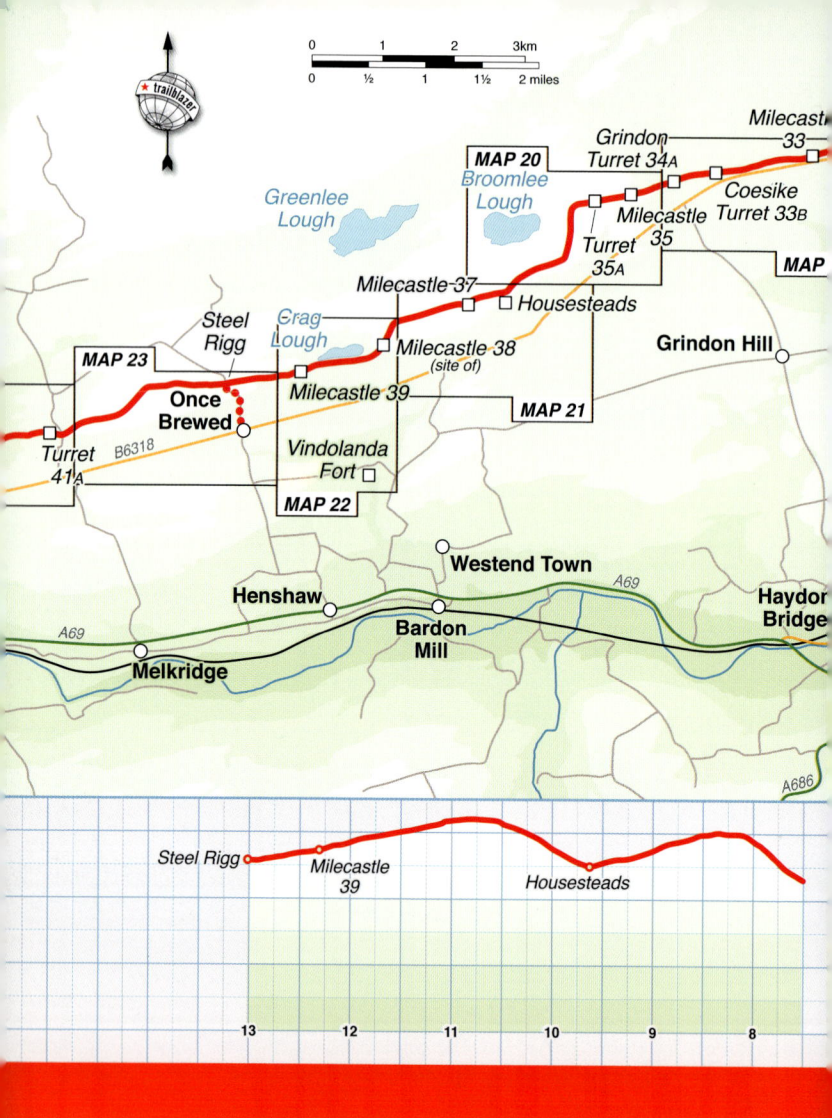

Maps 16-23
Chollerford to Steel Rigg

13 miles/21km — 5¼-6½hrs

NOTE: Add 20-30% to these times to allow for stops

Map Overview

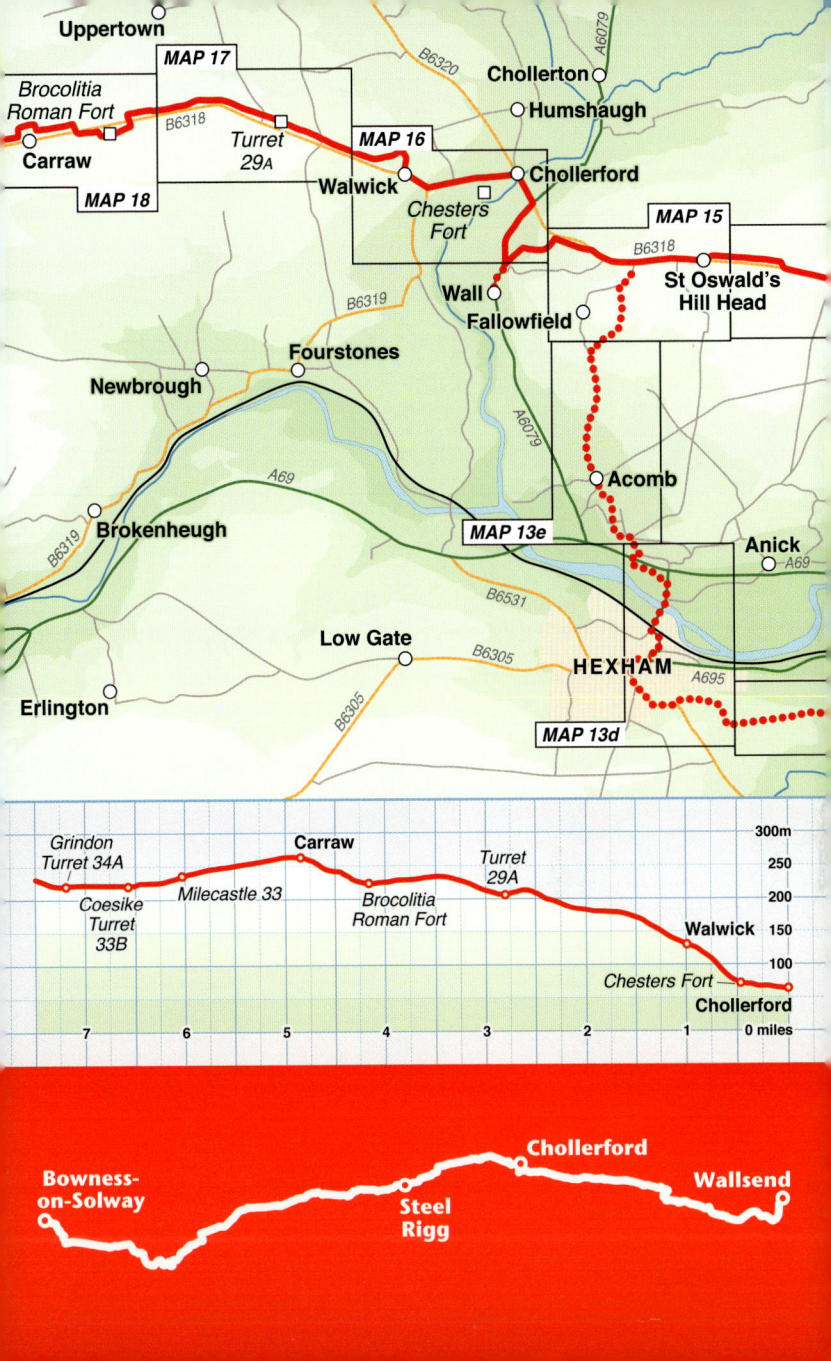

Locations on main map:
- Uppertown
- Brocolitia Roman Fort
- Carraw
- Turret 29A
- Walwick
- Chesters Fort
- Wall
- Fallowfield
- Chollerton
- Humshaugh
- Chollerford
- St Oswald's Hill Head
- Newbrough
- Fourstones
- Brokenheugh
- Acomb
- Anick
- Erlington
- Low Gate
- HEXHAM

Map references: MAP 15, MAP 16, MAP 17, MAP 18, MAP 13d, MAP 13e

Roads: B6318, B6319, B6320, B6305, B6531, A69, A695, A6079

Elevation Profile

Location	Distance (miles)	Elevation (m)
Grindon Turret 34A	7	
Coesike Turret 33B		
Milecastle 33	6	
Carraw	5	~250
Brocolitia Roman Fort	4	
Turret 29A	3	~200
Walwick	1	150
Chesters Fort		100
Chollerford	0	

Route Overview

Bowness-on-Solway — Steel Rigg — Chollerford — Wallsend

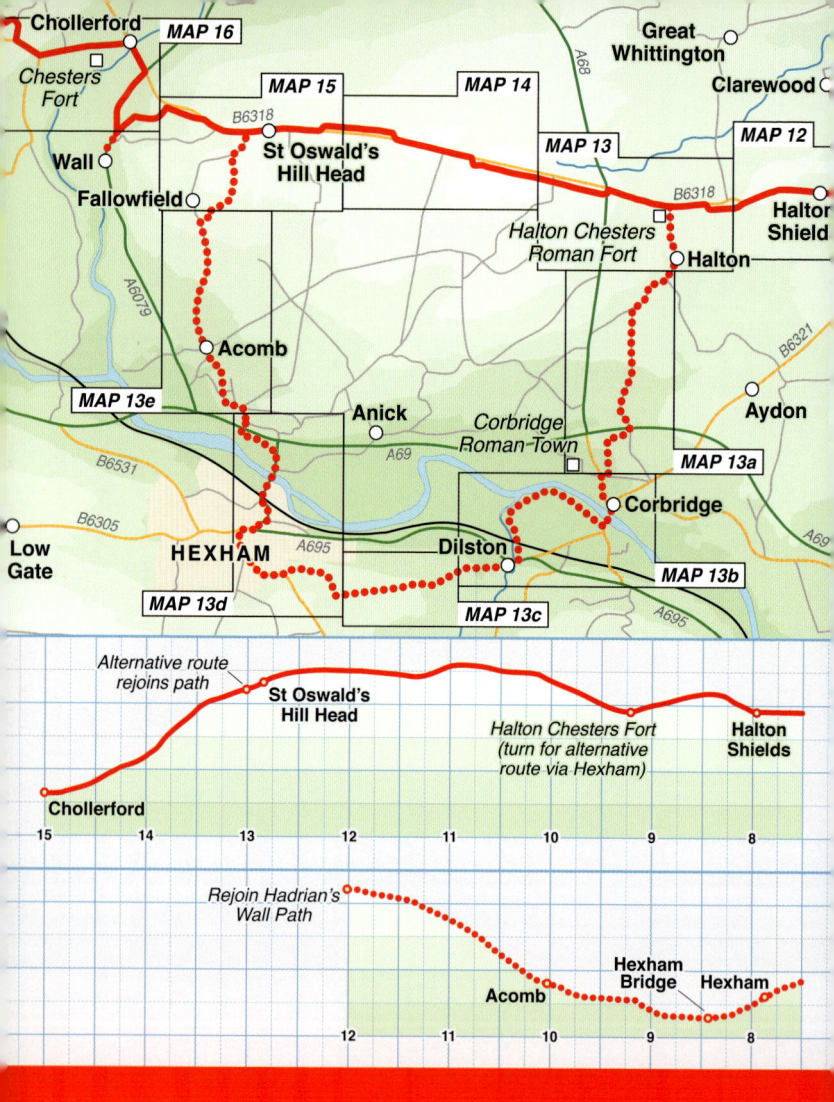

Maps 8-16
Heddon-on-the-Wall to Chollerford
15 miles/24km – 6¾-7hrs

Corbridge-Hexham-Acomb alternative route
12 miles/19.5km – 4½-4¾hrs

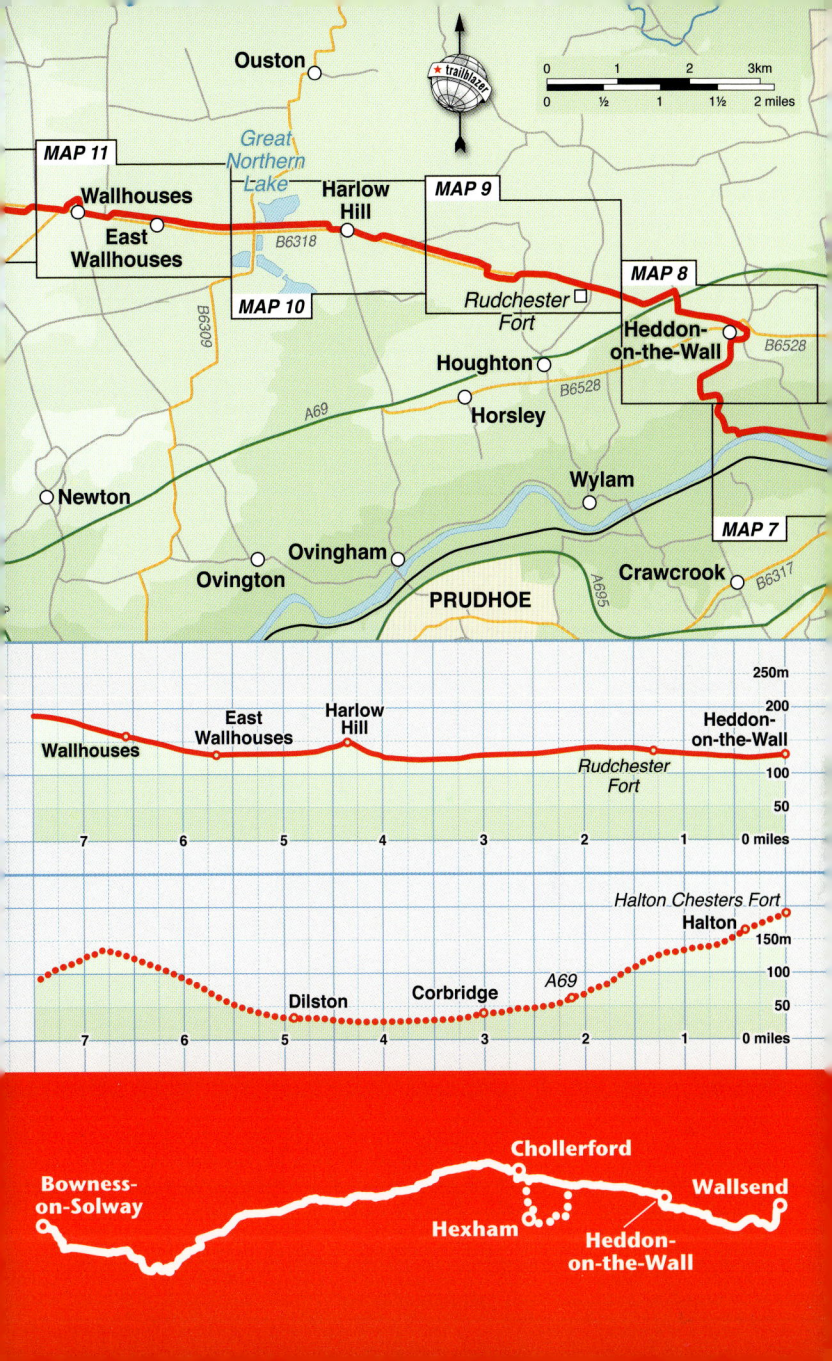

MAP 11
Wallhouses
East Wallhouses

MAP 10

MAP 9
Harlow Hill
Rudchester Fort

MAP 8
Heddon-on-the-Wall

Ouston
Great Northern Lake
Houghton
Horsley
Wylam

MAP 7
Newton
Ovington
Ovingham
PRUDHOE
Crawcrook

Wallhouses — East Wallhouses — Harlow Hill — Rudchester Fort — Heddon-on-the-Wall

Dilston — Corbridge — A69 — Halton — Halton Chesters Fort

Bowness-on-Solway — Chollerford — Hexham — Heddon-on-the-Wall — Wallsend

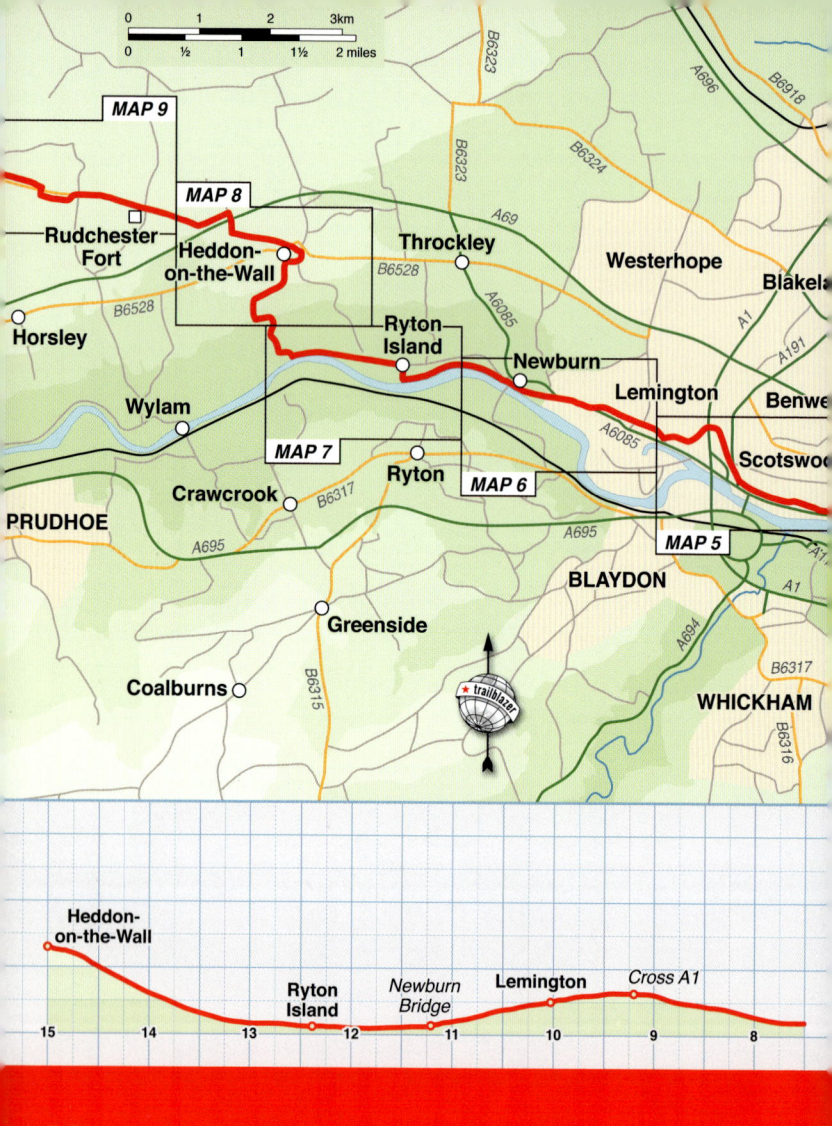

Maps 1-8
Wallsend to Heddon-on-the-Wall
15 miles/24km – 4¾-5hrs
NOTE: Add 20-30% to these times to allow for stops

NEWCASTLE UPON TYNE

wdon · Gosforth · LONGBENTON · Forest Hall · Battle Hill · Howdon · Jesmond · Heaton · WALLSEND · *Segedunum* · *MAP 1* · Walker · HEBBURN · *Redheugh Bridge* · *MAP 3* · City Centre · Byker · Monkton · *aradise* · Elswick · *Millennium Bridge* · GATESHEAD · Dunston · *MAP 4* · Mount Pleasant · *MAP 2* · Felling · Wardley · Dunston Hill · Team Valley · Leam Lane

Vickers		Redheugh Bridge		Millennium Bridge		Byker		Segedunum
7	6		5		4	3	2	1 0 miles

300m / 250 / 200 / 150 / 100

Bowness-on-Solway — **Heddon-on-the-Wall** — **Wallsend**

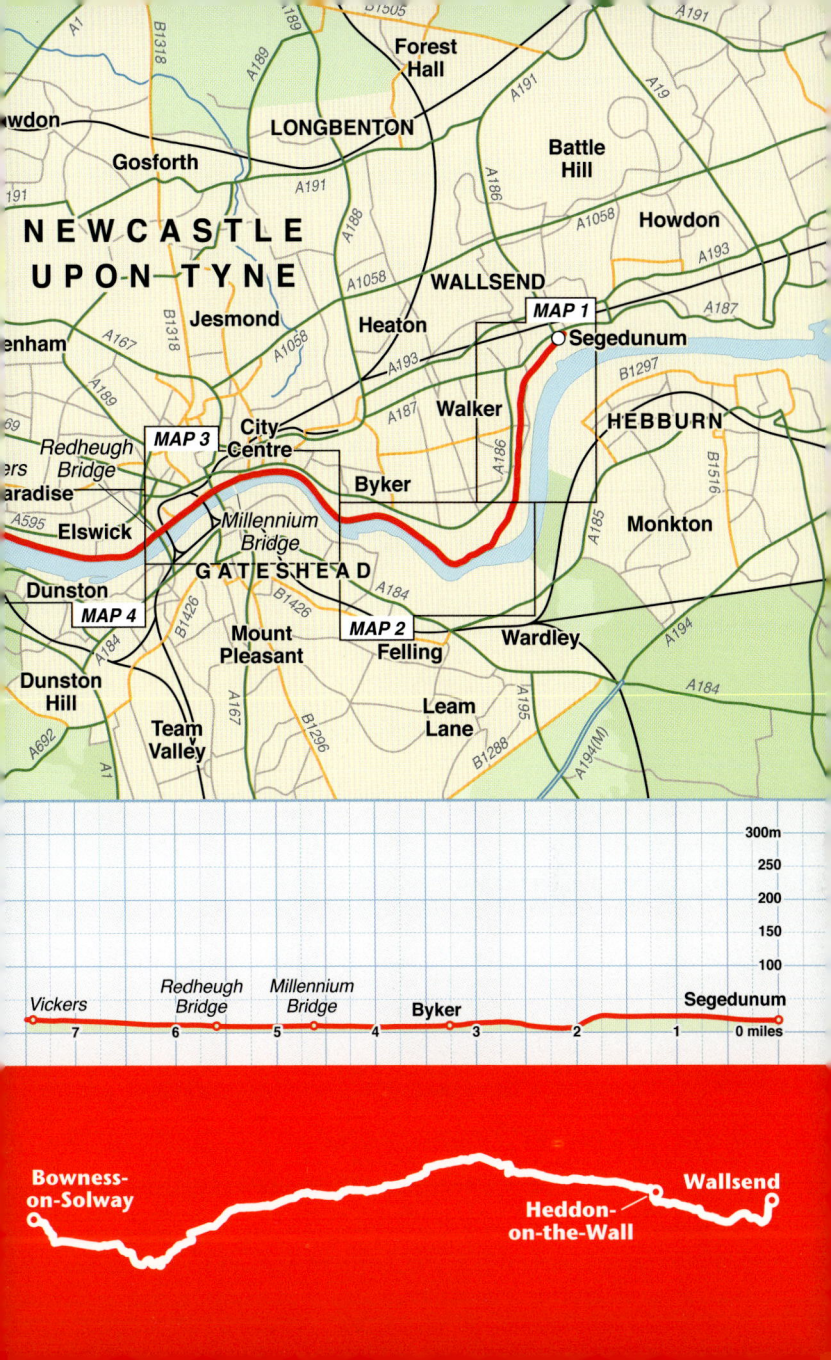

	Wallsend (Newcastle)	Newburn	Heddon	East Wallhouses	Port Gate	Wall	Chollerford	Housesteads	Steel Rigg	Carvoran	Gilsland
Newburn	11 / 17.6										
Heddon-on-the-Wall	15 / 24	4 / 6.4									
E Wallhouses	21 / 33.6	10 / 16	6 / 9.5								
Port Gate	25 / 39.9	14 / 22.4	10 / 16	4 / 6.4							
Wall	29 / 46.3	18 / 28.8	14 / 22.4	8 / 12.8	4 / 6.4						
Chollerford	30 / 47.9	19 / 30.4	15 / 24	9 / 14.4	5 / 8	1 / 1.6					
Housesteads	39 / 62.4	28 / 44.8	24 / 38.4	18 / 28.8	14 / 22.4	10 / 16	9 / 14.4				
Steel Rigg	43 / 68.8	32 / 51.2	28 / 44.8	22 / 35.2	18 / 28.8	14 / 22.4	13 / 20.8	4 / 6.4			
Carvoran	48.5 / 77.6	37.5 / 60	33.5 / 53.6	27.5 / 44	23.5 / 37.6	19.5 / 31.2	18.5 / 29.6	9.5 / 15.2	5.5 / 8.8		
Gilsland	51 / 81.6	40 / 64	36 / 57.6	30 / 48	26 / 41.6	22 / 35.2	21 / 33.6	12 / 19.2	8 / 12.8	2.5 / 4	
Birdoswald	53 / 84.8	42 / 67.2	38 / 60.8	32 / 51.2	28 / 44.8	24 / 38.4	23 / 36.8	14 / 22.4	10 / 16	4.5 / 7.2	2 / 3.2
Banks	55.5 / 88.8	44.5 / 71.2	40.5 / 64.8	34.5 / 55.2	30 / 48	26.5 / 42.2	25.5 / 40.8	16.5 / 26.4	12.5 / 20	7 / 11.2	4.5 / 7.2
Walton	58 / 92.8	47 / 75.2	43 / 68.8	37 / 59.2	33 / 52.8	29 / 46.4	28 / 44.8	19 / 30.4	15 / 24	9.5 / 15.2	7 / 11.2
Newtown	60 / 96	49 / 78.4	45 / 72	39 / 62.4	35 / 56	31 / 49.6	30 / 48	21 / 33.6	17 / 27.2	11.5 / 18.4	9 / 14.4
Crosby-on-Eden	65 / 104	54 / 86.4	50 / 80	44 / 70.4	40 / 64	36 / 57.6	35 / 56	26 / 41.6	22 / 35.2	16.5 / 26.4	14 / 22.4
Carlisle	70 / 112	59 / 94.4	55 / 88	49 / 78.4	45 / 72	41 / 65.6	40 / 64	31 / 49.6	27 / 43.2	21.5 / 34.4	19 / 30.4
Grinsdale	73.5 / 117.6	62.5 / 100	58.5 / 93.6	52.5 / 84	48.5 / 77.6	44.5 / 71.2	43.5 / 69.6	34.5 / 55.2	30.5 / 48.8	25 / 40	22.5 / 36
Burgh-by-Sands	77 / 123.2	66 / 105.6	62 / 99.2	56 / 89.6	52 / 83.2	48 / 76.8	47 / 75.2	38 / 60.8	34 / 54.4	28.5 / 45.6	26 / 41.6
Drumburgh	79.5 / 127.2	68.5 / 109.6	64.5 / 103.2	58.5 / 93.6	54.5 / 87.2	50.5 / 80.8	49.5 / 79.2	40.5 / 64.8	36.5 / 58.4	31 / 49.6	28.5 / 45.6
Glasson	80.5 / 128.8	69.5 / 111.2	65.5 / 104.8	59.5 / 95.2	55.5 / 88.8	51.5 / 82.4	50.5 / 80.8	41.5 / 66.4	37.5 / 60	32 / 51.2	29.5 / 47.2
Port Carlisle	83 / 132.8	72 / 115.2	68 / 108.8	62 / 99.2	58 / 92.8	54 / 86.4	53 / 84.8	44 / 70.4	40 / 64	34.5 / 55.2	32 / 51.2
Bowness-on-Solway	84 / 134.4	73 / 116.8	69 / 110.4	63 / 100.8	59 / 94.4	55 / 88	54 / 86.4	45 / 72	41 / 65.6	35.5 / 56.8	33 / 52.8

Hadrian's Wall Path

DISTANCE CHART

miles/*kilometres*
(approx)

Birdoswald	Banks	Walton	Newtown	Crosby-on-Eden	Carlisle	Grinsdale	Burgh-by-Sands	Drumburgh	Glasson	Port Carlisle
2.5										
4										
5	2.5									
8	*4*									
7	4.5	2								
11.2	*7.2*	*3.2*								
12	9.5	8	5							
19.2	*15.2*	*12.8*	*8*							
17	14.5	12	10	5						
27.2	*23.2*	*19.2*	*16*	*8*						
20.5	18	15.5	13.5	8.5	3.5					
32.8	*28.8*	*24.8*	*21.6*	*13.6*	*5.6*					
24	21.5	19	17	12	7	3.5				
38.4	*34.4*	*30.4*	*27.2*	*19.2*	*11.2*	*5.6*				
26.5	24	21.5	19.5	14.5	9.5	6	2.5			
42.4	*38.4*	*34.4*	*31.2*	*23.2*	*15.2*	*9.5*	*4*			
27.5	25	22.5	20.5	15.5	10.5	7	3.5	1		
44	*40*	*36*	*32.8*	*24.8*	*16.8*	*11.2*	*5.6*	*1.6*		
30	27.5	25	23	18	13	9.5	6	3.5	2.5	
48	*44*	*40*	*36.8*	*28.8*	*20.8*	*15.2*	*9.6*	*5.6*	*4*	
31	28.5	26	24	19	14	10.5	7	4.5	3.5	1
49.6	*45.6*	*41.6*	*38.4*	*30.4*	*22.4*	*16.8*	*11.2*	*7.2*	*5.6*	*1.6*

Bowness-on-Solway

Hadrian's Wall Path
WALLSEND – BOWNESS-ON-SOLWAY

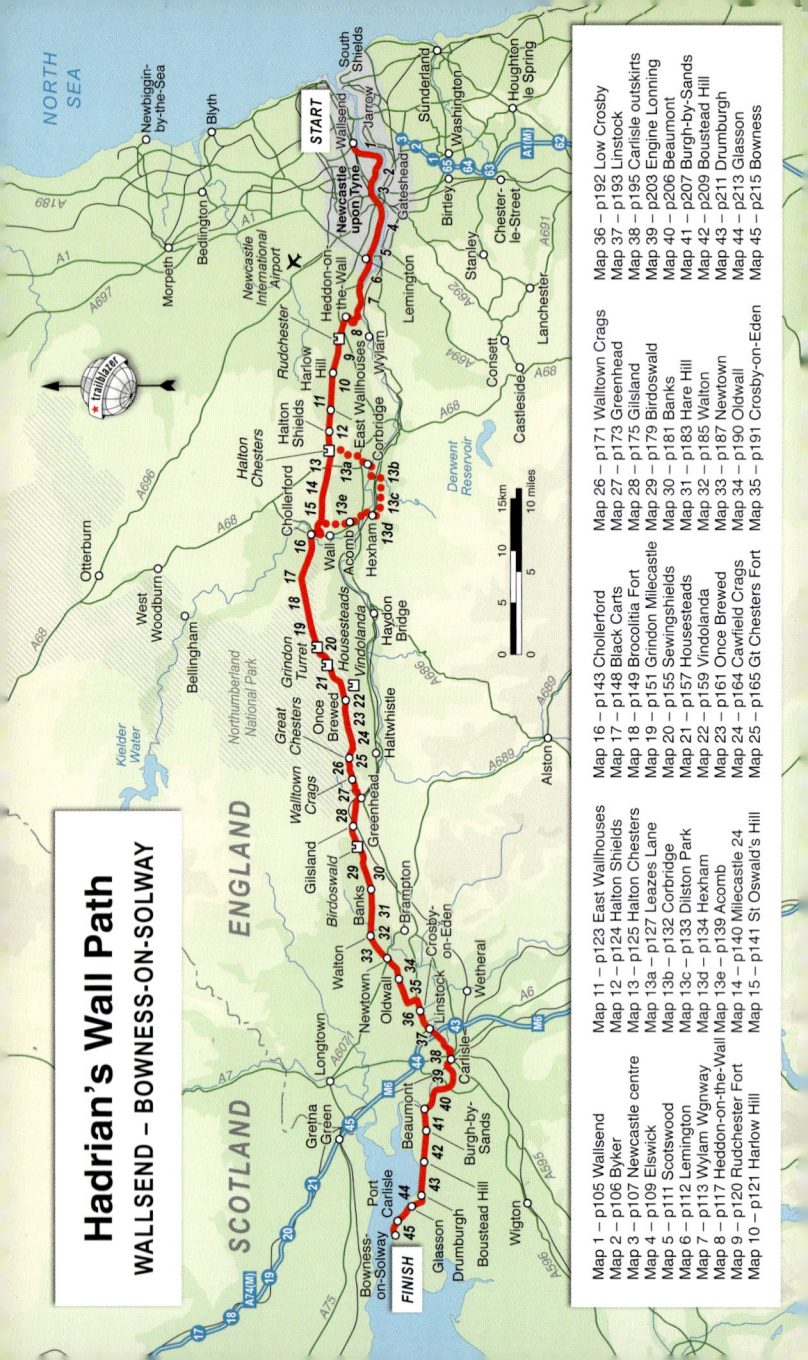

Map 1 – p105 Wallsend
Map 2 – p106 Byker
Map 3 – p107 Newcastle centre
Map 4 – p109 Elswick
Map 5 – p111 Scotswood
Map 6 – p112 Lemington
Map 7 – p113 Wylam Wgnway
Map 8 – p117 Heddon-on-the-Wall
Map 9 – p120 Rudchester Fort
Map 10 – p121 Harlow Hill
Map 11 – p123 East Wallhouses
Map 12 – p124 Halton Shields
Map 13 – p125 Halton Chesters
Map 13a – p127 Leazes Lane
Map 13b – p132 Corbridge
Map 13c – p133 Dilston Park
Map 13d – p134 Hexham
Map 13e – p139 Acomb
Map 14 – p140 Milecastle 24
Map 15 – p141 St Oswald's Hill
Map 16 – p143 Chollerford
Map 17 – p148 Black Carts
Map 18 – p149 Brocolitia Fort
Map 19 – p151 Grindon Milecastle
Map 20 – p155 Sewingshields
Map 21 – p157 Housesteads
Map 22 – p159 Vindolanda
Map 23 – p161 Once Brewed
Map 24 – p164 Cawfield Crags
Map 25 – p165 Gt Chesters Fort
Map 26 – p171 Walltown Crags
Map 27 – p173 Greenhead
Map 28 – p175 Gilsland
Map 29 – p179 Birdoswald
Map 30 – p181 Banks
Map 31 – p183 Hare Hill
Map 32 – p185 Walton
Map 33 – p187 Newtown
Map 34 – p190 Oldwall
Map 35 – p191 Crosby-on-Eden
Map 36 – p192 Low Crosby
Map 37 – p193 Linstock
Map 38 – p195 Carlisle outskirts
Map 39 – p203 Engine Lonning
Map 40 – p206 Beaumont
Map 41 – p207 Burgh-by-Sands
Map 42 – p209 Boustead Hill
Map 43 – p211 Drumburgh
Map 44 – p213 Glasson
Map 45 – p215 Bowness